C. S. LEWIS
The Authentic Voice

'Christian apologist, literary historian, scholar, critic, writer of science fiction and children's books, he was one of the more prolific authors of his time,' *The Times* obituary wrote of C. S. Lewis, following his death on 22 November 1963. 'As a Christian writer his influence was marked . . . he made religious books bestsellers and, in a nice sense, fashionable.'

In this imaginative and dramatic biography William Griffin allows the reader direct access to Lewis the man. He provides a narrative in which Lewis speaks for himself at every turn: we hear with delight the tones of the authentic voice.

From the pages of this book Lewis emerges as an active, energetic man, one who loved to walk and to talk, who was happiest in the company of friends. He was a brilliant scholar and a man of deep wisdom and humility. Known to millions through his books and broadcast talks, he patiently dealt with a vast correspondence, making new friends through letters. He came late but with great joy to the love of a woman and endured an agony of pain in her early death. From his first days as a reluctant convert he gave his whole heart and mind to the knowledge and love of God.

WILLIAM GRIFFIN — novelist, playwright and former religious books editor of *Publishers Weekly* — was for many years an editor at Macmillan in New York, one of Lewis's major publishers. His recent books have been translations of Latin spiritual classics by Augustine of Hippo and Thomas à Kempis.

'Lewis walks onto the stage almost immediately, speaking as if in a one-character show, and holds our attention . . . to the very end . . . One comes to experience him with a rare directness, as the biographer seems to disappear and leaves the reader standing face-to-face with his subject.'
CHICAGO TRIBUNE

'(Griffin's) dramatic biography is a mosaic based on diaries, letters, the reminiscences of friends and on his books — a kind of literary snapshot album of Lewis's life.'
BOSTON GLOBE

'Griffin has researched Lewis's literary scholarship as carefully as his more popular religious writings.'
BOOKLIST

'In this stimulating and imaginative narrative biography, author-playwright Griffin brings before us the man, as often as possible via his own words, throughout his long and energetic career at Oxford and Cambridge, particularly in his relations with friends, family, students, critics, editors, thus vividly revealing the warm personality of this keen logician with puckish humour.'
PUBLISHERS WEEKLY

'A crisp and moving account . . . Avoiding preachiness, omniscience, and tedious digressions, Griffin has opted to let C. S. Lewis do the talking.'
CHRISTIANITY TODAY

'The true Lewis, virtues and foibles, with much lively detail.'
BOOK WORLD, WASHINGTON TIMES

C·S·LEWIS

THE AUTHENTIC VOICE

WILLIAM GRIFFIN

LION

Dedicated to the memory of
my mother and my father

A Lion Book
an imprint of
Lion Hudson plc
Mayfield House, 256 Banbury Road,
Oxford OX2 7DH, England
www.lionhudson.com
ISBN-13: 978-0-7459-5208-6
ISBN-10: 0-7459-5208-9

First published under the title *Clive Staples Lewis:
A Dramatic Life*
by HarperCollins Publishers Ltd, New York

British editions 1988 & 2005
10 9 8 7 6 5 4 3 2 1 0

Printed and bound in Great Britain
by Cox & Wyman Ltd, Reading

CONTENTS

Evening Prayer' / Inland Revenue and Agape Fund / BBC scripts too long / third series of talks begun on BBC / enemy aircraft over Oxford / fifth talk of the BBC series / publications, reprinting, licensings / miracles sermonized / 'horse with a nosebag'

old age and resurrection / 'the perfect whisky cake' / lunch at Magdalen with Green, Baynes, Barfield

'As One Oldster to Another' / porcine charity / pleasure in thinking evil / Bruce dead and buried / latest Hercules from America / literary impact of the Authorized Version / planning summer vacation / map of Narnia / Mrs Moore to Restholme / Leavis and Russell savaged in verse / Ghouls and Boggles, Ogres and Minotaurs, Bird and Baby / 'What are we to make of Jesus Christ?' / periodicals in the Bodleian / Bide converted, confirmed, ordained / Korean War in British pubs / Flewett married to Freud / praise from an American widow / 'on the fringes of civilization' / Tynan and four-letter words / reunion, a three-cornered affair / high cost of holiday turkey / photographed for *Radio Times* / Twain's novels relished / the errors of Rome / Vanaukens at the threshold / CARE packages from Connecticut, confectionary from New York / Vanaukens about to bend the knee / 'cheerful insecurity'

Reading contemporary authors / Vanauken and vocation / 'a private gift of coal' / Mrs Moore, dead, buried, remembered / campaigning for Oxford Professor of Poetry / Day-Lewis elected / vacation anticipated / Easter Hare in the barber's chair / Pitter's glasses found / postvacation correspondence / Vanaukens converted / interviewed by Schofield / crossing swords with Milward / Green invited to be biographer / entertained by the Dominicans at Blackfriars / everything 'marvellously well' /
mumps and mortification / ghosts and faeries in Ireland / original sin / American gift forwarded / theism at the Socratic / CBE offered by Churchill / afraid of errors in OHEL / pig, Pitter, poetry

'The divine *Huckleberry*' / negative critique / *Kherub* and *Gryphon* / hiking in Malvern, pilgrimaging in poetry / photograph requested / 'Hero and Leander' at the British Academy / loathing prunes, writing for children / Mrs Hooker a.k.a. Mrs Lewis / divorce / Mathews marries Gebbert in California / Adams, his spiritual *directeur*, dead / Sappho and Lesbos / 'The World's Last Night' / about Steiner and anthroposophy / providence / Agape Fund / invited to lunch with Williams and Gresham / visit with Gebberts aborted / dining with Greshman at the Mitre / Gebberts' visit to Kilns cancelled by flu / Gresham entertained at Magdalen / veneration of the saints / Gresham at Magdalen again / philosophy at the Socratic / centres and fringes / 'Christians never say goodbye' / Christmas cake from South Carolina / Gresham at the Kilns for Christmas

Fogged in *Regress* / Christmas visitor / Boucher and Bradbury, *Fantasy and Science Fiction* / invited to speak by Clarke / boy healed by prayer / surprised pregnancy / 'books as a cathedral' / horrors of a first confession / conversion process / Medicine Hat Toothbrush Combine / coronation of Elizabeth II / Lewises proofing their books / 'Narnian Suite' / 'flesh and Pound' / visited by Kilby / visit to Green cancelled / too old to be attractive

PREFACE

C. S. Lewis: The Authentic Voice was meant to be an interim biography, somewhere between the first one published more than a dozen years ago and the definitive one yet to be written. It was originally undertaken primarily for the benefit of American readers, for although C. S. Lewis never visited America in person, his books continue to sell by the their million in the United States. But I have now been persuaded of its wider interest.

The biography treats Lewis's life in full, from his birth in Ireland on 29 November 1898 to his death in England on 22 November 1963. It details his university career first at Oxford, then at Cambridge; his service in the First World War as a second lieutenant and in the Second as a lay lecturer; his sermons in pulpits and his addresses at the British Academy; his misogyny as a bachelor and his scandal as a lover; his faithfulness as a friend and his loyalty as a brother; his public frugalities and his hidden charities.

He was a poet as contemporary as Auden and a versifier as funny as Gilbert, he was a satirist as slashing as Waugh and a social critic as clever as Coward, he was a scholar as sharp as Leavis and a mythologer as wise as Tolkien. He was a broadcaster with an enormous audience and a correspondent of staggering proportion. His esoteric work was published by university presses, his exoteric work appeared in *Punch* and *The Spectator*, in *Show* and *The Saturday Evening Post*.

The materials of Lewis's life I decided not to arrange according to themes, with appropriate chapter titles. Instead I chose to present the incidents and episodes in chronological order in the hope that the biography's narrative would flow not unlike a novel's.

The text progresses chronologically from 1925, when he was elected a Fellow of Magdalen, to that day in 1963 when he and Aldous Huxley and John F. Kennedy died. Each year begins a chapter-length segment; the running-heads provide a continuous chronological reference. Each chapter is approximately the same length and is full of incidents and episodes. Like the frames in a film, they flicker at first; but as the eye becomes used to them, they move rapidly, the figure of Lewis walks less jerkily, and there comes the semblance of life.

Emerging from this sort of narrative is an active, energetic man who looked like a farmer but talked like a philosopher, who would as soon lolligag in fairydom as joust in intellectual lists, who relished the love of friendship, was surprised by the love of a woman, and cultivated the love of God. He was also a funny man, Owen Barfield assured me in 1981; how rollicking he was in offhand conversation as well as in literary composition the reader will find many times in the pages that follow. There are warts too, scars of all kinds, sexual as well as spiritual.

The materials from which this biography was derived are the biography by Roger Lancelyn Green and Walter Hooper, and certain chapters in Humphrey Carpenter's *The Inklings*; the correspondence published in *Letters* and *They Stand Together*; the diaries of Warren Lewis published as *Brothers and Friends*; books of interviews and essays like Como's *C. S. Lewis at the Breakfast Table* and Schofield's *In Search of C. S. Lewis*; *The Bulletin of the New York C. S. Lewis Society* and *The Canadian C. S. Lewis Journal*; Lewis's unpublished letters and papers gathered at the Wade Collection, Wheaton College, and at the Bodleian Library, Oxford, especially *The Lewis Papers: Memoirs of the Lewis Family, 1850–1930*, eleven typewritten and bound volumes edited by W. H. Lewis; and the many people who allowed themselves to be interviewed by an American.

In *C. S. Lewis: The Authentic Voice* I have eschewed inference and psychoanalysis: Lewis speaks for himself at almost every moment and incident of his life. The reader who wants to know what Lewis thought on a particular subject or how his thought grew from one period of his life to another need only consult the index of this book, which contains not only people and places but also ideas.

I have also chosen not to use a time-honoured biographical technique. Although I flash backward many times during the course of the narrative, I never flash forward, anticipating future knowledge of events. Nor, in this narrative biography, do I distinguish between the major and minor events of Lewis's life; I present instead the continuing threads and emerging patterns of his daily life. Lewis's place in history, an evaluation some readers of Lewis lust for, is also outside the scope of an interim biography.

In *The Allegory of Love*, which was published in 1936, Lewis half-suspected that, even as he wrote, the novel of imagination was becoming biographical, and the biographical novel was becoming 'imaginative biography', a genuinely new form standing at the same distance from biography proper as the chronicle play stands from the 'just' history. This is the sort of biography I would like to think *C. S. Lewis: The Authentic Voice* is.

But would Lewis have allowed the 'imaginative biography' of himself to be so colloquial, so incidental, so trivial and even vulgar?

'A literature is and ought to be irreproachably "vulgar," ' he wrote in an essay entitled 'High and Low Brows,' and I will not do violence to that passage if I substitute the word *biography* for the word *literature*.

'It ought to deal strongly and simply with strong, simple emotions: the directness, the unelaborate, downright portraiture of easily recognizable realities in their familiar aspects, will not be a fault unless it pretends to be something else.' *C. S. Lewis: The Authentic Voice* has no further pretensions.

William Griffin

❧ 1925 ❧

'I wish you joy.'

The young man in academic gown had genuflected gracefully enough, but when he tried to rise, his heel caught. Silk tearing was not a pretty sound, and when Clive Staples Lewis — for that was the young man's name — rose from the red cushion, he was severely shaken. Five minutes' worth of Latin had just been read over him by Thomas Herbert Warren, president of Magdalen College, Oxford. When Lewis uttered *do fidem* or some such, Warren wished the new faculty member a full measure of joy.

The ceremony was over, or was it? Before Lewis could compose himself, Warren propelled him towards the Magdalen household, which had been gathered for the occasion.

'I wish you joy,' said A. L. Dickson. Mathematics. Moustached.

'I wish you joy,' said M. H. MacKeith through his nose. Natural sciences and anatomy.

'I wish you joy,' buzzed E. Hope. Science. A black Celt. Dark and small.

'I wish you joy,' intoned E. S. Craig, emperor of mathematics.

August 1925 was especially hot, and although the building was faced with stone, the walls panelled, the ceiling high, Lewis began to sweat.

'I wish you joy.' P. V. M. Benecke was ancient history.

'I wish you joy,' said T. D. Weldon, philosophy. A villain, if looks meant anything.

'I wish you joy.' S. G. Lee looked more like the hero of a romantic novel than the dean of a men's college.

Why, Lewis wondered as he worked his way around the largish room, pumping hands and mumbling words of gratitude to perfect strangers, why had no one warned him that if elected a fellow of Magdalen, he would have to do this?

'I wish you joy,' said someone, rather too closely. Ancient history, broils and strategems, lapel to lapel, H. M. D. Parker breathed conspiracy.

'I wish you joy,' said the law, chewing on a cigar. R. Segar was ugly enough to look at, yet suave enough to sell insurance.

In a French or Italian university, Lewis consoled himself, this would surely have come off with more *panache*, more *pennachio*!

'I weesha you joy!' shouted C. C. Foligno, Italian.

Perhaps only in a French university, fretted Lewis, having completed his round. If he were to tell these silly stupid gentlemen how utterly embarrassed he felt, they'd shoot him dead in his tracks.

❧

The ordeal by joy having been completed, Lewis left the assembly, thinking how far he had come since 1917. Oxford was lovely then, a 'tangle of spires and towers.' He was not able to accomplish much before the Great War; after it he was only one among the many athletes and pot-hunters and literary gents with a smattering of the political, the musical, and the philosophical. He got a first in classics and philosophy in 1922. When no job appeared on the horizon, he spent the next year getting a first in English. Still no job. He reviewed books for *The Guardian*, a weekly Anglican newspaper founded in 1846. He visited Trueman and Knightly, agents for tutors seeking permanent employment; when Williams, the local rep, found out that he did not want to move from Oxford, he advised him to put an advertisement in *The Oxford Times*. There was at least one response: a cheerful, healthy, contented-looking lad of eighteen who wanted help preparing for a classical scholarship examination.

'What Greek authors have you been reading?'

'I can never remember. Try a few names, and I'll see if I get on to any.'

'Have you read any Euripides?'

'No.'

'Any Sophocles?'

'Well, the *Alcestis*.'

'But isn't that by Euripides?'

'Then, by Jove, I *have* read some Euripides!'

A fellowship came up at University College, Reading, but Lewis would have to live there. Fellowships at St John's, Trinity, and Lincoln were announced; at least they were in Oxford; they would pay £500 per annum; but chances of his getting one were considered slim. In May 1924 there was an opening at University College; the philosophy tutor there would be going to the University of Michigan at Ann Arbor for a year; Univ. — as University College was called — asked Lewis to take on duties as philosophy tutor and perhaps to give a lecture or two. They offered £200 per annum. It wasn't much, but it was a beginning.

Early in the spring of 1925 a fellowship in English literature was announced at Magdalen College. Lewis put in for it as he had for the others, but he expected a person senior to himself to be elected. Early in May it was clear that he was in the running. He was invited to dinner at Magdalen together with some other candidates. He asked a friend what he should wear and promptly rented white tie and tails. When he arrived, everyone else was wearing black tie and dinner jacket.

'Do you like poetry?' asked the president of Magdalen during the course of the evening.

'Yes, president,' replied Lewis with what he hoped was deference. 'I also like prose.'

Not long after, he met the president on the street; they had a pleasant exchange. Three days later there was another interview, this time in the president's office. Warren asked the questions, expecting in most cases the answer *yes*. Did he realize that Magdalen undergraduates had special needs? Did he know that compensation was £500 a year with provision made for rooms, a pension, and a dining allowance? The term ran for five years, surely he must know that, with re-election almost assured. And then there was philosophy; would he be willing, if necessary, to add it to the English? At 2.30 the following afternoon, the telephone rang at Univ.; it was Warren calling to congratulate Lewis on his election.

The professorial establishment Lewis had once considered 'a close corporation of jolly, untidy, lazy, good-for-nothing, humorous old men,' and now he was one of them. Oxford he had once thought a stone wall unscalable, and here he was on 14 August, a fellow of Magdalen College, walking through the porter's lodge onto the High. Oxford was once again what it was when he had arrived in 1917: 'absolutely ripping!'

⁓

'Elected Fellow Magdalen.'

Lewis wired his father in Belfast not long after Warren shook his hand in congratulation. The 'prospect of being adrift and unemployed at thirty' had haunted both him and his father. In July 1923 he had allowed himself three more years to get permanent employment; his father agreed to provide further financial support; and time seemed to be running out when the good news came.

On the evening of 20 May at Little Lea, the family house on the outskirts of Belfast and at the feet of the Holywood Hills, Albert James Lewis was pouring a preprandial whisky when a servant announced the telephone. It was the post office. When Albert heard the words of the telegram, he was almost overcome. 'I went up to his rooms,' he recorded in his pocket diary later that night, 'and burst into tears of joy. I knelt down and thanked God with a full heart. My prayers have been heard and answered.' Two days later the election was announced in *The Times*. Albert, a solicitor in the employ of the city of Belfast, had no compunction about waving the evidence under the noses of the solicitors and clerks in the Belfast Corporation.

Soon thereafter Lewis put his thoughts into a letter. He thanked his father for the generous support of the last six years. Other young men, at least his equal in ability and qualifications, for lack of family support had had to abandon their dream of teaching at Oxford. 'You have waited, not only without complaint but full of encouragement, while chance after chance slipped away and when the goal receded farthest from sight. Thank you again and again.'

⌘

On what promised to be a hot summer day in Oxford, Lewis would rise early, pick out a book, and head up the Cherwell to a place called Parson's Pleasure. There, behind rickety wooden walls, parson or don, celibate or not-so-celibate, could divest himself and either dive from a makeshift board or simply walk into the water.

Liking nothing better than 'the real bite and shock . . . of a bathe,' Lewis plunged in and, using a crawl, swam to an elbow of the river. Each time his head rose, he could see the Cumnor Hills about a mile or so in the west. Certain that no females were lurking in the shrubs on the bank, he turned on his back and began floating. Looking up, he could see inch-long catkins and finely-veined leaves.

Looking back on his years at Oxford, he found little to be sad about. Indeed the years since the war seemed 'the happiest or only really valuable part' of his life. He had gained three firsts. His essay had won the chancellor's prize in 1921. He had even found a publisher for a slim volume of poems, 'mainly strung around the idea . . . that nature is wholly diabolical and malevolent and that God, if he exists, is outside of and in opposition to the cosmic arrangements.' This was the book he brought with him to Parson's Pleasure.

Emerging from the water, he felt refreshed. Towelling himself off, he remembered sending the manuscript of the poems to the most prestigious London publishing house he could think of, Macmillan. 'Some of the shorter nature poems seem to us to have no little charm,' read the rejection letter of 7 August 1918, 'but we do not feel that the collection as a whole would be likely to appeal to any considerable public.'

Next he sent the manuscript to William Heinemann. The publisher himself replied on 12 September, saying he would be 'pleased to become its publisher.' When a contract was not forthcoming, Lewis went to London. He was pleasantly received at the Heinemann office. The publisher was not there, said the receptionist; would he see the manager? Charles Sheldon Evans, Lewis found, was 'a young man, pale and fair and . . . a gentleman.' Heinemann eventually materialized. He was 'a fat little old man with a bald head, apparently well read, and a trifle fussy — inclined to get his papers mixed up and to repeat himself.' A deal was struck, Heinemann offering Lewis a royalty of 10 per cent of the profits on the published price of twelve out of every thirteen copies sold. In return, Lewis would offer Heinemann first refusal on his next work.

Letters were exchanged, some of them to do with the title of the work. *Spirits in Prison: A Cycle of Lyrical Poems* was the title Lewis favoured. The words were from the epistle of the apostle Peter; Christ 'went and preached unto the *spirits in prison*.' A book with the same title, however, had been published in 1908. Forsaking the New Testament for *Paradise Lost*, Lewis chose some words of Satan to the warrior armies:

> For this infernal pit shall never hold
> Celestial *spirits in bondage*, nor the abyss
> Long under darkness cover.

Spirits in Bondage it was then. But Lewis wanted another change on the title page. His first wish was to be published under the pseudonym of Clive Staples. Now he wanted to change the surname to Hamilton, his mother's maiden name.

Dry now, still in his baptismal suit, Lewis settled down on a tree trunk. He thumbed through the book from back to front, which was not an easy thing to do. His fingertips were like raisins, and his thumbs had unmovable joints. 'Death in Battle', the last poem in the book, had attracted the attention of John Galsworthy; he wanted to publish it in the February 1919 issue of *Reveille*, a new magazine whose profits would help disabled soldiers and sailors. Towards the middle of the book was a five-stanza poem entitled 'Oxford', celebrating the spirit of the city after the war:

> It is well that there are palaces of peace
> And discipline and dreaming and desire,
> Lest we forget our heritage and cease
> The Spirit's work — to hunger and aspire . . .

At the front of the book was the title page. The author was neither Clive Staples nor Clive Hamilton as he had wished, but Glive Hamilton.

The 106-page book was published in the last week of March 1919. Reviews did not rain upon publisher and author. Between the front endpapers Lewis found one commending him for a 'scholarly elucidation of a difficult subject'; the press-cutting agency had sent him a review of *The Principles of Symbolic Logic* by C. S. Lewis of the University of California. Tucked between the back endpapers was a piece of promotional material in which the author of *Spirits in Bondage* was listed as George Hamilton.

∽

It's been seven years now, said Mrs Moore in September, thinking of her son who had died in the Great War.

Paddy, as Edward Francis Courtenay Moore was called by family and friends, first met Jack, as Lewis had named himself when he was a child, in June 1917 when they entered the Officers' Training Camp. They were billeted at Keble, a newish brick fortress among the venerable stone-walled colleges of Oxford. At first Lewis found him 'a little too childish and virtuous for "common nature's daily food"', but soon Moore found they shared enthusiasm for certain authors. During the day they dug trenches and marched routes under a blazing sun. 'Soldiering is more than 'arf swank,' bawled the sergeant major; 'you've got to learn to walk as if the bloody street belongs to you!' At night they collapsed on pipe-frame beds with sagging spring and gasping mattress, talking perhaps of books, perhaps of patriotism, trying to keep their souls alive.

'I have no patriotic feeling for anything in England,' sighed Lewis, 'except Oxford, for which I would live and die.'

Weekends seem to have been free. Lewis stole away from Keble to his own room in Univ., where he enjoyed the luxury of sheets and pillows and sleeping late. Awake at noon, he and his new friends in OTC enjoyed punting on the Cherwell, the river that ran through Magdalen's property to join the Thames a few miles south; picnicking in Mesopotamia, the islet in the Cherwell near Magdalen; taking photographs to send home. One weekend Moore introduced Lewis to his mother, who liked having the boys out to tea and stuffing their cheeks with cake.

Mrs Janie King Askins Moore had been separated from her husband for some years, but she never stopped looking over her shoulder for a sign that the Beast was in hot pursuit. When Paddy left Ireland to go to Clifton College, she followed and set up house in nearby Bristol. When Paddy went to Oxford for the OTC, she followed once more with eleven-year-old Maureen in tow. 'I liked her immensely and thoroughly enjoyed myself,' wrote Lewis to his father after spending an August weekend with the Moores.

The passage from cadet to second lieutenant took four months. On 18 September the newly commissioned young men got four weeks' leave. Instead of hurrying to Belfast to visit his father, Lewis decided to accept Moore's invitation to go to Bristol. He brought a cold and a severe sore throat. Mrs Moore took his temperature, and when the mercury soared past 100 degrees she swept him under the covers. Days became a week; one week became two; sometime before the end of the third week Maureen remembered hearing Paddy and Jack, faced with the rapidly approaching reality of war and the possibility of death, pledge that if one of them got killed, the other would take care of the bereaved parent.

Lewis arrived home in Belfast on 12 October. No doubt the elder Lewis was hurt that his son spent three weeks in another family's bosom and chose to spend only one at his own true hearth. When he heard more about the stay in Bristol, however, he wrote to Mrs Moore, thanking her for her hospitality. In a week his son was gone. As the ferry pulled away from the slip in Belfast, parting father from son perhaps forever, the elder Lewis shivered. What was said and what was left unsaid eddied about him until the following day. In the first post he got a letter from Bristol. It was from Mrs Moore, saying she was only too pleased to meet the boys in the OTC and have them out to her house. 'Your boy, of course, being Paddy's roommate, we know much better than the others, and he was quite the most popular boy at the party; he is very charming and most likeable and won golden opinions from everyone he met.'

Lewis rummaged around the army encampment near Plymouth. Crown Hill was its name; it had 'nice cosy little bits of green country with cottages and water and trees, then woodier hills rising at last into big, open moors that make up the horizon.' In the morning he played the officer, leading recruits onto the parade ground where he handed them over to an instructor. In the afternoon he censored mail. In the evening there was dinner in the officers' mess, 'a sort of glorified golf club house', where there was serious business like bridge and snooker and rumours about whether the Third Somerset Light Infantry would be sent to Ireland to quell the Sinn Fein or to France to confront the Germans. France it was. On Thursday 15 November they got two days' leave before embarkation.

'Have arrived Bristol on 48 hours leave,' wired Lewis to his father. 'Return Southampton Saturday. Can you come Bristol. If so meet at station. Reply Mrs Moore's address 56 Ravenswood Road Redland Bristol.'

'Don't understand telegram,' wired his father in return. 'Please write.'

Lewis wrote and wired again, but boarded the troop transport without seeing his father. He crossed over to France on 17 November and reached the front on 29 November, his nineteenth birthday. He didn't know where Moore hit the trenches; he had been assigned to a rifle brigade.

In the months that followed, Lewis was wounded in the back, felled by friendly fire on Mt Bernenchon during the battle of Arras on 15 April 1918. What hit Moore was in the front and far from friendly. 'He was last seen,' wrote the adjutant in his brigade, 'on the morning of [24 March 1918] with a few men defending a position on a river bank against infinitely superior numbers of the enemy. All the other officers and most of the men of his company have become casualties, and I fear it is impossible to obtain more definite information.' Mrs Moore did learn later that Paddy was taken prisoner, overthrew his guards, and got back to British lines only to be sent over the top again. He was hit in the leg, and as he lay in a field, his batman trying to staunch the blood, a bullet tore through his head, killing him instantly.

∽

If Mrs Moore could not have Paddy, then she would have Jack.

She went to Lewis when he was returned from France to a military hospital near London. He recuperated the faster because of her affection, and when he was transferred to other medical establishments around the country, she was not far behind. When he returned to Univ. in 1919, she rented a house in Oxford. After three terms of living in rooms at Univ., he moved in with her and Maureen, moving house nine times before ending up on Western Road in Headington, a burgeoning community east of Oxford. The Beast in Ireland sent payments to wife and daughter; sometimes they arrived; sometimes they didn't. Lewis made up the difference from the allowance sent him by his father. Most months it was his income alone they lived on.

Living in a house named Hillsboro, he managed to combine 'the life of an Oxford undergraduate with that of a country householder.' He walked down to Oxford where he met his university appointments and shopped at the butcher's and grocer's. He walked about the countryside, sometimes with the family, other times by himself, almost always with a dog. In the kitchen he cut turnips and peeled onions and put ham on to boil. About the house he moved furniture, scraped and stained floors, cleaned the grate and lit the fire. In the garden he watered peas and beans. The lawn he mowed when the weather permitted.

'Have you ever sawed wood?' he wrote, trying to capture the experience on paper. 'If not, you probably have an idea that one sets the saw lightly on the log, gets to work, and continues steadily deepening until the two halves fall apart.' It was during the coal strike of 1921; his hands were indeed willing, but his thumbs would not bend to the task. 'Not a bit of it; you set the saw lightly on the log and then try to move it. It darts aside with a sound like a swallow, and you wrap a handkerchief round your hand; when the blood has soaked through this, you go into the house and get some court plaster.'

Not that he needed 'an alternative to idleness or to hateful thoughts', but if he did, 'domestic drudgery' was it; Mrs Moore laid it on with a trowel. He could have become quarrelsome, but he decided to be biblical. It was 'no one's fault,' he wrote to a friend; it was just 'the curse of Adam.' The drudgery, however, did not impede his intellectual progress. Rather it was like the clickety-clack of a train racing along iron track; it provided a continuous and not unpleasant background for reading and thinking and writing and dreaming about the future. It was also the sound of a well-adjusted family.

During lunch one day, just when Lewis was getting used to sitting at the head of the table, able to accept 'mild little wrangles about nothing,' one arose. There were two kinds of sweet on a plate; Maureen, aged fourteen, could not decide which to have; faced with yet another adolescent irritation, Mrs Moore begged her to pick one and shut up. Having no difficulty deciding which one he wanted, he picked up his fork and speared a tart. As if in retaliation, the plumpish pastry sent a fine shower of custard and juice all over the pater-familias, Maureen and her mother exploding with laughter.

Maureen was eleven years old and Lewis nineteen when they first met. She felt he had changed when he returned from the war, but she didn't bother to say how. She liked to read fairy tales; he encouraged her to move on to romance and poetry. The fact that she showed talent in music was pleasing, but her hours of practice on the piano often drove him from the house. He even tutored a young woman in Latin in return for her teaching Maureen the violin. He went with her to plays and recitals and accompanied her to church, sometimes against his better judgment. When she was confirmed in Christ Church Cathedral in December 1922, he was there. The 1662 Book of Common Prayer called the body and blood of Jesus Christ 'the most comfortable sacrament'; when she received it for the first time in January 1923, Lewis was there too; it made him feel most uncomfortable.

Minto, as Mrs Moore came to be called, had a wide acquaintance, was a fair observer of human nature, liked animals of all sorts, kept rein on her teenaged daughter's activities, and presided over her successive domains like an empress. She played bridge and croquet; she was seen on the golf course and the tennis court. As for her health, there were good days and bad days. Varicose veins bothered her; now and then there were shooting pains in her right arm; and depression periodically descended on her. But on the good days she was a lively conversationalist and could hold her own when Lewis' friends came to call.

❧

Of the five boys in the OTC who visited Mrs Moore in 1917, only Lewis was left. He had become her son Paddy not unwillingly; indeed he had flourished under her attentive and affectionate mothering. He was cautious at first about introducing his university friends to the Headington hideout, but sooner or later they were all invited. The first thing Mrs Moore wanted to know as she seated them at the kitchen table was about the war.

Rodney Pasley had served as second lieutenant in the Royal Field Artillery. Lewis first met him at Univ. Mornings at the college were for lectures and libraries; afternoons were for cricket and rowing and rugby and, for the non-athletic, walking. He and Pasley would walk their legs off and finally come to rest 'in a wood full of primrose.' Poetry was what they had in common. Lewis had a volume published. Pasley had a manuscript and was looking for a publisher. And wasn't it a shame 'how gushing generations have teased the language till the very name of primrose sounds sentimental'? The flowers were 'really rather attractive.'

Back in the kitchen at Headington, Mrs Moore served rabbit pie. Devouring it noisily, Pasley averred as how he was about to become engaged. Engagement Lewis immediately denounced as 'that fatal tomb of all lively and interesting men,' acknowledging of course that it might not be so in Pasley's case. What would he do for money? asked Mrs Moore. He was assistant master at Alleyn's School nearby; that paid enough to get started. Well, 'this marrying business' took money and lots of it, said Mrs Moore, and the conversation continued at a lively pace far into the night.

❧

Early on at Univ. Pasley had introduced Lewis to Leo Baker, who was living at Wadham College. Baker was playing about at the time with hypnotism and automatic writing; he also wrote poems. They immediately fell deep into conversation about 'ghosts and spirits and Gods.' Pasley had left by this time; Baker's eyes fell on Lewis'. Lewis got 'dazed and drunk in all he said.' By the conversation's end he 'was tired and nervous and pulled to pieces.'

What did he do in the war? asked Mrs Moore as she shoved a warm bowl of rice pudding under his nose. He was a flight lieutenant in the 80th Squadron of the RAF. Did he fly planes? My, the pudding was delicious and yes, he did fly planes. Lewis hastened to point out

that he flew 'under very deadly fire in France.' Well, that was because
— and could he have some more pudding? — he was 'out of body'
most of the time and could see someone else in the cockpit, roaring
with laughter and flying the plane between the anti-aircraft barrages.
He got the Distinguished Flying Cross for it, added Lewis. Not bad
for a conscientious objector, said Baker with a wink, and asked
Lewis how he had managed in the army.

'I loathed it.'

'Were you frightened in France?'

'All the time, but I never sank so low as to pray.'

Baker remembered the first, and indeed the only time he and
Lewis had talked about God. It was over tea at Wadham.

'You take too many things for granted. You can't start with God. *I
don't accept God!*' shouted Lewis, thumping the table and startling
the teacups.

If Baker could not talk with Lewis about God, Lewis could not
discourse to Baker on what was dear to his mind, German
philosophy.

'You will be interested to hear,' Lewis wrote to him a short time
later, 'that in the course of my philosophy on the existence of matter,
I have had to postulate some sort of God as the least objectionable
theory; but of course we know nothing.'

The two young men did talk about particular poems and poetry
in general, and where poetic inspiration came from. Could the poet
wish for it, hoping it would come? Could he will it, thereby demanding it to come? Did a muse have to descend from stage heaven and
drape it over the poet's shoulders?

Since 1916 the 'Swiss Family Sitwell' — as Lewis called Edith,
Osbert, and Sacherevell Sitwell — had been publishing *Wheels*, an
annual anthology of new poems whose form and matter were in
direct opposition to the prevailing poetry of the Georgians. 'Vorticists,'
Lewis branded them, deeming them nothing more than free-verse
mongers trying like Pound and Eliot to throw, right down the drain,
metre and rhyme and nature as a reliable source of imagery.

Pasley proposed, and Lewis and Baker were quick to accept, that
they should devise an anthology that would knock the locomotion
out of *Wheels*; it would contain the work of new poets, themselves of
course, and the poems would 'sing of contemporary life within
classical forms.' Lewis came up with the title *The Way's the Way*,
something he had fished out of John Bunyan's *Pilgrim's Prog· ·ss*.
Basil Blackwell, proprietor of Oxford's premier bookshop, promised
he would publish it and charge five, perhaps six shillings a copy.
Pasley got Margaret Giddings, a friend of his, to contribute; Carola

Oman, daughter of the historian at All Souls College, also joined the venture.

When the manuscript was sent to Blackwell, he stalled at first and then responded that for the work to be published, he would have to receive a subsidy from the poets. Pleading poverty, Lewis replied that he and the others 'could meet him to precisely the extent of £O-Os-Od.' That was in September 1920. By Christmas time, Lewis was returning the poems to the contributors. With Baker's he added eight lines that described in classical form at least one sad fact of contemporary life.

> *The Way's the Way* to bankruptcy,
> Paying cash down and heavy loss:
> And for this reason Edmond Gosse
> Those lovely lines will never see.
> And oh! to think with what a shock
> We crush the hopes of Clutton Brock;
> And luckless G. K. Chesterton
> Is fated not to look thereon.

Baker got his degree in 1922, but at the cost of complete physical collapse. Mrs Moore invited him out to Headington, where she mothered him back to health. His talents turned him away from the academe and onto the proscenium. While at the Moores he got a part in *Glorious England*, a play by Bernice de Bergerac, which was performed in the Priory Gardens of Christ Church on 31 July 1922. After that he was off to London where he joined the Old Vic. Lewis saw him several times, once as Earl of Westmoreland in Shakespeare's *Henry VI, Part III* in 1922 and in 1924 as First Lord in Shakespeare's *As You Like It*. After this he announced his intention to marry and brought around his intended.

༄

Baker had introduced a friend of his to Lewis. Owen Barfield was his name; he had taken the entrance examination to Oxford, and as was announced in *The Times* on 14 December 1916, got a scholarship to Wadham. Poetry again was the common bond, and on 24 May 1922, Lewis took the bus from Headington into Oxford to meet Barfield about 1.00 in the gardens of Wadham. It was a hot day; they strolled the rectangular path, then sat down on a heavy wooden bench under a purple copper beech. Lilacs bending in the breeze, herbaceous borders in full bloom, insects on the march and in mid-flight — could the bower of bliss in Spenser's *Faerie Queene* be better than this?

Literature had been in Oxford for centuries, but psychology had only just arrived, and the two young men tried to decide, by old candle and new torch, what made Christina Pontifex, the young woman who had won her husband-to-be from her sisters in a cardgame, tick. She was a character in *The Way of All Flesh*, an autobiographical work of fiction in which novelist Samuel Butler dealt gloomily and ironically with his own relationship to his father. They labelled the problem 'Christina's Dreams.' Lewis condemned them; 'the love dream made a man incapable of real love, the hero dream made him a coward.' Taking the opposite point of view, Barfield argued as fascinatingly and infuriatingly as a woman.

Next month Lewis invited Barfield out to Headington for supper. He saluted Mrs Moore and identified himself as having served in the Royal Engineers, rising from pioneer to second lieutenant; no fighting, no dangers, no anecdotes. After supper the men went for a walk in the woods. Sun setting, in the middle of a field, Barfield broke into a dance around a black and white cat named Pierrot. He did it, as Lewis remembered, 'with sublime lack of self-consciousness and wonderful vigour.' The cat was terrified, but it was amusing to Barfield and memorable to Lewis and three horses who happened to be standing by. The sun having set, they returned to the house, breaking into a 'burlesque poem in *terza rima*, composing a line each in turn,' trying to keep the *aba*, *bcb*, *cdc* rhyme bouncing merrily on. They continued it long into the night, eventually entitling the composition, done in the manner of Dante's *Divina Commedia*, 'The Button Moulder's Story.'

Barfield too succumbed to love; in April 1923 he was married. Maud was shy, homely in several senses, perhaps ten years older than her husband, or so Lewis concluded when he finally met her. He had the feeling, though, that he would like her and that she would improve Barfield where he needed improving. Sometime later Lewis and Barfield had a go-round about marriage in general; Mrs Barfield was not present; they soon found they felt pretty much the same about women and home life and especially about the unimportance of all the things that are advertised in common literature. There were differences between the two species, and it was more than biological. 'Either women or men are mad,' said Lewis. Barfield agreed, but added that at times he could see the woman's point of view with astonishing clarity.

◈

With Lewis and Barfield on that walk through the field that night, and also composing every third line of the *terza rima*, was Cecil Harwood. He matriculated at Christ Church; he too had been introduced to Lewis by Baker. He often caught the bus to Headington to enjoy Mrs Moore's hospitality and whatever might be coming out of her oven.

Starved by a spiritual hunger that demanded satisfaction, he would walk with Lewis and debate the great issues. Foremost in his mind one day was Rudolf Steiner, a German philosopher-artist-scientist, whose works were filtering across the English Channel. As theory evolved into movement, Steiner passed from Goethe to theosophy to anthroposophy.

What, Lewis demanded to know, was anthroposophy?

First of all, said Harwood, it was an advance on theosophy.

That was a relief, sighed Lewis.

It presented a world, a spiritual world comprehensible to pure thought, but accessible only to the highest faculties of mental knowledge.

That sounded like panpsychism to Lewis.

Steiner promised immortality.

That was a sugar plum, countered Lewis, that could be got in places better than Steiner.

Spiritual forces were everywhere. What could Lewis possibly oppose to that?

Shamelessly mythological people were everywhere, replied Lewis, but they were not spiritual forces; Steiner should know better than that, and so should Harwood.

Nonsense, said Harwood; he knew precisely what Steiner meant by spiritual forces.

The whole bag of tricks sounded like pagan animism to Lewis, and everyone, just everyone, knew what an anthropomorphic failure of the imagination that was.

Pagan animism might have been a failure, said Harwood, but anthroposophy would surely succeed.

Besides, said Lewis, wouldn't a knowledge of the life that was in trees and such like, real and unhuman, be more preferable?

If there were no such things as spiritual forces, asked Harwood, then how could one explain the similarity of the world's languages?

Probably, countered Lewis, by the similarity of the world's throats.

A hopeless materialist, Harwood branded Lewis.

An honest Horatio, Lewis complimented Harwood; for as their conversation grew louder, Lewis grew hotter, but Harwood sailed coolly, imperturbably, on.

∽

Lewis would have Minto — her pies and puddings were irresistible, and she was rollicking with his friends — if he could not have Flora. Photographs reminded him that his mother was pretty. Florence Hamilton was a clever girl, relatives told him. She got honours in logic and mathematics at Queen's College, Belfast; she wrote articles for magazines. But when she died in 1908, he was only nine years old.

There was still his father. Albert James Lewis was a lawyer with a practice that prospered. He had a large house built for his family. He loved to read, stocked the shelves of his library with books; as soon as his sons were able to make out the words, they began to devour the volumes. His wife, the half of his life that contained beauty and harmony and stability, died a painful death after an operation in the house, but he struggled to contain his grief. Although it would leave him only with housekeepers, he had no hesitation about sending his sons to be educated in England. Lonely but not unhopeful, he continued to live in the big house, expecting to enjoy periodic visits from his sons.

In 1925, however, July passed, August passed, September had already begun; still Jack hadn't come to Little Lea. What could a father think about a son who was consorting with a married woman except that he was having an affair? 'If Jack were not an impetuous, kind-hearted creature who could be cajoled by any woman who has been put through the mill,' wrote Albert in a letter, 'I should not be so uneasy.'

Jack explained the situation to him a hundred times. Courtenay Edward Moore was a scoundrel; Mrs Moore had no alternative, after the death of her son, but to seek sanctuary elsewhere. Albert could only wonder what the elusive Mr Moore would say in his own defence. He went on to develop the argument that the only reason he kept the big house open — with a succession of surly and unsatisfactory housekeepers — was for the boys to enjoy in their vacations, but if they were going to come home for only a handful of days each year . . .

It was September when Jack entered the front door at Little Lea. He did so with trepidation, but the dread was worse than the reality. He found his father well; Albert was cheered by the visit. Inevitably, the conversation turned toward money. Over the last ten years Albert had been never less than generous. When Jack won a prize or distinguished himself academically, Albert would fire off a fiver or tenner for celebrations; he would never forget his son's birthday. Jack was not slow in letting his father know about the dentist and the cobbler and the bookseller. The resulting cheque from Belfast was always received gratefully, even if it were deposited forgetfully between the pages of a book.

Soon he would be moving into new quarters at Magdalen and that, Albert pointed out, would mean new furnishings. Would he like some funds for that? Would he perhaps like to pick out a piece or two at Little Lea and have them shipped to Oxford? Jack thanked him but didn't think that would be necessary. His undergraduate rooms at Univ. had been furnished well enough; no doubt a fellow's rooms at Magdalen would contain everything he needed.

⤸

Lewis was depressed on leaving his father. At the beginning of October, seeking relief, he left Oxford and travelled by train to Cambridge, then on to Colchester. There, he headed for the military base where he met his brother, who was officer in charge of supplies. Warren Hamilton Lewis was three years older than Jack, unmarried, and happily a member of the Army Service Corps.

At the military barracks Warren had a motorcycle, by make a Daudel; he liked to pack his brother into the sidecar, together with a bag of sandwiches, and run about the English countryside. Earlier in 1925 they took a *Daudelspiel* southward to Salisbury. Approaching the city across the rolling downs, they could see the slender spire of the cathedral some fifteen miles away. The cathedral itself was enthralling, a moment of time petrified. What impressed Jack most was 'the force of mind; the thousands of tons of masonry held in place by an idea, a religion; buttress, window, acres of carving, the very lifeblood of men's work, all piled up there, and gloriously *useless* from the side of base utility for which we alone build now.'

Next morning of their spring trip they made a run to nearby Stonehenge. The megalithic limestone smelled of mildew. While they were wondering what the Bronze Age priests had used the place for, and taking photographs of each other lounging on the heelstone, they heard an artillery battery practising over the next ridge; it brought them back to the Great War. The long-barrelled guns sounded 'much louder and more sinister' than they had remembered.

As they made the run back to Oxford that day, Warren reminded Jack of the wild cycle ride he had made on 24 April 1918, almost seven years before. Warren was in France, some seven or eight miles behind the front, handling guns and ammunition, when he got a telegram from, of all places, Belfast, stating that Jack had been severely wounded. It was 1.30 p.m. Warren grabbed a motorcycle and set off, 'roaring along the straight bits of road and nursing [the] engine over the rough', trying to prevent fear from getting the worst of him and trying to squeeze the best out of his machine.

Some fifty miles and three hours later, he found the building that had been converted into a hospital. Jack was in bed; the left side of his face and his left hand were covered with bandages. As it turned out, there was only dirt in his eye and scratches on cheek and hand, but his left leg had been hit from behind and above the knee; shrapnel had entered the area just under his left armpit, passing through his rib cage and coming to rest in his chest. He seemed in good spirits, if in a little pain; they chatted for an hour or so, recalling old 'wheezes', stories their father liked to tell.

This particular weekend in October 1925 turned out to be uneventful. A motorized hike was out of the question, the Daudel having to be repaired in Colchester. Instead, the brothers dawdled through the Norman castle, which housed a collection of Roman antiquities. Then they ambled around what remained of Camulodunum, as the Roman colony at Colchester was called; stone walls and arched entranceways of the sort that Boadicea and her Britons tried to storm in AD61. After that it was to a pub they went. October was oyster time in Essex; the brothers washed them down with the local beer.

Jack left Colchester refreshed; Warren, as always on parting with his brother, felt depressed. He was happy about his brother's becoming a fellow at Magdalen. He was not exactly unhappy with Jack's situation with the Moores. He had even visited the house at Headington, sampled Minto's Celtic cuisine, and played croquet with Maureen. When he came to think of it, he was quite happy with his own position in the ASC. He could read, listen to music, entertain a lady of an evening, and Daudel about on weekends.

❧

Back at Magdalen, Lewis was assigned rooms in New Buildings, a single structure which in 1925 was already 190 years old. It was a rectangular, three-storey, cream-coloured pile built along classical eighteenth-century lines; at dawn and dusk it had the look of a ship anchored across the croquet lawn from the medieval buildings of the college. On the ground floor was a cloister that ran the length of the building in the front; in the basement were bathrooms and lavatories for the rooms above. On the three residential floors were apartments joined to each other vertically; that is to say, by staircases; which meant that each set of rooms had views both on the front and the back of the building.

Lewis had to move into New Buildings before Michaelmas term began in October. When he went to inspect the new quarters, he entered the colonnade in the middle and turned right. He found the gold numerals on a black plaque that indicated staircase 3 and climbed one flight to room 3. On entering he found a large sitting-room with two windows facing north, and facing south a bedroom with a window and a small sitting-room with a window.

To his amazement the rooms were empty. There was linoleum on the floor of the small sitting-room; there was a washstand in the bedroom; but there was nothing else. Expecting that he would not have to buy any furnishings, he had refused a grant from his father. In horror he fled to Mrs Moore, who, like a mother, said not to worry; they would go shopping in the morning.

'Carpets, tables, curtains, chairs, fenders, fire irons, coal boxes, table covers — everything — had to be bought in haste. It has cost me over £90, although I was able to pick up a few things secondhand. It sounds an alarming total,' he wrote to his father, 'but I do not think I have been extravagant; the rooms certainly do not look as if they had been furnished by a plutocrat.'

Lewis shared many things with Mrs Moore. Without her help, his new rooms would be in a shambles for months. But what he couldn't share with her, as he gazed out the window, was what he felt. His father would get an epistolary description of the place, but the full emotional content of the scene and what it meant to him could be understood only by a friend. He sat down to write to Alexander Kenneth Hamilton Jenkin, Esq.

Jenkin had been with him at Univ. and indeed would have stayed in Oxford if only he could have got a job. He was 'a little pale person with a smooth green face, not unlike a lizard's.' His health was not the best, but he hiked and biked; he had his own principle of push-biking, the maxim being that 'Where I go, my machine can go!' He practised his religion, hated art for art's sake, and wrote sad poetry about his native Cornwall.

Jenkin was also bookish. Lewis remembered once having memorized a rollicking sentence from one of the books on Jenkin's shelf, a tour of Cornwall written in the seventeenth century. Under the heading of 'Beastes', rats were described as 'not only mischievous by day for their devouring of clothes, writings, and meats, but cumbersome by night for their rattling and jousting as they gallop their galliards in the roof.' Jenkin, if anyone, could understand his feelings that night.

'The windows of my northern room look into the grove. There is a flat stretch of grass receding into big forest trees — all day long at present the leaves are eddying up the sky from them . . . There is nothing in sight, not even a gable, to remind me that I am in a town . . .'

Listening to the autumn leaves being crisped in the wind, Lewis fell asleep. 'A thin little hooting, rather like a faint cough, and most unearthly.' The noise woke Lewis; somebody or something was in the grove. It surely couldn't be the deer.

He lay back, trying to fall asleep again, the 'unearthly' noise bringing to mind the 'shocker play' he and Jenkin had always planned to write. As he recalled, they had created the characters. A Scientist with 'a bright red beard, Mephistophelian in shape but reaching to the waist, very thick lips, and one leg shorter than the other.' A Corpse whose body lay in a coffin packed with ice, but whose brain and nerves were kept alive by injections. A Hero and a Heroine who found 'a poor fellow whose face was badly smashed in the war' huddling by the fire, complaining of the cold and how the Scientist was always chasing him about. Of course, the Heroine would be the Scientist's next victim . . .

Lewis fell asleep, but the narrative, such as it was, continued in a dream. The Corpse escaped and ran amok, pursuing Lewis about the streets of London and down into the Underground. Lewis managed to reach the lift; the Liftman was terrified; and as the Corpse was about to strike, Lewis screamed, 'There's going to be an accidennnnnt!'

Awake now and sweating, Lewis heard that noise coming again from the grove; only this time it was 'most unpoetical and an anticlimax in the eyes of the unwise'; it seemed to be 'the grunting of old fat pigs.'

In the morning, shaving in the bathroom in the basement, Lewis looked up through the window and got 'a delicious, earthy freshness and a horizontal view of dew and cobwebs along the turf' of the grove. He also saw what had to be the cause of the disturbing noises the night before: 'a solitary stag nibbling quite close to the sill as if he were the first animal in the world.' Not quite the first, as he would learn later in the day. October was rutting season for the fallow deer in Magdalen grove.

❧

Lewis' first weeks at Magdalen were prosaic and somewhat different from his experience at Univ. There were more dons than at his previous college. They breakfasted and lunched in the common room; at Univ. he could have these meals sent to his rooms. They dined informally in hall, whereas at Univ. they wore formal attire. The one exception was when the president of Magdalen planned to be present; then a notice was sent to the dons to dress for dinner. The general tone of the place Lewis found 'rather slack and flippant.' The dons and undergraduates he found 'a little aloof.' But this was due, he sincerely hoped, to geography, the college being situated at the end of the town, on the edge of the suburbs.

Nights at Magdalen, however, had a poetic quality. On returning from dinner at another college, he would enter from the street, pass through the porter's lodge, then plunge into 'a long dark cobbled passage' opening into a cloistered quadrangle beshadowed by the moon, then plunge into another dark passage. Or, after leaving Mrs Moore and Maureen, he would enter the gate at the far end of the deer park, rain drumming on the ground, hoofs pounding away, and have to make his way through the clinging and comforting fog. The high point of both approaches was when 'the long lighted line of the cloisters in New Buildings' hove into view, and he scampered up staircase 3.

∾∾ 1926 ∾∾

In January, the beginning of Hilary term, Lewis gave his first lecture as fellow and tutor of Magdalen. Not wanting to appear immodest, he had chosen a small room in the college. On the day of the lecture some pupils studying English at other colleges, at the insistence of their tutors who were Lewis' friends, poured through the porter's lodge at Magdalen. When Lewis arrived, he could not get through the door, the room was so crowded. He turned and led the throng out to the porter's lodge and asked what other rooms were available. The porter pointed to the building across the street. With Lewis at the lead, academic gowns flying, they swarmed across the High. Brakes squealed, gears whined, and the smell of rubber hung in the cold, crisp air as they darted between charabancs with concertina hoods and bullnose Morrises made at Cowley.

Lewis had wanted to lecture on eighteenth-century precursors of the Romantic movement and did considerable work on the subject before he discovered in December, quite by accident, that F. P. Wilson, his English tutor at Univ., was going to lecture on English poetry from James Thompson, born in 1700, to William Cowper, died in 1800. 'Being neither willing nor able to rival Wilson,' he wrote to his father, 'I am driven to concentrate on the prose people, of whom at present I know very little.' During December and the first half of January he prepared furiously. When he finally mounted the dais, he lectured on Samuel Johnson and James Boswell, on Edward Gibbon, Adam Smith and Edmund Burke.

∾∾

Not long after the lecture, Lewis was felled by an aching head, swollen glands, inflamed eyes. German measles was the diagnosis; he retired to bed where he dozed, he daydreamed, he thought of the lecture. The men must have come to see what *it* was like. The women must have come to see what *he* was like. At least he got out alive, which was more than he could say of the lecturer in *Dymer*, a long narrative poem he had completed a few months before. In the middle of a dull and droning lecture, Dymer laughed out loud. When the lecturer said something like 'Silence, please!' the nineteen-year-old let out an 'idiot-like guffaw' and swung his right arm lazily, striking the lecturer on the head. 'The old man tittered, lurched, and dropt down dead.'

There was much that was feverish about *Dymer*, thought Lewis as he tossed and turned. Its two thousand lines narrated 'the story of a man who, on some mysterious bride, begets a monster; which monster, as soon as it has killed its father, becomes a god.' The story first came into his head in 1915. He attempted a prose version in 1916, but gave up after a year. He began again on 2 April 1922, this time in poetry. He chose rhyme royal, a stanza used by Chaucer and Shakespeare, William Morris and John Masefield. He worked continuously, almost daily, until August, perhaps September, 1925.

The story was set in Perfect City, an ideal locale reminiscent of Plato's Republic and Trotsky's Russia after the revolution, but redolent of British public schools and army life.

> There you'd have thought the gods were smothered down
> Forever, and the keys were turned on fate.
> No hour was left unchartered in that town,
> And love was in a schedule and the State
> Chose for eugenic reasons who should mate
> With whom, and when. Each idle song and dance
> Was fixed by law and nothing left to chance.

When Dymer was born, astronomers saw nothing unusual in their scopes. He was just another unit to be nourished and nurtured in the commune.

> For nineteen years they worked upon his soul,
> Refining, chipping, moulding and adorning.
> Then came the moment that undid the whole —
> The ripple of rude life without warning.
> It came in lecture-time one April morning

— Alas for laws and locks, reproach and praise,
Who ever learned to censor the spring days!

Febrile also was the character of the magician, who was inspired by William Butler Yeats. Lewis had met the Irish poet-playwright when he took up residence in Oxford in 1921. On a March evening Lewis and some other undergraduates walked up the Broad and turned in at No. 4. Climbing the staircase was like entering Hell. Demons and monsters stared out from the walls, etchings from the needle of William Blake. At the top of the stairs they were met by Georgie, the poet's new wife, and ushered into an oriental chamber, tall candles burning, flame-coloured curtains drawn. Facing the fireplace was a semicircle of chairs; sitting in the centre was Yeats. He looked 'very big, about sixty years of age,' in the firelight. On one side of him was a little man with a grey beard; on the other was a puckish cleric, whom Lewis seemed to remember as a lecturer somewhere in the university.

The young men hoped to hear some wisdom from the man who had edited the works of William Blake and wrote plays like *Cathleen ni Houlihan* and published poetry like *The Wild Swans at Coole*. But when they sat down on the antique chairs, he spoke in what sounded like French tones of 'cabbalism and "the hermetic knowledge."' If not wisdom, then perhaps they would hear gossip about William Morris or John Addington Symonds or Rabindranath Tagore; instead he talked, in Irish accents now, of 'magic and ghosts and mysteries.' 'What fluttering of the dovecote!' thought Lewis as he squirmed on the uncomfortable chair.

The poet spoke as if in monologue, but when there was a lull, Mrs Yeats and the priest proferred questions. The conversation, such as it was, turned eventually toward psychic phenomena.

'There's a professor living in Oxford at this moment,' said Yeats, 'who is the greatest sceptic in print. The same man has told me that he entered a laboratory where Mme Blavatsky was doing experiments; saw the table floating near the ceiling with Mme B. sitting on it; vomited; gave orders that no further experiments were to be done in his laboratory — and refused to let the story be known.'

'I don't believe it,' said the priest, whom Lewis now remembered as living at Campion Hall, the Jesuit residence in Oxford.

'Father Martindale,' said the poet mischievously, 'ye are a sceptic.'

This was 'the weirdest show' he had ever seen, Lewis would write to his father that night.

As the fire died, the conversation waned. Mrs Yeats rose from the divan to serve sherry and vermouth in long, curiously shaped glasses.

Martindale had whisky in an even longer, more curiously shaped glass.

And then, Lewis would write to his brother, 'the orgy was at an end.'

⤸

Recovered from the measles, able to walk about but not without ache, Lewis set out for Exeter College one evening. Nevill Coghill had invited him to dinner. He walked up the High.

Lewis first met Coghill in September 1922 at the beginning of Michaelmas term. Lewis had finished philosophy, Coghill had finished history, and jobs being hard to find, both were adding English as a second string to their bow. To Lewis, Coghill seemed to have stepped right out of *The Canterbury Tales*, full of such fourteenth-century virtues as 'chivalry, honour, courtesy, "freedom", and "gentilesse."' To Coghill, Lewis seemed to have wandered in from *The Faerie Queene*, a sixteenth-century allegorical poem in which dragons and giants, sorcerers and sorceresses did battle with the forces of virtue. 'Its knights, dwarfs, and ladies were real to him,' remembered Coghill long after, 'and became real even to me while he discussed them.'

Lewis turned right into Catte Street, 'street of the mouse-catchers' as it was called at the turn of the thirteenth century. The sun had set; streetlights illuminated the cobbles. On his left evensong was in progress at St Mary the Virgin; on his right dinner was being prepared in the kitchen of All Souls. Lewis remembered as he walked that he and Coghill liked the same poems, even the same passages in these poems, 'the epic scale of their emotions and their overmastering rhythmical patterns.' And Coghill would tolerate him when on one of their rambles about the countryside he would roar out the crashing rhythms of 'The Battle of Maldon' in Old English or *The Iliad* in Ionic Greek; indeed, Coghill would say that Lewis's voice had 'the taste of noble wine.'

In front of Lewis was the Radcliffe Camera, its dome like an Orthodox Easter egg. Past it, he turned left and headed towards Exeter. The Bodleian Library was now on his right. Then he passed under a huge horse chestnut into the fellows' garden of Exeter and thence into the college itself.

There, he was met by Coghill and ushered into the seventeenth-century hall, a high-ceilinged room beamed with Spanish chestnut and windowed like a cathedral; the fireplaces were aglow; shadows played on a carved Jacobean screen. He had finished *Dymer*, Lewis told his friend during dinner. Coghill asked to read it. He would have to keep it confidential, said Lewis; that he wrote 'pomes' might

41

be turned against him at Magdalen. Coghill agreed and asked if he had a publisher. Heinemann had published *Spirits in Bondage*, said Lewis, but that was eight years ago; Heinemann was dead now, died in 1920, and besides, they didn't sell that many copies.

The next day Lewis left the manuscript at the porter's lodge of Exeter. When Coghill opened it he found 'a thickish folder of type-written cantos.' He went into the fellows' garden and began to read. Well, it wasn't Eliot. Dymer was no Prufrock; Perfect City was no Waste Land; the poem was not a surgical exploration of the ills of urban society. It was more romantic and narrative, like *Dauber*, Masefield's reminiscences of his youth when he ran away to sea. It was a trifle antique but, like Eliot's 'The Hollow Men,' it ended with a bang. 'A good story well told,' Coghill felt he could say in a note that accompanied the return of the manuscript, 'supported by the sense of there being a powerful mind behind it, flashing out occasionally with an original expression.'

'It is as if you had given me a bottle of champagne,' replied Lewis on 4 February, 'a dangerous moment and difficult to reply to.'

〰️

In Trinity term, which ran from April to June and took its name from the first Sunday after Whitsun, Lewis undertook tutorials. Undergraduates trooped regularly to New Buildings, climbed stair-case 3, and thumped on door 3. There were De Peyer and Clark; 'a desperately stupid pair,' he noted in his diary for 1 May. There was Henry Yorke, a dark-complexioned young man who was writing a novel about what it was like to be blind. There was John Betjeman, an elfin creature with a winsome smile who was finding Oxford a garden of delights.

'I hope you don't mind as I have a blister.' Betjeman stood in Lewis' doorway, wearing a pair of flossy bedroom slippers.

'I should mind them very much myself,' said Lewis, 'but I have no objections to *your* wearing them.'

Had Lewis heard about the Fascists at the Labour Club last night? They broke into the meeting and interrupted the speakers, who were trying to drum up support for the wives and children of the strikers. Well, they were heckled, but before they left, they contributed to the relief fund set up for that very purpose.

How gloriously English! said Lewis, but Old English was more to the point. He handed Betjeman a reader with text on one side and glossary on the other. To the undergraduate, the Old English looked like modern English spelled badly. 'Cwic' was 'quick'; 'tingul' was 'twinkle.' When read aloud, it sounded worse, Lewis clucking his way through Alfred the Great's translations from Latin into the

English of the ninth century. Great fun, said Lewis, and reading the prose of King Alfred gave one more sense of antiquity than the poetry of Sophocles; but he couldn't convince Betjeman. The young man preferred almost anything to tutorials. He would motor strikers around Oxfordshire to gain additional support for the cause. He would spend long weekends as a guest at country estates, telephoning Lewis on Mondays to say that he had got measles and that the doctor forbade his picking up even a book. When he did show up, Lewis sat at his desk, back to the fireplace, and corrected papers while Betjeman stammered and stumbled over a text, not remembering whether this vowel was subject to J-mutation or that vowel to U-mutation. When the hour was exhausted, so was Lewis' patience. He demanded that the young man do more.

༂

On the night of 27 April Lewis had a fire going in his rooms and was sitting down to a book — Walter William Skeat on English language — when there was a knock on the door. It was Weldon. Without invitation he walked in and plumped down, wanting to talk. Thomas Dewar were his first two names, but he was called Harry. He was Lewis' age; he taught philosophy at Magdalen; in the late war he rose to captain; his conspicuous behaviour under fire had brought him mention in dispatches and, ultimately, a decoration on his tunic.

Whisky was splashed; it enkindled some light banter and not a little bawdy, Weldon laughing the louder and the longer. Whisky was splashed again, and the talk turned to *The Golden Bough*, James Frazer's study of comparative folklore, magic, and religion. According to Frazer, there were many parallels between the rites and beliefs of early cultures and those of early Christians. There were chapters entitled 'Incarnate Human Gods' and 'The Killing of tne Divine King' and 'Sacrifice of the King's Son.' Magic seemed to have preceded religion everywhere, was Frazer's thesis; Weldon, or so Lewis thought, would surely agree that man turned to religion only after magic had failed.

'Rum thing, all that stuff of Frazer's about the dying god,' said Weldon, accepting another splash. 'It almost looks as if it really had happened once.'

After admitting that the New Testament Gospels were more or less true, Weldon went on to reveal that he believed in the Trinity, at least as presented by Hegel, the nineteenth-century German philosopher. The kingdom of the Father was expressed in logic. The kingdom of the Son was expressed in philosophy of nature. The kingdom of the Spirit was expressed in philosophy of spirit, which appeared in the union of God and the faithful in the Church. The Triune God, said Weldon, attempting to quote Hegel from memory, was the Father and the Son, and this differentiation in the unity as the Spirit. The whole thing seemed to fit in.

It was well past midnight, but not long after a final splash, before Weldon stopped talking about the extraordinariness of mistletoe and the absoluteness of spirit and tottered off to his rooms. Lewis was tottering too, not so much from the alcohol as from the realization that the cynical, tough-minded Weldon was a Christian, even of this vague and philosophical sort.

೧೦

On Wednesday 28 April Lewis had tea promptly at 4.00 pm. He had promised the president of Magdalen that he would teach philosophy to 'a troupe of performing bagbirds' if he had to; his services had just been volunteered to a women's college. At 4.30 he crossed the deer park, made his way along the banks of the Cherwell, and sallied across the university park.

Oxford had not always been hospitable to women of talent and aspiration. In 1878 E. S. Talbot, a clergyman who would become a bishop, founded two halls for them, one Church of England, the other non-denominational. Somerville, named after mathematician Mary Somerville, who had died six years before at the age of ninety-two, began in a private house with twelve students. In another house, with nine students, Elizabeth Wordsworth, grandniece of the poet, began Lady Margaret Hall; she chose Henry VII's mother as patroness because 'she was a gentlewoman, a scholar, and a saint, and after having been three times married, she took a vow of celibacy.' What more could be expected of any woman? By 1920 Somerville and Lady Margaret Hall had become colleges; the young women of Oxford took the same examinations and were awarded the same degrees as the young men.

When Lewis arrived at Lady Margaret Hall at 5.00 and entered the red brick building, he was relieved to find six girls waiting for him. In numbers there was safety. One pupil, having a tutor to herself for a whole term, could play disciple so charmingly that tutelage would turn into marriage. None of them had read Plato. With a little help from Lewis, however, they were soon chattering away.

Colbourne, as he wrote in his diary that night, was 'dignified and fairly sensible.' Scoones was 'lanky, dark.' Grant was 'a very massive, lumpish person who never opened her mouth.' Thring was 'the most talkative.' House was 'nervy, a trifle soulful, and worried.' Johnson was 'perhaps the best.' A seventh girl, Carter, arrived well after the discussion had started; something about searching for a lost tortoise, she said; she was 'the prettiest and perhaps rather a bitch.'

They met once a week during Trinity term; for each session Lewis was paid £1. Plato having been dispatched, eighteenth-century philosophers such as Berkeley and Hume were exposed and discussed. Papers were read on causation, what really happened when one billiard ball kissed another, and scepticism. 'It is as if, not content with seeing your eyes,' said one of the girls during a discussion of how one comes to know her self, 'you want to take them out and look at them — and then they wouldn't be eyes.' 'The pretty ones are stupid,' wrote Lewis to his father, his bachelorhood intact at end of term, 'and the interesting ones are ugly.'

∽

Lewis met G. K. Chesterton, albeit in book form, in an army hospital in Le Tréport, France in 1918, where he spent three 'wholly delightful' weeks recovering from pyrexia, trench fever acquired from a louse that appears only during warfare and only among infantry. Chesterton's *Tremendous Trifles* and *What's Wrong with the World* were the only books in reach. The essays in the books had a Christian patina about them, but the burnish was not blinding to one who was not a Christian. What he enjoyed was the logic, the rhetoric, the cascade of figures of speech and thought. Also the essays were humorous, containing what Lewis, an inveterate reader even at the age of nineteen, with perhaps a thousand volumes behind him, liked best: 'not just "jokes" imbedded in the page like currants in a cake, still . . . less a general tone of flippancy and jocularity, but the humour which is not in any way separable from the argument, but is rather (as Aristotle would say) the "bloom" on the dialectic itself.'

The Everlasting Man was published in 1925, but Lewis was able to settle down with a copy only months later. The author intended it to be a sort of non-fiction romance; Lewis found it full of mythology and history. The wording of the argument was shot through with metaphor and simile like 'the winged thunderbolt of thought and everlasting enthusiasm'; 'the trumpet of liberty [blowing] over the land of the living'; 'the lightning made eternal as the light.' The argument itself was that the case for Christianity was less irrational than the case against it, and the argument was enhanced by paradox. 'The next best thing to being really inside Christendom is to be really outside it.' 'While the best judge of Christianity is a Christian, the next best judge is something more like a Confucian.'

G. B. Shaw, author of *Man and Superman*, and H. G. Wells, author of *The Outline of History*, were Chesterton's intellectual enemies. If the encounter could be envisioned as swordplay, then Lewis saw in

The Everlasting Man the oversized Christian wielding his Wilkinson, his back to the sanctuary wall. What gave Lewis especial pleasure was, not the sabres flashing, not the épées plinging, but the participants fighting for their intellectual and spiritual lives. When Chesterton concluded, somewhere near the end of the book, that Christianity 'met the mythological search for romance by being a story and the philosophical search for truth by being a true story,' Lewis had to admit that he was impressed. Indeed he was charmed, but only in the way that 'a man feels the charm of a woman he has no intention of marrying.'

∞

On 11 May Lewis walked towards Merton College, where scholars had been studying one thing or another since 1264. The college itself was a collection of grim, grey buildings, medieval in appearance, with battlements and gunports and a pinnacled tower over the chapel. Through the five-hundred-year-old gate, Lewis entered the grounds. He was there to attend a meeting of the English faculty of the university, made up of dons, professors and fellows and tutors who taught language and literature in the various colleges.

Standing around before the meeting began, he met 'a smooth, pale, fluent little chap', as he would write in his journal that night. J. R. R. Tolkien was his name; he was a graduate of Exeter, began teaching at Leeds in 1920, and returned to Oxford in 1925 as Rawlinson and Bosworth Professor of Anglo-Saxon. Making conversation, Lewis asked and Tolkien answered. Spenser? Couldn't read him because of the forms. Language? That was the real thing in school. Literature? It was written for the amusement of men between thirty and forty. The English faculty? If they were honest, they would vote themselves out of business. 'No harm in him,' recorded Lewis; 'only needs a smack or two.'

When the meeting began Tolkien proposed a revision of the syllabus. Acknowledging that the language people were in a constant state of war with the literature people, each demanding that the English pupil spend more time in the one area than in the other, he went on to suggest that the pupils be required to spend great amounts of time reading in both language and literature. A proposal of sweet reasonableness, it would have seemed. Literature, however, sent galleons like Shakespeare and Milton against language, who countered with galliots like philology and Middle English. When the smoke cleared and the wreckage sank, all that was left of Tolkien's proposal was ripples.

There was much in what he said, thought Lewis as he left Merton by way of Logic Lane. If only he hadn't pushed so hard for Icelandic!

∞

On 19 May Lewis attended a dinner sponsored by the Martlets, a college literary society whose membership was limited to twelve, which met four times a term, three terms a year. The first meeting had been held on 24 October 1892, in an undergraduate's rooms; a paper entitled 'The Causes Which Led to the Renaissance' was read.

Whoever first chose the name of the society must have been looking for something appropriate to literary and aesthetic fledglings. Heraldry seemed promising as a source, providing as it did a symbolic sequence for sons in a family. First sons were labels; second sons were crescents; third sons were mulets; fourth sons were martlets and were usually depicted without beaks and feet.

Lewis was elected secretary of the society on 31 January 1919. At this and the next seven meetings he recorded in longhand précis of the papers read and summaries of the discussions that followed. From 15 October 1919, until 13 June 1921, he served as president. Four times he addressed the society on writers as diverse as William Morris, Edmund Spenser, James Stephens, and James Boswell.

Occasionally — and this Wednesday night was one of them — the undergraduate Martlets were treated by the don Martlets to 'a very excellent meal with wine . . . in cool, brown, oaky rooms.' Perhaps the dinner was not dissimilar from the one served at the hundredth meeting in 1906:

> Consommé Mermaid
> Sauce Walter Scott
> Suprême de smale Foweles
> Mouton rôti à la C Lamb
> Chartreuse à la Martlets
> Diablotines à la Milord Byron

~

'I feel there can be no possible question as to its greatness,' replied Guy N. Pocock when Coghill sent him Lewis' *Dymer*. The editor had read the first few stanzas with a view to rejecting it and then getting on with the rest of his morning's correspondence, but once begun, he couldn't put it down. That was in March. In April Dent accepted the manuscript with 'extraordinary pleasure.' In May Lewis was reading proof. In June Pocock sent cover designs for approval. In July Lewis was reading revised proof and battling depression. 'I never liked it less,' he confided to his journal. 'I felt that no mortal could get any notion of what the devil it was all about.'

September 18, publication day of the poem as a book, passed without comment. On the following day, however, the first review appeared; in the months to come there would be others. 'The voyage

47

of the soul in search of the spirit,' said *The Sunday Times*, 'its struggle with fear, with the listlessness of dreams, and its final triumph, are set forth with an unusual sureness.' '*Dymer* is a fine piece of work,' wrote Arthur Quiller-Couch to Pocock, 'fine in conception and full of brilliant lines and images.' 'Here,' said *The Spectator*, 'is a little epic burnt out of vital experience and given us through a poet's eye.'

෴

At Oxford there were two groups of young men: the larger, the comparatively rich for whom there was little incentive to work or study; the smaller, scholars who had to work hard and live cheaply. Among the latter was Alan Richard Griffiths. He had read Latin and Greek at Magdalen the year before, but now he didn't want to push on into philosophy. Why was that? asked Lewis. Because he had lost faith in the intellect and its ability to reason. Why was that so? Because, said Griffiths, intellectualism was a disease from which they were all suffering and which was bringing their civilization to decay. Was there one thing in his life, asked Lewis, to which he constantly returned? Yes, said Griffiths; it was his experience in the presence of nature. But what did he hope to gain by abandoning philosophy and taking up the study of English literature? He hoped to come nearer the truth he was seeking. Lewis sympathized with the young man, eight years his junior, but protested that that was the wrong reason to switch subjects. Griffiths held his ground and in the terms that followed he carried on 'a crusade against Dryden and Pope and the age of reason, which had an almost religious fervour in it.' He even put his sentiments into a paper that he read before an evening literary society over which Lewis presided. The members 'had to find a new religion and of this, Wordsworth, Shelley, and Keats, and the other leaders of the Romantic movement were the prophets.'

෴

Dymer was a critical success for the poet, but a financial failure for the publisher. The royalty statement from Messrs. Dent, dated 31 December, indicated that, of the 1,500 copies printed, 108 had been given away as review copies, and 126 copies had been sold. With the statement was a cheque for £3 15s 7d. Would more copies have been sold if the review in the *Times Literary Supplement*, which Lewis knew for a fact had been written in September, had appeared before 13 January 1927? 'Mr Hamilton's poem is notable because it is in the epic tradition and yet is modern in idiom and reflects a profoundly personal intuition.'

Early in Hilary term Tolkien formed a literary club that would meet regularly in one college or another to read sagas and epics in Icelandic. He meant it for personal enjoyment, but he also thought that if he wanted to find a larger place for the study of Icelandic literature in the syllabus, he would have to convert members of the English faculty. *Kolbitar*, as he called the club, was 'an Icelandic word for old cronies who sit around the fire so close that they look as if they were biting the coals.' Lewis was among the coal-biters; as Tolkien would spread the text on his knees and begin to read the original and render it into English, Lewis was swept back to moments in his youth.

When he was nine he picked up *Tales of a Wayside Inn* by Henry Wadsworth Longfellow and read 'The Saga of King Olaf.'

> These, and many more like these,
> With King Olaf sailed the seas,
>   Till the waters vast
> Filled them with a vague devotion,
> With the freedom and the motion,
> With the roll and roar of ocean,
>   And the sounding blast.

This and other ballad-like stanzas gave the boy a fit of motion sickness, but he boarded the Long Serpent in his imagination and sailed northward to the ice-blue seas.

In that same volume he found 'Tegner's Drapa', a poem commemorating the death of Esaias Tegner, a Swedish contemporary of Longfellow's, whom the American poet considered was prefigured in Icelandic mythology.

> I heard a voice, that cried,
> 'Balder the Beautiful
> Is dead, is dead!'
> And through the misty air
> Passed like the mournful cry
> Of sunward sailing cranes.

The body of Balder the Beautiful, 'God of the summer sun, Fairest of all the Gods' was loaded onto his ship, decorated funerarily, put to the torch, and shoved off. It 'floated far away Over the misty sea,' but as he read the poem, he skipped aboard and he too was incinerated in the spirit as the funeral pyre slipped beneath the waves.

When he was thirteen and a student at Cherbourg, a small preparatory school at Malvern, he came across, in the Christmas 1911 number of *The Bookman*, a supplement reproducing some passages from *Siegfried and the Twilight of the Gods* translated by Margaret Armour and illustrated in colour by Arthur Rackham. 'I had never heard of Wagner nor Siegfried. I thought the twilight of the gods meant the twilight in which the gods lived. How did I know, at once and beyond question, that this was no Celtic or silvan or terrestrial twilight?'

The following summer, as he was perusing record catalogues, he came across, in a magazine entitled *Soundbox*, synopses of the *Ring of the Nibelungen*, the four Germanic operas derived by Richard Wagner from the Scandinavian myths. 'I read in rapture and discovered who Siegfried was and what was the "twilight" of the gods.'

When he was fourteen he was in a record shop in Belfast; he heard, quite by accident, the *Ride of the Valkyries*. 'To a boy already crazed with "the northernness," whose highest music experience had been [Sir Arthur] Sullivan, the *Ride* came like a thunderbolt.' From that moment on Wagnerian records became the chief drain on his pocket money and the presents he invariably asked for.

When he was fifteen, while visiting a cousin who lived near Dublin, he found on the drawing room table a copy of the very book itself, *Siegfried and the Twilight of the Gods*. Rackham's pictures seemed 'to be the very music made visible' and plunged him 'a few fathoms deeper' into delight. He seldom coveted anything as he coveted that book; and when he heard that there was a cheaper edition, he knew he could never rest until it was his.

When he was sixteen and studying with a tutor in Surrey he composed a tragedy in the Greek mode — with prologos and exodos and three epeisodia in between — but with materials from the mythology of the north. *Loki Bound* was the title, and as the best translator of Greek plays his aged tutor, William F. Kirkpatrick, had ever seen, he patterned his work after *Prometheus Bound*. Set in Asgard, the centre of the universe inhabited by the gods, Loki, the spirit of evil and mischief who had done Balder in with a spearpoint of mistletoe, challenged Odin for supreme authority; aided for a time by Fasold, a giant lovesick for Freya, goddess of love, Loki found himself at tragedy's end bound to a rock and blaspheming the supreme god and creator. In a letter dated 6 October 1914, he told Arthur Greeves about the play, which ran thirty-two pages in his notebook, and encouraged Greeves, who was his closest friend, to turn it into an opera; Greeves demurred, but said he would draw the illustrations for the book.

Barely six months before, in April 1914, Lewis had met Greeves for the first time. They lived across the street from each other in Strandtown, on the eastern perimeter of Belfast. Mrs Greeves telephoned the Lewis household one day to say that her son was sick in bed and would enjoy a visit from either of the Lewis boys. Jack went across the road none too enthusiastically, but when he saw a copy of *Myths of the Norsemen* at Greeves' bedside, he perked up. 'Do you like that?' they asked each other at the same time. Not only did they like the work as a whole — pointing at passages and talking excitedly — but also the same parts and in the same way.

❧

If Betjeman could not enter Lewis' world, he invited Lewis to enter his. Tea it was on 24 January. Lewis walked from Magdalen up High Street to Carfax, then turned left down St. Aldate's. When he climbed the stairs, he found himself 'pitchforked into a galaxy of superundergraduates.' The room was nice enough, walls panelled and windows looking out on spires; the conversation, however, was about arts and crafts, china and lace curtains, silver versus earthen teapots.

'He doesn't say much,' said Betjeman of Louis MacNeice, a young man Lewis found to be absolutely silent and astonishingly ugly, 'but he's a great poet.'

Lewis was not impressed; at 5.45 p.m. he returned to Magdalen with Betjeman in tow for a tutorial. Wulfstan was the author; he was archbishop of York for twenty years; when he died in 1023 he left to posterity a homily on the millenium entitled 'Address to the English'. The bishop's alliterative prose, however, failed to arouse Betjeman; Lewis entered in his diary that night, beside the name of his pupil, the adjectives 'ignorant' and 'stupid'.

Next session Betjeman surprised and delighted Lewis by reading an essay that demonstrated both thought and style. But when tutor began to question pupil, Betjeman fell apart. He had plucked the essay from a book and did not understand what he had plagiarized. 'I wish I could get rid of this idle prig,' confided Lewis to his diary.

❧

Frank R. Hardie, a tutor in classics, invited Lewis and some others to come to his rooms on Thursday 10 February to talk about issues raised in *Theaetetus*, that dialogue of Plato's in which Theaetetus as protagonist and Socrates as antagonist agonized over sense perception and could it ever really be called knowledge? Early in the day, Hardie sent a note round to Lewis, saying that the others couldn't make it but asking that he come anyway.

After dinner at Magdalen Lewis walked up the High, turned left at the Eastgate Hotel, and walked down Merton Street to the end. At the bottom of a tower with battlements was the entrance to Corpus Christi College. He passed through and stepped into a quadrangle paved with sixteenth-century stone. In the centre was a pillar, which in daytime was a sundial. Surmounting the pillar was a pelican, emblem of Corpus Christi; it was also a symbol of Christ sustaining his church, pecking her breast that her young may nurse on the blood.

Hardie and Lewis and, later in the evening, Weldon from Magdalen, with the help of honeyed mead, philosophized and theologized. 'Whether God can understand his own necessity' was especially mirthful. Hardie hunted down Thomas Aquinas' *Summa Theologiae* and fingered his way through the *index rerum*. Twelve types of necessity were listed there, but, Hardie had to conclude, at least under *necessitas*, '[God] doesn't understand a thing!' More mead or other malt beverage, and they were ready to consider 'God trying to explain the theory of vicarious punishment to Socrates.'

~

In April Lewis embarked on what he considered one of life's great pleasures, a tramp through the English countryside.

It began on a Tuesday. He and three others met on the station platform at Goring, some twenty miles south of Oxford. From there they set out due west across chalky hills. 'It was an afternoon of lovely sunshine,' wrote Lewis to his brother who was about to embark on a tour of duty in China, 'with a pleasant light and a lark overhead.' That night they slept at East Ilsley.

On Wednesday they continued on the 'close, smooth grass, deliciously springy to the foot; chalk showing through here and there and making the few ploughed places almost cream colour; and, about three to the mile, clumps of fir whose darkness made them stand out very strikingly from the low tones of the ground.' They had tea at Lambourn and slept at Aldbourne.

Thursday opened with discussions. The routes they wanted to follow were several, but none of them provided inns or taverns for lunch. They bought bread and cheese and butter and oranges, stuffed them into their packs and headed off. Only Lewis prophesied that this course of action would lead to disaster. He would carry the oranges, but he would not put butter among his socks and pyjamas.

Sometime during the day they came to rest in Shapely Bottom. There was much ribaldry about entering and leaving such a spot, and should they tarry there awhile and toss a pot of beer? The nays won; they went as quickly as they came. It put Lewis in mind, however, of those days, not so far past, when the sight of a shapely bottom had the power to stir his loins. There was that enchanted evening in 1917 when he saw, at a party, a lovely creature. 'Is she not absolutely perfect from head to heel,' he asked Greeves, 'and moreover, the necessary part of the body — one of the most beautiful anyway — shaped with an almost intolerable grace?' There was that dinner, also in 1917, celebrating the firsts two of his friends had got in examinations; he got 'royally drunk' and implored everyone in the room to let him whip them, one shilling a lash.

Only a person who had met Venus in a book would conclude that watching a shapely bottom walk across a room, however much layered with taffeta and batiste, was 'a liberal education.' Only a person who approached life through the printed page would seek help in a library; the man to be read on the subject, someone suggested, was Visconte de Sade. Only with Greeves did he share his lust, his friend feeling some attraction to the idea, if not the reality, of inflicting mild torture on another human being. When writing to him Lewis coined the name 'Philomastix,' Greek for 'one who loves the whip.'

At 5.00 p.m. that Thursday afternoon the hikers were descending a slope full of druidical stones into the village of Avebury. 'Imagine a green ancient earthwork with four openings to the four points of the compass, almost perfectly circular, the wall of a British city, large enough to contain broad fields and spinneys inside its circuit, and in the middle of them, dwarfed by its context, a modern village.' They had tea in an orchard and smoked pipes. Then in the back of a cart, leaning against milk cans, they 'bumped and rattled' their way into Marlborough, where they spent the night.

On Friday they walked about four miles into the Savernake Forest, 'the typically English kind of wood — nearly all big oaks with mossy spaces between them, and deer flitting in the distance.' They lunched in the village of Oare and afterward lay flat on their backs, with their packs for pillows, shutting their eyes and 'listening to the burring of the wind in the branches and an occasional early bumble bee.' That night they lay at Devizes.

On Saturday they struck south across the vale of Pewsey. 'No one can describe,' he wrote to his brother, 'the delight of coming to a sudden drop and looking down into a rich wooded valley where you see the roofs of the place where you're going to have supper and bed; especially if the sunset lies on the ridge beyond the valley. There is so much mixed in it; the mere physical anticipation, as of a horse nearing his stable, the sense of accomplishment and the feeling of "one more town," one further away into the country you don't know, and the old, never hackneyed romance of travelling.'

Next day they all returned home by train.

∽

In Trinity term a statute limiting the number of *wimmen* in the colleges was proposed. The octogenarians who thought that the education of women ran counter to the wisdom and experience of Christendom voted for it. The progressives of the 1880s, when feminism was first in flower, voted against it. The young and the postwar, Lewis among them, voted for it. 'Ignorance, romance, realism' was the way Lewis summed it up for his brother who was now in China. 'The first lot belong to the age of innocence when women had not yet been noticed; the second, to the age when they had been noticed and not yet found out; the third, to us.'

∽

'Mrs Moreton is here,' called Mrs Moore from the door of the Headington house. 'She says that Madame Balot tried to commit suicide twice today.' Lewis got up from the dining-room table and went to the hall. 'She's got a taxi here and wants me to go and see the doctor at the Warneford. We'll have to get a nurse for her.'

Exasperated at Mrs Moore's generosity — earlier in the year she had been on jury duty and spent the time holding the hand of a prisoner's wife — Lewis said he would go along. He stayed in the taxi while the women went into the doctor's and emerged with Nurse Jackson. As the taxi headed off, the question arose as to how the nurse could be introduced into the widow's home. Sane or insane, Madame Balot would certainly not agree to her presence.

'It's all perfectly simple,' said Mrs Moreton. 'I will stay in the Balot garden all night. Nurse can be put up in the bungalow opposite Madame's, and I will call her when the need arises.' Lewis wished he had stayed at home. 'If only I could have a man with me, I would feel less nervous about it.'

Mrs Moore led the nurse, not certain who the lunatic was, and got her installed across the street from Madame's.

'Nothing would be more likely to upset Madame,' said Lewis, trying to logic it out, 'than to find dim figures walking about her garden all night.'

'We must keep out of sight,' trilled Mrs Moreton, 'and go very quickly. We could put our stockings over our boots, you know.'

'Do you want something down there?' shouted a voice.

'We must keep our watch on the road and not in the garden,' insisted Lewis, moving down the road a fair distance. 'If we sit down by the paling, we'll be hidden from her window.'

Women from the neighbouring houses began to appear at their gates. Mrs Moreton, in the interest of maintaining Madame's privacy, let everyone know what was about to happen.

A watch such as this required some preparation. Grabbing Mrs Moore by the arm, Lewis returned home and drank a cup of tea, put on a greatcoat, and took some biscuits, smokes, a couple of apples, a rug, two cushions, and a waterproof sheet. Back at the fatal spot, he found Mrs Moreton, having been given provisions by the thoughtful women of the neighbourhood, ensconced in a chair, eating sandwiches and drinking from a thermos.

As night progressed, moonlight succumbed to clouds, and a fine rain began to fall. Mrs Moreton had not anticipated getting wet while performing a charitable act, nor had she expected to be so cold and so sleepy. Lewis fished an apple out of his pocket, took a bite, grimaced, and spat it out. Reaching into his pockets he found camphor balls, which he flung, together with the other apple and biscuits, all over the landscape. Half an hour before the songbirds rose, the crows croaked matins, unbenknownst to Madame Balot, who slept serenely unaware of the efforts of her friends and neighbours to save her from herself.

⧼⧽

In August Lewis and the Moores, together with a lovable fleabag named Papworth, packed and travelled like nomads southwest to the Atlantic shores of Cornwall, where they alighted at The Folly, Perranporth. In the leisurely days that followed Mrs Moore's veins and arteries relaxed. Lewis bathed in the surf, hiked and picnicked, wrote some letters. He also read *Martin Chuzzelwit*; the best parts were the ones about nineteenth-century America, but once he finished it, he had nothing else to read.

Looking for a bookshop, he headed for Truro some ten miles away. The city did have a cathedral, but it was a disappointing clump of stone. A cathedral had to mean clergy, however, and clergy meant a bookshop somewhere in this little market town. He saw an elderly parson tiptoeing towards him and asked for help.

'There is an SPCK depot further down the street,' he buzzed in Lewis's ear.

This was an unpromising lead since depots were never bookshops, but in the room above it he found a promising array of second-hand books. Among them was the poetical works of Armstrong, Dyer, and Green. It took only a moment to convince him that this book would provide entertainment for the rest of the summer.

Back at The Folly, deep in a chair from which he could see a 'blue sea and a golden sand, divided by twenty yards of pure white foam,' he opened the book and dived into 'The Art of Preserving Health,' a helpful treatise that might well have been written in prose but was done into Miltonic verse. Instead of saying that some people couldn't eat eggs, Armstrong proclaimed that

> Some even the generous nutriment detest
> Which in the shell, the sleeping embryo rears.

If one ate too much fat, Armstrong promised that

> The irresoluble oil
> So gentle late and blandishing, in floods
> Of rancid bile o'erflows; what tumults hence
> What horrors rise, were nauseous to relate.

Accounts of the vacation Lewis sent to Greeves in Belfast and to his brother Warren in Shanghai, but in both letters he pointed out that the Cornish jaunt was not official and hence should not be revealed to his father.

⟋⟍

The official vacation began in September. Lewis arrived in Belfast in time for breakfast at Little Lea on the 6th. Albert found him bright and cheerful and amusing as ever. He found his father looking older and acting stranger, his conversation having taken a turn for the coarse. An order of the day soon developed. He and his father would breakfast together. Then Albert would head downtown for Belfast, and Lewis would head upstairs to his study, an attic room really, at one end of the house. There he found the creations of his childhood. Pictures and drawings and pages cut from magazines were tacked on the walls. On the table were pen and inkpot, paintbox and writing books.

What Warren liked most as a child were trains and steamships; what appealed to Jack were dressed animals and knights in armour. Fated never to enjoy the athletics popular with other boys, he 'wrote about chivalrous mice and rabbits who rode out in complete mail to kill, not giants, but cats.' Eventually he provided a written history of Animal Land, as he came to call it. When he went to place it geographically, he put it rather close to India, his brother's favourite haunt of the imagination: 'an island with its north coast running along the back of the Himalayas.' Under pressure from their creators, Animal Land and India soon annexed each other to form a new principality named Boxen. Both kinds were retained — Benjamin VII of Animal Land, by species a rabbit, and Rajah Hawki VI of India, by species, a man — and they presided jointly over the one legislative body, the Dammerfesk.

Populating Boxen were characters like Sir Goose, Reginald Pig the shipowner, Viscount Puddiphat an owl, and the Duchess of Penzly, 'a heavy woman whom they all abominated.' Dominating the two young sovereigns and holding them in quasi-parental authority was their former tutor Lord John Big, by species a frog. He was 'immense in size, resonant of voice, chivalrous (he was the hero of innumerable duels), stormy, elegant, and impulsive.'

For several years now, on his periodic visits to Belfast, Lewis had been putting into order the surviving papers of this world long gone. When not working on the *Encyclopedia Boxonia* on this trip, he attempted a novel in a modern setting. Dr Easley, the narrator, who was an Englishman, sailed from Liverpool to visit his relatives in Belfast for the first time. Quite naturally, one of the first people he met at the rail of the ferry was an Irishman; they passed much of the trip exchanging amusing stories. He wrote seven thousand words before his interest ran out.

After lunch he would take a walk, setting out on paths to his own liking. The smell of autumn was in the air; it awakened in him, as it had not since childhood, the idea of autumn, which he had extracted from the works of Beatrix Potter. 'One autumn when the nuts were ripe,' she wrote in *The Tale of Squirrel Nutkin*, 'and the leaves on the hazel bushes were golden and green — Nutkin and Twinkleberry and all the other little squirrels came out of the wood, and down to the edge of the lake.' There were jokes and japes in the story, but there was also a sort of horror, even mystery, about lowly creatures having to deal with one bigger than themselves — in this case, Old Brown the owl — with one who lorded it over them without ruth.

After dinner Lewis would entertain his father with wheezes about characters in Oxford. One friend of his, while still an undergraduate, had to do a Mugger; that is to say, he was invited to tea by Reginald R. Macan, master of University College, in a way that he couldn't refuse. When asked by the ladies present about places suitable for spending the holidays, 'Not Devonshire,' he replied, trying to impress; 'it's not very salacious.' He thought 'salacious' was 'salubrious', and when the Mugger asked how he liked Oxford, 'Well, sir,' he replied, 'it isn't as salacious as I had hoped.'

ᘓᘓᘓ 1928 ᘓᘓᘓ

There were almost eight weeks between the end of Hilary and the beginning of Trinity terms. Lewis had begun a project of some magnitude that required research at the Bodleian Library. He left Magdalen after breakfast each morning and walked up the High. He turned right into Catte Street and after a couple of hundred paces turned left into the tower of five orders; rising out of the parapet above were pinnacles in Tuscan, Doric, Ionic, Corinthian, and Composite styles. He crossed the tight little quadrangle, which was enclosed by medieval buildings that used to house the school rooms of the university, and entered the door of the library.

Straight ahead was the Divinity School, a fifteenth-century hall in perpendicular Gothic with vaulted ceiling, ornamented with hundreds of crests and bosses. Turning left he climbed the worn circular stairs to the Duke Humfrey. Son of Henry VI, duke of Gloucester, Humfrey had patronized Italian scholars in England and helped finance the Divinity School. On his death he bequeathed to the university an enormous collection of texts and commentaries. To house them the university built a chamber on top of the Divinity School. The original collection with the cases housing it was destroyed in the middle of the sixteenth century; when Thomas Bodley saw the room in 1598, it was empty. From that moment on, he devoted his time and resources to restoring the library, which eventually acquired his name.

'Talk little and tread lightly' was the general admonition of the librarian; Lewis tried to keep his heels from clipping and clopping as he walked down the vaulted room. The ceiling was painted with open books and crests; portraits adorned the walls above the mullioned windows; coming out at right angles from the walls between the windows were bookcases laden with leather volumes and writing tables joined to the cases themselves. The windows were rarely opened, and the room smelled musty, of ancient hide and paper turning slowly to dust. Heating was introduced in 1821; electrification was possible by 1900, but it was still considered too expensive to install.

Books could not be removed from the library, though kings had tried it. Lewis ordered what he needed from the miles of stacks under the neighbouring buildings at the end of one day; the following morning he would find them delivered to his table. There was the 'faint murmur going on of semi-whispered conversations,' but he liked the 'hum of the hive.' Many of his fellow readers were regulars in the room; he did not know them, and they looked 'as if they were shut up with the other properties at night.' Taking off his coat, he looked out the window at the garden of Exeter College on 31 March and saw 'the sudden squalls of wind and rain driving the first blossoms off the fruit trees and snowing the lawn with them.' He arranged his writing instruments, opened his notebook, and sat down upon a very hard chair. 'If only one could smoke,' he wrote to his father, 'and if only there were upholstered chairs, this would be one of the most delightful places in the world.'

He had been rummaging through materials written in the sixteenth century and even had tentative plans to write a book about Desiderius Erasmus, the Dutch humanist who spent a good deal of time in England, writing and lecturing at Cambridge. The more he read, however, the more he felt he had to read, and the further back he had to probe. Eventually, as the spring vacation ended and he was leaving the Bodleian until he could return in the summer, he thought that the only obstacle to his book was finding a starting point. 'The only satisfactory opening for any study,' he concluded as he crossed the quad and looked up at the tower of five orders, embedded in which was a sculpture of James I handing copies of his work to Fame and University, was 'the first chapter of Genesis.'

∽

In March or April Lewis and the Moores spent a weekend in the Forest of Dean at 'a little old farmhouse.' It was approached by a road that seemed to pierce the timber and go for miles before emerging in a clearing, surrounded by a hedge. Fresh eggs, boiled fowl, and country butter pleased their palates. When they went to bed, they were scarcely able to identify the cries of fox, owl, and nightingale before sleep descended.

Walking among the lofty firs the next day — soundless, no bird singing, no brook babbling — Lewis felt that he had come to the end of it all, not the Forest of Dean, but the wood that was English poetry. He had read all the long poems; they had given him immense pleasure. But he knew that the next turn of path would not bring him to another *Faerie Queene* or *Paradise Lost* or *The Ring and the Book*.

∽

Lewis woke up at 5.00 a.m. It was cold and dark; if it had not been May Day, he would have rolled over. Instead, he got up, shaved, and dressed. Gathering up his gown and hood, he drank what was left of the previous night's milk and closed the door. He went downstairs, stopping for a moment at the lavatory, and then headed out into the paleness of first light. At the bottom of Magdalen Tower, he found a crowd gathering. He wormed his way through and began to climb the circular stone stair, then up a short ladder, finally through a narrow door onto the roof. There, standing on duckboards, were assorted members of town and gown as well as crimson-cassocked choristers. Looking down from the tower's edge, he saw pedestrians on the High and people bobbing in punts on the Cherwell. Looking out towards the east, he saw trees, meadows, houses with smoking chimneys, peaceful, like a painting.

In the collegiate calendar, which was not uninfluenced by the Julian *Kalendarium*, winter ended and spring began on the first day of May. The transition was marked in ancient Rome by dances and processions in honour of Flora, goddess of flowers; in Oxford it was celebrated with hymns and bells. As the sun rose it electrified the pastoral scene, sending shadows darting across the landscape. It started the choir singing '*Te Deum Patrem Colimus* (Thee God the Father We Worship),' a hymn derived from the Latin graces of the college. When the choir stopped, the bells began, all ten of them, making ears pound, the tower tremble. It was the choir's turn again; they sang a Vaughan Williams setting of an old English folk tune. The pre-dawn hush having been broken by the many harmonies emanating from the bell tower, the traffic began to flow on the High, the punts began to pole towards their moorings, and Lewis hurried to be among the first down the stair.

In spring 1927 Thomas Herbert Warren had announced his intention to retire as president of Magdalen. He was seventy-four; his mind was no longer nimble. When someone suggested 'the man who built Liverpool Cathedral' as an architect for a building that would be erected at Magdalen, he replied, 'oh I don't think we need anything that big.' In his time he might have reverenced a prince or duke too often, but he never despised a poor scholar from the grammar school. 'He has certainly had a run for his money,' wrote Lewis to his brother, 'and though a very laughable, is also a very lovable, old fellow.'

In spring 1928, with the election coming in November, things began to heat up. Warren was only the tenth president since the college was founded in 1458. The eleventh would have to be chosen carefully because, if precedent had any significance, he would be in office for decades. Once the electioneering began in earnest, the mood of Magdalen changed. 'This college is a cesspool, a stinking puddle,' wrote Lewis to his friend Barfield on 27 May, 'inhabited by ... things in men's shapes climbing over one another and biting one another in the back, ignorant of all things except their own subjects and often even of those; caring nothing less for learning; cunning, desperately ambitious, false friends, nodders in corners, tippers of the wink; setters of traps and solicitors of confidence; vain as women; self-important: fie upon them — excepting always the aged who have lived down to us from a purer epoch.

'I have written no poetry since last vacation,' he concluded on a happier note. 'I spent most in Bodley, starting a book on — what do you think? — *The Romance of the Rose* and its school.'

∽

Oxford was a swamp when the Romans arrived. Two rivers converging made it a poor site from a military point of view, but in peacetime the waterways served to make Oxford a thriving market town. Saxons walled it in the tenth century. Normans castellated it in the eleventh century. Scholars and pupils congregated in large enough numbers by the end of the twelfth century to form a university. Dominicans and Franciscans established houses of study in the thirteenth century and began teaching theology. On holy days and feast days in the next several centuries, there were processions to and from chambers. On occasions of academic significance in the centuries after that, the processions were to and from public buildings.

All these preceded the procession that was forming on Wednesday in the ninth week of Trinity term. It was *Encaenia*, the day on which the university commemorated its benefactors and bestowed honorary degrees. The procession began at 11.30 a.m. at the college of the vice-chancellor, the university's chief administrative officer, and wound its way through the streets of Oxford. Focal point was the chancellor, titular head of the university, who visited Oxford for the occasion; he was capped in black velvet with gold tassel and robed in black silk interspersed with twisted gold; his train was carried by an undergraduate in full evening dress. He was preceded by the university marshal and eight beadles with staves. He was succeeded by the high steward, the vice-chancellor, university burgesses, doctors and masters of the faculty, bachelors, scholars, commoners, and the registrar.

Always among the bystanders at the procession were the merchant tailors, evaluating their handiwork as it passed by on the hoof. Robes and gowns, cloaks and capes. Hoods trimmed with silk or lined with fur. Square caps and velvet bonnets. Starched bands or waterfall cravats. Bell-shaped sleeves and crescent-shaped sleeves or no sleeves at all. Cream silk and ribbed silk and art silk with apple-bloom embroidery. Ambling among the masters of arts, in black calf-length gown with crimson-lined hood, sporting a square cap, was Lewis, noting how 'few dons' faces are fit to bear up against the scarlet and blue and silver of their robes.'

Promptly at noon the procession entered the Sheldonian, once considered the grandest room in Europe. Completed in 1669, the theatre was named after Gilbert Sheldon, archbishop of Canterbury and chancellor of the university at the time; he had also financed it to the tune of £12,000 and commissioned Christopher Wren, who took his design from engravings of the Theatre of Marcellus in Rome. Its ceiling was a marvel of mechanics and mathematics: it measured 70 feet by 80 feet, and provided a pillarless hall accommodating 1,500 people in chairs on the floor and in tiers around the walls.

The chancellor stood before his throne. Proctors mounted two rostra projecting from the tiers, fasces with axe heads protruding from the lions' mouths carved on their fronts. 'God Save the King' was sung by the convocation, and all sat down. The public orator took each person receiving an honorary degree by the right hand up to the chancellor, bowed, and made a speech in Latin. The chancellor removed his cap, replied in kind, shook hands with the recipient, and motioned him to sit nearby . . .

Lewis' eyes drifted towards the ceiling whereon was painted an allegorical pageant entitled 'Truth Descending upon the Arts and Sciences.' Robert Streeter completed the work in 1669, and within a hundred years some poet — rather extravagantly, Lewis thought — penned the words 'Future eyes must confess we owe More to Streeter than to Michael Angelo.'

After all the recipients had been introduced and beseated, the public orator then launched forth in Latin, detailing the hills and valleys, the crests and troughs, the apogees and perigees, of the academic year just concluding . . .

What Lewis' eye saw, his imagination festooned. The allegorical characters in the painting were in a frenzy of activity. Logick was arguing. Chyrurgery was dissecting a brain. Theology wanted Truth to help her open the Bible. Law was parading about with Records, Patents, and Evidences.

Next thing Lewis noticed was that the orator had reached the final period of his peroration, and that the graduates were mounting the rostra, one on either side of the hall, to read extracts from their prize-winning essays. The scene brought him back to this same day in 1921 when he had won the chancellor's prize. It was blazing hot; he was wearing a boiled shirt and pumps, white tie and tails, cap and gown; he was soaking wet. When his turn came, he found the professor of poetry sitting in his way. He inhaled and inched by, but as he entered the rostrum he missed a step and fell backward. To those looking up from the floor he appeared, then disappeared as through a trapdoor, only to rise into view like a jack-in-the-box. He began to read nervously but concluded two minutes of 'Optimism,' essay topic for that year, in a firm, even a loud, voice. 'I'm glad things aren't getting any worse,' said the burly professor as Lewis squeezed past.

The three girls tossed from the heavenly ceiling deserved festooning, thought Lewis. Ignorance couldn't understand why nobody liked her. Rapine, dagger in one hand, torch in the other, dared anybody to come after her. Envy, with hag's breasts and snakey tresses, just plummeted hopelessly. '*Dissolvimus hanc convocationem,*' pronounced the chancellor, touching his cap; the throng poured out of the theatre in search of luncheons in the hotels and garden parties in the quadrangles.

❧

By the beginning of the long summer vacation he had decided that Erasmus would have to be another book. What lured him on was 'medieval love poetry and the medieval idea of love.' There were not too many facts to master, but there was a plethora of literature and a fair amount of paradox. 'On the one hand it is extremely supersensual and refined,' he wrote to his father, 'and on the other it is an absolute point of honour that the lady should be someone else's wife, as Dante and Beatrice, Launcelot and Guinevere.' He actually began to write in longhand in the hope that he would finish the first chapter in time to have it typed for his father to read in Belfast in August.

In July participating in the campaign for the presidency of Magdalen began to take a psychological toll on Lewis. What worried him was that 'the decent men seem to me to be all the old ones (who will die) and the rotters seem to be all the young ones (who will last my time).' In August he went to Belfast that he might be at Magdalen for September, which meant there would be a month of endless gatherings of political committees before Michaelmas began.

❧

'I am beginning to wonder whether biography, in our time, may not replace the novel as the dominant form,' wrote Lewis in review of *Matthew Arnold* by Hugh Kingsmill, for biography seemed to be 'the literary centre of this age towards which writers gravitate as inevitably as they gravitated towards allegory in the late Middle Ages or to drama in the reign of James I.'

'An interesting if not perfectly successful book,' he wrote in review of *Rossetti: His Life and Works* by Evelyn Waugh. 'We look forward with interest to Mr Waugh's next book.'

∽

In November the fellows and tutors met in the chapel of Magdalen to make a president. As Lewis would record it later, campaigning in the final months progressed in nine discernible stages.

Stage 1.   Hogarth put forward with almost universal approval. Hogarth dies.

Stage 2.   Chelmsford put forward by Weldon and his friends — to be their puppet.

Stage 3.   Benecke put forward by party including myself who dislikes both Chelmsford and Craig.

Stage 4.   Absolute determination of the Craig-ites not to have Chelmsford — absolute determination of the Benecke-ites not to have Chelmsford or Craig.

Stage 5.   Benecke leading by a long way.

Stage 6.   Proposal of Gordon. Satisfied Craig-ites as being at any rate better than Chelmsford; satisfies Benecke-ites as better than Chelmsford or Craig.

Stage 7.   Benecke vs. Gordon.

Stage 8.   No clear majority for Benecke possible. Fear of letting in Chelmsford of the Craig-ites, and Benecke-ites quarrel about Benecke and Gordon.

Stage 9.   Agreement of the two parties on Gordon, who then outvotes the remnant of the Chelmsford and Craig people.

'So,' Lewis wrote to his father, 'it is more or less of a compromise.'

1929

Lewis found religion attractive in books, which was odd because he was so unreligious himself. He read Shaw and Wells, Edward Gibbon and John Stuart Mill, writers who were not in the theistic tradition; he found them mildly entertaining, but they generally put him to sleep. Christian writers, on the other hand, with whom he was bound to disagree — Donne and Browne, Spenser and Milton, Johnson and Chesterton — he read again and again. The Christians might be wrong, but at least they weren't boring, he thought, as he boarded a red bus outside Magdalen for the run up Headington Hill.

If books had the power to move men's souls, he was feeling the pressure. In Hilary term he reread Euripides' *Hippolytus*, which made chastity into a martyr, and Alexander's *Space, Time, and Deity*, which distinguished 'enjoyment' from 'contemplation.' He reconsidered Hegel's philosophy of the absolute and festooned it with Berkeley's notion of the spirit. What resulted was a philosophical construct he called God. He could not know this God any more than Hamlet could know Shakespeare. But with this sort of concept, he felt comfortable. In fact, he felt free to accept it or reject it. When his stop came, he got off the bus believing what he had not believed when he got on, that an absolute spirit or God did indeed exist.

'The other night an undergraduate, presumably drunk, at dinner in the George, covered the face of his neighbour with potatoes, his neighbour being a total stranger,' he wrote in the middle of April to his brother. 'Whether this means simply that he flung the contents of the potato dish at him or (as I prefer to think) that he seized him firmly by the short hairs and systematically lathered him with warm mash, my informant could not say. But that is not the point of the story. The point is that, being haled before the proctors and asked why he had done so, the culprit very gravely and with many expressions of regret, pleaded in so many words, 'I couldn't think of anything else to do.'

How could he commune with absolute spirit? Lewis looked inside himself and was appalled by what he saw, 'a zoo of lusts, a bedlam of ambitions, a nursery of fears, a harem of fondled hatreds.' The immediate result of the introspection was that he no longer wanted to speculate about a philosophical construct; he wanted to pray. But to whom? He had gone about as far as a philosopher could go . . . and then it happened. The 'philosophical theorem, cerebrally entertained, began to stir and heave and throw off its gravecloths, and stood upright and became a living presence.' It was, he could hardly wait to write to Jenkin, a sort of 'theological shocker'. If it spoke, he heard it say 'I am the Lord,' 'I am that I am,' 'I am.'

Lewis was a private person; he called his soul his own; he did not pursue pleasure as a matter of course; most of his time he spent avoiding suffering. But the presence, the person, who had talked to him was unwelcome, discomforting, unreasonable; he was also unrelenting. Up staircase 3, sporting the oak of room 3, was the person Lewis dreaded most. 'I gave in, and admitted that God was God, and knelt and prayed: perhaps, that night, the most dejected and reluctant convert in all England.'

❧

In the first days of July he heard from his father, who was not feeling well. Sorry he was under the weather, Lewis replied, who went on to say that he was passing his days, now that Trinity term was over, 'among the dead' at the Bodleian. At the end of July he received two letters, one from an uncle in Scotland, another from a cousin in Ireland, to the effect that Albert was in pain, was losing weight, and was being put into Miss Bradshaw's Nursing Home for X-rays. 'I had heard the news and was anxious to write,' he wrote in response to a letter from his father, 'but hardly knew how to do so. I will, of course, come home at the first moment.' August 8th, 9th, and 10th he spent at Queens' College, Cambridge, examining for English literature. On the 11th he returned to Oxford, and on the 12th he left for the Liverpool-Belfast ferry, arriving at Little Lea on the morning of the 13th.

For ten days he cared for his father at home. After consulting with his cousin Joey — Dr Joseph Lewis, bacteriologist at Belfast Infirmary — he was able to write to his brother in Shanghai that Albert seemed to be 'suffering from a narrowing of the passage in one of the bowels.' He folded the letter and sealed it, then he went down to the cellar of Little Lea, twisted his father's key in the lock, and poured himself a 'mouthful of whisky.'

He tried his best to entertain his father with wheezes from Oxford. Had Albert heard the one about a certain professor Alexander, a philosopher at Leeds, who entered a railway carriage and sat down?

Well, sitting opposite him was a woman who soon wondered what was in the perforated cardboard box on the professor's lap.

'A mongoose, madam.'

'And what are you going to do with the mongoose?'

'I am taking it to a friend who is, unfortunately, suffering from *delirium tremens.*'

'And what use will the mongoose be to him?'

'Why, madam, the people who suffer from that disease find themselves surrounded with snakes.'

'Good heavens!'

'And of course a mongoose eats snakes.'

'But you don't mean that the snakes are real?'

'Oh dear me, no. But then neither is the mongoose.'

This wheeze, Albert assured his son, was a chestnut and a pretty old one at that.

'Things are not better,' Lewis wrote to his brother four days later, 'and I am really rather despondent about him.' Albert was delirious one night, his wild colloquies being heavily coloured with lavatorial imagery. Perhaps what Lewis thought of Rabelais, whose works he was reading during the day, could be applied to his father: 'very long, very incoherent, and very very stercoraceous.'

When not in his father's room, Lewis roamed the halls of Little Lea, opening windows his father always kept closed. 'Every room is soaked with the bogeys of childhood,' 'the awful "rows" . . . the awful returnings to school; and also the old pleasures of an unusually ignoble adolescence.' He sat in the dining room; in place of the 'gargantuan midday meal which was hitherto compulsory,' he ate 'a few biscuits and fruit.'

Greeves visited Little Lea every day. Often of an afternoon, when things were going well, he would take Lewis for a walk, thus freeing him for an hour from 'the retrogressive influence' of the house, plunging him 'back into the pleasures and pains of being a boy.' When the patient was settled for the night, Lewis went into the garden. The cool air was a change from the closed sickroom; the frogs in the field at the bottom of the garden were a pleasant sound.

'I am attending at the almost painless sickbed of one for whom I have little affection and whose society has for years given me much discomfort and no pleasure,' he wrote to Barfield, trying to put his father and the illness into some kind of philosophical perspective. 'Nevertheless, I find it almost unendurable.' He searched for the right word — was it 'intimacy' or 'familiarity' — to characterize the relationship? 'I suppose a good Greek was familiar with his wife and intimate with his *hetaira* [concubine]. But between men I suspect that intimacy includes familiarity potentially. Now with a woman of course, no degree of intimacy includes any familiarity at all: for that must be *storge* [familial affection] or *eros* [physical love] or both.'

Albert's pain persisted; Joey recommended an operation to correct what was blocking the colon; Albert was again removed to the nursing home. 'The operation, in spite of what they prophesied, discovered cancer,' wrote Lewis to his brother. 'They said he might live a few years. I remained at home, visiting him in the nursing home for ten days. There were ups and downs and some bad spasms of pain from flatulence (apparently the usual sequel to abdominal operations) going over the wound: but nothing really dreadful. Quite often he was himself and telling wheezes, though he was often wandering from the dopes.'

What did he remember of his mother's death? asked Albert. Not much, replied Jack. He remembered her giving him and Warren Bibles a few days before she died. He remembered crying out one night when he had a toothache, but she didn't come. Instead she stayed in her room with the doctors and nurses. He was told later that they operated on her and found cancer. Beyond that he knew nothing.

After her operation and for the next few days Albert sat with her and held her hand and listened to her as she wandered in and out of the anaesthetics.

'It's a pity,' she said when some Orangemen were beating their drums for hours on end not far from her window, 'that it takes so long to learn that tune . . .'

'If you speak when you come in before you are spoken to,' she said, hushing Nurse Black, 'you will be turned out of school . . .'

'When you get married,' she said to the nurse, 'see that you get a good man who loves you and loves God . . .'

'What have we done for Him?' she asked Albert in a conversation about heavenly things . . .

At 6.30 in the morning of 23 August 1908, Flora Augusta Hamilton Lewis died, 'as good a woman, wife, and mother as God has ever given to man,' wrote Albert in his diary that day; it was his forty-fifth birthday. 'Men must endure their going hence,' read the quotation of the day from the daily Shakespeare calendar on the mantelpiece of her room, 'even as their coming thither; Ripeness is all.'

'I have a growing respect for him,' Lewis wrote his brother. 'He faces the major issues very pluckily, and as for his reminiscences, in which he is at present indulging very freely, I get a more acute impression of the abominable rock from which he was hewn.'

September was receding and Michaelmas term approaching. Joey said things might not change for weeks either for better or for worse. Lewis, therefore, left Belfast on Saturday 22 September. On Tuesday he got a wire that his father had taken a turn for the worse. He left

Magdalen within the hour for the Liverpool ferry and arrived at the nursing home in Belfast the following morning. Too late. Albert had not wakened on Tuesday morning; his temperature rose during the morning; he died in the afternoon.

❧

'Sorry report father dead painless twenty-fifth September. Jack.' Thus read the cable Lewis sent to his brother on 27 September. It arrived at the Army Service Corps Headquarters, North China Command, before the letters describing the illness. Immediately Warren sat down at the Shanghai Club and composed a letter to his brother. More letters passed between the two in the next month, grieving, reminiscing, planning what to do about their father's estate. Albert had left more to Warren because of Jack's higher annual income, but Warren insisted that the proceeds should be split evenly. Then there was the house.

There was some expectation that Warren might arrive back in England by Christmas. When he wrote that April was the soonest he could manage, Mrs Moore wrote him a letter, saying that Mr Lewis' death 'was most merciful as it must have spared him such a great deal of suffering and illness which he would have hated, having been so independent all his life.' And when he arrived in England, she encouraged him to come directly to Oxford and consider Hillsboro as his home.

'Whatever else he was, he was a terrific *personality*,' Lewis wrote to his brother a month after the death. 'How he filled a room. How hard it was to realize that physically he was not a big man. Our whole world is either direct or indirect testimony to the same fact.' What the two brothers most rebelled against was gone. 'The way we enjoyed going to Little Lea, and the way we hated it, and the way we enjoyed hating it; as you say, one can't grasp that *that* is over. And now you could do anything on earth you cared to in the study at midday on a Sunday, and it is beastly . . .'

❧

'The return to college and its regular routine has done me good,' he wrote on 15 October to Greeves; 'the lag ends of recent horrors have begun to fade in my mind. I am very busy this term, but the beautiful weather overrides everything.' In the mornings, when not taking pupils, he did correspondence or set examination papers. At noon he would go to Headington for lunch, after which he would freshen the hen run and dig for worms, considering 'these humble twisters as poor relations' of the dragons in *Beowulf* and the *Edda*. 'Their kinship with the monstrous,' he remarked to Greeves, 'has taken from them the merely disgusting, and I can now lift them in my fingers without a shudder.' Even if he couldn't fondle them, he found earth such a lovely thing because it reconciled one to all its contents. A quick walk for Mr Papworth brought Lewis to tea time and a hasty retreat to Magdalen, where he would give a lecture at 5.00 p.m., take a pupil at 6.00, and dine at 7.15, sherry having been offered at 7.00. After dinner he might take a pupil at 8.30 or talk with Tolkien. On alternate weeks there would be the Michaelmas Club, the Linguistic Society, the Icelandic Society. There was correspondence relating to his father's estate.

One weekend at Headington, in the middle of the night, Papworth got so ill that a vet had to be called. Too much meat in the diet was the diagnosis, and the dog was given a sedative. The vet was an Irishman, and since he had come out at this ungodly hour — it was 2.00 a.m. — Lewis thought it only proper to stand the man to a brandy. Only Mrs Moore knew that the two men standing in the kitchen were not drinking brandy; she had filled the empty brandy bottle with mere whisky.

When Griffiths graduated from Oxford at the end of Trinity term, Lewis encouraged him to read the philosophers, and read he did Descartes' *Discourse on Method*, Spinoza's *Ethics*, Berkeley's *Principles of Human Knowledge*, and Kant's *Critique of Pure Reason*. As a result, when Griffiths visited him on 16 October, they spent a splendid evening of philosophical conversation, capped with a moonlit walk through the deer grove. The following morning they breakfasted together and went once round the river walks, both enjoying 'the bright yellow leaves floating on the water.'

Many times Lewis bent his knee before God in Trinity term, and since then he had tried to devote some part of each day to meditation. But his father's sickness and death put that plan away. It was autumn now; once again he got 'the sense, just as the mere nature and voluptuous life of the world is dying, of something else coming awake.' It was too cool to sit outdoors; it was too noisy to attempt to pray indoors. Last thing at night he was too sleepy. First thing in the morning he was not quite awake. Perhaps five minutes after breakfast would do, but could 'meditation,' he asked Greeves, 'be combined with emptying of the bowels?'

In October, to nourish his newborn spiritual life, he undertook to read *Diary of an Old Soul*, 366 poems for devotional reflection written in 1880 by George MacDonald. 'He seems to know everything,' he again confided to Greeves, 'and I find my own experience in it constantly.'

My surgent thought shoots lark-like up to thee.
Thou like the heaven art all about the lark.
Whatever I surmise or know in me,
Idea, or but symbol on the dark,
Is living, working, thought-creating power
In thee, the timeless Father of the hour.
I am thy book, thy song — thy child would be.

'As regards the literary quality, I am coming to like even his clumsiness.'

In November and December he read *Grace Abounding* and *Mr Badman*, and certain sentences struck home. 'But the milk and honey is beyond this wilderness.' 'I thought I could have spoken of His love and mercy even to the very crows that sat upon the ploughed lands before me.' 'I could not find that with all my soul I did *desire* deliverance.' In these devotional works, John Bunyan painted 'the horrors of religion and sometimes almost of insanity.' What did Greeves think of the darker side of religion they found in old books? asked Lewis rhetorically. 'Formerly I regarded it as mere devil worship based on horrible superstitions. Now that I have found, and am still finding more and more, the element of truth in the old beliefs, I feel I cannot dismiss even their dreadful side so cavalierly. There must be something in it: only what?'

Little Lea had to be cleared out and prepared for sale; the Christmas vacation seemed the ideal time to do this. Lewis would have liked to make the final visit with Warren; Mrs Moore would have to take his place. She would certainly be more helpful than Warren in placing a value on the things to be disposed of; perhaps there would be a few pieces that could be transported back to Headington. But would she be welcome at Little Lea? she wondered. Would there not be 'ghosts there who would not be happy to see her or anxious to make her happy?' Would it not look, thought Lewis, 'like the traditional insolence of an heir, trampling on the old king's laws before the crown is warm on his head'? The solution was to ask Greeves and his mother to put both of them up at Bernagh, their house across the street from Little Lea. Lewis would prime Mrs Moore, Greeves would prime his mother, and their 'cross purposes and misunderstandings,' if they didn't hurt each other, would be very funny. It was 'the cheekiest proposal' Lewis ever made, but Greeves accepted it and welcomed them for a week in early December.

On the eve of Christmas, Lewis with Mrs Moore and Maureen

walked to Magdalen. In the great hall there was a Christmas tree, a roaring fire, and green boughs festooned everywhere. From 9.00 to 10.00 p.m. the choir, with the uncertain accompaniment of a pianist, rendered Handel's *Messiah*, the first part of it. Then it was to the common room where there were sandwiches and wine mulled with sugar and lemon and nutmeg. Back to the hall, they saw that the only light was coming from the hundreds of candles on the tree. Carols — old English, medieval, Elizabethan — the choir sang a cappella. At midnight the vice-president of the college sent a message to the bell tower; the ringers were to begin their peals. Sack — dry, light, strong — was passed around in a loving cup for sipping and pledging one's blessing to others.

∽

'In this book I propose to describe the process by which I came back, like so many of my generation, from materialism to a belief in God.' It was Christmas Day; while the rest of the Headington household was at church, he riffled through the pages of a notebook and was reading what he had written so far. 'If that process had been an intellectual one, and if I were therefore simply giving a narrative form to a work of apologetic, there would be no place for my book. The defence of theism lies in abler hands than mine. What makes me bold to contribute to my own story is the fact that I arrived where I now am, not by reflection alone, but by reflection on a particular recurrent experience. I am an empirical theist. I have arrived at God by induction.'

∽

On Boxing Day Lewis went for a walk. He left Headington about ten in the morning and took the bus for Magdalen. There K. B. McFarlane, tutor in modern history, was waiting for him and both headed out of Oxford on foot. It was a trudge up Cumnor Hill, but then things began to brighten up. Walking on unfrequented paths, they met hardly a soul. 'The sky was palest blue, without a cloud or a breeze, and the weak sun laid a lovely unity of pale colour over the ploughed fields, the haystacks, and the church towers in each village.'

When they rounded a bend at the outskirts of Stanton Harcourt, they saw a farmyard in the foreground and beyond it a towered manor house and the village church. The ringers in the church were practising their peal as Lewis and McFarlane walked towards the farmyard where, looking at them across a half-gate, was 'a very fine old horse with a white star on his forehead.' 'It sounds poor on paper,' wrote Lewis to Greeves, trying to recapture the experience, 'but the thing about it was the sense of absolute peace and safety: the utter homeliness, the Englishness, the Christendom of it.'

Stalking him still was the presence that had brought him to his knees some months before, and before whom he had returned to his knees many times since. The presence seemed to colour everything he thought. When he enjoyed being snug and desolate in a wintry village, and when he contemplated the snugness and yet the desolateness not only of the scene but also of the universe, he could conclude only that it was the Absolute, the Spirit, who had made the universe and made it just the right size, not 'too vast and inhuman and alarming,' but just 'snug and dreamy and like cotton wool even in winter.'

'It's as different as chalk from cheese,' said Barfield. Lewis was visiting him in Long Crendon, east of Oxford. He had arrived on Sunday 29 December 1929, at 'a most delightful house, an ex-farmhouse with many out-buildings and an orchard'; he stayed four days. For the first two days Mrs Barfield and their newly adopted son Alexander were not at home; they had the house to themselves.

The temptation for the two friends was to talk all over the wordscape and walk all over the landscape, but they had promised each other to do 'some solid reading together.' In the mornings it was Aristotle in Greek, the *Ethics*; in the afternoons and evenings it was Dante in Italian, not the *Inferno* but the *Paradiso*, the cantos that Barfield found more caseous than cretaceous.

'It certainly seemed to me that I had never seen at all what Dante was like before,' Lewis wrote to Greeves on 2 January 1930, 'a sort of mixture of intense, even crabbed, complexity in language and thought and (what seems impossible) *at the very same time* a feeling of spacious gliding movement, like a slow dance, or like flying.'

Once they read the whole night through — 'Its blend of complexity and beauty is very like Catholic theology — wheel within wheel, but wheels of glory, and the One radiated through the Many' — hearing the crowing of a cock as they went to bed.

✥ 1930 ✥

Before Hilary term began Lewis was summoned to the house of
Arthur Spenser Loat Farquharson. He could not refuse because the
Fark, as he was called by the undergraduates, was senior tutor at
Univ., having been there since 1899. The Lieutenant Colonel, as the
Fark liked to refer to himself, having served with no memorable
distinction in the Great War, had introduced Lewis while an under-
graduate at Univ. to the logic and philosophy of ancient Greece.

Arriving at the 'tall, narrow house, cheek by jowl with Univ.
library,' Lewis was admitted by a servant; neither on this nor on any
previous visit did he see the tutor's wife. Little light seemed to filter
into the book-lined room. Some Heraclitean fire might not be inappropriate, thought Lewis as he waited. Heraclitus was a favourite of
the Fark's. Every summer for years he had put his name down as
lecturing on the Greek philosopher who held that fire was the essential element in the universe and that everything was in a permanent
state of change. Lewis was the only one ever to sign up for the course,
but the year he did the Fark said that Heraclitus was off.

'He came gliding towards me in the dusk,' wrote Lewis to
Greeves on 26 January, 'about five feet four inches high, his face
exactly like an egg in shape, with sandy hair fringing a bald patch, a
little military moustache, and eyebrows so far up his forehead that it
gives him a perpetual air of astonishment.'

'My dear fellow,' said the Fark, laying one hand on Lewis' shoulder
and using the other to wring Lewis' hand; 'this is very good of you.'

He was currently involved, and he was only one of many, in
producing a new Greek-English lexicon, and he just wanted to consult his former pupil on some obscure points of Attic and Ionic.
Interspersing scholarship with companionship, he preferred an
indecent story or two, which he would begin in all gravity and
attempt to end in some hilarity.

When the consultation was over, the Fark told Lewis how helpful
he had been.

Not all that helpful, said Lewis; he didn't know a thing about the
points that had been raised.

'It was the stimulus of your presence,' cooed the Fark in farewell.
✥

Towards the end of January Griffiths visited Lewis again. This
time the conversation turned towards the naturalistic novels that

were in fashion. To Griffiths they revealed 'the nature of the conscious mind and its natural processes on the one side and the unconscious soul with its deep instinctive feelings on the other.'

'He was all mucked up with naturalism, D. H. Lawrence, and so on,' wrote Lewis to Greeves a week later, 'but has come right and is, I do believe, really one of "us" now.' Lewis read Lawrence but in quite a different way from Griffiths; so powerful did Lewis think his own rhetoric, he convinced himself that he had talked Griffiths out of his admiration for at least one naturalistic novelist.

Griffiths, however, persevered in his opinion of Lawrence and felt that the novelist had made him see that civilization as it existed in England had desecrated the sources of life, that sex was essentially a holy instinct, and that sexual immorality was not only self-indulgence but also profanation of something sacred.

∽

After dinner on Monday 27 January Lewis headed up High Street to the Cornmarket, where he turned right. Several streets later he turned left at Friars Entry, where he walked down the wet cobbles. He stopped at No. 19, between a cinema and a public house, which housed the Oxford Broadside Club.

Three flights up narrow stairs, he entered a smallish room; standing about and smoking were perhaps thirty young men. On the walls he could make out drawings of what appeared to be powerfully built female nudes. Wasn't this a meeting of the Junior Linguistic Society? Assured that it was, he looked more closely at the drawings. The 'bellies and genitals showed a remarkable degree of development,' he noted, but the nudes had neither heads nor feet. Heads and feet were hard to draw, suggested one of the junior linguists. Judging from the wobbly hands, Lewis had to agree. The linguists had rented the room for the evening; they proved to be a congenial audience. Lewis delivered a paper entitled 'Some Problems of Metaphor.' After applause, he got involved in 'a long and philosophical discussion with a total stranger who appeared to be a lunatic.' He was home before midnight, but not by much.

∽

Robustious females were a sure cure for concupiscence, at least in Lewis' case, but it was not always so. The sexual enemy at one time could walk right up to him for a frontal attack. 'I seem to have been supported in respect to chastity and anger more continuously, and with less struggle, for the last ten days or so,' he wrote to Greeves, who had once been his co-conspirator in affairs sexual but now seemed more his father confessor; 'and have had the most delicious moments of *It*.'

By *It* he meant the 'sudden intense feeling of delight' that stopped him dead in his tracks during an afternoon walk. *It*, the psychoanalyst in Vienna would surely theorize, was nothing more than 'sublimated lust, a kind of defecated masturbation which fancy gives one to compensate for external chastity.' 'If he can say that *It* is sublimated sex,' countered Lewis, 'why is it not open to me to say that sex is sublimated *It*?'

⤬

Somewhere, perhaps in *The Vision of Piers Plowman*, Lewis came across a list of the seven deadly sins; somehow he thought plausible the theory that each person was afflicted or beset with one of the seven. Ranging over the list was a sobering experience, and he passed his observation on to Greeves. Avarice applied to neither of them. Envy would certainly apply to himself, anger also, but neither to Greeves. Gluttony would certainly be Greeves'. Unchastity embraced them both. Indolence of all the seven seemed to beset Greeves the most. Pride was undoubtedly Lewis' alone.

'It was not precisely Christianity,' he wrote to his friend Jenkin, 'though it may turn out that way in the end.' The question had once been, should he adopt Christianity? Now the question seemed to be, should Christianity adopt him? 'I now know [that] there is another party in the affair — that I am playing poker, not patience, as I once supposed.'

As he was writing, he remembered a rambling conversation he had with Jenkin some years before. It began with chivalry and ended with Christianity. The medieval knight, argued Lewis, ran his class code and his church code side by side in watertight compartments. The typical example of the Christian ideal at work, countered Jenkin was, not the knight, but St Paul. Apparently the gospel writers had seen something overwhelming, Lewis had to admit, but they had been unable to reproduce it.

⤬

On Monday 3 March he was the invited speaker at the Martlets. For his paper he chose a theme he had been developing since at least 1924. On 18 June of that year, at the 256th meeting of the Martlets, he spoke on James Stephens, an Irish writer whose works had been appearing regularly for at least a dozen years. That Stephens was born in either 1880 or 1882 and married either in 1917 or 1919; that he toddled around the slums of Dublin and lived much of his early life in an orphanage; that he worked for a time as a solicitor's clerk, then went to Paris to write; that he contributed to *Sinn Fein* and helped found *The Irish Review*; that he knew George Russell ('AE') and James Joyce; that he was small and slight with the face of one who dwelt forever in a world mocked and twisted by fairies: all these biographical details had — at least to Lewis' way of thinking — no bearing on the reading or meaning of *The Charwoman's Daughter* (1911) or *The Crock of Gold* (1912) or *Here Are Ladies* (1913) or *The Demi-Gods* (1914) or *Irish Fairy Tales* (1920) or *Deirdre* (1923).

Six years later Lewis had a name for his theory, 'the personal heresy'; on this topic, particularly in poetics, he addressed the 318th meeting of the Martlets. He began by recalling that an advertisement for an anthology published during the late war promised that readers would learn things the soldier-poets had not yet told 'their fathers or their sweethearts or their friends.' 'The assumption was that to read poetry means to become acquainted with the poet.' He went on to say that 'poetry is widely believed to be the "expression of personality": the end which we are supposed to pursue in reading it is a certain contact with the poet's soul; and "life" and "works" are simply two diverse expressions of this single quiddity.'

He cited specifically a book that had just been published, *Milton*, by E. M. W. Tillyard. In it 'we are told that the only critics of *Paradise Lost* who "seemed to tackle" the "problem" — for a poem is always a "problem" to psychological critics — in the "right kind of way" were the Satanists; and their rectitude consisted, apparently, in the fact that they "invested the character of Satan with all that Milton felt and valued most strongly".' This was a view that needed correction.

∽

He had fallen again sexually, he reported to Greeves. Chastity was still his goal. It was perhaps coincidental that he was, between Hilary and Trinity terms, working on the chastity found in *Comus*, a thousand-line poem in quasi-dramatic form by John Milton. The poem was really a masque, a script for a spectacular presentation of virtue under siege that had been commissioned for presentation before nobility on 24 September 1634. As he was composing, Milton left plenty of room for the prattling and prancing about of the amateur performers; he also allowed himself a good deal of room to theorize and moralize about chastity.

Milton was in his mid-twenties when he wrote *Comus*, and in those years chastity was the symbol of all virtue in life. It was not for nothing that he had been called 'the Lady' during his college days at Cambridge, and it was not surprising that when he came to personify chastity as the central character in the masque, he named her The Lady. It was her virtue that was pursued mischievously by Comus, the son of Bacchus and Circe. By the masque's end her virtue was still untouched, reason had overcome passion, and the soul, albeit mystically, had married God.

At the end of his study Lewis managed to discern yet another sort of chastity. Having enumerated five moments in the growth of the poem, and having taken into account the changes in successive manuscripts, he argued that the movement had been from disunity as a drama to unity as a poem, from dramatic promiscuity to 'poetic chastity.' Preferring poetics to histrionics himself, but acknowledging that the majority of critics disagreed with him, Lewis was quick to add, 'It is arguable that he [Milton] chose wrongly.'

∽

On Friday evening 4 April, Lewis, Barfield, and Harwood, together with Walter Field, left Oxford by car and headed south-west towards the Bristol Channel. The following morning, at Dunster, they began a walking tour and marked as they walked such places as Luccumbe, Dunkery Beacon, Stoke Pero, Wilmersham Farm, Cloud Farm, Lynmouth, and, some fifty miles and three days later, Challacombe.

Midway during the tramp they came to Badgeworthy Water, a fast-moving mountain stream, six inches deep in one place, perhaps five feet in another; the water was cold, Lewis found out as he barged across, and the bottom was slippery. More analytical, Barfield picked a narrower place, took off his boots, stuffed his socks into them, and tossed them across. Not far enough, noted Lewis and his friends with mirth; the boots fell right into the middle of the stream. 'After sailing a few yards like high-pooped galleons, [they] lit on the top of a fall where they stuck, rocking with the current, threatening every second to go sailing down into a whirlpool beneath.'

∽

On 16 April, having been 'out of England three years and five days, and after a journey of fifty days from Shanghai,' Warren Lewis disembarked at Liverpool, boarded a train at Lime Street, pausing for a moment to enjoy the acrid smell of an English railway station. On arriving at Euston, he registered at the station hotel, made his arrival report at the War Office, and settled in for the night. A coal fire had been laid in the bedroom grate. He telephoned his brother Jack, who was holidaying in Christchurch, on the south coast near Bournemouth.

The following morning he hired a couple of taxis and transported his luggage from Euston to Paddington Station. 'Then, it being a bright sunny morning,' he walked across Hyde Park, nodded to the statue of Peter Pan in Kensington Gardens, saluted the Guner War Memorial; at Victoria Station he went underground and took the tube under the Thames to Waterloo Station. There, at noon, the Lewis brothers embraced with Mrs Moore not far behind.

Jack and Mrs Moore were in the market for a new house, Warren was told, and hence they all piled into a taxi for Olympia where the Ideal Homes Exhibition was being held. As they strolled about the hall Warren regaled them with the homes he had seen when his ship berthed for a few days in Los Angeles: swimming pools, lawns without hedges or fences, pegged floors, raftered ceilings, even sumptuous bathrooms. When Jack and Mrs Moore were debating about how much they could afford, Warren suggested that if they had $125,000 which came out roughly at £25,000, they could buy a nine-roomer on a half acre in Hollywood.

~~~

On 22 April Jack and Warren boarded the overnight ferry that would take them from Liverpool to Belfast. They arrived at Donegal Quay the following morning and walked in the sunlight up Royal Avenue to No. 53, where the brass plate read A. J. LEWIS, SOLICITOR. J. W. A. Condlin greeted them; he had been Albert's managing clerk since 1917. He was an agreeable man; their questions he answered in a soft, dreamy sort of way.

Will the investments of the estate yield only £190 a year net? Warren wanted to know.

'Oh, it will be more than that for sure.'

What could they reasonably expect from the sale of the house? Jack wanted to know.

'It is worth £3,000 to a man that wants it.'

He assured the young men that he would send them a list of investments with the estimated annual yield and that he would ship the contents of the study at Little Lea to Oxford.

A taxi took the brothers to the cemetery. Jack remembered that where two paths met, there the 'circular plot of grass' was, containing the remains of all the Lewises and Hamiltons who had died in Belfast. 'The sight of [Albert's] grave with its fresh turned earth and a handful of withered daffodils at its head, alongside Mammy's,' Warren would write in his diary that night, 'was perfectly beastly.'

From the cemetery they took a taxi to Little Lea. Warren had remembered it as a huge house. Now it seemed like an ornate frame from which the portrait had been torn, so tremendous a presence had his father been. Mary Cullen, the cook and housekeeper for the last thirteen years, was at the door when they arrived and served them a light lunch. Refreshed, the brothers rolled up carpets they wanted shipped to Oxford and stashed them in the study. While there, they revised the list of books they wanted also shipped. Finally, there was the trunk of toys in the attic. In an exchange of letters some months before, they had agreed to destroy it. So they dragged it down to the vegetable garden, now wildly overgrown, and proceeded to dig a hole. Should they open the trunk for one last look at the stuffed animals and china figures they had used to populate the imaginative world of Boxen? They decided not to. As they were filling in the hole, they marvelled that they had created so much with so little.

Warren slept comfortably that night, but Jack awoke with toothache. About three he got up and took an aspirin. Looking out the window he saw 'a thick white mist gleaming from the lamps in the road, and a dripping from the leaves.' From that very window he could remember gazing many times in the past, 'in terror of ghosts, worry about [Mrs Lewis], toothaches, quarrels with Warren away back in early childhood.'

In the morning there was more packing. The brothers sorted through documents and diaries, photographs of themselves and the family; they gave the Witch of Endor, as they called Mary Cullen behind her back, the one she wanted of Albert. In the afternoon they walked down to Uncle Gussie's; Warren Augustus Hamilton was their mother's brother; he was co-founder of Hamilton & McMaster, marine boilermakers and engineers. After dinner Gussie drove them back to Little Lea, where they made him a present. From the cellar of the house they fetched to the car the contents of the drinks cabinet. As they did so, the brothers felt that all of their previous life had come to a close, Albert having guarded the cupboard so sternly and dispensed its contents only with discretion and always with ceremony. After bidding goodbye to Gussie and Mary, they took Gillespie's taxi to the quay where they boarded the overnight ferry for the return trip to Liverpool and Oxford.

༄

On Thursday 1 May before sunrise, Warren awoke just moments before the Magdalen scout knocked on his door. Not long after, Jack appeared in hood and gown. He treated Warren to a cup of tea. Then the two of them headed across the quad to Magdalen Tower. They climbed to the top where they found that they were far from the first. College noblesse and town bourgeoisie as well as the choir preceded them. The sun rose, the choir sang, the bells peeled, the tower shook noticeably. May Day had officially begun. Then running across Magdalen Bridge below, Warren saw 'a crowd of ridiculous little figures . . . being hustled on by a fool with his bladder, and in their wake the rest of the Morris dancers.'

Reaching the ground some minutes later the brothers hurried up the High, crossed over to the Broad, then ambled up to Balliol College, outside of which the Morris dancers were capering about. There were seven of them, as Warren would record in his diary that night, 'dressed in white shirts and trousers with green cross belts and rosettes and bells at their knees, one old man also in white but with red cross belts who did a solo, and a couple of fools; one man played a concertina; the dancers had a white handkerchief in each hand.'

Warren's days in Oxford were numbered. He got notice from the War Office that his leave would extend only until 15 May. Between now and then he pottered about Blackwell's, sampling the new and second-hand books; he picked up pies for Mrs Moore and music for Maureen; he walked Tykes, as Papworth was now called, all over the town and hills. Headington he found 'a delightful village with its stone-walled lanes and irregular houses of all sorts'; the church too was good, especially in twilight. In the evenings he read Elizabeth Barrett Browning and William Wordsworth. One Saturday night he and the others went to *Sir John in Love*, an opera by Vaughan Williams based roughly on Shakespeare's *Merry Wives of Windsor*.

He spent a good deal of time with his brother. He drew up a plan for organizing the family papers that were being shipped from Little Lea. That would take up the first year of his retirement, which shouldn't be too far in the future. Jack talked of his coming to live with them on a permanent basis. The switch from institutional to familial life, he warned, might not be an easy one. There would be Mrs Moore's mare's nests and Maureen's practising on the piano and violin. There would be the perpetual interruptions of family life, even a partial loss of liberty. Lewis had made the choice some years before, and how did he like it? On the whole his judgment was that domestic life derived him a great many pleasures and saved him a great many pains. The earliest he could retire, said Warren, was 1933; if there were a new house by then, he felt he could move in easily. He insisted that Jack draw on the estate for as much as £500 if needed for the down payment; he himself would contribute £200 to the venture.

On 13 May Warren received his orders. On 15 May he took the afternoon train to Bulford, ten miles from Salisbury, within walking distance of Stonehenge.

On 30 June Lewis journeyed the fifteen miles east of Oxford to an idyllic cottage in Long Crendon. There, 'amid thatched roof and the crooning of hens, with a pony and a donkey in the orchard and honeysuckle over the door,' he visited Barfield and his family for a few days. In the mornings the two men finished reading, aloud and in Italian, *Il Paradiso*, which they had begun on a visit in January. 'Can you imagine Shelley at his most ecstatic combined with Milton at his most solemn and rigid?' wrote Lewis to Greeves. 'It sounds impossible, I know, but that is what Dante has done.' They also read in Old English some *Beowulf* with a farmer's daughter, a plump young woman who had gone to London for an English degree and returned home to milk cows and take occasional pupils. In the afternoons the two friends went to a reach in the Thames where Barfield taught Lewis to dive head first; then they lounged 'naked under the pollards on a flat field; mowers in the next; and tiny young dragon-flies — too small to be frightful yet — darting among the lilies.' In the evenings they planned the Bacchic Festival they would hold a year hence, celebrating the wine they were making from the vine that grew over the cottage. 'The adopted baby is to be the infant Bacchus. Harwood with his fat shiny face, on the donkey, will be Silenus. Barfield and I, Corybantes. Mrs Barfield, a Maenad. Barfield and I will write poetry, and she will compose a dance,' wrote Lewis to Greeves. 'You ought to come.'

∽

Mrs Moore had heard that there was a house for sale a mile or two away. She went to see it herself and returned to Hillsboro most excited. She encouraged Lewis to see it. On Sunday morning, 6 July, he and Warren, who had come from Bulford to spend the weekend, walked up Headington Hill, then over to the 'northern foot of Shotover.' Following her directions they found 'a very bad and little used road.' Halfway up, they turned right and proceeded up a narrow lane flanked by a row of trees. Two kilns hove into view, looking like upside-down funnels from among the kitchen utensils, only they were made of brick and surrounded by sheds. Next came the house, which appeared larger than Hillsboro: two chimneys, two dormers protruding from the sharply sloping slate roof, a pleasing front door. In front of the house was a nice lawn and a hard tennis court. Passing by the house and heading further up Shotover they came to a pond, 'a large bathing pool, beautifully wooded, with a delightful circular brick seat overlooking it.' Still further up they found 'a steep wilderness broken with ravines and nooks of all kinds' running 'up to a little cliff topped by a thistly meadow,' at the far end of which was 'a thick belt of fir trees.'

Should they buy the Kilns, as they now called the place, or shouldn't they? That afternoon they sat down at the kitchen table at Hillsboro to talk it over. Jack proposed that they consider the buying of the house as though it were the canonization of a saint in the Roman church. Minto and Warren would put forth arguments for buying it, and he, *advocatus diaboli*, arguments against buying it.

It had two more rooms than Hillsboro, said Minto.

But what they really needed, countered Jack, was four more

rooms.

Well, we'll just add two more rooms onto the house when we buy it, concluded Minto.

But building two more rooms will just add to the cost of the house.

Only £100, said Minto, and she would pay for that.

Certainly no more than £200, said Warren, and he would throw in the £100 he was expecting any moment from Albert's estate; after all, the study and bedroom would be for him.

But the Kilns was not within walking distance of Oxford.

There was always the bus, said Minto.

But that was not within walking distance of the shops in Headington.

Let me worry about that, said Minto, knowing in her heart that she would press the two brothers into delivery service more often than they could imagine.

But did they really need eight acres?

The garden was such stuff as dreams were made of, sighed Warren.

But for the money they would have to spend, shouldn't they get a house that was located closer to things and had a better garden?

Many a £10,000 house was worse situated and had a poorer garden, said Warren.

But £3,500, the asking price of the Kilns, was more money than they had.

The sale of Little Lea should certainly make the Kilns affordable, said Warren.

To ascertain just how much money was immediately available from Albert's estate, Jack fired off a letter to J. W. A. Condlin in Belfast. Almost by return came a notice that the balance in the Bank of Ireland account was £1,381. This was £700 more than Jack had expected. Immediately Warren urged him to put 'some of this elusive fairy gold into the new house.'

Thus was the Kilns canonized, and in a month's time the house was theirs.

⌘

Coghill had a friend that he wanted to introduce to Lewis. Henry Victor Dyson Dyson was his name, but he insisted on being called Hugo; he got a B.A. from Exeter College in 1921 and a B.Litt. from the university in 1924; he was now a lecturer and tutor in English at Reading University, and was in Oxford for a brief visit. On 28 July Lewis invited them both to dinner at Magdalen, during which and for many hours thereafter serious conversation was interspersed with laughter. 'How we roared and fooled at times in the silence of the night,' he wrote of the occasion to Greeves, 'but always in a few minutes buckled to with renewed seriousness.' Magdalen's gates were locked by the porter every night at 12.00; when 3.00 a.m. came and went, Lewis had to escort his friends 'through pitch black cloisters to let them out by the little gate' near Magdalen Bridge, where the street lamps illuminated the bell tower. By 10.00 the following morning, he was awake and 'feeling rather morning-after-ish,' but there lingered pleasantly the memory of Dyson as 'a man who really loves the truth, a philosopher and a religious man, who makes his critical and literary activities depend on the former — none of your damned dilettanti.'

Barfield sent Lewis a novel he had written entitled *English People*; it contained many fine passages, Lewis thought, but Barfield was not able to find a publisher. Lewis began 'the first instalment of a new romance', which he eventually entitled *The Moving Image*. He planned to write a chapter a week and send it to Greeves for critical evaluation; the project lasted no longer than eight weeks. Greeves too wrote a novel, the completed manuscript of which he had the temerity to show to Forrest Reid, a novelist living in Belfast; Reid did not think it publishable; Greeves quickly concluded that he was a literary failure. Lewis also read the manuscript; he did not say that Reid was wrong in his evaluation; instead he pointed out that, although he had had two books of poetry published, he was still as disappointed an author as his friend, so few copies of *Spirits in Bondage* and *Dymer* having been sold. 'Suffering of the sort that you are now feeling is my special subject, my profession, my long suit, the thing I claim to be an expert in.'

Moving day was Friday 10 October, a beautiful autumn day, trees ablaze with colour. Jack loaded a Jowett car and drove up Headington Hill as though he were navigating a Cunard liner. Furniture was dumped in the house. Cartons of books were stashed in the garage. Boxes of dishes were carried into the kitchen. Warren arrived in the middle of the afternoon and added the sidecar of his Daudel to the cartage and haulage.

On Saturday Minto and Maureen worked to put things right inside the house. Jack and Warren walked up to the pond where they decided to do something about the unsightly weeds breaking through the watery surface. They pushed a punt out from the shore and started drawing the weeds out from the muddy bottom, piling them at one end of the punt. When the boat began to ship water they poled to shore, where Warren pitchforked the evil-smelling pile out of sight.

Sunday was a day of rest. In the afternoon some friends of Mrs Moore's dropped by for a visit. A tour of the estate followed. When Mrs Armitage saw the pond, she boarded the punt and insisted that someone pole her into the middle. Tykes hopped aboard, and with reluctance Jack stepped aboard also. Balance was hard to maintain since both he and the woman were standing, and one lurch sent Mrs Armitage — with a scream and a flash of flaming red bloomers — down onto an inch of slime covering the seat of the boat. Good sport that she was, she laughed at herself, and the others laughed themselves to tears.

After tea and some lament from Minto that half of her 'unmatchable tea things' had been broken in the move, Mrs Armitage and her daughter departed. While Minto began to think of the evening meal, Jack and Warren roamed down Shotover towards the quarries and past the Headington Quarry parish church, which was dedicated to the Holy Trinity. The windows were pleasantly lighted, and evensong filtered out into the autumn air. Now that they were landed gentry, suggested Jack, perhaps they should begin to patronize their local church; Warren agreed.

In the weekends that followed, Jack caught the bus from Oxford and Warren cycled up from Bulford to the Kilns, where they continued unpacking and made further plans for the landscaping. A forestry expert was invited to inspect the timber; he said it would fetch a good price on the market. They weren't that hard up, said Jack, declining to sell it. If they ever were in arrears, suggested Warren, they could always charge admission to Americans to see their pool, which the brothers had just learned was known locally as Shelley's Pond, a place where the poet used to brood and meditate and sail his boats.

In April Lewis' bedside reading had been the fourth gospel in Greek. In May he had perused *The Practice of the Presence of God* by Brother Lawrence of the Resurrection. In June he had traversed *Centuries of Meditation* by Thomas Traherne. By October he was going to bed earlier and rising in time to go to morning chapel at eight. He would pass through the ante-chapel, walk through the altar screen, past the lectern, and with a resounding thud sink to his knees in one of the carved wooden stalls. If Weldon had spied him attending dean's prayers, he would never hear the end of it; but the chapel was the last place in Oxford Weldon would look.

'I think the trouble with me,' he wrote on Christmas Eve to Greeves, 'is *lack of faith*. I have no *rational* ground for going back on the arguments that convinced me of God's existence; but the irrational deadweight of my old sceptical habits, and the spirit of this age, and the cares of the day, steal away all my lively feeling of the truth; and often when I pray, I wonder if I am not posting letters to a non-existent address.'

⤳ 1931 ⤳

'He and I even went to church twice,' wrote Lewis of his brother and himself to Greeves on 10 January; 'and — will you believe it — he said to me in conversation that he was beginning to think the religious view of things was after all true. Mind you (like me, at first) he didn't *want* it to be, nor like it; but his intellect was beginning to revolt from the semi-scientific assumptions we all grew up in, and the other explanation of the world seems to him daily more probable.'

⤳

'It is now six months since I submitted to you the manuscript of an article entitled "The Personal Heresy in Criticism,"' he wrote on 19 April to T. S. Eliot, founder and editor of *The Criterion*. He didn't expect an affirmative answer; in years gone by he and Coghill and a few others who preferred old poetry to new had written mock-Eliotic poems and sent them to modernist magazines like *The Criterion* in London and *Dial* in New York; not 'one of these filthy editors' fell into the trap, and their 'literary dragonnade' fizzled. Nine months more, wrote Eliot when he replied a month later; it might take that long before a publishing decision could be made. That he probably thought the article mock-Eliotic criticism was Lewis' only consolation

⤳

'Our usual plan here is to spend a term on Chaucer and his contemporaries,' he wrote on 18 June to a young man who would be entering Oxford in the autumn. Vacations should be spent reading texts in order to master the story, the situation, the style. For example, if he were going to read Chaucer and his contemporaries next term, he should read, before the term began, *Piers Plowman*, *Confessio Amantis*, *Sir Gawain and the Green Knight*, and as much other fourteenth-century prose and poetry as he could find. To try to do both Chaucer and Shakespeare in the same term would be 'a hazardous experiment.'

〜

Having met Dyson for the first time the previous July, and seeing the verbose and vivacious little man four or five times since then, Lewis was beginning to rank him as a friend of the second class, first class being reserved for Barfield and Greeves. Saturday, 19 September, was one of those times. He was invited to Magdalen to dine; Tolkien was also invited. After dinner they set out for a stroll on Addison's Walk, a woody pathway along the Cherwell that had got its name from Joseph Addison, a fellow of Magdalen in the late seventeenth century. It was a warm, still night. The conversation turned towards myth and metaphor.

Myths were enjoyable in themselves, argued Lewis; he had certainly enjoyed them more than most, but they were believed only by children. Adults knew better; myths were lies; although the better ones had been breathed through silver, they were none the more believable for that. Tolkien and Dyson were quick to disagree. However untrue they might seem to be, they contained elements of the truth. Created as he was by God, the myth maker was himself a creator, albeit a sub-creator, when he undertook to spin a tale or develop a plot, and when he did so shafts of truth were bound to dot the forest floor.

The argument was 'interrupted by a rush of wind.' It began to rain, or so they thought at first. Leaves pattered down on their shoulders, not raindrops, but they decided to head back to New Buildings, where the conversation turned towards Christianity and its doctrines.

He was having difficulty, Lewis said, not so much in believing a doctrine as in knowing what a doctrine meant. When asked for an example he gave the doctrine of redemption. Drunkenness could lead a person down the primrose path where only a redemptive act could save him. He could see that, but what he couldn't see was 'how the life and death of someone else (whoever he was) 2,000 years ago' could help them there and then — except insofar as his *example* helped them. He had read the gospels, but nowhere did he find this *example* business; instead he found 'propitiation' and 'sacrifice' and 'blood of the lamb', expressions that he could interpret only in the sense that seemed to him 'either silly or shocking.'

What was wrong with sacrifice? asked Tolkien, who was Church of Rome, and Dyson, who was Church of England. There was nothing wrong with the idea of sacrifice, Lewis had to concede. He had always liked 'the idea of sacrifice in a pagan story', 'the idea of a god sacrificing himself to himself', 'the idea of a dying and reviving God.' But the idea of such notions of sacrifice were entirely out of place when it came to interpreting the gospels.

If pagan stories were 'God expressing himself through minds of poets, using such images as he found there,' then Christianity might very well be construed as 'God expressing himself through what [they called] "real things".' Why couldn't the story of Christ be construed as a myth, argued Tolkien and Dyson with vigour, but a myth that was true? 'A myth working on [them] in the same way as on the others, but with this tremendous difference, that *it really happened*'?

What about the doctrines derived from the one true myth? Were they in any sense truths? Whatever else they were, they were 'translations into [their] *concepts* and *ideas* of that which God has already expressed in a language more adequate, namely the actual incarnation, crucifixion, and resurrection.'

As the evening wore on, Lewis grew more certain that the Christian story had to be approached in the same way he approached the other myths and that it was 'the most important and full of meaning.' By three in the morning he was almost certain that it had really happened. He and Dyson made haste to let Tolkien out 'by the little postern on Magdalen Bridge.' Then they returned to New Buildings where they paced the colonnade until 4 o'clock.

Some days later, invigilating in the Examination Schools building, Tolkien tried to recapture that evening by beginning a verse letter from one who loved myth to one who hated it.

> 'Dear Sir,' I said — 'Although now long estranged,
> Man is not wholly lost nor wholly changed.
> Dis-graced he may be, yet is not de-throned,
> and keeps the rags of lordship once he owned;
> Man, Sub-creator, the refracted Light
> through whom is splintered from a single White
> to many hues, and endlessly combined
> in living shapes that move from mind to mind.
> Though all the crannies of the world we filled
> with Elves and Goblins, though we dared to build
> Gods and their houses out of dark and light,
> and sowed the seed of dragons — 'twas our right
> (used or misused). That right has not decayed:
> we make still by the law in which we're made.'

'I have just passed on from believing in God to definitely believing in Christ — in Christianity,' wrote Lewis twelve days later to Greeves. 'My long talk with Dyson and Tolkien had a good deal to do with it.'

∽

Lewis could not accuse Hamlet of being slow to decide. He was reading the text of the play with care. He studied 'all the innumerable theories' about the play. He soaked himself in the atmosphere 'made up equally of the prevalent sense of death, solitude, and horror.' The character he found extraordinarily gracious and lovable. He surrendered himself to the magic, regarding it, not as a play, but as a poem, a romance.

∽

As Monday 28 September dawned in Headington Quarry, the ground was carpeted with fog. During breakfast Maureen rehearsed the reasons for and against their planned excursion to the Whipsnade Zoo. At 11.15 Warren started the Daudel, Jack hopped into the sidecar, and the brothers roared off; the others would follow by car. Halfway there, the fog broke and the sun shone through. Having stopped for beer and fuel on the way, they still arrived at the village of Whipsnade before one o'clock. There, they spread the Daudel's waterproof on a slope of short turf, opened bottles of beer, and recovered from the vibrations of the forty-mile run. At 2.20 the Singer arrived. Mr Papworth bounded from the window of the car; Maureen emerged from behind the wheel, followed by her mother and her mother's friend Vera Henry. Sandwiches were passed around, which the brothers devoured. At 3.00 they entered the zoo; all, that is, except Jack, who had to mind the dog. He felt pleasantly relaxed, emotionally refreshed, as 'a man, after long sleep, still lying motionless in bed, becomes aware that he is now awake.' Lounging on the waterproof, he became aware that, sometime during the last few hours, he had come to a conclusion without the intervention of the intellectual process. When he set out from Headington he hadn't believed, and when he arrived in Whipsnade he did believe, that Jesus Christ was the Son of God. At 4.00 Warren emerged from the gates and took over the watch. He suggested Jack pay special attention to the kangaroos hopping about in Wallaby Wood; to the American timber wolves, 'evil, noiseless-looking beasts'; and the bears, 'skinny, black, duck-toed fellows with white noses'; there was a 'delightful, brock-brown, plethoric one who sat up and saluted for buns.' When Jack emerged about 5.30, he found Warren eating Whipsnade Rock, on sale at the zoo's gate. He said he too liked the brown bear the best. It was the sort of creature they would wish to have included among the menagerie they created for Boxen. 'Bultitude' would be the perfect name for him. The brothers cycled off; the others drove off; and when Jack stepped from the sidecar at the Kilns, he was a bit stiff, but the belief that Jesus Christ was the Son of God was still fresh in his mind.

The following Monday, 5 October, the brothers again made the run to Whipsnade, this time without the other members of the family. It was a farewell trip. On Wednesday Warren would embark for China for what he hoped would be his final tour of duty before retirement. It was foggy at the beginning, but it was sunny by noon. They ate at a restaurant with cloisters at the zoo; then they walked about the grounds. Again Bultitude was the animal that pleased them the most.

〰️

On 19 October Griffiths visited Lewis and presented him with a rare, poorly bound copy of *An Appeal to All that Doubt, or disbelieve the truths of the Gospel whether they be deists, Arians, Socinians, or nominal Christians*. The eighteenth-century work had become something of a devotional classic. William Law, a clergyman who refused to take the oath of allegiance to George I, was the author; both Griffiths and Lewis had drawn spiritual fruit from his *Serious Call to a Devout and Holy Life, adapted to the state and condition of all orders of Christians*: 'a very severe but wholesome draught,' as Lewis described to Greeves on 18 May.

How was the grand experiment working out? Lewis was referring to the dramatic step Griffiths and two of his friends had taken the year before. Communism was emigrating from Russia; extremism was infecting politics; factories were poisoning the atmosphere: it was a time of extreme crisis for them. They felt that the only course of action was to retreat to an earlier century and 'live without all the products of the industrial revolution.' They picked 'a plain little village at the bottom of a valley with a small stream running through it,' Eastington; they thought it had the simple beauty of everything that was in harmony with nature. They bought 'a four-roomed cottage built of solid Cotswold stone with Cotswold tiling, but without water, drainage, or lighting of any sort.' Daily life approached the idyllic. They milked cows, herded sheep, and grew their own vegetables. In the evenings they lit tallow dips, stuck them into an iron candelabrum, and read poetry and philosophy. Eventually they began to pray, not in the warmth of the kitchen, but on the cold stone outside. They had an annual income of £800. 'Allowing not only for food and clothing and all household expenses but also for books,' they needed only £100 for themselves. The remaining £700 they felt they should invest in morally worthwhile tasks. They even offered

Barfield £100 a year for the next few years to subsidize his editing of the unpublished works of Coleridge.

As Michaelmas term began, Lewis' life once again fell into an orderly pattern. He was awakened by a scout with a cup of tea at 7.15. He was able to stretch his legs in Addison's Walk before adjourning to chapel for dean's prayers. Breakfast at 8.20. Pupils from 9.00 to 1.00, at which time Maureen was waiting with a car at Magdalen's gate. After lunch at the Kilns he would often take a spade and head northward on the property to do some landscaping. 'The scurry of the waterfowl as you pass the pond, and the rich smell of autumnal litter as you leave the drive and strike into the little path,' he wrote on 22 November to his brother, 'are always just as good as new.' At 4.45 Maureen would drive him back to Magdalen, where he had pupils from 5.00 to 7.00. Dinner at 7.15 and on Tuesday evenings pupils reading *Beowulf* from 8.30 to 11.00.

The second week in November he went to Reading, where he spent the night at the university as Dyson's guest. 'A burly man, both in mind and body, with the stamp of the war on him,' was the way Lewis described him to his brother; 'he is a Christian and a lover of cats.'

Sometimes accompanying him on his afternoon jaunts were Martin Lings and Adrian Hugh Patterson; both were pupils of his, both poets, both fast friends of each other. Lings was about five feet tall, 'very ugly, very dark'; looking one hundred years old and hurrying noiselessly along the cloisters, he reminded Patterson of a furtive mouse rushing to escape calamity. Patterson had an Italian face, was moody and inclined to be effeminate; he had spent his first two terms at college 'sitting in his rooms, listening to the feet of people on the staircase, always hoping that it was someone coming to call on him.'

One afternoon a week Lewis ventured forth with Edward Foord-Kelcey, a neighbour of his. He was perhaps eighty years old, drove his own car, mended everybody's wireless; at the moment he was carpentering a new cover for the font at Holy Trinity. What Lewis liked about him was that he was a voracious reader, at least of Sterne, Boswell, and Dickens, and that he cared for no poetry but Shakespeare's. He was 'deliciously limited,' he wrote to Greeves, yet he was 'redolent of English country life as an old apple in a barn.'

That he was a retired country parson put no strain on Lewis' credulity during their weekly rambles. The old man distrusted all mysticism and imagination. He disbelieved in the virgin birth. He had doubts about the immortality of the soul. He thought drunkenness a greater sin than murder or incest, and he was high on practical charity; 'we must learn to love those we can't like.' On Christmas Day Lewis was able to write to his brother something seasonable about Foord-Kelcey: 'he objected to the early chapters of St Luke (the annunciation) on the ground that they were — *indelicate*.'

ᥫᥬ 1932 ᥫᥬ

Since 1929 Lewis had been working on textual problems in the works of Chaucer; part of that work came to fruition in 1932 when his essay entitled 'What Chaucer Did to *Il Filostrato*' appeared in *Essays and Studies*.

The story of Cressida and her lovers Troilus and Diomede originated in twelfth-century France. It was retold in the fourteenth century first by Boccaccio, then by Chaucer; Shakespeare would retell it in the sixteenth century and Dryden in the seventeenth. Chaucer, in rendering the medieval Italian poem into acceptable Middle English, meandered into philosophical discussions about fate and free will, brought life to the rollicking character of Pandarus, and generally ordered the relationships of the lovers, not along slapdash Italian lines, but according to courtly love, a code of behaviour then in fashion that encouraged romantic love out of wedlock; although unchristian, it seemed to have had a refining influence on society, treating love as a fine art and its pursuit as a liberal education. Lewis concluded his analysis by saying that 'courtly love . . . is at bottom more agreeable to those elements in human . . . nature . . . than the cynical Latin gallantries of Boccaccio.' He went on to theorize that 'certain medieval things are more universal, in that sense more classical . . . than certain things of the Renaissance' and than — he could not resist including — the novels of D. H. Lawrence; *Lady Chatterley's Lover* had just been published.

Another reason why Lewis might have preferred Chaucer to Boccaccio, and one not unconnected to his theory of personal heresy, was that as an author Chaucer was a comparative unknown who had to depend for his success on how well he told the story. Boccaccio, on the other hand, was so widely and critically received before he wrote *Il Filostrato* that, as is inevitable with all successful authors, he himself became the product; his audience looked forward to the next Boccaccio, no matter what the story was or how well it was told.

⌘

'The efficacy of prayer is . . . no *more* of a problem than the efficacy of *all* human acts. That is, if you say "It is useless to pray because Providence already knows what is best and will certainly do it," then why is it not equally useless (and for the same reason) to try to alter the course of events in any way whatever?'

By the end of 1931 Lewis was going not only to church on Sunday but also to communion. By the end of February, he was coming to some conclusions about the efficacy of prayer; above, he addressed to his brother in Shanghai; below, to his friend in Belfast.

'When you ask me to "pray for you" . . . I don't know if you are serious, but, the answer is, I do. It may not do you any good, but it does me a lot, for I cannot ask for any change to be made in you without finding that the very same needs to be made in me; which pulls me up and also by putting us all in the same boat checks any tendency to priggishness.'

⌘

'To enjoy a book . . . I find I have to treat it as a sort of hobby and set about it seriously. I begin by making a map on one of the end leafs; then I put in a genealogical tree or two; then I put a running headline at the top of each page; finally I index at the end all the passages I have for any reason underlined. I often wonder — considering how people enjoy themselves developing photos or making scrapbooks — why so few people make a hobby of their reading in this way. Many an otherwise dull book which I had to read have I enjoyed in this way, with a fine-nibbed pen in my hand: one is *making* something all the time and a book so read acquires the charm of a toy without losing that of a book.'

⌘

The attunement of himself with the harmonies of the natural and supernatural world, which he called joy, he tried to capture in what he hoped would be a long narrative poem:

> I will write down the portion that I understand
> Of twenty years wherein I went from land to land.
> At many bays and harbours I put in with joy
> Hoping that there I should have built my second Troy
> And stayed . . .

'I am not yet satisfied with any part I have yet written, and the design is ludicrously ambitious,' he wrote on 6 May to Barfield. 'But I feel it will be several years anyway before I give it up.'

&

Since 1911, when he first saw plot synopses of *The Ring of the Nibelungen* with illustrations by Arthur Rackham, and later, when he heard the music on a gramophone, he was under the sway of Richard Wagner. The operas composing the *Ring* fell like waterfalls on his imagination and eventually fed, like underground streams, his sense of northernness. He was surprised in 1932 when *Siegfried*, third opera in the *Ring* cycle, was being presented in London, by the return of his 'boyish appetite' to see a show. He badgered Barfield to go to Covent Garden Theatre in advance and buy the 'cheapest bookable' seats for Monday 16 May; he even offered to pay for Barfield's ticket.

He had already seen *The Valkyrie*, second of the cycle, on 14 June 1918; he was recuperating from his war wounds at the time; although he could only hobble about, he did manage to get to the Drury Lane Theatre. He could remember it still, and no doubt he rehearsed it for Barfield. His seat was off to the side; the person in front of him kept jumping up and down; someone else, obviously with the score on his lap, kept whispering 'Louder!' or 'No, no, no!' disagreeing at almost every note with the conductor, Thomas Beecham. He even had to leave before it was finished, 'but the performance,' he reported to Greeves at the time, 'was beyond all words.'

The images created by this latter production remained with Lewis for years. 'The lighting gave a really unusual impression of spring moonlight, and that combined with the glorious love music of the orchestra . . . simply swept you away — and then all the time creeping in under this, the faint horn-motif of the sword and the far-off tinkling hammers to remind you of the Nibelungs . . .' Since that time irruptions in the natural world nearly always reminded him of one part of the *Ring* or another. 'Trees plunging like terrified but tethered horses, leaves eddying, chimneys howling, and under all the lesser and lighter noises, a great solid roar above the house': to lie in bed at night and revel in a Wagnerian storm thundering about the Kilns was an aesthetic experience, second only to sitting in a stall at Drury Lane or Covent Garden.

&

He had tried it in prose a few years before; he had tried it in verse a few months before; he wanted to try again to record his conversion from atheism to Christianity in some literary way. His passage had indeed been a pilgrimage, albeit an interior one, and pilgrimage literature was no stranger to him. *Everyman* was perhaps the most successful, a fifteenth-century Dutch play, which had been translated early in the sixteenth century. The central character was, not one individual, but all individuals. Summoned by Death and hence facing the final pilgrimage, Everyman looked among his friends for a companion. Only one of them, Good Deeds, would accompany him through death and to judgment beyond. Pilgrimage was indeed the motif Lewis was looking for, but a dramatic model was of no use to him.

There was 'The Dream of the Rood', an Old English poem in which the poet, in vision, talked with the cross that Christ was crucified on, and the cross talked back. There was *The Vision of William concerning Piers the Plowman*, a sprawling allegorical poem written by William Langland in the second half of the fourteenth century. There was also *The Pilgrim's Progress, from This World to That Which Is to Come, Delivered under the Similitude of a Dream*, a prose allegory published in 1678. The dream-vision would be a far better model than drama; it would allow for the many uses of allegory. Lewis could move backward and forward in time without respect to causality. He could fabricate the incidents of the allegory in such a way that they had one meaning for the characters and an additional meaning, perhaps several meanings, for the reader. What was philosophically complex in his own pilgrimage, therefore, Lewis felt he could make ridiculously simple and not a little interesting.

Dreams were no strangers to Lewis. When he was a child, ghosts visited him frequently at night, and insects — 'their angular limbs, their jerky movements, their dry metallic noises' — terrorized him as they lumbered forward with the inexorability of French locomotives.

A few years before he had dreamed — and woke to remember — that he went to the kitchen to get something to eat. Opening the cupboard door, a package rolled off the shelf and hit the floor with a thud. Thinking it a cabbage, he picked it up and, unwrapping the brown paper, he found, looking up at him with baleful eye, a woman's head, Mrs Lovell's, the woman who had done odd jobs for Mrs Moore but in recent weeks had disappeared without a trace.

Then there was the dream about his father. 'I was in the dining room at Little Lea, with all the gases lit, and talking to my father,' was the way he described it to Greeves. 'I knew perfectly well that he had died, and presently put out my hand and touched him. He felt warm and solid. I said, "But of course, this must be only an appearance. You can't really have a body now." He explained that it was only an appearance, and our conversation, which was cheerful and friendly, but not solemn or emotional, drifted onto other topics.'

With much of this on his mind, Lewis left Oxford on the night of Monday 15 August for Liverpool, where he boarded the overnight ferry for Belfast.

Personified and prancing about allegories like *Piers Plowman* and *The Pilgrim's Progress*, he recalled as he leaned against the railing of the boat, were characters like Death and Good Deeds, abstractions of a sort he was sure he could use in his own work. In Langland there were a trio of Do-ables (Do Well, Do Better, Do Best), the Seven Deadly Sins, and Tom-true-tongue-tell-me-no-tales-nor-lying-stories-to-laugh-at-for-I-loved-them-never. In Bunyan there were Evangelist, Worldly-wiseman, Faithful and Hopeful, Passion and Patience, Obstinate and Pliable, and virgins named Prudence, Piety, and Charity.

If Langland could invent Lady Holychurch to stand for Christianity, then he could create Mother Kirk. Mr Enlightenment could represent the intellect triumphing over religion; his son Sigismund could stand for psychology tromping on rationality. Mr Sensible could stand for reasonableness in search of happiness. And there could be three young men — Mr Neo-classical, Mr Neo-angular, Mr Humanist — who would found a community based on classicism, Catholicism, and humanism.

As allegories created characters out of abstractions, so also they created out of nothing places that had no geographical reality. Bunyan exnihilized Vanity Fair, the Slough of Despond, the Valley of the Shadow of Death, Doubting Castle and Palace Beautiful and the Delectable Mountains. Langland placed, on already existing topography, the Tower of Truth, in which dwelled God the Father, and the Castle of Care, in which lived the Father of Falseness, and the earth itself he called 'a fair field full of folk.'

In his own work, for which he would eventually draw a map, Lewis — and he was writing rapidly now at a table in Greeves' house — dotted the landscape with places like Thrill, Claptrap, and Puritania. He laid down the Isthmus Sadisticus and the Isthmus Mazochisticus. There was a North, where people were pale, austere, taciturn; there was a South, where people were dark, indulgent, loquacious. Slashing across the landscape that had once been paradise but was now crevassed with a fault of spiritual origin, was the Grand Canyon, an exotic name from the American West. If he were not in Shanghai, Warren would surely insist on a military railway, one that would link such major population centres as Zeitgeistheim, Occultica, and Orgiastica; after all, he had devised the principal steamship routes on the map of Boxen.

The central character of an allegory was usually the author himself and, as that author fervently hoped, a multitude of readers would identify themselves with that character. Langland was Long Will;

many a medieval prelate and clerk would recognize himself in Will. Bunyan was Christian as he set out on the sort of journey all Puritans could understand. And Lewis was John, the twentieth-century pilgrim who would be drawn inexorably towards the island and mountain of his desires. In a sense, he began his work where Bunyan left off. Christian had to face every temptation the seventeenth century had to offer; John, setting out from Puritania, met, first of all, the eighteenth century in the character of Mr Enlightenment; in the next seventy-two chapters he would meet personifications of every philosophical, literary, and political movement from that time right down to the 1930s.

To root the allegory somewhere in the theological firmament, there had to be a creation myth, and Lewis decided to have Mother Kirk tell it to John about halfway through. There was a Landlord who had a farm. He 'decided to let the country to tenants, and his first tenant was a young married man.' Under the influence of the Enemy, who was one of the Landlord's children, the farmer's wife ate 'a nice mountain apple,' something she had been told not to do. 'And then — you know how it is with husbands — she made the farmer come round to her mind.' *Peccatum Adae* it was called by Mother Kirk in her own peculiar language, 'the sin of Adam.' Indigestion was followed hard by earthquake, and the paradisal park became a gorge.

Having traversed half the world in search of the Landlord, having been beguiled by a variety of temptations and interpretations of existence, but seemingly no closer to the island or mountain of his desires, John uttered a cry for help. He prayed, and 'a Man came to him in the darkness' and spoke.

'Your life has been saved all this day by crying out to something which you call by many names, and you have said to yourself that you used metaphors.'

'Was I wrong, sir?'

'Perhaps not. But you must play fair. If its help is not a metaphor, neither are its commands. If it can answer when you call, then it can speak without your asking. If you can go to it, it can come to you.'

'I think I see it, sir. You mean that I am not my own man; in some sense I have a Landlord after all?'

Like a common criminal to a police sergeant, John turned himself in. He accepted the veracity of the myth and the credibility of Christianity. Equanimity restored, John found himself retracing his former steps. The temptations and interpretations that had so tormented him before, he now saw with clearer eyes. Like the yachtsman in Chesterton's *Orthodoxy*, who had sailed around the world only to discover that what he sought was on the coast of

England, John arrived back in Puritania. The pilgrimage was within, he concluded; the philosophical battles were fought quite independent of geography; and the many temptations had to be wrestled with on the topsoil of one's soul.

As a guest in the Greeves' household Lewis had been writing furiously, and by the end of his two-week stay he had completed a first draft. *The Pilgrim's Regress, or Pseudo-Bunyan's Periplus* would not be an inappropriate title, he thought; for a subtitle he considered 'An Allegorical Apology for Christianity, Reason and Romanticism.' An allegory it certainly was. A defence of Christianity it was without doubt, John having taken a header into the pool of belief at the foot of Mother Kirk. Reason as man's primary philosophical tool had been argued at length, reason being more than a knight cloaked in blue, a virgin who triumphed with naked sword or confounding riddle. But was it romantic enough?

❧

'It is a very consoling fact that so many books about real lives — biographies, autobiographies, letters, etc. — give one such an impression of *happiness*, in spite of the tragedies they all contain,' wrote Lewis on 4 December to Greeves. 'Perhaps the tragedies of real life contain more consolation and fun and gusto than the comedies of literature?'

❧

After eighteen years, two months, and twenty days in the army, Warren returned from Shanghai to the Kilns. It was as beautiful as he had remembered it when he arrived on 14 December; there was a new wing, which consisted of a study and, beyond it, a bedroom for him. On the morning of the 21st, he awoke to find at the door of that bedroom a copy of *The Times*. He riffled through the pages until he came across the small announcement: 'Capt. W. H. Lewis retires on ret. pay.' 'So far from grousing' — it had been almost a year since he had written in his diary — 'I am deeply, and I hope devoutly, thankful.'

First order of business would be the Lewis family papers. He would arrange them in chronological order, make a representative collection, put them into a fresh typescript, and bind the pages into as many volumes as necessary. He was also looking forward to a three-day walking tour with Jack in January. 'How many men are there,' he continued in his diary, 'who, before they are forty, can struggle free and begin the business of living?'

Griffiths, since seeing Lewis last, had taken a number of significant steps on the road to conversion; each step he shared with his former tutor in letters.

Having abandoned all traces of pantheism, idealism, and atheism, he embraced the Church of England. Having received communion regularly for a time, he felt the need to repent. Having come to grips with his sinfulness in general, he knelt beside his bed one night and began to pray. Having risen from his knees the following morning, he heard a voice tell him to make a retreat. Having found an Anglo-Catholic church nearby and learned what it was he was supposed to make, he was told that one was to begin that very morning. Having heard an old priest discourse with some warmth on 'the fundamental doctrines of original sin and redemption, of the incarnation and the Holy Trinity,' he felt 'the simple truth of the faith' penetrate to his soul. Having happened upon Anglo-Catholicism in a form that touched his heart, he came to ask what its relationship was to the Church of England and indeed to the Church of Rome. Having found a Catholic church in Winchcombe, he knocked on the door and met 'a Father Palmer, the son of an old English Catholic family,' who lent him some books and soon introduced him to a monastery in the neighbourhood. Having spent six weeks at Prinknash Priory, living the life of the community and reading such books as *Christ the Ideal of the Monk* by Dom Columba Marmion, he decided to become a Roman Catholic himself. Having been received into the Catholic Church at Winchcombe on 24 December 1932, he decided to enter the priory as a postulant at the end of January 1933 and would be clothed as a novice sometime the following December.

∽

'In a hole in the ground there lived a hobbit . . .' It was the beginning of Hilary Term, and Lewis was reading a manuscript Tolkien had given him. Tolkien had been telling his four children about hobbits for years now. On encouragement from Lewis and a few others, he had embroidered the bedtime stories, committed them to chapters, and pounded the handwritten script into typescript on a huge Hammond machine. As he read Lewis was swept away into a world he thought only he and Greeves had the door to. Bilbo Baggins even looked and sounded like Tolkien, and Tolkien was not slow to admit it. Over a glass in the pub at the Eastgate Hotel of a Monday morning, he said that he was, of course, not as well-to-do as Baggins, but he was indeed middle-aged; he dressed in sensible clothes but with a splash of colour in his waistcoat; he liked food unrefrigerated, and he would, if given the field, pick his own mushrooms.

Lewis liked everything about the story except, perhaps, the end. He had adjustments yet to make, said Tolkien. It succeeded with his children, but would it interest others? That remained to be seen. One thing the work did succeed in being was romantic, not in the sense that the novels of William Morris were romances or the exploits of the characters in a novel by Dumas or Sabatini . . .

Romantic, thought Lewis; *The Prilgrim's Regress* was romantic. What drew John from the serenity and security of Puritania and set him on the road was 'a sweetness and pang so piercing' that he could scarcely resist. Such a ringing desire sustained him throughout the pilgrimage, and as he neared the end, he came to the realization that 'the wanting, though it is pain too, is more precious than anything else we experience.'

One thing both Lewis and Tolkien agreed on as they rose from their tables at the Eastgate. For a truly successful work, for a truly romantic work, it should give one an entrance into another, perhaps a better, world. One should 'hear the horns of elfland.'

∽

Sometime after Christmas, Lewis sent the manuscript of *The Pilgrim's Regress, or Pseudo-Bunyan's Periplus* to J. M. Dent and Sons in London. By the beginning of February Dent replied that they would publish the work if he met certain conditions. He would have to simplify the title, shorten the manuscript, and submit to illustrations. If these conditions were acceptable, they would have galley proofs by mid-April and bound books by the end of May.

If Dent left *An Allegorical Apology for Christianity, Reason and Romanticism* intact, Lewis would drop the last three words from the title. If they forewent illustrations, he would draw a *mappa mundi* of the various places mentioned in the text. And he would look through the manuscript again for passages that might possibly be cut. Dent was agreeable. A contract was struck.

Lewis had already sent the manuscript to several of his friends, asking them to read it for 'confusion, bad taste, unsuccessful jokes, contradictions'; Greeves replied at length. He pointed out 'passages where one word less would make the difference.' Many of the words Lewis did use he found too 'idiomatic and racy,' not classical enough. Lewis replied to the effect that he preferred the colloquial to the literary and was only following Bunyan's example in this respect.

The characters in the allegory too often quoted from previously published works and in languages other than English. They were almost always from the mouth of Mr Sensible, countered Lewis, and almost always this character was misquoting. Besides, 'one of the contentions of the book is that the decay of our old classical learning is a contributory cause of atheism.'

Regress was divided into ten books, and each one was preceded by as many as four epigraphs. Too many, said Greeves, and too confusing. Most readers, said Lewis, never look at epigraphs anyway, and why, if he was pleased by them, should he remove them?

The argument of the allegory Greeves found too complex, even though he already knew the sinuous and tortuous path of his friend's conversion. 'The *intellectual* side of my conversion was *not* simple,' complained Lewis, 'and I can describe only what I know.'

When Dent offered Lewis a contract, however, and as he set about preparing the manuscript for composition, he made many of the changes indicated by Greeves and he rewrote those passages in which he couldn't accept his friend's suggestions.

'I suppose you have no objection to my dedicating the book to you?' he asked rhetorically of Greeves in a letter dated 25 March. 'It is yours by right — written in your house, read to you as it was written, and celebrating (at least in the most important parts) an experience which I have more in common with you than anyone else.'

❦

On the evening of 14 April the brothers, with Minto and Maureen, went to a little church in the Chilterns where they attended a passion play. It was Good Friday. The play consisted of five scenes. The choir sang hymns; the vicar read the story of the passion with reverence. 'The acting was, of course, bad,' wrote Warren in his diary before going to bed, 'but it was the badness of naiveté — no ranting or anything of that kind; and they had avoided the pitfall of having a professional or a trained amateur in the anonymous cast "to help the show along".' On Easter Sunday morning they attended what turned out to be a choral service and went to communion. Jack winced at the singing; Warren railed against receiving 'a prepared wafer instead of the ordinary bread'; but Jack could not prevent himself from praying.

'Since I have begun to pray,' he wrote to Barfield, 'I find my extreme view of personality changing. My own empirical self is becoming more important, and this is exactly the opposite of self-love. You don't teach a seed how to die into treehood by throwing it into the fire· and it has to become a good seed before it's worth burying . . .

❦

On 2 May, a Tuesday, Lewis took a train for London where he and Barfield went to Wagner's *Das Reingold* at the Covent Garden Theatre, first of the four operas in the *Ring* cycle. It would take a great deal to destroy such an evening for Lewis. The seats were bad, however, and the man who played Alberich shouted instead of sang.

To restore his friend to good humour, Barfield began to recite a poem:

> I stand before thee, bottom upward;
> I see thy beauty gradually unfold,
> Daily and hourly, more and more.
> How many full-sail'd verse express,
> How may measured words adore
> The full-flowing harmony
> Of thy swan-like stateliness,
> Bottom upward?

It had to be by Tennyson, thought Lewis. Could it have been 'Mariana'?

> The luxuriant symmetry
> Of thy floating gracefulness,
> Bottom upward?

It was 'Eleänore,' and Barfield was substituting 'bottom upward' every time the poor girl's name was mentioned.

> Every turn and glance of thine,
> Every lineament divine,
> Bottom upward,
> And the steady sunset glow,
> That stays upon thee?

In the last week of May *The Pilgrim's Regress* was published by Dent, and in the first week of June *Memoirs of the Lewis Family, 1850-1930* arrived from the bindery, at least the first volume of it. Since the beginning of the year Warren had been sifting and sorting the mound of material that had come from Little Lea and arranged them in manageable piles. There were seven leatherbound diaries in the handwriting of Albert's father-in-law, the Rev. Thomas Hamilton. There were thirteen volumes of his own diaries dating from 1912 to 1930. There were eight volumes of Jack's diaries dating from 1922 to 1926. There were fragments of other diaries kept by Albert and

Jack. There were unsorted papers from Albert's father, Richard Lewis. There was a large mass of letters written to and by Albert, dating from the late 1870s to his death in 1929.

From these Warren chose entries from 17 October 1850, to 23 September 1880; they would comprise volume one. He typed them single-spaced, margin to margin, on his American-made typewriter. He arranged the pages in nineteen chapters; the typescript ran to 337 pages. He listed the publisher as Leeborough Press, after their home in Strandtown near Belfast. He picked as epigraph something from Daniel Webster to the effect that the present generation was a link between the past and the future.

Jack pronounced the work a great success, and by 2 June Warnie, as his brother called him, had already hunted and pecked fifty pages of volume two.

〜

On 17 August the brothers went to see *Cavalcade*, a film of Noel Coward's musical pageant presented the year before in the West End. It chronicled British history from New Year's Eve 1899 to New Year's Eve 1930 as experienced by the members of two families. As play and film began so they ended, with champagne glasses raised, the families having survived the Boer War, the death of Queen Victoria, the Great War, and the shimmering if disillusioning twenties. The news was spelled out in lights. Newsboys shouted the headlines. Steam rivets, loudspeakers, jazz bands, airplane propellers — the noise grew in decibels until, as Coward intended, the general effect was one of 'complete chaos.' As if to bring order out of chaos, coming into focus on the screen was the Union Jack, and the discord changed to 'God Save the King.'

'I thought it would be historically interesting, and so I suppose it was; and certainly very clever,' wrote Lewis to Greeves. 'But there is not an idea in the whole thing from beginning to end; it is a mere brutal assault on one's emotions, using material which one can't help feeling intensely. It appeals entirely to that part of you which lives in the throat and chest, leaving the spirit untouched. I have come away feeling as if I had been at a debauch.'

Just after the final toast in the film, but before the Union Jack, there was a brief scene in a night club. Fanny was seated on a piano. The set was, as Coward intended, 'angular and strange'; the song she sang, which Coward had written, was 'oddly discordant.'

VERSE

Why is it that civilized humanity
Must make the world so wrong?

In this hurly burly of insanity
Your dreams cannot last long.
The Press headline — every sorrow,
Blues value is News value tomorrow.

REFRAIN

Blues, Twentieth Century Blues, are getting me down.
Who's escaped those weary Twentieth Century Blues?
Why, if there's a God in the sky, why shouldn't he grin?
High above this dreary Twentieth Century din,
In this strange illusion,
Chaos and confusion,
People seem to lose their way.
What is there to strive for,
Love or keep alive for? Say —
Hey, hey, call it a day.
Blues, nothing to win or lose.
It's getting me down.
Blues, I've got those weary Twentieth Century Blues.

If England suffered from anything on New Year's Eve 1930, it was artistic and spiritual bankruptcy. At least that was Coward's diagnosis; from close and continuing contact he too seemed to have contracted it. Lewis identified the same virus, and he treated it, he thought, with devastating effect in *The Pilgrim's Regress*. Into the mouth of Guide, who was helping John the Pilgrim pass through Ignorantia, he put a song:

Iron will eat the world's old beauty up.
Girder and grid and gantry will arise,
Iron forest of engines will arise,
Criss-cross of iron crotchet. For your eyes
No green or growth. Over all, the skies
Scribbled from end to end with boasts and lies.
(When Adam ate the irrevocable apple, Thou
Saw'st beyond death the resurrection of the dead.)

Clamour shall clean put out the voice of wisdom,
The printing-presses with their clapping wings,
Fouling your nourishment. Harpy wings,
Filling your minds all day with foolish things,
Will tame the eagle Thought: till she sings
Parrot-like in her cage to please dark kings.
(When Israel descended into Egypt, Thou

Didst purpose both the bondage and the coming out.)

> The new age, the new art, the new ethic and thought,
> And fools crying, Because it has begun
> It will continue as it has begun!
> The wheel runs fast, therefore the wheel will run
> Faster for ever. The old age is done,
> We have the new lights and see without the sun.
> (Though they lay flat the mountains and dry up the sea,
> Wilt thou yet change, as though God were a god?)

Cavalcade had brought Coward bags of mail, raves from reviewers, crowds at the box offices, and there were those who said that the patriotic pageant would eventually result in a peerage from the grateful monarch. But what, Lewis thought to himself, would the publication of *Regress* bring him?

⁓

'That litany makes one feel as if the royal family were not pulling their weight,' said Lewis of a Friday morning in summer. It was 8.15; he was emerging from dean's prayers.

'Why is that?' asked Adam Fox, who would have been dean of the chapel if such a title existed at Magdalen; he was known instead as the dean of divinity.

'If they were, then we wouldn't have to sandwich their welfare in between "holy church universal" and "all Christian rulers and magistrates".'

P. V. M. Benecke kept step with the younger men as they headed for breakfast. He was sixty-five years old, walked quickly still, and wore clothes until they frayed. He was a senior fellow of the college, tutored ancient history, collected images of pigs on his mantelpiece, and played the piano as a grandson of Mendelssohn should.

Awaiting them in the common room was J. A. Smith, Waynflete professor of moral and metaphysical philosophy and senior fellow of the college. He slept fitfully in his seventieth year, but not so uneasily as to need chapel in the morning. When the others arrived, he gave the impression that he had been waiting for them, albeit casually, but also for hours, perhaps even the whole night.

'What a dreadful thing it would be, I thought last night when I couldn't go to sleep, for a learned Chinese to go blind.'

'Why?'

'The ideograms that make Chinese writing so beautiful convey meaning to the eye, but some have no sound attached to them.'

Fox had also had trouble falling asleep. He got up and went for a walk. It was after midnight when he heard a terrible noise. An undergraduate scrambling over the high wall fell on his knees right at Fox's feet.

'Oh, my God!' shouted the young man as he looked up and saw the dean of divinity.

'No,' said Fox with all the aplomb he could muster, 'just his accredited representative.'

'I see *Fury*'s in trouble again,' said Benecke, reading from *The Times*.

'Is Fury an old member of the college?' asked Lewis, who never read the newspaper and only rarely scanned the headlines.

'*Fury*,' said Benecke, disappointed that his colleague was not so well informed as he, 'is his majesty's warship, and it has run aground.'

'Hone, that fellow I had to dinner last night,' said Lewis. 'He's a senior man and a Rhodes scholar, but I shouldn't have asked whether he played games. I should pay more attention to these things,' said Lewis, rising to leave, 'but he's captain of a cricket eleven somewhere in the university.'

༄

On 1 September, as the Lewises emerged squinting from the matinee of *King Kong* and walked up Beaumont Street, evaluation of the film was inevitable. Warnie felt that it was as good a film as he had ever seen; the special effects were exhilarating. Fay Wray's screaming still echoing in his ears, Jack wondered whether this was yet another cinematic debauch of the imagination.

The film was certainly escapism at its hairiest. It was also a fairy tale, containing as it did morsels from Beauty and the Beast as told by the Brothers Grimm. But was it not also a feast for the Freudians? Would they not call it a psychodrama of the collective unconscious? Wasn't the hairy ape a symbol of the black man enslaved, the white man's inability to dominate nature, sexual desire unsatisfied, love unconsummated?

Sexological interpretations of existence Lewis could never accept; in *Regress* he had John confront it directly. He was captured by Sigismund Enlightenment, a character symbolizing the intellectually fashionable psychology emanating from Vienna, who tried to convince him that the island so achingly sought as the fulfilment of desire was merely a pretence to conceal his own lusts. Lusts he did indeed have, having lain many times with a brown girl and sired a hundred other brown girls. But the Landlord, Sigismund went on to argue, existed not in reality but only in John's mind. So convincing was Mr Enlightenment that Lewis had to send an *equites ex machina* to rescue him. 'There is some force in the wish-fulfilment doctrine,' said Reason, a virgin in blue cloak who was also a knight with naked sword. 'Whatever force it had was in favour of the Landlord's existence, not against it.'

That films like *King Kong* were a success and that Freudianism was rampant, saddened Lewis as he and his brother passed the Maggers McWugger, the spire to commemorate the Protestant martyrs Cranmer, Latimer, and Ridley. What hope was there for his own work, celebrating, among other things, the bankruptcy of psychology?

∞

'Suppose you are taking a dog on a lead through a turnstile or past a post,' wrote Lewis to Greeves in September; it was blazing hot, Papworth was panting in the shade, and Lewis was trying to console his friend on the loss of his dog Paddy. 'You know what happens (apart from his usual ceremonies in passing a post!). He tries to go the wrong side and gets his head looped around the post. *You* see that he can't do it, and therefore pull him back . . .' By the end of the letter of condolence, Lewis had extended the canine metaphor beyond belief and converted it into a metaphysical conceit.

∞

'The Jews have made no contributions to human culture,' pronounced Adolf Hitler, 'and in crushing them I am doing the will of the Lord.' He had become chancellor of Germany in January; by the end of the year he would be burning books, beating workers, and murdering Jews. 'The blaspheming tyrant has just fixed his absurdity for all to see in a single sentence,' wrote Lewis on 5 November to Greeves, 'and shown that he is as contemptible for his stupidity as he is detestable for his cruelty.'

To some in England another war seemed impossible. 'Drink to the war, then, if you want to,' said the upper-class matron in *Cavalcade*, about to send her son off to the Great War; 'I'm not going to; I can't!' When the Oxford Union sponsored a debate on 9 February, the resolution of which was, That this house will in no circumstances fight for its king and country, there were 275 ayes, 153 nays.

To others war seemed inevitable. Fr. Rothschild in Evelyn Waugh's *Vile Bodies* had seen the war coming, although the prime minister in the novel hadn't. All the politician wanted to know from the omniscient Jesuit was why his stepson 'should drink like a fish and go everywhere with a negress.' 'I think they're connected, you know,' said the Jesuit, whose character was modelled on C. C. Martindale, 'but it's all very difficult.' Waugh ended the novel on a battlefield of the future with a character named Chastity snuggling up to a bemedalled general in the back seat of a disabled Daimler.

In *Regress* Lewis had developed a Hitler-like figure in Savage. A giant in the North, he dressed in animal skins, wore an iron helmet with horns protruding; standing at his side was a Valkyrie named Grimhilde, wings adorning her helmet, breasts bursting her bodice. Vertue, John's travelling companion for much of the pilgrimage, had dinner with the giant; roast pork it was, handled by fingers, washed down by strong, sweet mead; soon, promised Savage, he would be drinking blood from men's skulls. There was singing and shouting and philosophizing. The giant talked about the genetics of dwarfs and the breeding of subspecies like Marxomanni, Mussolimini, and Swastici for an eventual attack on the South. No belief in the Landlord for Savage. His way of life was measured by heroism, master morality, violence. 'If I am to live in a world of destruction, let me be its agent and not its patient.'

༄

On Friday morning, 17 November, not long after eleven, Dyson bounded up staircase 3 of New Buildings and burst into sitting room 3. 'Your favourite reading's *Orlando Furioso*, isn't it?' He had said that to Warren the first time they met, and he was not averse to saying it again.

'Maps, Hugo, maps,' said Warren, waving the routes of his next walking trip with his brother.

'Sorry, sorry, my mistake,' said Dyson. Warren pointed to the small study; the door was closed; Jack was with pupil. 'It's such a cold morning,' shivered Dyson, 'that I shall have to adjourn almost immediately for a brandy.'

'If you're prepared to accept a whisky,' said Warren, 'it's available in the room.'

'It would indeed be an unpardonable rudeness to your brother,' said Dyson, sniffing the decanter, 'to leave any of this.'

Warren recalled, as Dyson poured a glass, what a splendid time he and Jack had had when invited to Dyson's house in Reading last March. He had especially enjoyed meeting his wife; a 'slim and very fair, rather pretty and pleasant' woman, as he recorded in his diary that night, 'but too anxious to make one at home to be quite successful.'

'Whatever became of that Polish girl,' asked Warren, 'the one with the unpronounceable name? A lecturer at the university, wasn't she?'

'Still working on the CON section of the *N.E.D.* [*New English Dictionary*].'

When the poor woman had arrived — 'good looking,' wrote Warren in his diary, 'in the unusual style of grey eyes and black hair'

— she was greeted so boisterously by Dyson that he spilled his glass of sherry right down the front of her dress.

'I suppose we can't be heard in the next room,' said Dyson, cocking an ear in the direction of the small study. 'Oh, it's all right. It's the pupil talking — your brother won't want to listen to him anyway.'

Impatient for noon to arrive, Dyson left for Blackwell's and persuaded Warren to accompany him. As they walked up the High and crossed over to the Broad at Catte Street, they said little in the cold. After that fateful dinner, Warren remembered, Dyson took him and his brother to a small book-lined study. There they had coffee, and Dyson read them some verses of his own written in imitation of Alexander Pope. 'Shall we join the ladies?' he asked, just when the brothers were getting comfortable. 'I wonder what would happen,' whispered Jack to Warnie, 'if one of us just said, "Well, I think we're very comfortable where we are".' At No. 50 Broad Street, Dyson turned into Blackwell's.

'I want a second-hand . . . Shakespeare. Have you got one?'

'Not a second-hand one, sir, I'm afraid,' said a shop assistant.

'Well, take a [new one] and rub it on the floor and sell it to me as shop-soiled. I have no objection; have you?'

'What's all this?' he asked when no answer was forthcoming from the assistant; he pointed towards a large table on which were arranged some fifteen or twenty leather-bound volumes.

'An exhibition of old bindings, sir.'

'Why, *just* the thing you're looking for,' said Dyson to Warren as he picked up a Milton costing £20. 'Put it in your pocket, my boy; put it in your pocket.'

Bookless, Warren slowly walked towards the door.

'You look pale, my boy,' said Dyson as he turned back to the assistant. 'You must beware of overwork.'

On 23 November, a Thursday, Lewis addressed the Martlets. 'Is Literature Art?' was the title of the paper; as he read it to the members of the society, he couldn't help but think of *Regress*. Was it art? Was it literature? Was it anything? *Spirits in Bondage* and *Dymer* had been published under a pseudonym and so, like Chaucer when he came to write the *Book of Troilus*, Lewis had no audience waiting for him; reviewers would not be tempted to the personal heresy; the book would have to make its own way.

'"Oxford" should be diagnosed from the neatness with which the extravagances of psychoanalysis are hit off in the eighth chapter of the third book,' wrote the reviewer in *The Times Literary Sup-*

plement dated 6 July 1933, 'and the essentials of Hegelianism packed into a nutshell in the last four chapters of the seventh . . .

'When John . . . begins to find the way to salvation, he is inspired to break into fragments of song . . . revealing a poetic gift that may rightly be called arresting: it pulls the reader up in the midst of the smooth-flowing narrative to admire its energy and profundity . . .

'John the Pilgrim is consigned to Mother Kirk . . . [a] solution that will win applause from some, while others may see in it one more illustration of the spiritual infecundity of our day — since it would appear . . . that the old fables which terrified John's childhood . . . are not to be essentially transformed but only vindicated, with a subtlety, indeed, that would have delighted Newman, but with a rigour that excludes any true religious development.'

One thousand copies of the book had been printed, or so Lewis was able to worm out of Dent, and fewer than seven hundred had been sold in the six months since publication. 'C. S. Lewis,' it seemed, was about to become as unknown to British readership as 'Clive Hamilton.' It was Greeves' fault, he would say, for he not only dedicated the work to his friend but also followed many of his suggestions.

✍

A is the Absolute: none can express it.
The Absolute, Gentleman! Fill up! God bless it!

B is for Bergson who said: 'It's a crime!
They've been and forgotten that Time is Time!'

C is for Croce who said: 'Art's a stuff
That means what it says (and that's little enough!)'
And also for Cambridge, that kindest of nurses,
Where 'tissues' write essays and 'ganglia' verses.

D is for Descartes who said: 'God couldn't be
So complete if he weren't. So he is. Q.E.D.'
And also Democritus (Atoms and Void
Were the only two things the man really enjoyed.)

For a year now Lewis and Barfield had been reducing philosophy to foolishness and putting the results into rhyme.

L is for Leibnitz who said: 'It's the best
Of all possible worlds. I've examined the rest.'
(He also invented a nice calculation
To pull up fast trains — like a portable station.)

M is the Many, the Mortal, the Body,
The Formless, the Female, the Thoroughly Shoddy.

N is for Not-Being which sinks even deeper,
More formless, more female, more fooling — and cheaper.

But it's O for the One. Hallelujah! Callay!
Glory be! (and see also above under A);
For the One is all round like an accurate sphere
And its function is simple, my son — to cohere.

The result was 'Abecedarium Philosophicum,' which readers of *The Oxford Magazine* saw in the 30 November issue.

༄

On Monday afternoon, 11 December, the surface of the pond at the Kilns had hardened enough to support the brothers Lewis as they cavorted about on silver skates. Although their legs ached they managed to stay upright most of the time, and they were able to enjoy the wintry colours of the wood around them, especially 'the purplish colour of the tops of young trees.' Old Foord-Kelcey ambled by; he stopped to watch; when 4.00 approached, he was invited to tea. In the kitchen at the Kilns, the octogenarian expressed his continuing disbelief in the virgin birth, his old doubt about the immortality of the soul, and his new interest in spiritualism.

He, if anyone, was the perfect specimen of a Christianity that had been modernized or liberalized, thought Jack, and as such he had put him in *Regress* as the character of Mr Broad. John the pilgrim came upon Broad's 'red house, old and ivied, and well back from the road.' Broad went forward to introduce himself and to invite his visitor to have tea on the 'smooth lawn, surrounded by laurels and laburnum.'

'As I grow older, I am inclined to set less and less store by mere orthodoxy,' said Broad, offering John a chair in the shade. 'So often the orthodox view means the lifeless view, the barren formula. I am coming to look more and more at the language of the heart.'

Broad's wife, Martha, joined them. 'Maidservants in snowy aprons opened the long windows of the library and came over the grass with tables and trays, the silver teapot and the stand of cakes.'

'Logic and definition divide us,' continued Broad, offering some honey to John. 'It is those things which draw us together that I now value most — our common affections, our common delight in this slow pageant of the countryside, our common struggle towards the light.'

Mrs Moore couldn't agree more with Foord-Kelcey, offering the retired pastor another cake, and nagged at Jack for believing so much of that ancient stuff. Lewis felt sorry now that he had adorned the character of Mother Kirk with so many of Minto's mannerisms.

⁓

On Sunday evening after supper, in the new study, Warren presided at his mammoth gramophone. Jack and Minto settled into chairs, Papworth curled up in his basket, and Warren set needle to disc. For the next hour or so they would listen to a Beethoven symphony. It was also New Year's Eve. Instead of being out at a party, Jack thought of the party in *Vile Bodies*, attended by the Bright Young People in a captured German blimp. What those poor satirized creatures wouldn't have given, thought Jack, to crash the party he threw in *Regress*. It was held in 'a big room rather like a bathroom; it was full of steel and glass, and the walls were nearly all window.' 'Drinking what looked like medicine and talking at the tops of their voices' were the Clevers. 'They were all either young, or dressed up to look as if they were young. The girls had short hair and flat breasts and flat buttocks so that they looked like boys; but the boys had pale, egg-shaped faces and slender waists and big hips so that they looked like girls — except for a few of them who had long hair and beards.'

In what followed at the party, Lewis laid out — like patients anaesthetized in an amphitheatre — the proponents of 'the poetry of the silly twenties,' 'the swamp literature of the dirty twenties,' and 'the gibberish literature of the lunatic twenties.' Victoriana sang a song that was not appreciated and had the temerity to accompany herself on a toy harp. A bearded man wearing 'a red shirt and a codpiece made of the skins of crocodiles' 'began to beat on an African tom-tom and to croon with his voice, swaying his lean, halfclad body to and fro and staring at them all, out of eyes which were like burning coals.' And then there was Glugly, 'very tall and as lean as a post; and her mouth was not quite straight in her face.' 'Globol obol oogle ogle globol gloogle gloo.' It was unclear whether she was attempting to sing or to recite, but she 'ended by pursing up her lips and making a vulgar noise such as children make in their nurseries.'

⚓ 1934 ⚓

A clerk in Barfield's office had made arrangements with a river transport firm for one of its barges to take on passengers for a round trip on the Thames. Thus it was that Barfield boarded an empty lighter, gingerly assisting his wife, Maude; Lewis followed, toting a supply of beer for both passengers and crew; and the three of them settled down on canvas chairs to enjoy the sights and sounds and smells. They were pushed down the winding river past Greenwich to Woolwich. By late afternoon, loaded now, with three or four others lashed to it, the lighter was nudged upriver to its pier. Disembarking, the Barfields and Lewis were aglow with a most pleasant and unusual experience.

⚓

'You are being metaphorical.'

'You are just as metaphorical as I am, but you don't know it.'

'No, I'm not. Of course, I know all about *attending* once having meant *stretching*, and the rest of it. But that is not what it means now. It may have been a metaphor to Adam — but I am not using it metaphorically. What I *mean* is pure concept with no metaphor about it at all. The fact that it *was* a metaphor is no more relevant than the fact that my pen is made of wood. You are simply confusing derivation with meaning.'

Reading a paper at the University of Manchester, Lewis was trying to present, in dialogue form, the substance of a debate that was taking place in philological circles. On the one side were C. K. Ogden and I. A. Richards who, in their book *The Meaning of Meaning*, which was published in 1923, had stated that it was impossible to handle a scientific matter in metaphorical terms. On the other side was Barfield who, in his book *Poetic Diction: A Study in Meaning*, which was published in 1928, maintained that all language had a figurative origin and that the so-called scientific terms used by Ogden and Richards — 'organism', 'stimulus', 'reference' — were not miraculously exempt.

The immediate problem Lewis was addressing was the mass, or mess, of metaphors floating like flotsam and jetsam, dead or discarded, down the stream of living language. How far, if at all, he asked, was thinking limited by these metaphors? He identified himself to the audience as a rationalist, one for whom reason was the organ of truth and for whom the condition of that truth was very often metaphor. New or old, not dead but perhaps revivified, a metaphor was the product of the imagination and, like a barge on a working river, it was freighted with meaning.

∽

At the beginning of May, Lewis was felled by chills and fever, and his body ached all over. He cancelled his lectures and tutorials and telephoned the Kilns for help. Warren drove in to Magdalen and fetched his brother back to Headington. The next day he too succumbed to the same symptoms. Mrs Moore rang for help. Their doctor had died recently; she only hoped that another was manning the practice. Shortly thereafter, Robert Havard turned up at the Kilns with a little black bag. Mrs Moore met him at the door.

Yes, he had taken over for the late Dr Wood. Yes, he was going to maintain surgeries in both Headington and Oxford. How long had she been suffering from the flu?

No, the doctor wasn't for her; it was for Professor Lewis, she said, and led the way up the stairs. She made the introductions and then proceeded to list all the sick man's symptoms.

That he might examine the patient, Havard asked her to leave. He took Lewis' recent medical history, learning that he suffered frequent relapses into colds and fevers and anything else that would put him joyfully into bed with a book.

It wasn't parrot-fever, said Havard, trying to be reassuring. Just a little influenza. A lot of that was going about, and there wasn't really much one could do about it. Rest, lots of bed rest. Liquids, lots of watery liquids. In the later stages of recovery spirits added to the liquids had been known to help.

Somewhat relieved, Lewis proceeded to take the doctor's history.

Yes, he was an Oxford man. Read chemistry at Keble before going on to medicine. No, he hadn't abandoned literature and philosophy. Had Lewis ever met Tolkien? Well, Tolkien was one of his new patients, and he expected that the philologist would keep him informed on the latest in Icelandic. And what was Lewis' specialty? The Middle Ages? Well then, did he know Ronald Knox, another patient of his, chaplain to the Catholic undergraduates for the last ten years? It was impossible not to know Knox; he was supposed to be the funniest man in Oxford.

They talked for thirty minutes before Mrs Moore appeared at the door. Professor Lewis was not the only sick man in the house. Captain Lewis was also suffering. Down the stairs she went, and off to the captain's wing. Again she introduced Havard. Again she listed the symptoms. Again he asked her to leave. Again he diagnosed influenza.

The brothers had fallen ill while winter was hanging on. When they revived spring seemed to have arrived. Bluebells were everywhere as they walked slowly about the property. The cat had five kittens; the swans had three cygnets; a hawk was menacing a heron; and the woods were awash with new rabbits.

∽

'I have read your pathetical letter with such sentiments as it naturally suggests, and write to inform you that you need expect from me no ungenerous approach.' It was 7 May; Lewis was writing to Harwood. 'It would be cruel if it were possible, and impossible if it were attempted, to add to the mortification which you must now be supposed to suffer.' It seemed that he had asked his friend of fifteen years to accompany him to that year's production of the *Ring* cycle, but first to get the tickets. 'Where I cannot console, it is far from my purpose to aggravate; for it is part of the complicated misery of your state that while I pity your sufferings, I cannot innocently wish them lighter.' Harwood had failed to get the tickets and had confessed his failure. 'He would be no friend to your reason or your virtue, who would wish to pass over so great a miscarriage in heartless frivolity or brutal sensibility . . .' Lewis had accepted the apology, but he could not restrain himself from replying in the highly upholstered prose of the eighteenth century. 'As soon as you can, pray let me know through some respectable acquaintance in what quarter of the globe you intend to sustain that irrevocable exile and perpetual disgrace to which you have condemned yourself.' Lewis had enjoyed being a guest of the Harwoods in Sussex, swinging and swimming with their children and playing heads, bodies, and tails with them; and when he returned he would write a bread-and-butter letter to Mrs Harwood that was slathered with charm. 'Do not give in to despair.' He was subjecting his friend to the full Johnsonian blast. 'Learn from this example the fatal consequences of error, and hope in some humbler station and some distant land that you may yet become useful to your species.'

∽

'I should warn you that what you apparently expect to lie behind the lecture is both more and other than is really there.' He was responding to a letter that had arrived in the morning mail. 'In lecturing to students who know nothing about the Middle Ages, I have had to be clear and brief, therefore dogmatic; and I have probably — though I hope this was not my intention — appeared more learned than I am.'

The woman he was writing to was attending his 'Prolegomena to the Study of Medieval Poetry.' As he strode into the lecture room that first day in Trinity term and put his notes on the lectern, he started speaking before he looked up. There would be nineteen lectures in all. They would cover such topics as courtly love and allegory, *The Romance of the Rose* and the *Book of Troilus*, John Gower and Thomas Usk. When he did look up from his notes and around the hall, what he saw, as if in dream vision, was the Prioress from *The Canterbury Tales*. 'Full seemly her wimple pinchèd was'; her nose was elegant, her eyes smoke, her mouth small, her lips soft and red.

As the course progressed, he fell ill and had to miss three lectures. When he returned, he announced that he would entertain suggestions for the topics of the lectures that remained. She wrote to him, identified herself as Sister Mary Madeleva, a sister of the Congregation of the Holy Cross; she was an American, and she wished he would not cancel Boethius. The next three lectures he devoted to *Consolations of Philosophy*. From the convent of the Holy Child, where she could see swans on the Cherwell and hear the bells of Magdalen, she wrote to thank him and asked if there were not a bibliography he might provide her with.

'There are probably such printed bibliographies as you mention,' he replied on 7 June, 'but I have no knowledge of them.' He went on to describe the origin and nature of his series. 'The process is inductive for the most part of my lecture; though on allegory, courtly love, and (sometimes) on philosophy, it is deductive; i.e. I *start* from the authors I quote.'

He gathered that she was a teacher, but he did not really know her purpose in asking. Modesty of a sort unknown to the Prioress prevented her from mentioning that she had a PhD in English from the University of California and that her speciality was Chaucer.

'The two things to know really well are the *Divine Comedy* and *The Romance of the Rose*. The student who has really digested these (I don't claim to be such a person myself!) with good commentaries, and who also knows the classics and the Bible . . . has the game in his hands and can defeat over and over again those who have simply burrowed in obscure parts of the actual Middle Ages.'

Again she wrote him a note of thanks and offered him the only gift a nun can give: hospitality in one of her convents if ever he should visit the United States.

⸎

He had been working on a long narrative for years. In 1918 it began as a poem entitled 'Hippolytus'; in 1920 it had been transmogrified into 'Wild Hunt'; by 1927 it was entitled 'The King of Drum,' and he was writing large chunks of it in a variety of rhymes and metres; by 1934 the theme was firmly fixed in place, and he was calling it 'The Queen of Drum.' The narrative began with lovers embroiled, or so it seemed at first blush, in courtly love complexity. The King was old and slept his nights in bed. His Queen was young and, save for an hour each night, traipsed about the landscape in search of she-knew-not whom or what. The setting of the poem was medieval, but the diction was twentieth-century; when King, Chancellor, General, and Archbishop convened, Lewis did the scene as an Oxford college meeting.

> Heavily the hours, like laden barges passed
> — Motion, amendment, order, motion. Now at last
> The trickling current of the slow debate
> Sets toward that ocean sea, where soon or late
> Time out of mind their consultations come,
> — The everlasting theme 'What's wrong with Drum?'
> When, marvellous to dull'd ears, elf-brights between
> Two droning wastes of talk, one name — 'The Queen'
> Broke startling. And the scribbler dropped the pen
> And sleepers rubbed their eyes and whispering men
> Drew heads apart watching.
>   Yes. Sure enough.
> The Chancellor's on his feet and taking snuff
> And writing and grimacing with a bow
> In the article of deprecation . . . Now,
> Listen!
>   . . .'and also seen by vulgar eyes
> In her most virtuous, yet, perhaps, unwise,
> Occasions' . . . 'a King's house contains the weal
> Of all. He is the axle of the wheel,
> The root of the politic tree, the fountain's springs' . . .
> 'Nothing is wholly private in a King.
> For what more private to each man alone
> Than health, my lords? Yet, if the monarch groan,
> The duteous subject . . .'

Something was indeed wrong in Drum; if it were easy to point the finger at the Queen, it was not so easy to figure out why she had to roam about at night. As the Queen's confessor and confidante, the Archbishop would know, or so the King surmised. It wasn't the Queen, said the Archbishop; it was the General, who then took advantage of the drunkenness of the King and Chancellor to lock them both in the dungeon, there to sober up or die off. An ancient dictator in modern diction, the General proclaimed that it was 'a new world now', that he was its leader, and that he was taking possession of the realm.

> The General stood there, so vast
> With legs astride, so planted, that he seemed to bear
> The weight of the whole house upon his shoulders square.
> His red, full blood grandiloquently in his cheek
> Spoke so that you could almost say his body shouted
> And was his garish blazon ere his tongue could speak,
> Saying, 'I am the leader, the event, the undoubted,
> All potent Fact, the firstborn of necessity,
> I am Fate, and Force, and Führer, Worship me!'

As his first spoils, the General claimed the young Queen, whom he would invade whether she protected her borders or not. Thinking assignation the better part of assassination, she promised to meet him in her bower. The General then turned towards the Archbishop and talked with him about joining, in holy conspiracy, the church and the state. He was reasonableness itself as he spoke.

> Now, in this new regime, of course your Grace
> Must certainly retain his present place
> And power and temporalities. Indeed,
> If I might criticize, we rather need
> Not less but more of what you represent;
> For up till now — pray, take this as it's meant,
> Kindly — a certain somnolence has come
> To be the hallmark of the Church of Drum,
> For several years. Henceforward that won't do;
> And naturally I rely on you.
> Faith-martyrdom — and all that side of things
> Concerns Dictators even more than Kings.
> Can you contrive a really hot revival,
> A state religion that allows no rival?
> You understand, henceforward it's got to be
> A Drummian kind of Christianity —
> A good old Drummian god who has always some
> Peculiar purpose up His sleeve for Drum,
> Something that makes the increase of our trade
> And territories feel like a Crusade,
> Or, even if neither should in fact increase,
> Teaches men in my will to find their peace.
> These are the general principles.

Weak man that he was, old and well-fed and with the soft, pink skin of a baby, the Archbishop nevertheless had faith enough to refuse; calling out 'to Christ to be forgiven,' he was beaten to death by the General's henchmen.

Instead of confronting Mussolini, Hitler, and Franco head on and thus coming to a conclusion about the dictatorships threatening the stability of Europe in 1934, Lewis' narrative swung back to a simpler time. The young Queen, on the way to her bower, gave her guard 'a lovely blow' across the mouth with an armlet of gold and sent him 'bloodied and blubbering' to the pavement. Sprinting for freedom out into the landscape she used to roam at night, and plunging herself into a stream to shake the bloodhounds, she eventually met a pale king riding a white horse. He warned her that she was rapidly approaching a triple crossroads. If she veered to the right, she would go to Heaven. If she swerved to the left, she would go to Hell. His best advice to her was:

> Keep, keep the centre! Find the portals
> That chosen mortals at the world's edge enter.
> Isles untrampled by the warying legions
> Of Heaven or Darkness — the unreckoned regions
> That only as fable in His world appear
> Who seals man's ear as much as he is able . . .

In December he got a letter from Griffiths, inviting him to visit Prinknash Priory. He told Lewis he was completing his term as novice and would become a full-fledged Benedictine monk on 21 December when he professed vows of poverty, chastity, and obedience.

Lewis accepted. As he approached the priory he expected to find a graceful ruin, some remnant of Henry VIII's rampages against the monasteries of his time. Instead, he found a pleasant old Cotswold manor house standing on the side of a hill which sloped down onto a plain, studded with leafy trees, that stretched for miles towards Malvern. He was welcomed at the door by Griffiths, a huge dark Celt magnificent in white habit. That was a *himation*, wasn't it? A tunic, said Griffiths. A *chlamus*? A scapular; since professing his vows a few days before, he was allowed to wear a cowl, a heavy outer garment with long sleeves that was the choir dress of a monk.

What should Lewis call him now? When clothed as a novice Griffiths had taken the name of Bede, after the seventh-century monk who wrote the *Ecclesiastical History of England*. Before reading that book, he had thought that the ecclesiastical system in England

and indeed in Europe was corrupt and awaiting only the purification of the Protestant Reformation. Instead, he was delighted to find 'that the Church of England had been founded by a Roman pope and that the first archbishops of Canterbury and York had been sent from Rome.' Altogether, Bede was a shining example for a twentieth-century monk, an illuminated page from a manuscript written centuries before.

Bede it was then, and he led the way to the midday meal. Silence reigned in the refectory full of white-robed figures, the sole voice being that of a monk reading from the pages of a book, that the spirit might also be refreshed while the body was receiving its sustenance. After the meal, the community processed to the chapel, Lewis in tow, chanting an anthem or psalm, for yet another word of thanksgiving.

The afternoon belonged to the tutor and his pupil. Was the life hard enough for him? Lewis reminded Griffiths that in his Oxford days he had never used tobacco, ate meat rarely, and avoided hot baths because they were voluptuous, enervating, and led to an effeminate love of the clean. Life in the monastery was not an easy one, said Griffiths, but it was 'far less austere' than he had expected. 'The meals were simple but they were generous, and though there was no meat, there was an abundance not only of fruit and vegetables but also of cheese and eggs and fish and cereals.' He was used to wooden beds with straw mattresses. A chair and a desk in his cell served his intellectual needs. But he had to admit that the community's 'hot baths and central heating and other luxuries of that kind' took some getting used to.

This particular Benedictine community, and Lewis would be interested to hear this, was originally founded in the Church of England. 'After some years, however, they found no authority for their way of life in the Church of England and they asked to be received into the Church of Rome.' Perhaps Lewis himself would soon be following the Benedictines', and indeed, Griffiths', example.

'If I object at all to what you said, I object, not as a friend or as a guest, but as a logician,' wrote Lewis on 26 December. 'If you are going to argue with me on the points of issue between our churches, it is obvious that you must argue *to* the truths of your position, not *from* it.'

'Don't be alarmed,' he wrote on the same day to Greeves; 'the effect on me was purely aesthetic, not religious, and during the afternoon, my host talked nonsense enough to put me off the conventual life for ever and a day.'

'Good morning, good morning,' said Lewis to the pupil who had just passed through his 'oak' (the outer door of his rooms).

'Good morning, sir,' said E. L. Edmonds.

'Don't call me *sir*, Edmonds. I'm not a sir.'

He motioned the young Canadian to the easy chair while he looked among his 'vast array of pipes,' some short, some long, one white with a long stem fit for a churchwarden in a Dutch painting.

Had he ever seen *The Student Prince*? asked Edmonds, disappearing into the folds of the huge chair. He had just seen the operetta and was enthralled. Medieval life in a German university town. Undergraduates marching to the Golden Apple Inn. *'Gaudeamus igitur juvenes dum sumus.'* A luscious, ill-fated romance between a prince and a waitress.

'So you enjoyed it, did you?' asked Lewis, not resounding to Edmonds' joy abounding. He finally selected 'a short, curvy-stemmed, chubby, rosewood' pipe. Not finding his pouch of tobacco, he picked up a tin — 'Three Nuns', he said to Edmonds with a wink — thumbed a wad into the bowl, and lit up, sending a cloudy blue ring towards the ceiling.

Edmonds had brought 'far too much knowledge' into previous tutorials, or so the tutor had said; he had scoured far too many recognized authorities in search of the perfect critical opinion. This tutorial would be different. He would give his own opinion of Jonathan Swift. Perching on the edge of the soft chair he attacked *Gulliver's Travels*. The 'unnecessary vulgarity,' especially in parts III and IV, was surely 'the first signs of depravity and . . . "*saeva indignatio*" ' that would eventually lead the author, who was also an Anglican priest, to the very brink of madness.

'Have you ever been to an officers' mess?' asked Lewis when Edmonds had finished reading his twenty pages. 'Men talk like that, you know'; and he proceeded to draw a distinction between the coarse and the lewd. Edmonds' writing style, which Lewis adjudged turgid, could learn much from the directness of Swift's prose.

~

On 28 April he picked up his pen, dipped the nib into the ink, and with contrite heart began to write a long-overdue letter. Some years before, longer than he cared to remember, he had exploded in anger, not once but twice, at his friend Baker. Whatever caused it, remembrance of it was now dim. He apologized fully and sweetly and offered, if Baker was willing, 'to pick up some of the old links.' Then he brought Baker up to date on events in his own life and in general philosophized about growing older. 'I suppose we have all lived to discover that we are not great men, and not to mind. There are better things than that in the world, and out of it. We have so spoiled our language that I cannot even say "God bless you" without pausing to try and explain that I mean the words in their literal sense.'

∽

Tolkien had begun composition of a long poem entitled 'The Fall of Arthur'. He was making extensive use of alliteration, a technique found in Old Norse and Old Icelandic as well as in Anglo-Saxon poems. Not much had been written about the interaction of alliteration and metre, Lewis found, certainly not much for the non-specialist; hence he conducted a survey of his own with a view to eventual publication.

'In any English country taproom,' he concluded, 'the student may hear from the lips of labourers speech-groups which have a certain race and resonance in isolation.' 'A cold kipper.' 'Shoddy shipbuilders.' 'Hell's housekeeper.' 'Hard haymaking.' 'Born bootlegger.' 'Shipbuilders show.' All these had a certain 'richness and fullness of sound'; they were indeed the elements of a metre congenial to English; and they offered 'possibilities of resonance which have not been exploited for a thousand years.'

The first thing a reader of alliterative verse had to do, according to Lewis, was to ignore the spelling and attend only to sounds. Then he or she had to distinguish between long and short syllables as well as between accented and unaccented syllables. Each line of alliterative verse consisted of two half-lines, which were independent metrical organisms and which were connected only by alliteration. Each half-line was made up of two lifts, and these lifts could be combined with dips in at least five different ways. As a preliminary example of what he meant, he offered the following six lines, the lifts being indicated by uppercase letters, the dips by lowercase letters:

We were TALKing of DRAGONS,|TOLKiEN and I
In a BERKshire BAR.|The BIG WORKman
Who had SAT SILent|and SUCKED his PIPE
ALL the EVEning,|from his EMPTy MUG
With GLEAMing EYE|GLANCED toWARD us;
'I SEEN 'em mySELF,'|he SAID FIERCEly.

Perhaps another reason for his treating alliterative verse at some length was that it seemed, after a thousand years, to be coming back into style. Not only was Tolkien using it but also Wystan Hugh Auden. He was a former pupil of Coghill's; Lewis remembered Coghill's first description of the young man: 'the forbidding scowl, the uncombed flop of blond, revolutionary hair, the large expressive mouth, the big bones of the face, and the sandy complexion that had a certain roughness of surface.' Auden began at Christ Church in Michaelmas term, 1925. He played the piano, cultivated eccentricity, courted homosexuality, and was rumoured to have on his mantelpiece an orange, decaying, as symbol of the decline of the West. Biology had consumed his first year, but because he wanted to be, not just a poet, but a great poet, he switched to English language and literature. Hearing Tolkien recite the opening lines of *Beowulf* in a lecture convinced him that Anglo-Saxon was his dish. But all the help that Coghill, Tolkien, and his tutor in philology C. L. Wrenn would give him was to no avail; he got a third in 1928.

Auden wrote verse as an undergraduate, several pieces of which appeared in *Oxford Poetry*, an anthology published annually. In the 1926 volume he treated the impossibility of believing in God:

> . . . We draw our squares about the Universe
> To make the habit of it suit our purse . . .
> Expound our neat cigar-philosophies,
> With God above, as harmless as you please,
> The keeper of a Paradise for fools,
> A dear Arch-Monad in horn spectacles.

Eventually, a sheaf of Auden's poems found its way to Eliot's desk at *The Criterion*. They were a jumble of psychology and politics; here and there — 'Doom is dark and deeper than any sea-dingle' — there was the sort of alliteration usually found in the Icelandic and the Anglo-Saxon. They had enough merit, thought Eliot, who was also an acquisitions editor at Faber and Faber, and under that imprint 'a slim volume bound in cord with a blue wrapper' entitled *Poems* by W. H. Auden appeared in the autumn of 1930. *The Times Literary Supplement* found the poems so personal to the poet and so eccentric in their terminology that instead of communicating an experience of value to the reader, they merely created a problem in allusions to solve. 'Am I really so obscure?' Auden wrote to a friend. 'Obscurity is a bad fault.'

The initial printing of the book was one thousand copies; sales, although not spectacular, continued with regularity enough to encourage Eliot to offer him another contract. This time it was for *The Orators: An English Study*, a collection of prosaic and poetic pieces dealing with people who spoke up, allegorical personages like Leader, Young Man, and Enemy. It seemed a random collection of pieces, but at least one reviewer, the one in Eliot's *Criterion*, thought he discovered a single theme running throughout; it was 'the true value of leadership' or 'society' or 'the importance of group organization over the individual' or perhaps a combination of these. The hero was certainly a revolutionary, but the work itself might be pro-Fascist; it might be anti-Fascist; it might even be a joke. It was welcomed, however, as another *Waste Land* because it described 'a sick England with a sick people, its industries closed and its workers idle; the middle classes fearful and defensive, afraid of change, afraid of life; and the young, feeling the need for action, for a journey beyond the border of the familiar into a new life, but uncertain and afraid, and wanting a leader.'

In September 1932 Auden began a narrative poem in alliterative verse, the first lines of which echoed the opening of *Piers Plowman*:

> In the year of my youth when yoyos came in
> The carriage was sunny and the Clyde was bright
> As I hastened from Helensburgh in the height of summer
> Leaving for home in a lounge suit . . .

Publication of Dover Wilson's *Manuscript of Hamlet* in 1935 drove Lewis to consider just what the genuine text of the work was, for it had tremendous implications not only for the interpretation of *Hamlet* but also for the future development of literary criticism. 'The conclusion would seem to be that we must do one of two things,' he wrote to *The Times Literary Supplement*, which published the letter in the 2 May issue. 'We must either reject the conception of a Shakespeare who "thought in terms of the stage" and replace it with that of a literary author to whom performance was as accidental as to Milton or Tennyson; or we must define the "genuine text" to be "the whole performance insofar as Shakespeare did not explicitly disclaim it." If we do the first, then the manuscript is the genuine text; if we do the second, we must cease to talk of theatrical "contamination"; we must start with the assumption that the prompt-book is genuine, and the *onus* will lie on anyone who says that it is corrupt.'

'I have now finished my book *The Allegorical Love Poem*,' wrote Lewis on 18 September to R. W. Chapman at Oxford University Press, 'and am in search of a publisher.'

He first got the idea for the book in July 1923. F. P. Wilson, one of his tutors, had invited him to tea to discuss the future. There were no jobs in the university at that time. Wilson asked him if he had a book in his head. An epic poem, perhaps, replied Lewis; perhaps 'a study of the romantic epic from its beginnings down to Spenser, with a side glance at Ovid.' By 1928, fully employed and established at Magdalen, he was spending vacations in the Bodleian, discovering anew the world of allegory and courtly love. 'Don't you think this rather jolly?' he wrote in April of that year to his brother. 'In one of those gardens in a dream, which medieval love poetry is full of, we find the tomb of a knight, dead for love, covered with flowers.' Then he translated some Old French:

And birds that for the soul of that signor
Who lay beneath, songs of true love did pour:
Being hungered, each from off the flowers bore
A kiss, and felt that day no hunger more.

'The odd thing,' he continued, 'is that one would expect the same rhyme going all through to be monotonous and ugly; but to my ear it produces a beautiful lulling like the sound of the sea.'

The Allegorical Love Poem as a whole, concluded Lewis in his letter to Oxford University Press, 'has two themes. 1. The birth of allegory and its growth from what it is in Prudentius to what it is in Spenser. 2. The birth of the romantic conception of love and the long struggle between its earlier form (the romance of adultery) and its later form (the romance of marriage).'

By return mail, on 20 September, he got a letter from Kenneth Sisam to the effect that the delegates of OUP would consider the work at their first meeting in Michaelmas term. On 29 October the delegates made the publishing decision and said they expected the work to be in bookshops by the end of May next.

What to study? That was the question perplexing most first-year students as they approached Oxford. Freshmen members of the English Society had made at least the first choice; as they waited for Lewis to address them, they wondered what in particular he would have to say about English literature. When he arrived he lectured them on education in general and introduced the notion of leisure as a possible end of such activity. He distinguished educational discipline from vocational training. He encouraged them to see the difference between education, the day-to-day activity of the university, and learning, the lifetime quest for knowledge.

He could not let the occasion pass without attacking the composite syllabus, which was a possible choice for the undergraduate. That was a course of studies made up of 'a little philosophy, a little politics, a little economics, a little science, a little literature.' Some of his colleagues had thought that one up, and Lewis took violent exception to it. 'In reading such a school . . . you would not be turned loose on some tract of reality as it is, to make what you could of it; you would be getting selections of reality selected by your elders — something cooked, expurgated, filtered, and generally toned down for your edification.' English literature, on the other hand, was a vast tract of reality on which the undergraduate could roam, learn how the people smelled, loved, lived, and died. But even this subject was too vast for study in just three or four years. 'We begin by cutting off a hundred, or two hundred, or any reasonable number of years from this end' — the sudden and quick amputation of such contemporary writers as Auden and Eliot, Coward and Lawrence drew groans from his audience — 'and still we have too much left.'

Before they groaned again, Lewis hastened to develop a metaphor. He pictured English literature as a tree growing in a soil composed of the history of the English people, a compost of economics, philosophy, sociology. 'I imagine that neither you nor I wish to draw attention to this; for if you look into the statutes, you will find that examiners are at liberty to set questions on it, and it is always possible that if we talk much about it, they may wake up and really do so.'

Picking up English literature as though it were a tree balled and burlaped from a nursery, he plucked the coverings off to examine the roots. The lesser roots were Greek, Spanish, Italian, French, and German. The greater roots were Old French and Latin. The greatest root, the taproot, was Old Germanic developing into Old English or Anglo-Saxon. 'The man who does not know it remains all his life a child among real English students. There we find the speech-rhythms that we use every day made the basis of metre; there we find the origins of that romanticism for which the ignorant invent such odd explanations.'

Having lopped the newest branches, having pruned the lesser roots, Lewis presented the undergraduates with the study of English literature. To study only one subject was narrowing, of course, but better to be enslaved by one's own selection than by the committee that made up the composite syllabus. As though an angel at paradise, he threw open the gates and beckoned the undergraduates to enter and choose their own path. 'Here's your gun, your spade, your fishing tackle; go and get yourself a dinner.'

'I didn't much like having a book of mine, and specially a religious book, brought out by a papist publisher, but as they seemed to think they could sell it, and Dent's clearly couldn't, I gave in. I have been well punished . . .'

Some months before, Lewis had been visited by Frank Sheed, co-founder with his wife, Maisie Ward, of a new publishing firm in London. Sheed had read *The Pilgrim's Regress* and was impressed; he was sorry to hear that it had gone out of print but would gladly put it back into print if the author were agreeable. Lewis was reluctant to express his misgivings. He had been encouraged from his Belfast days to mistrust papists and from his Oxford days to beware of philologists. Tolkien was both, but he was not an ardent apologist for Catholicism. Sheed and his wife, however, were rumoured to take to the benches in Hyde Park of a Sunday afternoon to defend the triple tiara against all tirades.

Answering before he was asked, Sheed said that his firm did not sell crucifixes, statues, rosary beads, or medals; only books. Yes, they had been referred to as Catholics who were publishers, but they preferred to be known as publishers who happened to be Catholics. 'Just above the middle of the brow' was where Sheed and Ward books were aimed. And did Lewis know that they now had an office in New York City? Amused and somewhat relieved, Lewis had to admit that *Regress* was not exactly a sectarian work; he finally agreed.

Dent printed 1,500 copies with the Sheed and Ward imprint. Sheed himself set about writing new copy for the dust jacket. The work was full of wit, he said; Lewis was certainly funnier than Bunyan; the pilgrimage began in Puritania; Lewis was born in Ulster . . . Lewis was furious when he read it, the copy implying that he had forsaken Northern Ireland and was now repudiating the Church of Ireland; but it was too late; the new edition was already in the bookshops. 'If you ever come across anyone who might be interested,' wrote Lewis to Greeves, 'explain as loudly as you can that I was not consulted and that the blurb is a damnable lie told to try and make Dublin riff-raff buy the book.'

Whether Catholics in the Republic of Ireland did indeed buy the book Lewis never found out, but Catholic periodicals began to review it. 'The revival of the allegorical method is very successful,' said the 4 January 1936 issue of *Blackfriars*, journal of the English Dominicans who happened to have a house of studies in Oxford. 'This brilliantly written volume is a caustic, devastating critique of modern philosophy, religion, politics, and art,' said the May 1936 issue of *Catholic World*, published by the Paulist Fathers in New York City; 'a clear-cut, logical, and effective apologia of reason and the

Christian faith.'

The book also got reviewed in the secular American press. 'It is undoubtedly a picture of genuine mystical experience, rationalized by philosophy,' said the 8 December issue of the *New York Times Book Review*. 'A modern man's intricate journey through the worlds of thought and feeling and desire; his passionate search for truth; his need to correlate the primitive in his own nature and the highly complex mental processes that distinguish him from creatures of a different order are resolved, here, into the utmost simplicity by means of a logical and provocative allegory.'

Did the dust jacket copy really indicate that the pilgrim's final destination was Rome? Certainly not Rome, said *Blackfriars*, which found the dust jacket 'tasteless and inappropriate'; the reviewer was George Sayer, a Catholic, twenty-two years old, and a former pupil of Lewis.

But W. Norman Pittenger, an Anglican priest teaching at General Theological Seminary in New York City, when reviewing the book in the 11 January 1936 issue of *The Living Church*, concluded solely on the evidence in the book that the pilgrim 'lands up in the end in a resting place which we fancy is none other than the Church of Rome ... We are sure that the book will find many delighted readers, even if they do not all arrive in the happy haven of Roman Catholicism.'

〰

'I hope ... that binding, paper, etc., will be — in our old formula — excellent, exquisite, and admirable,' wrote Lewis about his OUP book to Greeves. 'In other words, if you can't read it, you will enjoy looking at it, smelling it, and stroking it. If not a good book, it will be a good pet! It will be 400 pages, they say. (It will be very funny, after this, if they do it in double columns and a paper cover.)'

The Press began to question the title, and even sent the first two chapters, 'Courtly Love' and 'Allegory', to a patristics scholar for review. Galley proofs arrived at Magdalen before the end of December. 'I am correcting the first bunch of proofs for my book,' he wrote to Greeves on 29 December, 'and am ... tearing my hair because it doesn't look at all the size of page I expected. It will not be as *tall* a book as I had pictured — and what is the good of a scholarly work if it does not rise like a tower at the end of a shelf?'

〰

'Dear children of God, my sermon this morning will be a very short one ...'

That was something to be grateful for, thought Lewis to himself.

'I wish only that you should ponder and meditate the deep meaning and mystery of our masses on Christmas Day ...'

What else would one do on Christmas Day? asked Lewis. The only reason he himself was not in church was that he had a heavy cold and was feeling miserable.

'Not only do we at the feast of Christmas celebrate at once our Lord's birth and his death, but on the next day we celebrate the martyrdom of his first martyr, the blessed Stephen . . .'

Reading this book was a martyrdom of a special sort, groaned Lewis as he rolled uncomfortably about his bed.

'A Christian martyrdom is no accident. Saints are not made by accident . . .'

Thomas à Becket preached the sermon Lewis was reading, and the martyrdom he sensed approaching was his own.

'A martyr, a saint, is always made by the design of God, for His love of men, to warn them and to lead them, to bring them back to his ways . . .'

The words were not those of the Archbishop of Canterbury in 1170; rather, they were the words put into the mouth of the character Becket by Lewis' arch enemy.

'I would have you keep in your hearts these words that I say, and think of them at another time . . .'

Not a chance, said Lewis to himself as he closed the little book and put his head back onto the pillow. He had heard better sermons in his own parish church. The book he closed was *Murder in the Cathedral*, a play mostly in verse that had been produced in June. It was 'designed for a Christian stage and a Christian public,' which might have accounted for its success at the Canterbury Festival. It appealed also to audiences who did not accept its theological premises, dealing as it did not so much with ecclesiastical rights and privileges as with the limits of temporal power. Hitler was taking giant steps across the cartography of Europe; audiences who saw the play at the Mercury Theatre in London in November did not miss the point.

Eliot was the author of the play. He had undergone a conversion and returned to the Church of England, especially to High Church, which seemed only a hop, skip, and jump from Roman Catholicism. In particular, Lewis found him to be a rarefied intellectual who debunked romanticism, that sort of sweet desire that had led Lewis from darkest atheism to brightest Christianity. When he created the character of Mr Neo-angular in *Regress*, he had Eliot in mind. When the pilgrim John said that he sought an island because, as the object of his desire, it had to exist, Mr Neo-angular replied that that way lay nonsense. When John said that Mother Kirk had assured him that the island existed, Mr Neo-angular replied that, 'You had no business to talk to her except through a qualified steward' like himself. When John said that Reason had also assured him of the island's existence, Neo-angular warned him that 'the only safe commerce with Reason is to learn from your superiors the dogmata in which her deliverances have been codified for general use.' If Neo-angular had to sum up John's desire, it would have to be in the words 'romantic trash.'

'I *tasted* what you call romantic trash,' replied John angrily; 'you have only talked about it . . . Forgive me if I am rude; but how is it possible that you can advise me in this matter? Would you recommend a eunuch to a man whose difficulties lay in realm of chastity? Would a man born blind be my best guide against the lust of the eye?'

Not even the fact that Eliot had used a variety of alliterative verse in *Murder in the Cathedral* could allay the misery Lewis felt as he lay in bed on Christmas Day.

✌ 1936 ✌

'Have you found, or is it peculiar to me, that it is much easier to pray for others than for oneself?' asked Lewis of Griffiths in a letter written on 8 January. 'Doubtless because every return to one's own situation involves action; or to speak more plainly, obedience. That appears to me more and more the whole business of life, the only road to love and peace — the cross and the crown in one.

"Did you ever notice a beautiful touch in the *Faerie Queene*:
    a groom them laid *at rest in easie bedd*,
    His name was meek Obedience."

What indeed can we imagine Heaven to be but *unimpeded* obedience. I think this is one of the causes of our love of inanimate nature, that in it we see things which unswervingly carry out the will of their Creator, and are therefore wholly beautiful; and though this *kind* of obedience is infinitely lower than ours, yet the degree is so much more perfect . . .'

Here and there a snowdrop or aconite appeared along the paths around Oxford as Hilary term began. Peter Philip crossed the lawn towards New Buildings. He was nervous. He had not done all the reading for his tutorial; he had stayed up all night writing the essay; he had an important question to ask the tutor. An Oxford don he had imagined to be 'elderly, thin, pale, austere, scholarly, and rather aloof.' Lewis he found, instead, to be rotund, jocose, looking like 'a well-to-do tenant farmer' who padded about the college grounds in tweed jacket and deerstalker hat; he seemed the athletic type and just might possibly answer the pupil's question in the affirmative.

Philip climbed staircase 3, passed through the oak of room 3, and found Lewis on the sofa lighting up his pipe. He settled into a chair, produced his essay, and yawned. Instead of putting the question right to Lewis, he decided to read. 'How interesting that that should be the South African pronunciation,' said Lewis now and again during the essay, offering the pronunciation preferred in England. Twenty minutes or so passed before Philip finished. Lewis asked some questions, inquiring what proof there was for one assertion, even offering proof for another assertion. Then he gave Philip an assignment for the coming week and suggested an armful of books that would surely prove useful in writing the next essay.

Had Lewis seen the newspaper? asked Philip, before exiting through the oak. 'Oxford Crew Starts Training' read the headline. Well, it seemed that he, Philip, had been asked to cox the college eight. That would mean long, hard hours sculling up and down the Oxford waterways. But surely such practice would be time well invested when Oxford met Cambridge at the university boat race round about Easter time.

What was he getting at? asked Lewis.

Of course, it was impossible to forgo all tutorials and essays for the rest of Hilary term, stammered Philip, but was it possible to skip some of them?

If he had time for sculling, replied Lewis in anger, then he had time for studying, and he heaped a few more titles on the already mountainous reading list for the following week's tutorial.

～

'The King's life is moving peacefully towards its close.' It was 10.00 p.m. on Monday 20 January. Minto and Warnie were listening to the BBC report of the doctors attending George V. Then through the static there was a short prayer for the King's soul in its passing. He died at 11.55. 'What a reign of it he had!' wrote Warnie in his diary the following day. 'Lords Reform, the Ulster crisis, the war, the years of unrest and unemployment. And how well he did! He, who was looked upon as "the husk of a king", was the only one to weather the storm. Emperor, Kaiser, Tsar, Ferdinand of Bulgaria, Constantine of Greece, all swept away, and he came out of it with enhanced prestige.'

On the morning after the King's death, Lewis went to chapel at Magdalen and heard for the first time the prayer for his gracious lord, King Edward VIII. Soon thereafter he began composition of a poem that he would entitle 'Coronation March':

> Blow the trumpet! guardee tramp it!
> Once to lord it thus was vulgar;
> Then we could afford it; empire simpered,
> Gold and gunboards were an ace of trumps.
> Ranting poets then were plenty,
> Loyalty meant royalties. Life is changing . . .

❧

One night in Hilary term Lewis was invited to Exeter by Coghill, where they dined in the great hall, fireplaces blazing. Lewis was seated on the right of the rector of the college, Robert Ranulph Marrett. Conversation was friendly, and frequently took a fresh turn.

'I saw in the papers this morning,' said the rector, 'that there is some scientist-fellah in Vienna called Voronoff — some name like that — who has invented a way of splicing the glands of young apes into old gentlemen, thereby renewing their regenerative powers. Remarkable, isn't it?'

'Unnatural,' said Lewis.

'Come, come! Unnatural! What do you mean *unnatural*? Voronoff is part of nature, isn't he? What happens in nature must surely be natural? Speaking as a philosopher, don't you know, I can attach no meaning to your objection. I don't understand you!'

'I am sorry, rector, but I think any philosopher from Aristotle to — say — Jeremy Bentham would have understood me.'

'Oh, well, we've got beyond Bentham by now, I hope. If Aristotle or he had known about Voronoff, they might have changed their ideas. Think of the possibilities he opens up! You'll be an old man yourself one day,' he said, turning to Lewis.

'I would rather be an old man,' said Lewis, turning to Coghill, 'than a young monkey.'

Hilarity continued into the common room and on into the night. As they were parting, Coghill pressed a book into Lewis' hands and said he should read it. *The Place of the Lion*. Charles Williams wrote it. Just the sort of book Coghill felt Lewis would like.

❧

'I . . . feel no *duty* to attack you,' wrote Lewis to Griffiths, who persisted in listing the differences between Rome and Canterbury, 'and I certainly feel no *inclination* to add to my other works an epistolary controversy with one of the toughest dialecticians of my acquaintance, to which he can devote as much time and reading as he likes and I can devote very little.'

∽

'It isn't often nowadays you get a *Christian* fantasy,' wrote Lewis on 26 February to Greeves. He was referring to the book Coghill had given him a few days before; he found it 'a really great book.' The novel, which had been published four years before, was a shaggy angel story, the narrative energy of which propelled the central characters on an intellectual journey to determine why the world they lived in was irrupting. A lion — or was it a lioness? — was roaming about the countryside, evading capture. Soon a 'crowned snake' was slithering about, seeking whom it might entwine. Then a butterfly with a two-foot wingspan appeared in a garden, ravishing a lepidopterist.

Hottest in pursuit of the mystery was Anthony Durrant, sub-editor of a literary weekly called *The Two Camps*, and Damaris Tighe, the young woman with whom he was in love. 'Pythagorean Influences on Abelard' was the title of the thesis she was preparing for her university degree; in the process she was drawing from a variety of ancient and medieval sources. Her research, which led her from Platonic ideas to Dionysian angels, would eventually provide the key to the mystery.

Early in the novel, Tighe was inveigled into delivering a particle of her research to a group of women seeking mild intellectual entertainment. 'The *Eidola* and the *Angeli*' was the title of her talk. Although it was introduced to the thick-legged audience as 'The Idler and the Angels,' she managed to retain her composure, but this did indicate to the reader of the novel that the world of reality was being invaded by the world of ideas.

Lewis finished reading the book on Ash Wednesday; he found it good preparation for Lent. 'It shows me (through the heroine) the special sin of abuse of intellect to which all my profession are liable, more clearly than I ever saw it before,' he put in a letter to Greeves. So enthusiastic about the novel was he that he sent Coghill's copy to Harwood with a note to forward it next to Barfield.

∽

'I was very sorry to hear about Tommy. I am particularly sorry for John,' wrote Lewis on 26 February to Greeves. 'I am afraid it is most unlikely that he will find anyone to take Tommy's place . . . Try to be as nice to him as you can — but I have no doubt you are doing that already.'

Tommy and John were Greeves' dogs; and Lewis went on to say that Mr Papworth, also known as Tykes, had been gathered to his fathers earlier in the month. The dog was fourteen years old, had been ailing for some months, wore an ulcer on his chin, imbibed on the night of 15 February 'a strong sleeping draught' — whisky, according to Warnie — and went to sleep like a baby, never to wake again.

ᘰ

Lewis was reading the galley proofs of *The Allegorical Love Poem* as fast as OUP could send them to him, but *The Place of the Lion* was never far from his mind. He was thinking of adding to his own book an appendix or two on the significance of 'genius' and 'danger' in ancient, medieval, and Renaissance literature. At the same time he couldn't help remembering, with amusement, Damaris Tighe who planned, as one of six appendices to her *Pythagorean Influences on Abelard*, a colossal graph of human thought, 'three graphs actually, from 500 BC to AD 1200, showing respectively the relation of official thought, cultural thought, and popular thought to the ideas of personalized and depersonalized natural powers.'

On Wednesday 11 March Lewis decided to convey his complete enthusiasm for the novel to Charles Williams by writing to him at the OUP office in London. 'If you had delayed writing another twenty-four hours,' wrote Williams the following day, 'our letters would have crossed. It has never before happened to me to be admiring an author of a book while he at the same time was admiring me. My admiration for the staff work of the Omnipotence rises every day.'

Williams had been reading the proofs of *The Allegorical Love Poem* with a view to writing a description of the work 'for travellers and booksellers and people.' He enclosed what he had written for Lewis' perusal. The reason he fell so heavily for the work was that it was 'an aspect of the subject with which my mind has always been playing . . . I regard your book as practically the only one that I have ever come across, since Dante, that shows the slightest understanding of what this very peculiar identity of love and religion means.'

ᘰ

During Lent Lewis read Augustine's *Confessions*. The intellectual parts, the parts full of soulful cerebration, he perused with great relish. From the devotional parts, the parts dripping with sentiment, he drew little fruit. Encouraged by a sermon to undertake some form of self-denial during the penitential season, he uncovered 'a constant temptation to over-asperity' every time he took his pen in hand. Examining his pleasure in using the English language forcefully, he discovered, not a species of anger, but a form of pride. Which left him confused even into Eastertide.

'The question is,' he wrote to Griffiths on 24 April, 'how you decide whether an ability and strong propensity for some activity is a temptation or a vocation. You will answer that it all depends whether we can or do offer it to God. But frankly — and I want your answer very much — have you made any approaches to a state in which the conscious offering to God can be maintained *concurrently* with the actual donkey work of doing the job? I find I can do those things (even) which I believe that God wills me to do (such as writing this letter) by forgetting God while I do them. I don't mean forgetting intellectually (which would be absurd in the present instance) but turning away — not offering. Is this due to sin or to the very nature of human consciousness?'

When Oxford University Press expressed a dislike for the word 'allegorical' in the title of the work, Lewis suggested the word 'Busirane', the name of the 'vile Enchanter' symbolizing unlawful love in the *Faerie Queene. The House of Busirane* might do the trick, but to Williams and others at the press that sounded like the title more of a romantic novel than a study in medieval tradition. *The Allegory of Love* proved to be an acceptable compromise.

In the preface Lewis paid his 'unambiguous debts' to a Benedictine priest and patristics scholar and to the medieval society of Manchester University; to his companions at Magdalen, C. T. Onions, B. McFarlane, and J. A. Smith; to Tolkien and Dyson. To his father for keeping a house full of books he paid special thanks, and he dedicated the book to Barfield, 'wisest and best of my unofficial teachers.'

'I think both your old attitude to poetry (when you looked for religion in it) and your present one (in which you reject it as a bridge you have now finally crossed) are equally based on an error common to all modern critics — that of taking poetry as a substantive thing like chemistry or agriculture.' Lewis and Griffiths were continuing their wrangle. 'In fact, in a sense there is no such thing as poetry,' wrote Lewis on 14 September. 'It is not an element but a *mode*.'

'Have a gasper.'

It was Thursday night in Michaelmas term. Some undergraduates had been invited to Lewis' rooms. As each arrived Lewis held out a yellow packet of Gold Flake cigarettes. Once ignited, the yellow peril, as it came to be called in the English trenches of the Great War, was almost as deleterious to the human lung as poisonous gas from

German bunkers. Soon there was more ash than ashtrays; Lewis flicked his to the floor. Ashes were good for a carpet, he maintained; something women had been slow to discover. Beer was poured from pitchers. When a quorum was achieved, Lewis moved to the centre of the room and shouted '*Hwaet!*'

Listen the undergraduates did to this and the other Anglo-Saxon words that followed. It was a poetic line he was reading. The metre was alliterative, which meant that the pauses were meaningful; the alliteration in each line was like the sound of silver tinkling. Lewis' baritone voice, resonant enough to fill a great hall, transported the small group back through time to the eighth and seventh centuries, when Christianity was eastering in England, before Bede was venerable, after monks had planted the martyrs' seed.

Someone, somewhere, most probably in a monastery, instead of venturing forth to harvest the Angles and the Saxons, sat instead at a *scrinium*, interweaving pagan tales with Christian verities and expressing the new work in a language, not of northern sagas or southern epics, but of the Germanic peoples who thrived on the island.

When Lewis had read a hundred lines or so, he handed the text to an undergraduate, who stumbled on with Lewis' help. He and the others had studied Anglo-Saxon grammar and syntax and indeed had mastered a measure of vocabulary; they had studied Grimm's and Verner's laws of consonantal change; some might even have read the work in modern translation.

Lewis himself had read *Beowulf* long before he arrived in Oxford as an undergraduate. He had bought William Morris' translation of the poem, and in a letter dated 1 November 1916, he conveyed his enthusiasm to Greeves. 'When I was reading it, I tried to imagine myself as an old Saxon thane sitting in my hall of a winter's night, with the wolves and storm outside and the old fellow singing his story. In this way you get the atmosphere of terror that runs through it — the horror of the old barbarous days when the land was all forests and when you thought a demon might come to your house any night and carry you off.'

More beer, more gaspers, and another undergraduate took up the text. The young Beowulf and his fourteen companions had just arrived at the great hall of Heorot. They paid their respects to the Danish king Hrothgar, whose only complaint in life was that his glorious hall had been invaded by a giant. That night, as every night for the last twelve years, Grendel burst through the doors of the hall and ate a thane. When he reached for another Beowulf grabbed his arm, twisted it, and although both thrashed about the hall, Beowulf managed not only to retain his grasp but eventually to twist the monster's arm right out of its socket.

As another undergraduate continued the story, Lewis hoped that the group was perceiving something of the splendidness of the poem. He himself had been fighting for the centrality of the work in the English literature syllabus. Some would have preferred that undergraduate students read classical epics like the *Iliad* in Greek and the *Aeneid* in Latin instead of *Beowulf* in Anglo-Saxon. Others would have the pupils read *Romance of the Rose* in Old French. No one valued the classical as well as the continental languages and literatures as much as Lewis — 'I do not know where the last ditch in our educational war may be at the moment; but point it out to me on the trench map, and I will go to it' — but he felt the proper place for the study of these languages was before or after, but not during, the study of English.

Some of Lewis' colleagues, Tolkien among them, would drop in on the 'beer and Beowulf' parties, as they came to be called; each took his turn reading the text. Tolkien was especially interested in the poem; his lectures on it, which were memorable affairs, laboured to demonstrate that criticism of the poem over the centuries was as varied as it was inaccurate. The poem was neither 'the confused product of a committee of muddle-headed and probably beer-bemused Anglo-Saxons' nor 'a string of pagan lays edited by monks.' Neither was it 'a translation from the Danish' nor 'imported by Frisian traders.' It might well be a burden to the English syllabus, but it was well worth studying.

These and other remarks on the poem Tolkien organized into a lecture entitled 'Beowulf: The Monster and the Critics', which he delivered to the British Academy on 25 November. In it he defended the work not only as a poem but also as a poem with powerful passages, high tone, and dignity. It was not an epic poem; rather it was a heroic elegiac poem describing two great moments in one man's life, both of which had to do with monsters. In the flower of his youth Beowulf slew both Grendel and his mother, evil spirits both; in the autumn of his life he bested a dragon, a firedrake guarding a treasure trove of symbolic importance. All the while the hero was demonstrating the virtue that seemed to be the essence of northernness, courage, a coolness in the face of adversity, even with none of the promises of revelation.

'Mr Lewis is indisposed,' read the handwritten notice tacked to the outer door of room 3, staircase 3, New Buildings, 'and regrets that he cannot hold any tutorials this week.' The week passed; the following week half-passed before Norman Bradshaw found out, much to his horror, that Lewis was well again and that he himself had missed a tutorial. At the next appointed time he tapped the door of room 3, entered, and apologized. 'I'm not your schoolmaster,' bellowed Lewis, waving the apologies off, indicating at the same time that the loss, such as it was, was not his own but the pupil's.

The essay was on the poetry of the first half of the sixteenth century; Bradshaw discoursed on the lyrics, many of which were really the words of songs. Some were good as poems even without musical accompaniment. Others were simply dull without flute or oboe. Dullest of the lot, and Bradshaw had chosen it particularly, was one attributed to Henry VIII.

> Whereto should I express
> My inward heaviness,
> No mouth can make me fain
> Till that we meet again

'Well, I must go and have a pee,' said Lewis rising from the sofa and heading towards the bedroom and the chamber pot. When he returned, he had a strip of cloth in his hand, trying to attach the hook on the left waistband onto the tailor's eye on the right waistband. 'It's like having a grey flannel penis hanging out.'

Bradshaw had produced a recorder from his coat and proceeded to play an air that would have been a suitable accompaniment: the three-hundred-year-old words danced into life. Lewis was agreeably surprised. Both tutor and pupil agreed that it was as unfair to criticize the words of a song without having heard its music as it was to evaluate a play without having seen it acted on stage.

❧

John Donne was overrated, or so Lewis maintained in conversation with Joan Bennett of Girton College during one of his regular visits to Cambridge. Fifty years before, the seventeenth-century poet was considered inconsequential, but now he was numbered among the greats. One thing critics weren't doing, Lewis protested, was distinguishing between Donne's *best* poetry and his *most characteristic* poetry.

Both Lewis and Bennett had been invited to contribute an essay to a festschrift volume to honour the seventieth birthday of Herbert Grierson, who had retired two years before after forty years of teaching rhetoric and literature at the universities of Aberdeen and Edinburgh. Donne was one of Grierson's many specialities; his definitive edition of Donne's poetry was published by Oxford University Press in 1933. Donne's love poetry hadn't been scrutinized lately — that appealed to Lewis as a topic. Bennett asked if she could read his essay before she wrote her own; she too wanted to write on the love poems.

He immediately set about discovering three levels of sentiment. The 'celebration of the simple appetite' was the lowest; 'ostensibly virtuous love' was the highest; and in between lay the vast majority of the poems and the many varieties of love. He also discerned five themes, 'all of them grim ones — on the sorrow of parting (including death), the miseries of secrecy, the falseness of the mistress, the fickleness of Donne, and finally the contempt for love itself.'

Concentrating on the love poetry, Lewis acknowledged in the essay, meant leaving out much of the poet's best work. But no matter, he sailed on, on the one hand attacking 'literary Manichaeism, that distrusted the pleasures of the imagination while preaching the pleasures of the body, and on the other hand extolling the Irishness of the English poet's wit, which demonstrated not only the playfulness but also the irritability of his intellect.

How far was Donne's poetry calculated to interest the human imagination? he asked at the end of the essay. 'Its interest, save for a mind specially predisposed in its favour, must be short-lived and superficial, though intense. Paradoxical as it may seem, Donne's poetry is too simple to satisfy. Its complexity is all on the surface — an intellectual and fully conscious complexity that we soon come to the end of. Beneath this we find nothing but a limited series of "passions" — explicit, mutually exclusive passions which can be instantly and adequately labelled as such — things which can readily be talked about, and indeed, must be talked about because, in silence, they begin to lose their hard outlines and overlap, to betray themselves as partly fictitious.'

When Bennett read the essay he sent her, she was perplexed. Donne didn't think sex was in and of itself sinful; Lewis was wrong there; and contempt of women wasn't one of the general characteristics of Donne's love poetry. She wrote to Lewis, asking if he would mind if she wrote a refutation of his arguments, or at least a clarification of his points, an essay that would also be included in the commemorative volume.

'It is not a question (for your sake and that of the festschrift, not mine) whether a general pro-Donne paper called "Donne and His Critics" — a glance at Dryden and Johnson and then some contemporaries including me — wouldn't be better than a direct answer. C.S.L. as professional controversialist and itinerant prize-fighter is, I suspect, become already rather a bore to our small public, and might in that way infect you. Also, if you really refute me, you raise for the editor the awkward question, "Then why print the article?" However, do just as you like . . . and good luck with whatever you do.'

How could one man, Bennett asked herself, a middle-aged bachelor and confirmed Christian to boot, think well of the love poems of another man for whom, at least when he wrote the poems, chastity meant nothing? She at least was a woman, had fallen in love and married, and was teaching literature at Cambridge University's only college for women. She was working in a man's world, which gave her little advantage, but surely in reviewing and evaluating love poetry of whatever century, being a woman had to be some advantage. And she quite simply thought that Donne was one of the greatest poets in the English language.

Donne was 'perpetually excited,' Lewis had written in his essay, 'and therefore perpetually cut off from the deeper and more permanent springs of his own excitement.' Ridiculous, thought Bennett. Love *was* an exciting experience, was the obvious answer to that charge, and great love poetry was bound to communicate excitement. But when she began to write, she felt she had to say more on this point. 'Love is exciting, but it is also restful. Unreciprocated love is a torment of the spirit, but reciprocated love is peace and happiness . . . Donne is a great love poet because his poetry records and communicated these diverse experiences.'

⟡

Dons, expected young John Lawlor when he arrived in Oxford the year before, were 'sports-jacketed figures in pastel ties, reclining under the great chestnut tree at Balliol in apparent indolence, but all the while razor-keen to detect inconsistencies in attitude or standpoint.' But when he entered Lewis' rooms at the beginning of Michaelmas term, he found a bald, red-faced man in rumpled jacket and baggy trousers with a tie that was not pastel and 'obviously in no mood to waste time.'

That term Lawlor was introduced to Anglo-Saxon and 'worked up from the early sentences to the piece on King Edward.' Now that it was Hilary term, he was reading about Edmund Spenser and dipping heavily into *The Faerie Queene.* The pupil picked a spot on the sprawling settee. The tutor plumped down into an armchair, listening to the essay, smoking vigorously, pencilling notes, drawing caricatures.

After the essay Lewis asked questions. Giving fewer answers than he would have liked, Lawlor was forced to quote Ronald Knox in his own defence. 'The prevailing attitude . . . was one of heavy disagreement with a number of things which the reader has not said.'

When asked what if anything he was doing besides preparing for tutorials, Lawlor had to admit there was the civil war in Spain; he was 'busy organizing lunches for refugee funds, collecting money by point-blank asking, and getting up meetings and demonstrations in support of the Spanish government.'

No, he did not want to contribute, said Lewis before he was asked. He had a rule about not contributing 'to anything that had a directly political implication.'

∽

On 28 March, which was Easter Sunday, Lewis wrote to Greeves to warn him that when he visited England next, he would find 'the Kilns changed much for the worse.' A rash of small houses had sprung up in the neighbourhood. Lewis was quick to point the finger at William Richard Morris, chairman of Morris Motors Ltd. and since 1934 Lord Nuffield. His factory buildings lay about a mile from the Kilns, occupying ninety acres of what was before the war prime agricultural land. From its assembly line, fourteen and three-quarters miles long, rolled five hundred Morris Eights every working day. The employees were well paid, were even shareholders. They began work at eight, had an hour off at lunch, and worked again till five. Then they bicycled away, 'six abreast, to the villa, the bird bath, the wireless, the garden, and a bi-weekly visit to the pictures.'

The creeping urbanization of Headington in general and of Shotover Hill in particular, the more Lewis thought about it, would affect not only the future of his own household but also the future of forestry.

> How will the legend of the age of trees
> Feel, when the last tree falls in England?
> When the concrete spreads and the town conquers
> The country's heart; when contraceptive
> Tarmac's laid where the farm has faded,
> Tramline flows where slept a hamlet
> And shop-fronts, blazing without a stop
> From Dover to Wrath, have glazed us over? . . .

∽

Early on a Saturday morning in April, pupils wandered into Magdalen College dining hall for tutor's collections. It had been six weeks since Hilary term had ended; with the university sermon in St Mary the Virgin's the following day, Trinity term would begin. During this six-week vacation pupils were supposed to have done assigned readings; the collections were the tutors' way to find out how much and how well. There were twelve examinations; for each one booklets composed of sixteen blank pages were passed out. The pupil wrote his name and subject matter at the top of the first page and began to answer questions like the following:

Write on one of the following: Henryson, Dunbar, Gavin Douglas, etc.

What did (a) Chaucer do to Boccaccio and (b) Malory to the 'French Book'?

Why has Shakespeare been so much more highly regarded than other dramatists of his time?

Tutors could mark an examination with alpha, beta, or gamma, enhanced or diminished by pluses or minuses. Lewis marked Bradshaw's with alphas mostly, some betas, no gammas. 'Good, but begins badly,' he wrote in pencil at the end of one answer. 'You start by saying that there is only *one* "tangible" explanation (whatever that means) and then come very near to giving two. The whole use of "magic of poetry" as an explanation is bad. Some of your examples could be analyzed further, couldn't they? Don't bring in "magic" till you are sure explanation can go no further.'

⁂

Bray the trumpet, tumble tragic
Drumbeat's magic, sway the logic
Of legs that march a thousand in a uniform,
Flags and arches, the lion and the unicorn
Romp it, rampant, pompous tramping . . .
Some there are that talk of Alexander
    With a tow-row-row-row-row-row.

It was Wednesday 12 May. Crowned King of England was, not Edward VIII, for he had abdicated in December, but George VI. At 8.15 that night in Magdalen hall there was a dinner celebrating the occasion. Green melon and lobster salad; roast chicken, sausages, and vegetables; coffee meringue. A toast: glasses of Bollinger select Cuvée, vintage 1921, raised to church and king, the ecclesiastical establishment coming first in memory of the time in 1698 when the fellows of Magdalen locked themselves inside the college and threw the keys into the Cherwell rather than submit to James II's Roman Catholic nominees for president and fellows. A second toast: glasses passed over the tops of the water-jugs — in form like the Jacobite toast to Stuart pretenders James and Charles — in salute to Edward VIII who was now in France. A third, the Magdalen toast — *jus suum cuique* ('to each man his just deserts') — and each drank from the huge loving cup as it was passed from man to man.

⌘

'A don in the middle of long vacation is almost a non-existent creature,' wrote Lewis in 1937. 'College neither knows nor cares where he is, and certainly no one else does.' He was already into the second chapter of a piece of narrative prose when he penned those words; to ensure continued progress during the summer, he absented himself from human society as much as possible. He did emerge one night a week, though. He and his friends — Tolkien, Coghill, Dyson, Wrenn, and the like, and of course Warren — would forgather in collegiate rooms and read aloud a chapter or two of a work in progress. *The Hobbit* had made its premier appearance to adults in this forum. A cooling draft would be downed; the material just read would be raked with friendly criticism.

The central character of Lewis' work would be a cross-country walker. 'Do you do it for money, or is it sheer masochism?' asked one of the characters. 'Pleasure, of course,' replied the Lewis-like character. When the other suggested that he must have enjoyed the army, he replied, 'It's just the opposite of the army'. He went on to point out that the walker, unlike the soldier, could choose when and where and how long to go.

Lewis began the novel by putting a map in his chief character's hand and a pack on his back and by setting him on the road. Most of the men in the room listening to the author read the first chapter had been on just such a tramp with him at one time or another; they fully expected to discover themselves, or bits of themselves, in the narrative as it unfolded.

'He walked fairly fast, and doggedly, without looking much about him,' read Lewis in a sonorous voice, 'like a man trying to shorten the way with some interesting train of thought. He was tall, but a little round-shouldered, about thirty-five to forty years of age, and dressed with that particular kind of shabbiness which marks a member of the intelligentsia on a holiday. He might easily have been mistaken for a doctor or a schoolmaster at first sight, though he had not the man-of-the-world air of the one or the indefinable breeziness of the other. In fact, he was a philologist, and a fellow of a Cambridge college. His name was Unwin.'

The men, especially Tolkien and Wrenn, were much amused by the first paragraphs. Lewis moved quickly to confront Unwin with two rude characters. Devine, a Cambridge man who was trying to turn his scholarship towards the making of millions, contained more than a few traces of T. D. Weldon, Magdalen's philosopher. Weston, a physicist who made interplanetary travel possible and now wanted to make it profitable, was a scientist not unlike J. B. S. Haldane, a biochemist at Cambridge and later at London University and a Marxist at both places; in the last chapter of his *Possible Worlds*, a book of essays published in 1927, he had stated that, if the human race were to continue to survive and progress, mankind would have to colonize the planets.

First chance Devine and Weston got, they drugged Unwin, and not long thereafter all three found themselves on Malacandra, a planet not at all unlike what Lewis and his friends knew of Mars. Populating the planets were *nau* (plural of *hnau*), Malacandrian for 'rational animals'. Unwin soon discerned three different species and being a philologist, learned their languages with comparative ease. There were *hrossa*, horse-like creatures not unlike hippopotami, who farmed and fished. There were *sorns* or *seroni*, giraffe-like creatures roaming the Malacandrian savannah, who were the intelligentsia, living off the fruits of others. And there were *pfifltriggi*, small hairless, snouted creatures, who with their many fingers mined ore and made objects of utility and beauty.

Because Unwin like Lewis made his morning devotions, prayed when in danger, and lived a life influenced by theological verities, Malacandra would also have a supernatural framework. There would be *eldila*, planetary intelligences not unlike angelic presences. Chief of these would be *Oyeresu*, one of whom, an *Oyarsa*, ruled each planet in the universe. Of greatest importance to the superstructure, if of little importance to the narrative, would be Maleldil, God the Father, and Malaldil the Young, God the Son.

One of the conventions of space fiction, dominated at that time by H. G. Wells, was that the characters had to pass from a good planet, Earth, to a bad planet. The fact that Unwin and his kidnappers travelled from an evil planet to a good planet, thought Lewis' friends, was a nice twist. Earth was ruled by an *Oyarsa*; once creature of light, he had rebelled and since that time was known as the Bent One, wandering about the earth seeking whom he might warp.

Being somewhat short in astrophysics, Lewis did not spend many words on the interplanetary voyage. Instead he lavished attention on what might be called astrolinguistics, something his Oxford audience was more appreciative of. *Hrossa* were 'great speakers and singers.' *Pfifltriggi* let their artifacts do most of the talking for them. *Sorns* tended to philosophize, their concepts being intelligible in all languages. Holed up in a guest house one night with all three species, Unwin even thought he could discern their sense of humour. '*Sorns* seldom got beyond irony, while the *hrossa* were extravagant and fantastic, and the *pfifltriggi* were sharp and excelled in abuse.'

Lewis finished the first draft of his novel by the end of August. *Out of the Silent Planet*, he entitled it, 'silent planet' being the English equivalent of *Thulcandra*, the Malacandrian word for 'Earth'. A number of scenes in the work he knew would give special delight when read to his donnish audience. On first encountering a *hross*, Unwin struck up a conversation in a way not unreminiscent of Henry Higgins establishing phonetical contact with Eliza Doolittle. Kneeling in the bow of a boat paddled by a *hross*, Unwin speared an alligator-like water dragon with a skill that would have made Edgar Rice Burroughs smile. And at the novel's end, when Unwin returned to earth, escaped from the space vehicle before it blew up, and stumbled down a lane, a road, a village street, he would say, on entering the first pub, 'A pint of bitter, please.'

There was general approval among Lewis' friends when Weston and Devine were finally captured by a posse of armed *hrossa* and put on trial before the *Oyarsa* of Malacandra. There was even applause when they heard the scientist, with guards on either side, pleading for his life. 'I am prepared without flinching to plant the flag of man on the soil of Malacandra,' shrieked Weston; 'to march on, step by step, superseding, where necessary, the lower forms of life that we find, claiming planet after planet, system after system, till our posterity — whatever strange form and yet unguessed mentality they have assumed — dwell in the universe wherever the universe is habitable.'

For some reason not consistent with angelic metaphysics, *Oyarsa* could not understand Weston as he orated like Shaw's St Joan at the stake. Unwin had to translate into Malacandrian and by so doing Lewis was accomplishing what every controversialist dreamed of; he was transmitting not only what the opposition had to say but also interpreting what the opposition's words meant in a larger, and indeed a theological, context.

'I may fall,' cried Weston in peroration. 'But while I live, I will not, with such a key in my hand, consent to close the gates of the future of my race. What lies in that future, beyond our present ken, passes imagination to conceive: it is enough for me that there is a Beyond.' Resting his case and exhausted, he looked around for a place to sit. Much to the merriment of the roomful of dons at Magdalen, Lewis threw one final spear at Haldane. When the scientist gave the same sort of speech as Weston's he would at the end sink into a chair as the applause began. But on Malacandra, when Weston finished, there was no chair; the silence was deafening.

What did it all mean? In *The Pilgrim's Regress*, Lewis thought he had made his meaning clear, but as the years passed and sales were slim, he came to the conclusion that he had made a blunder. The pilgrimage he described, which he had thought would be as familiar to a reader as a train ride from Euston to Crewe, turned out to be as rough and smelly as a camel ride through the Gobi. He would not make that mistake again.

In his thriller, after the close of the narrative, he added a chapter. In it he revealed that Unwin was a pseudonym and that he, Lewis, had heard the tale directly from the good doctor, who in his naiveté encouraged him to put it into fictional form in order to ensure the widest possible circulation. In real life also there was a Weston; the force or forces behind him, warned the novel, would 'play a very important part in the events of the next few centuries, and, unless we prevent them, a very disastrous one.'

'What we need for the moment,' said the doctor in conclusion, 'is not so much a body of belief as a body of people familiar with certain ideas. If we could even effect in one percent of our readers a change-over from the conception of space to the conception of Heaven, we should have made a beginning.'

⧉

'Oh good, an Anglo-Saxon,' said Lewis the moment Harry Blamires, a fair-haired, blue-eyed northerner, entered room 3. 'I've had nothing but Celts today.'

Blamires was accustomed to find his tutor seated on the Chester-field sofa, stoking the bowl of his pipe and searching about for a light. Today, however, he was striding about the room, reciting aloud a line of poetry.

Was it 'Úp the airy Moúntain' or 'Úp the aíry Móuntain'? Lewis asked Blamires for an opinion. Was it 'Dówn the rushy glén' or 'Dówn the rúshy glén'? Were they two-stress lines or three-stress lines? The reason he had to decide was that the lines following — 'Wee folk, good folk' and 'Green jacket, red cap' — were even more difficult to scan. Blamires hazarded a conjecture; Lewis thanked him, commenting that his pupil's metrical ear was not one of his strong points. Anyway, it was time for the young man to read his essay.

Most of the preceding six days Blamires had spent on Abraham Cowley, a seventeenth-century poet and diplomat who was as at home with metaphysical conceits as with coded messages. Blamires paid special attention to an epic, unfinished, on the biblical history of David written in extraordinary couplets. Looking up as he read, he saw not only that he had captured Lewis' attention but also that his tutor was rocking back and forth trying to control his mirth.

'You don't mean to say you've actually read the thing!'

'Every word.'

'I'm terribly sorry,' said the tutor in gravest apology. 'But think of it,' he said brightening up. 'You must be the only man in the country, perhaps the only man alive, to have read every word of Cowley's *Davideis*!'

More often than not, Blamires got an alpha for his essays. The discussions that followed were sometimes difficult. At least this time Lewis didn't ask him to compare the *Davideis* with *Peter Rabbit*. 'I think Dr Johnson's judgment on Oliver Goldsmith applies to you,' said Lewis to Blamires, who was preparing to leave. 'You write like an angel and talk like poor Poll.'

∽

'The publishers claim that *The Hobbit*, though very unlike *Alice*, resembles it in being the work of a professor at play,' wrote Lewis in the 2 October issue of *The Times Literary Supplement*. 'A more important truth is that both belong to a very small class of books which have nothing in common save that each admits us to a world of its own — a world that seems to have been going on before we stumbled into it but which, once found by the right reader, becomes indispensable to him.'

∽

'Fervent medievalists have been noticed progressing well in the shadow of Mr C. S. Lewis,' began a paragraph in 'Catmeat', a column of whimsical observation and comment in the Michaelmas issue of *Cats*, literary publication of St Catherine's Society, whose pupils, usually of limited means, were members of the university without at the same time incurring the costs of belonging to a specific college. 'We discover that in the privacy of their lodgings,' the paragraph concluded, 'thick brown dressing gowns and hair shirts are *de rigueur*.' Although unsigned, the squib was surely the work of one, perhaps two, young men who had just joined the magazine committee.

Alan Rook had wanted to read medieval English at Oxford since he was at preparatory school. At St Catherine's he read twelve hours a day, seldom went to lectures, and took tutorials with Lewis. The tutor was impressed and invited him several times to dine at high table at Magdalen. After dinner they would stroll across the lawn to New Buildings where they had fruit and Madeira; when one or two others arrived, they would talk philosophy until dawn. It was an intellectually stimulating, if psychologically draining, experience.

'Rook, you think of me as a medievalist and a scholar. You're making a mistake. I'm nothing of the sort,' said Lewis to a stunned and bewildered young man. 'I'm a butcher, a rough and brutal man.'

Not long thereafter, the tutor made a startling but welcome suggestion. 'Rook, your mind and mine are too much alike. If you continue with me, you'll become just another Lewis. You don't want that. You'd better go on to someone else.' And he did indeed go on, to Charles Wrenn, university professor of Anglo-Saxon.

Peter Bide, having left behind a promising career in chemicals and dyestuffs, went to Oxford for literature. Lewis was not his tutor, but he did attend Lewis' lectures introducing the study of medieval and Renaissance literature. So bedazzled was he with the one on John Lydgate, a fifteenth-century versifier, that he went directly from the lecture hall to the Oxford Union, where he found *The Falls of Princes* on the library shelf. Not long after he began reading the poem, he fell asleep. He blamed the somnolence when he awoke, not on the fact that it was winter and he was sitting near a fire, but on the very real possibility that Lewis' enthusiasm for the work — 36,000 lines of benumbing rhyme-royal — far exceeded its literary merits.

༄

William Morris was underrated, or so Lewis thought when he reviewed, for *The Times Literary Supplement* of 29 May 1937, a book entitled *The Works of Morris and Yeats in Relation to Early Saga Literature* by Dorothy M. Hoare.

Since childhood Lewis had been amassing a psychological debt to the nineteenth-century artist and artisan. Poetic works like *The Story of Sigurd and the Fall of the Niblungs* (1876) had the power to transport the young Lewis to another world, and prose romances like *The Well at the World's End* (1896) awakened in the adult Lewis an aching desire for the great unknown. But to readers in England in the 1930s, Morris' poetry seemed mere escapism, and his novels, tattered tapestries.

When asked by the Martlets to address them in Michaelmas term, Lewis decided to collect his thoughts about Morris. The language Morris invented for his poems and perfected in his prose romances, Lewis conceded, was never spoken in any English household or at any English public gathering. And the imaginary world Morris created, Lewis conceded also, was made out of scraps and pieces of medieval stuff that might, or might not, have been authentic.

Entering Exeter College in 1853, Morris had been, from the start, enthralled by the Middle Ages, not the 'Christian mysticism, Aristotelian philosophy, courtly love,' but 'the world of sagas, at once homely and heroic.' Malory's *Morte d'Arthur* struck him on the heart; he subsequently painted 'Queen Guinevere' as a fresco in the Oxford Union, and *The Defence of Guenevere, and Other Poems* (1858) was his first published book. He even designed what one contemporary called 'some intensely medieval furniture.' In 1859 he founded an interior decorating firm that revolutionized English taste in wallpapers, textiles, and carpets.

When they assembled on 5 November 1937, the Martlets dawdled through their banquet, dreading the paper on William Morris that awaited them. He may have been a giant in the nineteenth century, but in the twentieth he was just another stuffed and mounted pachyderm in the Ashmolean Museum of Arts and Antiquities. Lewis, though, had the reputation of defending the indefensible with vigour and colour, and so the evening might not be a loss after all.

What he found especially appealing about Morris, Lewis told the Martlets, was his sense of northernness. The seven or eight prose romances Morris wrote in his fifties and sixties were flooded with glints and lights from the Old Norse, Icelandic sagas. They were full of geography, not just scenery; they were evocative, not just photographic; Morris did not paint the landscape in words, as other nineteenth-century novelists did; he told the lie of the land, and the reader painted the landscape for himself. Morris, Lewis seemed to detect, had a passion for immortality 'as wild, as piercing, as orgiastic and heartbreaking' as his characters seemed to have for immorality.

In his prose romances, which Lewis felt were 'the real crown of his work,' Morris described, not just the extraordinary exploits of the single hero, but 'the daily life, health, and preservation of the community.' Onto his medieval creations Morris projected a kind of modern socialism.

In his own century Morris had lectured as often as he could on the principles of socialism and demonstrated in the streets to the point of arrest. He became a member, successively, of the Social Democratic Federation and the Socialist League. Although he died in 1896, he was 'in one sense as good "totalitarian" as ever came out of Moscow or Berlin.'

Morris did not believe in God. 'It's so unimportant,' he said to an interviewer in 1892. He was 'the most irreligious of all our poets — *anima naturaliter pagana.*' Prejudiced neither by theism nor by atheism, he described 'the actual going on of the communal life, the sowing, planting, begetting, building, ditching, eating, and conversation,' all the tensions of life without prescribing solutions, logical, ideological or even theological .

'The modern literary world is increasingly divided into two camps, that of the positive and militant Christians and that of the convinced materialists.' Lewis did not want to send the young Martlets out into the night without offering them something useful for November 1937. 'It is here that Morris may be of incalculable value in saving us from "dissociation"; for both camps can find in him something that they need.'

Christian readers could find all 'the natural virtues and the natural desires from which all philosophical religion must start — the question which all theologies claim to answer.' Communist readers could find a political creed that was, in principle at least, the same as their own but that was combined with an absolute refusal to paint out 'the great bar of black that runs across the shield of man.'

All readers, if they read long enough, would find that Morris 'presented in one vision the ravishing sweetness and the heartbreaking melancholy of our experience, . . . shown how the one continually passes over into the other, and . . . combined all this with a stirring practical creed, this is to have presented the *datum* which all our adventures, worldly and otherworldly alike, must take into account.'

Not so many years before, 1930, Lewis had traded in his Bombay Edition of the *Works of Rudyard Kipling* for the *Collected Works of William Morris*, thirty-one volumes for twenty-four volumes; since that time he had dipped regularly into them for refreshment. How many of the young Martlets would show up at Blackwell's on the morrow, a Saturday, wondered Lewis as he walked back to Magdalen, looking for *The Earthly Paradise* (1868-1970) or *The Wood Beyond the World* (1894).

✑ 1938 ✑

When Lewis got the manuscript of *Out of the Silent Planet* back from the typist, he sent it off to Dent in London. They demurred on the ground that *The Pilgrim's Regress* did not encouraged them to invest in another work by the same author. Refusing to consider Sheed and Ward, he consulted Tolkien. Why not Allen & Unwin, publisher of *The Hobbit*? After all, the hero of the novel and the chairman of the publishing house bore the same family name.

Forthwith Lewis sent the novel to Stanley Unwin. Shortly thereafter, on 18 February, Tolkien followed it with a letter. 'I read it, of course; and I have since heard it pass a rather different test, that of being read aloud to our local club (which goes in for reading things short and long aloud). It proved an exciting serial, and was highly approved. But of course we are all like-minded.'

Unwin sent the novel to a reader, who returned a report to the effect Malacandra and everything on it were *bunk*. Disturbed, Unwin sent the reader's report to Tolkien and asked for a report on the report. 'At first blush,' replied Tolkien on 4 March, 'I feel inclined to retort that anyone capable of using the word "bunk" will inevitably find matter of this sort — bunk.' The work had artistic shortcomings, Tolkien was quick to agree, but he found the blend of *vera historia* with *mythos* 'irresistible'.

The reader had missed it, but just in case Unwin had missed it, Tolkien went on to make clear that the myth was the fall of the angels and the subsequent fall of man. 'I cannot understand how anyone can say that this sticks in his gullet, unless (a) he thinks this particular myth "bunk," that it is not worth adult attention (even on a mythical plane); or (b) the use of it unjustified or perhaps unsuccessful.' He himself had found the work enthralling; once started reading, he could do nothing else until he finished it.

Instead of soliciting the opinion of yet another reader, Unwin withdrew the manuscript from Allen & Unwin and gave it to an editor at The Bodley Head, of which he was also the chief. There it was found acceptable; if Lewis would change the last name of his main character, he could look forward to publication in the fall. Would 'Ransom' be acceptable, replied Lewis, and when might he expect proofs?

✑

Three years having passed since Griffiths had professed vows of poverty, chastity, and obedience, he was free to leave Prinknash Priory or to stay. If he wanted to stay, the Benedictine community would have to assemble in chapter and vote his admittance. He received the required two-thirds majority easily. On Tuesday, 21 December, he made his solemn profession as a Benedictine monk, which included a vow of 'stability, conversion of life, and obedience.' Not long thereafter he was appointed guestmaster at the priory. It was his job to welcome the weekend visitors, a trickle in winter, a torrent in summer. With these people, who were seeking refreshment of one sort or another, Griffiths was able to talk on everything from the most superficial to the deeply supernatural. All of the visitors needed help, and the help the Benedictines offered best was prayer. It was on this level that Lewis and Griffiths communicated best. Lewis even sent him a poem about the dynamics of prayer that had about it a whiff of mysticism.

> They tell me, Lord, that when I seem
> To be in speech with You,
> Since You make no replies, it's all a dream
> — One talker aping two.
>
> And so it is, but not as they
> Falsely believe. For I
> Seek in myself the thing I meant to say,
> And lo! the wells are dry.
>
> Then, seeing me empty, You forsake
> The listener's part, and through
> My dumb lips breathe and into utterance wake
> The thought I never knew.
>
> Therefore, You neither need reply
> Nor can; for while we seem
> Two talking, Thou art one forever; and I
> No dreamer, but Thy dream.

What Lewis and Griffiths did not share was how the division between the Churches of England and Rome might be healed. They were like two terriers tearing at opposite ends of a treasured towel.

'I feel that whenever two members of different communions succeed in sharing the spiritual life so far as they can now share it, and are thus forced to regard each other as Christians,' wrote Lewis to Griffiths on 29 April, 'they are really helping on reunion by producing the conditions without which official reunion would be quite barren. I feel sure that this is the laymen's chief contribution to the task, and some of us here are being enabled to perform it.

'You, who are a priest and a theologian, are a different story; and on the purely natural and temperamental level there is, and always has been, a sort of tension between us two which prevents our doing much mutual good. We shall both be nicer, please God, in a better place. Meanwhile, you have my daily prayer and good wishes.'

Before winter had completely melted into spring, Lewis was strolling along Addison's Walk. While galanthus and yellow eranthis were bursting from the muddy landscape. He wondered what would happen if bird life could coax plant life into blossoming by promising immortality. What a poem that would make, and he began putting verses together as he walked.

> I heard in Addison's Walk a bird sing clear
> 'This year the summer will come true. This year. This year.
>
> 'Winds will not strip the blossom from the apple trees
> This year, nor want of rain destroy the peas.
>
> 'This year time's nature will no more defeat you,
> Nor all the promised moments in their passing cheat you.
>
> 'This time they will not lead you round and back
> To Autumn, one year older, by the well-worn track.
>
> 'This year, this year, as all these flowers foretell,
> We shall escape the circle and undo the spell.
>
> 'Often deceived, yet open once again your heart,
> Quick, quick, quick, quick! — the gates are drawn apart.'

Full bloom would indeed come in the fullness of time, but what a deception! Autumn would blow, and winter would chill, but poetry, was it not? was made of such deceptions.

'You look very pleased with yourself,' said Coghill approaching him on the muddy track.

'I believe,' said Lewis, feeling another deception coming on, 'I *believe* I have proved that the Renaissance never happened in England. Alternatively, that if it did, it had no importance!'

'Why do you never drop in and see me?' wrote Lewis on 28 May to Betjeman. He was returning, apologetically, two books his former pupil had lent him years before. Betjeman's own book, *An Oxford*

153

University Chest, a trove of sketches on academic life, pastoral pleasures, and architectural critiques, was about to be published by
Oxford University Press. When Betjeman replied, suggesting Monday
6 June, Lewis wrote to say he couldn't make it.

᪥

Final examinations were approaching. To relieve the pressure,
Bradshaw and his friend W. R. Fryer, whom the tutors called *stupor
mundi* for his nonstop forty-minute essays, went to see Gilbert and
Sullivan's *The Gondoliers*. The music relaxed them, the rhyming
ditties tickled them; when Don Alhambra del Bolero, the grand
inquisitor, made a stunning entrance, they almost exploded. He
looked exactly like Lewis; when one of the characters cast a doubt as
to the whereabouts of another, His Distinction replied in perfect
Lewisian idiom.

'A doubt? Oh dear, no — no doubt at all! He is here, in Venice,
plying the modest but picturesque calling of a gondolier. I can give
you his address — I see him every day! In the entire annals of our
history there is absolutely no circumstance so entirely free from all
manner of doubt of any kind whatever! Listen, and I'll tell you all
about it.'

As His Distinction sang, Bradshaw and Fryer laughed the louder,
for the refrain contained words perfect either for Lewis' motto or his
epitaph:

> Of that there is no manner of doubt —
> No probable, possible shadow of doubt —
> No possible doubt whatever.

᪥

Barfield proposed a weekend walk along some chalky downs or
cretaceous hills with Lewis and Harwood. Harwood accepted, but
Lewis wrote back on Friday 10 June to say that he had a mountain of
papers to correct and, even if he hadn't, he had run a needle into his
foot. In swiftest retaliation, Barfield expelled Lewis from the College
of Cretaceous Perambulators. If he wished to be readmitted, he
would have to take a written examination. On the last night of the
walk, in the Red Lion Hotel, Basingstoke, Barfield and Harwood took
a piece of stationery and wrote a sample question. 'Who were: Owen
Glendower, Owen Nares, Robert Owen, Owen More, Owen Barfield,
Vale Owen, Owain, Ywain, Rowena, Bowen, Rovin', Sowin', Growin',
Knowin', and Gloin'?'

On their return, Lewis was presented with the entire examination. Part I, containing the questions, at least four of which, but no
more than six of which, he had to answer in sixty minutes, tested the

broad knowledge any cross-country perambulator might reasonably be expected to possess. ('"... *centre de Tourisme incomparable!"* MAUROIS. Justify this contemporary estimate of Cheltenham.') Part II was an essay on one of six topics, for which he was allowed forty minutes. ('The Quirinal — Its Uses and Abuses.') Part III was practical: 'Candidates will be expected to show reasonable proficiency in the game of darts, and to read a chapter to the satisfaction of a recognized bishop of the Established Church.'

Lewis decided that the best way to handle the chastisement by his friends was to take the examination seriously. He got an examination booklet, and feigning as best he could the script, syntax, and punctuation of an undergraduate, drove his pen across the page. 'Quirinals are things that no one would wish to take with him on a walking tour . . .'

✎

'Speak! Irene! Wife!'

Lewis was reading aloud from *Irene Iddesleigh*, a novel by Amanda M'Kittirick Ros. He had invited the pupils who had taken the final exams to dinner in his rooms. After the scouts cleared away the dishes, while all were enjoying postprandial spirits, he plucked from his shelves the nineteenth-century novel and challenged all present, beginning with himself, to read at random from the book for one minute without laughing.

'Do not sit in silence and allow the blood that now boils in my veins to ooze through the cavities of unrestrained passion and trickle down to drench me with its crimson hue . . .'

Peter Philip was not there. As his third year at university came to a close and final examinations approached, he quailed. Sympathetic to the young South African, Lewis wrote to his father to recommend a fourth year; he also volunteered to make the arrangements with the university.

Bradshaw was there. He had taken the final exams, but he had not got a first. The tutor was surprised, the pupil dismayed. Some months later when Bradshaw asked Lewis for a letter of recommendation, the tutor was able to write quite warmly about his former pupil. 'His scholarship is accurate and sensitive, and he is sufficient of a musician and musical historian to illuminate his literary studies from that neglected angle. He is a *very* agreeable man to work with, and I can recommend him unreservedly.'

✎

'Tollers, there is too little of what we really like in stories,' said Lewis on more than one occasion. 'I am afraid we shall have to write some ourselves.' They considered themselves *mythnomers* or *mythonomers*; they made plans to write some excursionary thrillers into which, for their own amusement, they would smuggle mythopoeic elements, even thimbleful of theology. Lewis had staked out 'a space journey' and in what seemed no time at all finished *Out of the Silent Planet*. Tolkien wished his friend didn't write so quickly; he himself at a more leisurely rate confected a 'time journey' entitled *The Lost Road*. Beseeched by Allen & Unwin for a novel to follow the success of *The Hobbit*, he sent it to London even though it was still a work-in-progress; even if he were to finish it, came word from his publisher, it would not be commercially viable. He put it aside and turned his efforts towards *The Lord of the Rings*.

Buoyed by the good reviews his space journey was getting, Lewis decided that he would try a time journey. 'If there is to be any more space-travelling, it would have to be time-travelling as well . . . !' That was the last sentence of *Out of the Silent Planet*, and from that he developed the first sentence of a work tentatively entitled *The Dark Tower*. ' "Of course," said Orfieu, "the sort of time-travelling you read about in books — time-travelling in the body — is absolutely impossible." '

∽

'Look, Prisca!' squealed the nine-year-old girl as a dancer in red tights whirled across the stage. 'There's Professor Tolkien!' She had come to the playhouse with Priscilla Tolkien, also nine years of age, to see the Professor perform a solo of sorts. But he wasn't playing King Mark in a ballet based on *Tristram and Iseult*; that was an undergraduate. The professor was going to read a long Chaucerian passage faithful in pronunciation to the fifteenth century.

It was August. A number of diversions or entertainments had been planned for presentation at the Playhouse during the first week of the month. Three plays would be presented by collegiate dramatic societies. There would be two concerts by the Oxford Chamber Orchestra. There would be the ballet and a festival of narrative poetry recitation. John Masefield had been involved in orchestrating the diversions for the last fifteen years; this year he asked Coghill to help. Coghill passed on to Lewis the letter inquiring about a fresh narrative poem by a contemporary poet with a good amateur voice. On 17 May Lewis replied to Masefield that he did indeed have such a poem and that it was entitled 'The Queen of Drum.'

'Please let me say now that I have greatly enjoyed it,' wrote Masefield after reading the poem twice, 'and feel an extraordinary beauty in the main theme — the escape of the Queen into Fairyland.'

Since the poem had five cantos and ran to some 1,500 lines, Lewis suggested that he read only the first two or three cantos, 500 or 700 lines, and that the audience be invited to suggest how it might end.

After reading the poem a third time, Masefield felt that the second canto was wrong and that the Archbishop made a saga all by himself.

Did he still want to use the poem in the diversions? Lewis had to ask.

Of course, replied Masefield. 'It is a very fine thing, and very beautiful; but the great difficulty is one of length.' He asked Lewis to cut it to forty minutes; modern audiences, if past experience meant anything, began to 'squirm and shuffle' after that time.

The first and the last cantos, 600 lines, Lewis decided to read, and perhaps some of the second.

～

Many of Lewis' academic acquaintances denounced what they considered lowbrow books, *Out of the Silent Planet* among them. They could not have acquired the wherewithal to denounce, assumed Lewis rightly, if they had not already read the books and indeed derived some enjoyment from them. They would welcome, assumed Lewis wrongly, a theory that would justify the perusal of lowbrow books and still preserve for the highbrow readers some measure of immunity.

Lowbrow books were characterized by adjectives like 'popular,' 'common,' 'commercial'; they were certainly cheap, trashy, and trivial; they provided escape, diversion, mere entertainment; and, presumably, they were bad. Highbrow books, on the other hand, were characterized by adjectives like 'literary,' 'classical,' and 'serious'; they were certainly grave, weighty, and momentous; they offered artistic, aesthetic, or spiritual satisfaction; and, presumably, they were good.

Using Haggard's *She* as an example, a novel he had enjoyed reading more than once, Lewis immediately conceded its lowbrow style and dialogue, but he asserted that the work had a theme that was alluringly presented and a narrative that wouldn't stop. It was a lowbrow book, all right, but it was not a bad book. It was a book that was good in some respects and bad in others. As analysis of other books would show, there were both good and bad highbrow and lowbrow books.

In an essay he was writing, which he would read to the English Society, Lewis went on to point out that the highbrow books of today were most often those that had been lowbrow when first published, like the novels of Fielding and the plays of Shakespeare, like the poems of Ovid and the plays of Molière. If he could find out what the passage of time did to books, he felt, he would then know something about the nature of highbrow and lowbrow. Time certainly added a patina to some works of rich construction. Time even made the reading of most works more difficult; the older the book was, the longer the commentary that seemed to be needed.

But would time make a lowbrow book less vulgar? Less vulgar, not in the sense of base, mean, ignoble, but in the sense of not subtle, not delicate, not many-sided? But literature, argued Lewis, ought to be vulgar. 'It ought to deal strongly and simply with strong, simple emotions: the directness, the unelaborate, downright portraiture of easily recognizable realities in their familiar aspects, will not be a fault unless it pretends to be something else. If it essays, without delicacy, that which demands delicacy, it will then become faultily vulgar . . .'

All attempts to divide books into two categories have to fail, he concluded, because the distinction between highbrow and lowbrow rested 'upon a confusion between degrees of merit and difference of kind.'

∽

War in Europe was fast approaching, as events in Munich seemed to indicate. It upset Lewis to discover how attached he had become to his books, his friends, his daily round. 'If we are separated, God bless you, and thanks for a hundred good things I owe you, more than I can count or weigh,' he wrote on 12 September to Barfield. 'In some ways, we've had a corking good time these twenty years.'

About a Christian's bearing arms in defence of his country, he had no qualms. Indeed he would offer several good reasons to anyone who needed them, but the stark reality of war as he had experienced it once was less than comforting. 'I was terrified to find how terrified I was by the crisis,' he wrote on 5 October to Griffiths. 'Pray for me for courage.'

∽

Lewis thought it odd that he, 'a layman and a comparatively recently reclaimed apostate,' should be invited by a religious society to say a few words on Christianity and literature. There really wasn't much to say. The rules for writing a good passion play or a good devotional lyric, it seemed obvious to him, were simply the rules for writing tragedy or lyric in general. Success in sacred literature, he was convinced, depended on the same qualities of structure, suspense, variety, diction, and the like that secured success in secular literature. In framing his letter of rejection, however, he did think he might say something about the Christian approach to literature; the society replied that it looked forward eagerly to the result.

If he juxtaposed certain ideas in the New Testament with certain key words in modern literary criticism, he just might begin to develop some principles of Christian literary theory and criticism. But when in the course of the address he had laid the biblical passages dealing with the hierarchy of creation and the imitation of Christ over against assumptions like 'creativity', 'originality', and 'spontaneity', he hoped to find some contradictions. He didn't. What he did find was a great difference of temper.

'A man whose mind was at one with the mind of the New Testament would not, and indeed could not, fall into the language which most critics now adopt. In the New Testament the art of life itself is an art of imitation. Can we, believing this, believe that literature, which must derive from real life, is to aim at being "creative," "original," and "spontaneous"?

'"Originality" in the New Testament is quite plainly the prerogative of God alone; even within the triune being of God it seems to be confined to the Father. The duty and happiness of every other being is placed in being derivative, in reflecting like a mirror. Nothing could be more foreign to the tone of scripture than the language of those who describe a saint as "a moral genius" or a "spiritual genius," thus insinuating that this virtue of spirituality is "creative" or "original".

'If I have read the New Testament aright, it leaves no room for "creativeness" even in a modified or metaphorical sense. Our whole destiny seems to lie in the opposite direction, in being as little as possible ourselves, in acquiring a fragrance that is not our own but borrowed, in becoming clean mirrors filled with the image of a face that is not ours.'

⤜ 1939 ⤛

On 6 February a five-thousand-line poem entitled *Flowering Rifle* was published in London by Jonathan Cape. The author, Roy Campbell, was not unknown to Lewis. He had arrived in Oxford in October 1919 from South Africa, hoping to enter Merton College. After several desultory years, he abandoned the degree course and the university town to earn a living as a poet. *The Flaming Terrapin*, an allegorical poem about Noah and his arkful being towed halfway around the world to Europe by a turtle of intermittent flame, was published to some notoriety in 1924. His subsequent persona as a sort of white Zulu with flowing hair and colourful clothes made him a darling of the London literary set. He was a drinking and a fighting man; like a lion he laid the females that paused in his path. But when he learned in November 1927 that his wife Mary was attracted to, indeed had been seduced by, Vita Sackville-West, the news was like a spear to his heart. 'Fancy being cuckolded by a woman!' When someone in a pub said this to Campbell, he stormed out into the night, victim of yet another shaft, this one right in the centre of his pride.

Flowering Rifle was subtitled 'A Poem from the Battlefield,' and the preface ended with the words VIVA FRANCO! ARRIBA ESPAÑA! The poem itself praised the nationalist forces and attacked such republican opposition as 'Charlies,' 'Wowsers,' and 'rednecks.' It was flooded with propaganda, repetitious as though hastily written and never reread; the couplets were as clumping as the hoofbeats of Franco's cavalry. Lewis' reaction to the book was instantaneous and uncomplimentary; he framed his remarks in poetic form:

> Rifles may flower and terrapins may flame
> But truth and reason will be still the same.
> Call them Humanitarians if you will,
> The merciful are promised mercy still . . .
>   . . . — who cares
> Which kind of shirt the murdering party wears?
> Repent! Repent! Some feet of sacred ground,
> A target of both gangs, can yet be found . . .

On 1 April Franco won unconditional and complete victory, and in the 6 May issue of *The Cherwell* magazine, Lewis' poem appeared.

Lewis felt a sort of call to arms. Against the six conditions for a just war laid down by theologians, and reported by E. L. Mascall in 'The Christian and the Next War' in the January issue of *Theology*, he mounted a counterattack. He fired off a longish letter in which he took a number of exceptions and made a number of distinctions. But the practical question, it seemed to him, had to do with authority. Who decided that the preconditions of war had been fulfilled? There were at least two answers. The first, the modern answer, was that the private conscience of the individual was empowered to make the decision, and that each one could make it for oneself. But another answer, an older answer, was that 'the ultimate decision as to what the situation at a given moment [was] in the highly complex field of international affairs' had to be delegated. He went on to point out that Christendom had made at least two efforts to handle the evil of war, chivalry and pacificism, and that if chivalry's record was bad, pacifism's was worse. Perhaps there was a third way. Perhaps if all Christians bore arms, they would be in a position not to obey orders that were clearly anti-Christian. 'I feel certain,' he concluded his letter to *Theology*, 'that one Christian airman shot for refusing to bomb enemy civilians would be a more effective martyr (in the etymological sense of the word) than a hundred Christians in jail for refusing to join the army.'

Having expressed the concept of bravery so forcefully, he immediately felt brave himself. He was still subject to military recall until 29 November, his forty-first birthday. But as he expressed to Griffiths in a letter on 8 May, he was soon overcome with fear. 'My memories of the last war haunted my dreams for years. Military service, to be plain, includes the threat of every temporal evil . . . I'm not a pacifist. If it's got to be, it's got to be. But the flesh is weak and selfish, and I think death would be much better than to live through another war.'

He seemed to draw some consolation from prayer, especially from meditation on Christ's agony in the garden of Gethsemane. So much had to be suffered, so much had to be gone through; suffering and death must come before resurrection; the cross preceded the crown. It made him tremble with fear. Expectation there was and even in the face of the promises of the New Testament, there was not a little fear. 'The process of living seems to consist in coming to realize truths so ancient and simple that, if stated, they sound like barren platitudes. They cannot sound otherwise to those who have not had the relevant experience: that is why there is no real teaching of such truths possible, and every generation starts from scratch.'

$\backsim$

'In his brilliant essay on "The Personal Heresy in Criticism" printed in last year's *Essays and Studies* of the English Association,' wrote E. M. W. Tillyard, fellow of Jesus College, Cambridge, 'Mr C. S. Lewis mentioned my *Milton* as a book in which poetry was treated as the expression of personality.'

Lewis had originally delivered his remarks on the subject at a meeting of the Martlets in 1930. When later he submitted the manuscript to Eliot's *Criterion*, he had to wait more than a year before it was rejected. He then submitted it to *Essays and Studies*, where it was published in 1934. Tillyard was moved to reply; his rejoinder appeared in the 1935 volume of the same journal.

'I do not say that much of Mr Lewis' essay is not extremely provocative and controversial. With some of it I disagree; and as the matters of disagreement seem to me well worth dwelling on, I offer the comments that follow.'

'Dear Dr Tillyard,' replied Lewis in an open letter, which was published in the 1936 issue of *Essays and Studies*. 'A friend of mine once described himself as being "hungry for rational opposition." The words seemed to me to hit off very happily the state of a man who has published doctrines which he knows to be controversial, and yet finds no one to voice the general disagreement that he looked for. It was with just such a hunger that I sat down to read your formidable "Rejoinder" to my essay on the "personal heresy." In such matters to find an opponent is almost to find a friend; and I have to thank you very hastily for your kind and candid contribution to the problem.'

Lewis was not an athlete. He did not play rugby as an under-graduate nor as a tutor did he countenance rowing as a reason for a pupil's absence. Yet his sporting instinct was aroused by an academic controversy such as this; he approached it aggressively and with a will to win, yet not without litotes here and there and a helping hand to the other side.

'As I glance through the letter again,' he wrote in conclusion, 'I notice that I have not been able, in the heat of argument, to express as clearly or continuously as I could have wished my sense that I am engaged with "an older and a better soldier." But I have little fear that you will misunderstand me. We have both learnt our dialectic in the rough academic arena where knocks that would frighten the London literary coteries are given and taken in good part; and even where you may think me something too pert, you will not suspect me of malice. If you honour me with a reply, it will be in kind; and then, God defend the right! I am, my dear sir, with the greatest respect, your obedient servant, C. S. Lewis.'

The controversy, which was now beginning to assume the aspect of a joust between two giants, Lewis championing Oxford and Tillyard championing Cambridge, left the printed page to continue in the public fora. The final result was six essays, three by each man, which, together with a co-authored preface, was published by Oxford University Press in 1939 under the title *The Personal Heresy: A Controversy*. Who won the annual jousts? Lewis felt that he had been unhorsed on more than one occasion. Tillyard felt that he had been hacked to mincemeat more than once. Readers and reviewers tended to take sides. 'Throughout the debate it is Mr Lewis who dominates the whole subject,' wrote Thomas Merton in the Sunday, 9 July edition of the *New York Times*, 'maintaining an intensity of conviction and a forcefulness of dialectic that his opponent cannot overcome. This is frequently so obvious, indeed, that Mr Tillyard seems only to be presenting a mere foil for Mr Lewis' ideas, which serves to clarify and strengthen them as the debate proceeds.'

∽

The Shakespeare Festival at Stratford-upon-Avon was celebrating its fiftieth year in 1939. The season began in the third week of April and would run until the middle of September. Eight plays were scheduled for presentation; among them was *The Taming of the Shrew*. On this play and some of the others, Lewis was invited to lecture in the middle of August. 'Can you supply me with any items?' he wrote on 23 July to Barfield. 'It is difficult to make that tedious farce the peg to hang something on.' He tried, but in vain, to arrange a weekend with his friend at or near Stratford, but Barfield was reluctant to leave his wife and children in London as war approached.

∽

'It is not easy to find the right type of story book for sisters who are resting or convalescing after illness,' wrote Sister Penelope Lawson on 5 August to Lewis. She was librarian at the convent of the Anglican community of St Mary the Virgin at Wantage, some fifteen miles southwest of Oxford. 'At ordinary times we do not read novels at all, as you may imagine; but the right novel at the right moment can have a real spiritual value.' She had read Mascall's review of *Out of the Silent Planet* in the April issue of *Theology*, ordered the book for the library, and was the first in the convent to read it. 'All along the line it provokes thought in just the directions where I have always wanted to think; and wherever it is most delightfully suggestive, one senses the most profound scriptural basis . . .' Enclosed with the letter was a copy of a book of hers, *God Persists*, a short survey of world history in the light of the Christian faith, which had just been published by Mowbray in Oxford.

'You will be both grieved and amused to hear,' wrote Lewis in reply on 9 August, 'that out of about sixty reviews only two showed any knowledge that my idea of the fall of the Bent One was anything but an invention of my own. But if there only was someone with a richer talent and more leisure, I think that this great ignorance might be a help to the evangelization of England; any amount of theology can now be smuggled into people's minds under cover of romance without their knowing it.'

The first reading of her book gave him great pleasure. He recommended other books to her, mostly by George MacDonald and Charles Williams, that might make convalescence more bearable if not more speedy. 'Though I'm forty years old, I'm only about twelve as a Christian,' he concluded his letter, 'so it would be a maternal act if you found time sometimes to mention me in your prayers.'

∽

At noon on Saturday 26 August Lewis and Dyson met at Folly Bridge and climbed down to Salter's Boatyard where they boarded the *Bosphorus*. Warren had arranged the trip in his boat some time before, but with the impending hostilities he was expecting to be recalled by the Royal Army Service Corps. To take his place, Jack commandeered Havard, who immediately volunteered to act as navigator. Up the Isis at the head of the Thames they motored, stopping for dinner at the Trout in Godstow. Germany and Russia had just signed a mutual non-aggression pact, but there was little talk of that. What gloriously arose was an argument about whether the Renaissance had really happened, Jack enjoying the negative. The next days were spent lazing through the countryside and sampling the riverside pubs. Buckland, Radcot, Lechlade, with a side trip to the Thames and Severn Canal.

Several days later they returned downstream. Whenever the engine sputtered and died, Jack and Hugo hopped ashore and began to tow the cruiser, Humphrey (as Havard was called) remaining at the helm. When the engine revived, they continued their trip and were able on Friday 1 September to lunch at the Trout. There, they heard the news that the Germans had breached the Polish border at eleven points at 4.45 a.m. and that the Polish cavalry had been shredded by the *Panzerdivisionen*. War for England, it seemed, was only hours away. They didn't talk much as they puttered back to Folly Bridge and tied up at Salter's. When they met that evening at the Clarendon Hotel for a conclusory dinner, Lewis argued the positive. 'Well, at any rate, we now have less chance of dying of cancer.'

∽

On 4 September Warren received a letter from the War Office, recalling him to active duty. It was, to him and to others, as though they had fallen asleep during the last war, had a delightful dream of some years' duration, and were just being rudely awakened. He went to Catterick, Yorkshire, to prepare for embarkation to the continent.

During the autumn Lewis kept his brother posted on developments on the home front. The government had decided not to take over New Buildings; therefore, he and the other fellows would not have to leave their rooms. Boys under twenty years of age were not yet being drafted; therefore, there would be a Michaelmas term. At morning chapel almighty God was already being invoked to prosper England's cause.

At the Kilns he was covering all the windows with dark material; marauding enemy aircraft would find nothing a-twinkle after dark on Shotover Hill. Children were being evacuated from London; the Kilns could accommodate as many as four, Mrs Moore decided; the first group had just arrived. The girls were nice enough, he reported; their carryings on brought him right back to his own childhood. One immediate disadvantage of the evacuees was that they all seemed to go to the eight o'clock service on Sunday morning. 'Surrounded by a writhing mass of bored urchins who obviously have no idea what's going on or why,' he found it even more difficult to sustain his devotion.

&

'A university is a society for the pursuit of learning. As students, you will be expected to make yourselves, or to start making yourselves, into what the Middle Ages called clerks: into philosophers, scientists, scholars, critics, or historians. And at first sight, this seems to be an odd thing to do during a great war . . .'

It was Sunday 22 October. Lewis, at the request of T. R. Milford, vicar of St Mary the Virgin, the university church since the thirteenth century, was preaching the sermon at evensong. Anxiety among the majority of undergraduates and not a few dons was running high. It was the second Sunday of the Michaelmas term. The church was packed before eight. The nave was dimly lit; the hymns were sung from memory; but there was enough light in the pulpit for Lewis to read from his prepared script.

'We are mistaken when we compare war with "normal life". Life has never been normal. Even those periods which we think most tranquil, like the nineteenth century, turn out, on closer inspection, to be full of crises, alarms, difficulties, emergencies . . . [Men] propound mathematical theorems in beleaguered cities, conduct metaphysical arguments in condemned cells, make jokes on scaffolds, discuss the last new poem while advancing to the walls of Quebec, and comb their hair at Thermopylae. This is not *panache*; it is our nature . . .'

The title of the sermon, which had been posted about the university beforehand, was 'None Other Gods: Culture in Wartime'; Lewis hoped it would indicate, to the biblically literate at least, that the men and women of Oxford, as Moses and Israel before them, should put none other gods between themselves and the Lord God, especially idols like culture and war. For the text of his sermon, he chose

'A Syrian to perish was my father' from Deuteronomy (26:5), a passage in which Moses described Jacob as being in danger of destruction and his people Israel as facing the possibility of annihilation.

'Before I went to the last war, I certainly expected that my life in the trenches would, in some mysterious sense, be all war. In fact, I found that the nearer you got to the front line, the less everyone spoke and thought of the allied cause and the progress of the campaign; and I am pleased to find that Tolstoi, in the greatest war book ever written, records the same thing — and so, in its own way, does the *Iliad* . . .'

Midway through the sermon he looked up and saw that the undergraduates were still there. They seemed attentive, but he remembered that the lads in 1742 hissed John Wesley out of the same pulpit after two hours, even though he was preaching the beginning of Methodism. He would not preach that long, and he would never again criticize Eliot for putting a sermon in the middle of *Murder in the Cathedral*.

'The learned life, then, is, for some, a duty. At the moment it looks as if it were your duty. I am well aware that there may seem to be an almost comic discrepancy between the high issues we have been considering and the immediate task you may be set down to, such as Anglo-Saxon sound laws or chemical formulae. But there is a similar shock awaiting us in every vocation — a young priest finds himself involved in choir treats and a young subaltern in accounting for pots of jam . . .'

Near the end of the sermon he identified three enemies that had always beleaguered scholars during wartime — excitement, frustration, and fear — and prescribed some mental exercises to strengthen them against sudden attack. He also defused simplistic notions about death that were lying about, and even suggested that death in wartime was better than death in peacetime; at least on a battlefield there was a reasonable prospect of dying without pain.

'But if we thought that for some souls, and at some times, the life of learning, humbly offered to God, was, in its own small way, one of the appointed approaches to the divine reality and the divine beauty which we hope to enjoy hereafter,' he said in peroration, 'we can think so still.'

Duplicated copies of the sermon were handed to the undergraduates as they tumbled into the aisles and out of the door of the south porch onto the High. *Age quod agis*, 'do what you are doing,' seemed to have been Lewis' message, a theme as old as asceticism itself; war and the threat of war could no longer be used as an excuse for unfinished assignments, for missed tutorials. A statute of St Mary the Virgin holding her child looked down on them from a niche above the porch, and looking down on her would have been two winged angels if their heads hadn't been victims of centuries of erosion.

⤠

In the middle of August Sister Penelope had sent Lewis a book. In gratitude, he had asked Sheed to send her a copy, complimentary if possible, of *The Pilgrim's Regress*. On reading it in October, she wrote to the author to inquire whether the tableland represented high Anglicanism or low. 'I'm . . . not what you call high,' he replied on 8 November. 'To me the real distinction is not high and low, but between religion with a real supernaturalism and salvationism on the one hand and all watered-down modernist versions on the other.'

⤠

'Are not all lifelong friendships born at the moment when at last you meet another human being who has some inkling . . .' It was Thursday night in Michaelmas term. Lewis was reading his latest composition to a roomful of friends. They were referring to themselves now as Inklings. The name was not original to them; it had been the name of an undergraduate literary society earlier in the decade; unused, it was arrogated by the donnish group who gathered weekly to read one another the fruits of their pens.

During the summer he got a letter from Ashley Sampson, an editor at Geoffrey Bles. Sampson had once had a press of his own, Centenary; Bles had bought it; now both Sampson and Bles were publishing, under a dual imprint, popular theological books with the series title 'Christian Challenge'. Having read and indeed relished *The Pilgrim's Regress*, Sampson invited Lewis to write a book for the series on pain. It was an unpopular subject, he acknowledged, but an important one; he thought Lewis might just be equal to the impossible task of producing an attractive book. Lewis agreed, but on one condition, that he write anonymously; he could not possibly live up to the principles he would have to enunciate. Prefaces were created for no other purpose, replied Sampson, than to reveal the author in all his nakedness.

'When I think of pain,' Lewis would insert somewhere in the manuscript, ' — of anxiety that gnaws like fire and loneliness that spreads out like a desert, and the heartbreaking routine of monotonous misery, or again of dull aches that blacken our whole landscape or sudden nauseating pains that knock a man's heart out at one blow, of pains that seem already intolerable and then are suddenly increased, of infuriating scorpion-stinging pains that startle into maniacal movement a man who seemed half dead with his previous tortures — it "quite o'er-crows my spirit." If I knew any way of escape, I would crawl through sewers to find it.'

He began to plan the book almost immediately. He would have to treat such divine attributes as omnipotence and goodness and such human realities as wickedness and pain in all its varieties. He would refer to Aquinas' *Summa Theologiae* and Luther's *Theologica Germanica*, to Kenneth Grahame's *Wind in the Willows* and James Jeans' *The Mysterious Universe*, to Traherne's *Centuries of Meditations* and Law's *Serious Call to a Devout Life*. He would mobilize such engines of rhetoric as syllogism and dilemma, analogy and antithesis.

The connection between pain and sin would surely have to be made, but it would be difficult to make it plausible to the casual Christian. The sense of sin so essential to Christianity seemed to have slipped in the last hundred years. Virtues like kindness and mercy were in the ascendant; rocketing from the depths of the new psychology were trajectiles like repression and inhibition. Their target, after the whistling had stopped and the plunge to earth begun, was the sense of shame so essential to Christianity. Once 'one of the ramparts of the human spirit,' it was now considered 'a dangerous and mischievous thing.'

What about animal pain? No one had treated that subject before in a serious book with theological pretension. Would there be animals in the afterlife? 'Where will you put all the mosquitoes?' Dyson would surely ask. 'A Heaven for mosquitoes and a Hell for men could very conveniently be combined,' Lewis could certainly retort.

What about Heaven? Scripture and tradition have habitually put the joys of Heaven into the scale against the sufferings of earth, he would argue; no treatment of the problem of pain that did not take this into account could be called a Christian one. 'There have been times when I think we do not desire Heaven, but more often I find myself wondering whether, in our heart of hearts, we have ever desired anything else.'

On Thursday 9 November all the Inklings were present, except Coghill. Dinner at the Eastgate, during which Dyson became 'a roaring cataract of nonsense', was followed by retirement to rooms, where Tolkien read a section from his sequel to *The Hobbit*; Williams, who had recently moved to Oxford, read a nativity play entitled *The House by the Stable*; and Lewis gave them another dose of *Pain*.

On Thursday 30 November only Lewis and Tolkien were free. That evening Lewis walked up High Street, turned left at Carfax, and walked down St Aldate's to Pembroke College, where Tolkien was now a professorial fellow. The quadrangle walls were covered with

Virginia creeper, leaves aflame from a late autumn. Upstairs the two men sipped gin and lime juice and read, Tolkien from his new work that would bear the title *The Fellowship of the Ring*, Lewis again from *Pain*.

All the Inklings had heard at least one of the chapters of *Pain* read aloud, except Warren; he was now at the No. 3 Base Supply Depot at Le Havre, France. Jack kept him informed of affairs at the Kilns and of the minutes of the Inklings, and was pleased to tell him that he was dedicating the book on pain to Inklings both near and far.

∽

'Good morning, Mr Lewis,' said the young man at the door of room 3. Christopher Derrick was his name; he was from Douai Abbey School, Woolhampton, Berkshire; he was applying for entrance to the university. Lewis ushered him in and immediately put him to the test.

'T. S. Eliot writing about *Paradise Lost* objects to Satan's speech to the Sun as being rhetorical. Would you care to comment?'

'I'll comment if I may, sir, by asking you two questions.'

'Good.'

'First of all, rhetoric was for a very long time a major part of a gentleman's reputation, a most important skill. When did the word "rhetoric" stop being properly used?'

'Good, good.'

'The other question is this, sir. We hear on this state occasion the Prince of Darkness addressing the orb of day. It is a great, an heroic, an epic moment. Would Mr Eliot prefer the diction used on such an occasion to be relaxed, slangy, conversational, American, or something like that?'

'Good, good, good. That will be all, Mr Derrick. You'll be hearing from us.'

Derrick left the room, glad that he had taken the trouble to get some coaching for the interview from Chesney Horwood of St Cat's. The next day he got in the mail a letter stating that he had been elected to a demyship, the highest undergraduate scholarship.

❧ 1940 ❧

On Thursday 1 February, the Inklings met in Lewis' rooms. Havard, the doctor of more than one person present, read 'a short paper on his clinical experiences of the effects of pain.' No Inkling was experiencing pain that evening, rum having been served at the outset. 'Pain provides an opportunity for heroism,' concluded Havard; 'the opportunity is seized with surprising frequency.' The paper was approved.

'The Inklings is now really very well provided,' wrote Lewis a few days later to his brother in France, 'with Adam Fox as chaplain, you as army, Barfield as lawyer, Havard as doctor — almost all the estates — except of course anyone who could actually produce a single necessity of life — a loaf, a boot, or a hut.'

❧

'There is some good poetry in the world, such as that of the Anglo-Saxons, which uses no similes. And there is some poetry, such as that of popular song, which uses about the same amount of simile as ordinary conversation: a woman is as fair as a flower, or a dancer as light as a leaf on a lime tree.' It was the night of Tuesday 13 February. Lewis was addressing the Oxford Dante Society on the simile as a fully fledged poetic device. He distinguished three classes of simile — and he proceeded to show, at the risk of 'breaking a butterfly upon the wheel', to demonstrate why he believed that Dante's poetry was the greatest he had ever read.

Afterwards some undergraduates gathered to test 'the fallacy of maximum differentiation' that Lewis had enunciated during the talk. 'A thing is most itself, in the sense of being most recognizable,' he had said, 'when it is most unlike everything else: but that does not mean that it is then in its best state.' They took some whisky and to find out whether it was a spirit, they applied a lighted match to it. Celebrating their discovery, they poured more whisky, splashed it with soda, and raised their glasses to Cézanne and Picasso, the painters whom Lewis seemed to identify as Italians.

❧

'Did you fondly believe — I did — that where you got among Christians, there at least you would escape from the horrible ferocity and grimness of modern thought? Not a bit of it.' Lewis was writing to his brother on 18 February, lamenting the fact that for 'people of the square-rigged type' like themselves, pocket battleships, *Untersee*

Boots, and other aspects of modernity like politics and economics were becoming 'too much'. Seeking respite one day he sailed into theology and, instead of finding sanctuary in the harbour, he was attacked. 'I blundered into it all, imagining that I was the upholder of the old, stern doctrines against the modern quasi-Christian slush; only to find that my sternness was *their* slush.' He was surrounded by talkers, clambering like 'Covenanters and Old Testament prophets' up and down his rigging; they did not think that 'human reason or human conscience' had any value at all; they even maintained that God's dealing with men had to appear neither as just nor merciful.

᯽

Of British policy, foreign or domestic, Lewis knew nothing. He bewailed the loss of happier days 'when politics meant tariff reform and war was with the Zulus.' He even wrote of starting 'a Stagnation Party, which at general elections would boast that during its term of office *no* event of the least importance had taken place.' But when a few young Christian intellectuals attacked Colonel Blimp and the businessman, he found fault with their logic. Replying in the 15 March issue of *The Guardian*, under the title of 'Dangers of National Repentance', he speculated that the businessman under the gun was their hardworking father, who paid their way through university.

᯽

'If I am a pacifist, I have Arthur and Alfred, Elizabeth and Cromwell, Walpole and Burke, against me. I have my university, my school, and my parents against me. I have the literature of my country against me, and cannot even open my *Beowulf*, my Shakespeare, my Johnson, or my Wordsworth without being reproved.'

He had been invited to address a pacifist society in Oxford. He accepted, although he thought he was the last person the undergraduates wanted to hear. He had no sympathy with the modern view that killing or being killed was 'a great evil'; his pupils, pacifist among them, knew it. Perhaps they wanted to test their rationalizations. Perhaps also they hoped to win this influential Christian to their side.

᯽

Griffiths sent an announcement of his ordination to Lewis, a small card adorned with a woodcut of Melchizedek. Lewis replied on 16 April, offering his congratulations, if that was the right word. Also he noted how appropriate Melchizedek was, 'a figure who might have been intended . . . for people who were being led to the truth by the peculiar route that you and I know.' With the note he enclosed a copy of his *Rehabilitations, and Other Essays,* which had just been published by the Oxford University Press.

∽

'A woman, an ex-pupil of mine called Mary Neylan,' he wrote as a postscript on the letter to Griffiths, 'seems in her last letter to be hovering on the brink of conversion to Christianity — a proper subject for your prayer.'

Neylan had written at some length shortly after the new year. She had apparently read the New Testament and was disappointed with what she found there. In the same situation he had read the gospels and was severely depressed by them. Lewis had been led to expect a lovable figure in the person of Jesus; instead, he met a stern and unbending one. He had been told that he would find moral perfection in Jesus, but why did Jesus accept a dinner invitation from a Pharisee only to drench him with a torrent of abuse?

'Now the truth is, I think,' replied Lewis on 26 March, 'that the sweetly-attractive-human-Jesus is a product of nineteenth-century scepticism, produced by people who were ceasing to believe in His divinity but wanted to keep as much Christianity as they could. It is not what an unbeliever coming to the records with an open mind will (at first) find there.'

In April she wrote to Lewis again, this time regarding the appropriate opinion a modern woman should have towards sex and marriage. Replying on the 18th, he thrashed the modern idea of a man and woman being in love as the basis of marriage. He preferred 'something universal and solid — the biological aspect', as expressed in the Prayer Book.

Words like 'sober and godly matrons' bothered a modern woman like Neylan. 'They may be a stickler if you haven't read the English school; but *you* ought to know that all the associations you are putting into it are modern and accidental. It *means* "married women" (matrons) who are religious (godly) and have something better and happier to think about than jazz and lipstick (sober).'

∽

They were having such a lovely time, the three schoolgirls from the Convent of the Sacred Heart in Hammersmith near London. Margaret, Mary, and Katherine had arrived at the Kilns in January; they would be leaving in July. Today it was warm and sunny; they were having lunch with Mrs Moore and Mr Lewis in the summer-house, which was not too many yards from the main house.

'Minto,' as Mr Lewis called Mrs Moore, who wore Victorian clothes and dangled a cigarette from her lip, ruled the roost like a fairy-tale stepmother. There were things the girls could do and could not do. They slept in the room above Lewis' library; they studied in a little bungalow on the grounds; they did not have dinner with the family; for supper they would have marie biscuits, apples, and milk.

'Boyboys,' as Mrs Moore called Mr Lewis, was more like an uncle. He showed them the books in his study, helped them with their homework, encouraged them to listen to his records. Armed with walking stick, adorned with deerstalker, he invited them for walks in the woods and occasionally for a stroll down to Headington where he bought them boxes of fish and chips. They were welcome for four o'clock tea at Magdalen; on May Day they were all at the top of the bell tower. Of an evening he might send food secretly up to the girls' bedroom or ask them across to his own bedroom, where they could search the skies through his telescope.

As they were eating lunch on that fine spring day, the sky grew overcast, and heavy rain began to fall. When everyone had finished, Mrs Moore called out to the parlour maid to fetch the umbrella and galoshes for Mr Lewis. Of all the people in the summerhouse that afternoon, he was the one who wouldn't get wet.

~

Was the poem rubbish, or was it 'an inevitable outcome, and an illuminating symptom, of the poet's repressions?' This was the question Lewis posed in a talk delivered at the invitation of the Martlets during Trinity term. 'Why, and how, should we read this poem?' which had once been the critical question, was being replaced by the newer, purely historical question 'Why did he write the poem?' or 'Impelled by what causes did he write it?' Freud was the father of the new literary criticism, and Lewis delved into his *Introductory Lectures on Psychoanalysis* both to expound the principles and to attempt a critique. Two Freudian positions were particularly prominent.

The first was that 'all art is traced to the fantasies — that is the daydreams or waking wish-fulfilments of the artist.' Lewis was quick to note that this was a theory as much about readers as about writers. He was quick also to distinguish, Freud having given him the lead, that there were two kinds of daydreams, one in which the dreamer was a character, but another in which he was not. Lewis admitted that he had had dozens of the former, but he could not recall a time when he did not have the latter. The self was present as hero in one sort of dream but was absent from another. In the one instance the imagination was free to produce 'the fantastic or mythical, or improbable type of literature.' In the other, the imagination was constrained to generate, 'what may, in a very loose sense, be called the realistic type.'

The second Freudian position was symbolism. Dreams contained images, of that there was no doubt, but were these images a sort of secret or symbolic language, which, once decoded, had universal meaning? Did a *house* really signify the human body; *kings and queens*, fathers and mothers; *fruit, landscapes, gardens, blossoms*, the female body or various parts of it? Eden, or Milton's description of it, Lewis was willing to concede, might contain latent sexual interest in the unconscious, but it also contained, he had to insist, a thousand other things. 'If it is true that all our enjoyment of the images, without remainder, can be explained in terms of infantile sexuality, then, I confess, our literary judgments are in ruins. But I do not believe it is true.'

~

Lewis was worried about his brother. Last September he had been recalled for military service; his spirit was willing, but his flesh went crawling. In October he was assigned to Le Havre. He had been in hospital twice for fever, in October and again in January. Jack kept him informed of events by letter, trying always to keep the news on the light side. 'I was going into town one day and had got as far as the gate,' he wrote on 21 April, 'when I realized that I had odd shoes on, one of them clean, the other dirty . . .'

In April Norway was invaded. In May the Low Countries were overrun. Neville Chamberlain resigned as prime minister on 10 May. Winston Churchill took his place; on 13 May he told the House of Commons that his policy would be war and his aim would be victory; in the meantime he promised 'blood, toil, tears, and sweat' in the immediate days ahead. In the second half of May, as German armies approached, French armies collapsed; British units fighting in support of the French were falling back to the channel cities of Calais, Boulogne, Dunkirk, and Le Havre.

Besides writing to Warnie, Jack could only say some prayers. Words came into his head, poetic lines; before long he was scribbling in his notebook.

> How can I ask thee, Father, to defend
> In peril of war my brother's head today,
> As though I knew, better than thou, the way,
> Or with more love than thine desired the end?
> When I, for the length of one poor prayer, suspend
> So hardly for his sake my thoughts, that stray
> And wanton, thrusting twenty times a day,
> Clean out of my mind the man I call my friend;
> Who, if he had from thee, no better care
> Than mine, were every moment dead. But prayer

Thou givest to man, not man to thee: thy laws
Suffering our mortal wish that way to share
The eternal will: at taste of whose large air
Man's word becomes, by miracle, a cause.

Evacuation from the ports continued, almost 400,000 from Dunkirk by 4 June, and by 12 June the port of Le Havre was in flames.

⟡

Were they, or weren't they? It was a balmy summer afternoon. Lewis and Williams were wandering in the meadow behind Magdalen when they came across, still in the middle distance, what appeared to be a couple *in flagrante delicto*. With delicacy they detoured through the high grasses. What the young people were doing was not at all clear to Williams. 'The boy's ass was pumping like a fiddler's elbow,' said Lewis. Who they were was not discernible from such parts of the anatomy as were visible. Lewis supposed they were undergraduates. Williams supposed they were married. Lewis was sure his editor-friend was naive.

Williams could have countered with something to the effect that if the incarnation had happened just once, just once then could a couple coupling in a field be married. Whatever he said, he would have argued vigorously, maintaining that sexual energy had immortal longings. He had put something like that in *Shadows of Ecstasy*, his novel which was published in 1933; in it the central character even stated that immortal energy could be found in Milton's verse. Not so long ago, on Monday 5 February he had extolled not only Milton's verse in general but also *Comus* in particular, because it contained a peculiar if little known form of energy called chastity. On the day, at 10.45 in the Divinity School of the university, in a beautifully carved room centuries old, he had addressed undergraduates and faculty alike. He did not begin with Middleton Murray, T. S. Eliot, or other contemporary critics, but rather with Milton himself, and developed a theme no other contemporary critic would touch: 'the sage and serious doctrine of virginity.' Not only was it criticism of the highest order, it was sermonizing as well. 'It was a beautiful sight,' wrote Lewis on 11 February to his brother, 'to see a whole room full of modern young men and women sitting in that absolute silence which can *not* be faked, very puzzled, but spellbound: perhaps with something of the same feeling which a lecture on *un*chastity might have evoked in their grandparents — the forbidden subject broached at last. He forced them to lap it up, and I think many, by the end, liked the taste more than they expected to.'

Dyson had not been present that morning in the Divinity School, nor indeed had he celebrated with Lewis and Tolkien at the Mitre afterward. But when he heard some weeks later that Williams had lectured on the unlecturable, he said he had heard it all before; indeed wasn't there a danger in speaking of so delicate a subject at all? 'The fellow's becoming a common *chastitute*!'

Detesting the liturgical music that he would have to encounter at the sung Eucharist at 10.30 a.m., Lewis regularly kept holy the Sabbath by attending Holy Communion at 8.00 a.m., the Rev. T. E. Bleiben officiating at Holy Trinity. Perhaps during, but certainly after, the service on Sunday 14 July, he got the image of a poor soul's making his life's pilgrimage escorted by a guardian angel on the one hand and on the other by a fallen angel. As Lewis walked up the hill from Holy Trinity to the Kilns, the image developed into a story with characters. The soul would probably be as much like himself as John in *The Pilgrim's Regress* was. The narrative would begin with the man still young. He would be either an atheist or an agnostic, but theism would be fast approaching, followed not long after by conversion and commitment to a church. He would have an overbearing mother not unlike Mrs Moore, but unlike Lewis he would eventually marry a nice Christian girl. Back from the 'blood feast,' as Mrs Moore liked to call the communion service, he went to his library and looked for his copy of *Confessions of a Well-meaning Woman* by Stephen McKenna. An epistolary novel published in 1922, it contained twelve letters from the heroine to a 'friend of proved discretion.' The letter-writer was humourless, but the work itself managed to be quite humorous; there seemed to be a 'moral inversion — the blacks all white and the whites all black.' Perhaps this was the sort of format that would be appropriate for his story.

War, of course, would be raging — the story being set in the present — and the young man would have to entertain such possibilities as patriotism and pacifism. Bombs would fall, death would be imminent, choices would have to be made. But the real battle would be taking place, not on British or European soil, but in the spiritual firmament. Good angel might have to do battle with bad angel. Instead of trying to create a blitzkrieg of Miltonic proportions, however, Lewis decided to pitch the battle at a somewhat lower level.

'The idea,' he wrote on 20 July 'would be to give all the psychology of temptation from the other point of view.' That not only would make the story more interesting but also would enable him to say something about the nature of Hell. Hell would have to be 'something like the bureaucracy of a police state or the offices of a thoroughly nasty business concern' with 'clean, carpeted, warm, and well-lighted offices' run 'by quiet men in white collars and cut fingernails and smooth-shaven cheeks who do not need to raise their voice.'

He then created a lowerarchy, which no doubt enjoyed the 'miserific vision,' and assigned specific tasks. Triptweeze, Toadpipe, and Scabtree were names that had a devilish ring about them. Tempters there would be: Glubose would harangue the young man's mother; Slumtrimpet would harass his wife. Slubgob would head the Training College. Wormwood, just graduated from that ignoble institution, would be assigned to the young man. For advice the stripling tempter would correspond with his uncle, a tempter of no small reputation, now elderly and retired, but able still to sign himself 'his Abysmal Under Secretary, Screwtape, T.E., B.S., etc.'

Lewis took some notepaper, sat down at his desk, and dipped his nib into the ink. 'My dear Wormwood.' It was as though he were writing to one of his friends; his pen fairly flew across the page.

∽

At half-past midnight on Saturday 10 August, he put the armband on his left arm and left Magdalen. The street lamps were dark, but he had no trouble finding his way up the High. The moon was shining. He was heading for a rendezvous; there was no telling how many men he'd meet; since he had only two sandwiches, he decided to eat them on the way. He was a member now of the auxiliary defence force initiated by the prime minister. Middle-aged men like himself, fit and hearty and having served with distinction in the Great War, Churchill had decided to mobilize. There had to be half a million of them on the island. With whatever weapons they could find — shotguns and hunting rifles; bayonets squirrelled away after the armistice; even golf clubs, crowbars, pitchforks — they would watch for the invasion that would surely come.

At Carfax he turned left and headed down St Aldate's. He had heard that some members of the Home Guard, albeit in London, used rollerskates to propel themselves around the city, the quicker to confront the Nazis should they suddenly materialize from the skies. Skating down St Aldate's, however, whether in daylight or moonlight, would be a perilous proposition; no doubt someone in the Oxford Home Guard would soon suggest it. Past the Town Hall and Christ Church, past the post office and the police station, walking down the hill, he stiffened somewhat, his stride lengthened, and he found himself marching, the cadence in his ears, the drill sergeant shouting to come on then, bawling that he was slower than the second coming of Christ!

Approaching Folly Bridge he broke step, an army of one, and

crossed the Thames. For no special reason as he walked, he remembered Wallie, a company commander in the Great War; he was 'a farmer, a Roman Catholic, a passionate soldier', the only man he had ever met who loved to fight and capture and kill. There were four or five turnings before he reached Lake Street. Simple enough in the daylight, but someone with a sense of what it was like to be a stranger in a foreign country had removed the street signs. Jerry, if and when he should invade, would not be able to tell precisely where he was. Like a tourist he would have to stop to ask directions. By that time some member of the Home Guard would have poured sugar in his petrol or hurled a grenade loaded with paraffin.

Sergeant Ayres, a dear man from the Great War, Lewis also remembered as he walked; an ordinary man who, when he found that his lieutenant was utterly hopeless, suggested deferentially what the better military option would be. When Lewis asked, why not poop a rifle grenade towards a German post not so far away, 'Just as 'ee like, zir,' replied Ayres; 'but once 'ee start doing that kind of thing, 'ee'll get zummit back, zee?' And that was indeed what happened. The shell that wounded Lewis in the back provoked the shell that killed Ayres.

At Lake Street arm badges were checked; names were ticked off by the light of a torch; general strategy was discussed. No gas masks yet, but each man was issued a rifle; it was made in America, and needed wiping off, having been stored in grease for the last twenty years; ten cartridges were allowed each man; more would be forthcoming if the going got hot. At precisely half-past one Lewis and his companions crossed St Aldate's and ambled across cricket fields towards the Thames. The rifle was heavier than he remembered. Soon they reached the verandah of a college pavilion, where, with a wide view of the Oxford savannah, they perched for a while.

It was a mild night, some wind, more than enough moonlight for an aerial invasion. But no parachutists descended, no gliders bounced to the ground, no U-boat surfaced on the shallow Thames. As three o'clock became four, cool met damp; condensation appeared across the cricket grounds. In the far distance, Lewis saw, or thought he saw, field-grey figures, perhaps as many as sixty, moving towards him, wearing military uniforms — Germans all right — but with no weapons, their hands in the air. They wanted to surrender, Lewis remembered from the Great War; even now, twenty-two years later, he did not point his rifle at them.

Talk, such as it was among the Home Guardsmen, turned to war and the philosophy of war. Was this the one that would end all wars? They thought not. Would human misery ever be abolished from the face of the earth? There was some discussion; Lewis thought not; the man with some schooling thought not. 'Then,' asked the labouring man of the moonlit meadow, 'what's the good of the ruddy world going on?'

On 16 August Warren got what he had been so ardently hoping for. With the rank of major now, he was transferred from active service to the reserve of officers. He left Wenvoe Camp in Cardiff and headed for Oxford where he promptly joined the Sixth Oxford City Home Guard Battalion.

On Tuesday 27 August Maureen Moore, aged thirty-four, married 'a music master called Blake,' wrote Lewis to Greeves; 'a very small, dark, ugly, silent man who hardly ever utters a word — which is perhaps just as well for anyone married to such a chatterbox as Maureen!'

In September two more evacuees walked up the road to the Kilns. 'Are you the gardener?' asked Patricia and Marie José, also known as Microbe because of her interest in germs. The shabbily clad, rather portly gentleman in the yard roared with laughter. 'Welcome, girls,' said Lewis and ushered them into the house. He showed them his books and his records; he encouraged them to use them often and well. Mrs Moore, now that she was a daughter short, helped the girls settle in. He now had 'a houseful of really delightful children refugees,' he would write a friend; 'I am a bachelor and never appreciated children till the war brought them to me.'

'I once had a patient, a sound atheist, who used to read in the British Museum. One day, as he sat reading, I saw a train of thought in his mind beginning to go the wrong way. The Enemy, of course, was at his elbow in a moment. Before I knew where I was, I saw my twenty years' work beginning to totter . . .' It was a Thursday night in Michaelmas term; Lewis was reading from the first letter of Screwtape to Wormwood. 'If I had lost my head and begun to attempt a defence by argument, I should have been undone. But I was not such a fool. I struck instantly at the part of the man which I had best under control and suggested that it was just about time he had some lunch.'

The concept of a senior devil instructing a junior devil in the act of temptation was amusing enough, but could he really carry it off in a roomful of men who were already Christians? Sentences like, 'We have trained them to think of the future as a promised land which favoured heroes attain — not as something which everyone reaches at the rate of sixty minutes an hour, whatever he does, whoever he is' were welcomed with warmth. Sentences like, 'The age of jazz has succeeded the age of the waltz, and we now teach men to look like women whose bodies are scarcely distinguishable from those of boys' were greeted with enthusiasm. Sentences like, 'I have known a human defended from strong temptations to social ambitions by a still stronger taste for tripe and onions' sent the Inklings rolling on the floor with laughter.

Human laughter, Screwtape would make the point in one of his letters, could lead one down the primrose path to the eternal bonfire. Like a scholastic philosopher he divided the causes of human laughter into joy, fun, the joke proper, and flippancy. 'You will see the first among friends and lovers reunited on the eve of a holiday . . . Fun is closely related to joy — a sort of emotional froth arising from the play instinct . . . The joke proper . . . turns on sudden perception of incongruity . . . But flippancy is best of all . . . economical . . . clever . . . always assumed to have been made . . . a thousand miles away from joy.'

'The long, dull monotonous years of middle-aged prosperity or middle-aged adversity,' wrote Screwtape to Wormwood, 'are excellent campaigning weather.' He might as well have been writing to the Inklings: Havard was thirty-nine; Tolkien, forty-eight; Dyson, forty-four; Warnie, forty-five; Williams, fifty-four; Lewis, forty-two. 'You see, it is so hard for these creatures to *persevere*. The routine of adversity, the gradual decay of youthful loves and youthful hopes, the quiet despair (hardly felt as pain) of ever overcoming the chronic temptations with which we have again and again defeated them, the drabness which we create in their lives and the inarticulate resentment with which we teach them to respond to it — all this provides admirable opportunities of wearing out a soul by attrition.'

'I am going to make my first confession next week,' wrote Lewis on 24 October to Sister Penelope, 'which will seem odd to you, but I wasn't brought up to that kind of thing. It's an odd experience. The *decision* to do so was one of the hardest I have ever made: but now that I am committed (by dint of posting the letter before I had time to change my mind), I began to be afraid of the opposite extremes — afraid that I am merely indulging in an orgy of egoism.'

Before this time auricular confession had been anathema to him, whether practised by Roman Catholics who told their sins to a priest or by itinerant evangelists who told undergraduates to confess their sins to each other. He had always wanted to attack the practice whenever he found it, but 'if you try to suppress it,' he wrote on 31 March 1928 to his father, 'you only make martyrs.'

'Well — we have come through the wall of fire,' he wrote on 4

November to Penelope, 'and find ourselves (somewhat to our surprise) still alive and even well. The suggestion about an orgy of egoism turns out, like all the Enemy propaganda, to have just a grain of truth in it, but I have no doubt that the proper method of dealing with that is to continue the practice, as I intend to do. For after all, everything — even virtue, even prayer — has its dangers and if one heeds the grain of truth in the Enemy propaganda, one can never do anything at all.'

∽

'The hero was half-sleeping by his bivouac fire in the woods while a redskin with a tomahawk was silently creeping up on him from behind . . .'

It was Thursday 14 November. Lewis was addressing an undergraduate literary society at Merton College on a subject he thought much neglected by literary critics, 'story considered in itself.' In ancient Greece Aristotle had concluded that story or plot was the most essential ingredient in a tragedy; in medieval Italy Boccaccio had developed an allegorical theory of story to explain ancient myths; in twentieth-century Switzerland Jung and his followers had produced a doctrine of patterns that were primordial and images that were archetypal. But there was more yet to be said about story; Lewis was using the tales of James Fenimore Cooper to prove his point.

A good story, he said, might be enjoyed in two different ways. First there was the feeling of excitement, 'the alternate tension and appeasement of imagined anxiety.' That was what a person got from the first reading of a book. 'Dangers, of course, there must be: how else can you keep the story going?' But then there was something else, which could be gained only from reading a book the second time. The unliterary person might read a book only once, he said, but literary men, like the ones listening to him that night, would read a book a second time; they would receive for their efforts 'certain profound experiences,' an atmosphere, even a new world. Dangers there were, but they were redskin dangers; it was the 'redskinnery' that the reader got the second time around, 'the feathers, the high cheek bones, the whiskered trousers.' What he wanted, and what he encouraged the undergraduates to want, was 'not the momentary suspense but that whole world to which it belonged — the snow and the snow shoes, beavers and canoes, warpaths and wigwams, and Hiawatha names.'

∽

'Dirty fingernails, a sluggish liver, boredom and a bad English style may often in a given case result from disobedience, laziness, arrogance, or intemperance.' Lewis was trying to put to rest an argument that had continued all too long, one that had begun in the March 1939 issue of the Anglican periodical *Theology*. In it Brother George Every argued for the necessity and even the excellence of a literary magazine entitled *Scrutiny* and inquired whether it was proper for a Christian, especially a Christian cleric, to have good literary taste and indeed possess culture, and further implied that it was alarming if he didn't.

Before reading the article, Lewis had given little thought to the question; now he felt he had to reply. In 'Christianity and Culture', which appeared in the March issue of that year, he immediately noted that sensitivity and good taste had never been marks of the one, true Church and that 'coarse, unimaginative people' were as likely to be saved as the 'refined and poetic.'

Then he surveyed the literature on culture, or at least the literature that he himself had read. The authors who claimed revelation 'seemed, if not hostile, yet unmistakably cold to culture.' Emitting varying degrees of warmth on the subject were authors who had to rely on reason: Greek philosophers like Aristotle and Plato, fathers of the Church like Augustine and Jerome, medieval clerics like Aquinas and à Kempis, Elizabethan playwrights like Shakespeare and Webster. Milton cast some shadows in *Areopagitica*; Newman shed some light in *University Education*; but Lewis was unable to make their conclusions his own.

He, therefore, felt that he had to construct his own argument. First, it was necessary to earn a living, which, for people like himself, meant working in cultural pursuits. Second, Christians like himself who earned their living as purveyors of culture acted as antidotes to those culturalists who were non-Christians. Third, cultural pursuits were rationally justifiable, but they weren't in and of themselves meritorious. Fourth, certain of the values inculcated by culture might be considered 'sub-Christian' in that they were almost, if not quite, Christian.

'Culture is a storehouse of the best (sub-Christian) values,' Lewis was able to conclude with some logic. 'These values are in themselves of the soul, not the spirit. But God created the soul. Its values may be expected there to contain some reflection or antepast of the spiritual values. They will save no man. They resemble the regenerate life only as affection resembles charity, or honour resembles virtue, or the moon the sun. But though "like is not the same," it is better than unlike. Imitation may pass for initiation. For some it is a good beginning. For others it is not; culture is not everyone's road into Jerusalem, and for some it is a road out.'

In the May issue of that year there was a ten-page reply to the positions he had taken; he hastened to write a letter, which arrived at *Theology*'s office in time for publication in the June issue. Every wrote a six-page rejoinder, which appeared in the September issue; it defended literary criticism. In reply Lewis penned a nine-page article entitled 'Peace Proposals,' stating that he did not see that his doctrines contradicted those of his critics; it appeared in the December issue. He did maintain that there were two kinds of good, one moral and the other literary, and that it was sometimes devilishly difficult to disentangle the two. Finally, there were bad reasons why a Christian, even a cleric, had bad taste and was uncultured, and there were even some good reasons.

'The man's ears may be unwashed behind, or his English style borrowed from the jargon of the daily press because he has given to good works the time and energy which others use to acquire elegant habits or good language. Gregory the Great, I believe, vaunted the barbarity of his style. Our Lord ate with unwashed hands.'

∾ 1941 ∾

It was with delight that Lewis got, in the first post of the year, a letter from Neylan. Although she had not satisfied all her objections to becoming a Christian, she had solved enough of them to take the big step. But something seemed to have gone wrong. After having climbed so long and so hard, she was out of breath, and an endless plateau seemed to stretch before her. 'Don't be worried about feeling flat, or about feeling at all,' he wrote to her on 4 January. 'And remember that religious *emotion* is only a servant.'

On receiving his letter she took his words to heart and wrote to thank him. But it was he who had to do the thanking. 'My own progress is so very slow (indeed sometimes I seem to be going backward),' he wrote to her on 29 January, 'that the encouragement of having in any degree helped someone else is just what I needed.'

∾

In recent weeks *The Guardian* had been printing much about the growing desire in the Christian minority for a party, a front, a platform in politics. With such a concept Lewis had grave difficulties; in the 10 January issue he made his case.

To throw his argument into bold relief, he characterized three different positions. Philarchus was convinced that monarchy worked. Stativus favoured democracy. Spartacus would be happy only with a leftward revolution. All three were devout Christians, but each, to achieve his political end, would accept some measure of aid from the enemy: the Fascist, the Communist, the Millionaire. Whichever of the three triumphed — they could not co-exist for long — Lewis did not seem to feel mattered; things would become different; they wouldn't necessarily become better.

At this point he introduced another character, the Devil, a sort of fourth columnist who was already at work in all three campaigns. He was disguising himself as the Holy Ghost and clouding Christian leaders' minds into thinking that 'treachery and murder' were allowable for a holy cause and that 'faked trials, religious persecution, and organized hooliganism' were necessary to maintain the new fabric. But all this, as Lewis hoped would be obvious, was nothing more nor less than taking the name of God in vain. Which was why he entitled the article 'Meditation on the Third Commandment.'

What, then, was a Christian supposed to do, form an inter-denominational Christian Voters' Society and write to members of Parliament, insisting that they operate on strictly Christian principles? 'Yes: just that. I think such pestering combines the dove and the serpent. I think it means a world where parties have to take care not to alienate Christians, instead of a world where Christians have to be "loyal" to infidel parties.'

There was, of course, another way. Christians could become the majority in England. 'He who converts his neighbour,' concluded Lewis, 'has performed the most practical Christian-political act of all.'

౼ౢ

'I write to ask whether you would be willing to help us in our work of religious broadcasting.' It was Monday, 10 February. Lewis had just opened a letter from the Rev. J. W. Welch, director of the BBC's religious broadcasting department. 'The microphone is a limiting and often irritating instrument, but the quality of thinking and depth of conviction which I find in your book ought surely to be shared with a great many other people; and for any talk we can be sure of a fairly intelligent audience of more than a million.' Lewis was amazed. He hardly listened to the radio and could not remember having heard a religious programme.

Welch suggested two possible topics. The first was 'the Christian, or lack of Christian, assumptions underlying modern literature'; Lewis felt he could talk about that. The second subject was 'a positive restatement of Christian doctrines in lay language.' 'Even if you feel you cannot help us in our work,' said Welch at the end of the letter, 'may I take the opportunity of thanking you for *The Problem of Pain*?'

It was the second subject that caught Lewis' fancy. He took up his pen and responded that he would indeed give some talks, but that they would have to be during the long summer vacation. 'The law of nature, or objective right or wrong,' he wrote, would be just right for him. New Testament writers assumed that the Hebrews knew this law even when they disobeyed it. 'In modern England we cannot at present assume this, and therefore most apologetic begins a stage too far on.' Christianity, if it were mentioned at all in the talks, would have to come at the end. 'Some title like "The Art of Being Shocked" or "These Humans" would suit me.'

~

In March 'a nervous, provincial, grammar-school boy' waited in a small book-lined study. From the Crypt School, Gloucester, he was about to be examined orally for a scholarship at Magdalen. Ushered into a large and pleasant sitting room, he found some dons sitting in armchairs. One, the one with the red face, asked him a question about Johnson. 'Which Johnson do you mean?'

'Oh, either.'

'I know nothing about either.'

But Derek Brewer answered enough questions that morning to be elected to a demyship. When he wrote to thank Lewis, he inquired what he should read before going up to Magdalen in the autumn. Lewis sent him suggestions; 'your book bill ought to be your biggest extravagance.'

~

On a cold, rainy night in Hilary term, Lewis in dressing-gown met two visitors in military uniform at his Magdalen door. They had been expected. After checking to see that the windows were securely shaded, they moved to the fire and warmed themselves with a drink. The two men — Rev. Maurice Edwards, chaplain-in-chief of the Royal Air Force, and Rev. Charles Gilmore, his assistant — told Lewis of the 'battle of Britain,' as it was beginning to be called. From July to October of the preceding year, when air fighting was over British soil, the fighter command had shot down or otherwise destroyed perhaps as many as 2,500 German aircraft. An astonishing victory really, against overwhelming odds. The RAF had losses too; perhaps as few as nine hundred; but that meant nine hundred British families were grieving; of course, the losses would continue as long as the war.

When Lewis asked what he could do, they replied that he could give a few lectures to the men at aerodromes, talk some religion, keep their spirits up. The government would, of course, pay his expenses; the fees for his lectures would be paid by the dean of St Paul's out of some monies at his disposal. In fact, it was the dean who had suggested Lewis in the first place.

Who would his audience be?

All would be in uniform. One quarter of them would be professional military. The others, civilians who had just joined up.

He couldn't speak to a group like that. He was just a professor who had trouble making himself understood by undergraduates who paid for the privilege of listening to him.

The RAF might be less intelligent than the average Oxford undergraduate, countered the chaplains, but for them there was a sense of urgency that would make them listen most attentively to Christian truths enunciated with the sort of clarity found in *The Problem of Pain*.

Where would he have to go? He couldn't travel far during term time.

Abingdon would be a good place to start.

When?

As soon as he was able.

It was against his better judgment to accept, but accept he did. When he arrived at Abingdon, about five miles south of Oxford, the first thing he saw was Nissen huts, hundreds of them. The first thing he heard was loudspeakers. Would he be able to speak over their din?

'I've no use for all that stuff!' An officer had just stood up in the middle of his talk, a hard-bitten old coot at that. 'But, mind you, I'm a religious man too. I *know* there's a God. I've *felt* him: out alone in the desert at night: the tremendous mystery. And that's just why I don't believe all your neat little dogma and formulas about him. To anyone who's met the real thing, they all seem so petty and pedantic and unreal!'

The man was telling the truth, thought Lewis on his way back to Oxford. When the officer turned from the desert to the creed, he was turning from something real to something less real, from the desert itself to something like a map of the desert. The real experience had been like a pushpin on a map. But if the man ever wanted to get out of the desert and back to England, if he ever wanted to build on that one-time experience, he would have to use that map. In a sense, cartography was a little like theology. That was what he should have said to the officer, he thought, as he trundled up staircase 3; his talk had to be classified 'a complete failure.'

'Thank you very much for the book. It has given me real help.' Sister Penelope had sent him a copy of her *Windows on Jerusalem*, which had just been published by Pax House; he was responding on 10 April. 'What I particularly enjoy in all your work, specially this, is the avoidance of that curious drabness which characterizes so many "little books on religion".'

When he learned that she had been lecturing the WAFS [Women's Auxiliary Fire Service], he wanted to compare her experiences with his at the RAF. She couldn't have been as bad as he thought himself. 'One must take comfort in remembering that God used an *ass* to convert the prophet,' he wrote to her on 15 May; 'perhaps if we do our poor best, we shall be allowed a stall near it in the celestial stable — rather like this.' He filled the rest of the piece of stationery with a drawing of an ass in the foreground, flanked by a figure in a wimple and a figure under a mortar-board; in the background was the heavenly city.

⁂

The wistaria was about to flower on the walls above the colonnade of New Buildings that spring afternoon. Two young men in military uniform had crossed from the cloisters and were about to enter staircase 3 when Lewis descended in academic gown and mortar-board. Fryer and Hewitt they were. Of course, he recognized them. He remembered all former pupils. But it was a bad time for him; he was on his way to a college meeting; he did have fifteen minutes; would they care to stroll down the colonnade?

Fryer went right to the point. He had a question about non-resistance to evil. Christ, it seemed, had offered 'an absolute and total prohibition of even forcible self-defence.' What about the hard case of a soldier defending his country?

'Most commands of high authority, even dominical authority, are laid down in universal terms which seem to admit of no exceptions,' replied Lewis in fulsome terms. 'But there are often necessary and justified exceptions where, if we followed the letter of the law, we should do — and encourage — more harm than if we diverged from it. All such commands must be taken *exceptis excipiendis*,' concluded Lewis; 'and one of them is the Lord's command to "resist not evil".'

It was almost 2.30. Lewis bade them farewell, inviting them back whenever they could make it, and darted across the grass towards the cloisters.

⁂

Early in May Lewis showed up at the BBC for a dry run. The Rev. Eric Fenn, a Presbyterian, whose job it was to supervise the preparation and delivery of the talks, gave him some printed material and pointed to a microphone. Lewis read; a recording was made. When it was played back, Lewis was flabbergasted. 'I was unprepared for the total unfamiliarity of the voice,' he would write to Greeves; 'not a trace, not a hint, of anything one could identify with oneself.' Fenn was impressed, though, but Lewis would have to read smoothly, continuously, with no pauses for rhetorical effect. In such interstices Lord Haw Haw, the British traitor broadcasting from German territory on BBC frequencies, was known to insert false, misleading, even insulting remarks.

Would the four Wednesdays in August be acceptable as broadcasting dates? When Lewis said yes, Fenn asked when the scripts would be ready. He had begun them, but why would Fenn need them so soon? Because they would have to be read by the censor. Changes were requested in most scripts; the changes themselves would have to go through the censorship process. Remember, said Fenn to Lewis as they parted, be as colloquial as you possibly can.

'Will this do?' wrote Lewis on 17 May. With the note he enclosed the manuscript of the four talks. 'I find the more colloquial you are in the actual talks, the harder it is to make a close précis.'

◈

After Lewis finished the thirty-first and final communication between Screwtape and his nephew Wormwood, he was urged by the Inklings to have a fair copy made of the manuscript and to send the sheaf off, maybe not to a publisher, but certainly to his friend at *The Guardian*. The editor liked both concept and execution; beginning with the 2 May issue, he published one a week; the last would appear in the 28 November issue. Two pounds was an appropriate fee for each letter; Lewis insisted that it be sent to a charity. Would a cheque for £62 to a fund for the widows of clergy be acceptable?

◈

'Mammon proposes an *ordered* state of sin with such majesty of pride that we are almost led astray,' wrote Lewis at the beginning of 'Satan's Followers', chapter fourteen of a book he was preparing for the press, *Preface to 'Paradise Lost.'* 'Perhaps Milton has touched here so essentially the nature of sin that if it were not for the suspicious *live to ourselves* (II,254), we should not recognize it as such, so natural is it to man.'

These sentences, however, were not his; they sounded like Williams' on *Comus*; but they were Muriel Bentley's. She was an undergraduate at Somerville College; he had read her persuasive comments in an examination paper. She gave him permission to quote when he asked, even though when she had asked him to take her on as a pupil in English literature, he refused. He didn't like female pupils, rumour had it; if it was any consolation, neither did Oxford, what with the debating union, even the chapel at Pusey House, being closed to them.

Lewis did take female pupils, though. There were the ladies of St Hugh's, Patricia Thomson and Rosamund Rieu. He rose when they entered his sitting room and treated them with some chivalry. That is, until the reading of the essay; then it was visors down, and one couldn't tell under all the mail who was the male and who the female.

He said she had reminded him of a Shakespearean heroine, commented Rosamund casually to Patricia as they went down staircase 3, but did he mean Rosaline in *Love's Labour's Lost* or Rosalind in *As You Like It*? It made a difference, the one being 'a wightly wanton with a velvet brow with two pitch balls stuck in her face for eyes,' the other having 'a pretty redness in [her] lip, a little riper and more lusty red than that mix'd in [her] cheek.'

∽

Early Sunday evening, 8 June, Fred Paxford, gardener, sometime cook, general factotum at the Kilns, drove Lewis down Headington Road and St Clement's, over Magdalen Bridge and up the High. Lewis alighted in front of St Mary the Virgin's. Solemn evensong was approaching; Milford had asked him to speak again. By the time Paxford parked the car and returned to the church, he had to fight his way in. The seats, the benches, the galleries, even the window ledges were hung about with undergraduates.

The vicar presiding, the organist intoned, the congregation sang, Lewis winced. How Screwtape hated 'that detestable art which humans called music', he couldn't help remembering, and how ironic that Screwtape would feel 'something like it occurs in Heaven'. When quiet descended the nave, Lewis ascended the pulpit — the very pulpit from which began not only Methodism but also the Tractarian movement — and placed his manuscript on the lectern. 'The Weight of Glory,' it was entitled. He began to read, his voice deep, his tone serious, his appearance cheerful.

Reward for Christians was Heaven, he stated, but he quickly pointed out how for a hundred years 'the evil enchantment of worldliness' had led people to believe that man's true home was on earth, that earth could be made into a sort of Heaven, or that if there were a heavenly Heaven, it was a long way off. Philosophies like progress and creative evolution promised happiness, but even if they could deliver it, he countered with a little logic, 'each generation would lose it by death, including the last generation of all, and the whole story could be nothing, not even a story, for ever and ever.'

He went on to articulate the spiritual longings of humankind. He paid special attention to desire, 'a desire which no natural happiness will satisfy', a 'desire, still wandering and uncertain of its object and still largely unable to see that object in the direction where it really lies.'

'Meanwhile, the cross comes before the crown, and tomorrow is a Monday morning,' he said at the end. He wanted the undergraduates to leave the church, not thinking about celestial glory, which would come at some unknown point in the future, but about practical charity towards one's immediate neighbour. 'The load, or weight, or burden of my neighbour's glory should be laid on my back, a load so heavy that only humility can carry it, and the backs of the proud will be broken.'

As Lewis stepped down from the pulpit, the organ swelled, the congregation sang 'Bright the vision that delighted', and the preacher beat a hasty exit onto the High.

'Give it to 'em all right,' muttered Paxford all the way home in the car; 'Mr Jack really give it to 'em!'

‿

The Screwtape Letters, which had been appearing every Saturday in *The Guardian*, caught the eye of Sampson, editor of *The Problem of Pain*. He convinced Bles that the *Letters* were a good publishing risk and wrote to Lewis, offering him a contract, which would mean publication probably in the spring of 1942. Lewis was delighted. After the end of Trinity term he made yet another fair copy of the manuscript. Then he wrote a preface in which he stated that the correspondence had just fallen into his hands, that the Devil was a liar, and that the war the Devil was interested in was not the European one currently in progress. He slapped two epigraphs into the front matter, one from Luther to the effect that the best way to drive the Devil out is 'to jeer and flout him', the other from Thomas More to the effect that the Devil 'cannot endure to be mocked.' He dedicated the project to Tolkien. He dated the whole thing 5 July and sent it off in the mail to London.

‿

On Wednesday afternoon, 6 August, Lewis boarded the train at Oxford and headed south-east towards London. As the carriage coach clickety-clacked down the line, he looked over the typescript sent to him by the BBC. 'Right and Wrong as a Clue to the Meaning of the Universe' was the overall title of the four talks. When he arrived at Broadcasting House he was met by Fenn, who conducted him to a studio. They rehearsed the talk. As 7.45 approached, the studio door was closed. Lewis sat poised at the microphone. 'On the air' was flashed, Fenn gestured, Lewis began to read. 'Everyone has heard people quarrelling. Sometimes it sounds funny and sometimes it sounds merely unpleasant; but however it sounds, I believe we can learn something very important from listening to the kinds of things they say . . .

'A man occupying the corner seat in the train because he got there first, and a man who slipped into it while my back was turned and removed my bag are both equally inconvenient,' he said in his second talk on 13 August. He was dealing with the reality of the law of nature and sharing an experience that had happened to him more than once.

∽

'The classic English topic of conversation, the weather, has vanished for the duration,' wrote Mollie Panter-Downes in the summer to William Shawn, 'and now would be good for animated chat only in the event of a brisk biblical shower — of oranges, cheese, cornflakes, and prunes instead of manna.' She was a Londoner; he was editor of *The New Yorker*, publishing her reportage of life in the blitzed capital as often as her letters got through.

Between rehearsal and broadcast at the BBC, talk was often of food too. According to Fenn, the shelves at Fortnum and Mason were as appetizing as ever, but what good were sauces and chutneys if there were no fish or flesh or fowl to put under them?

From Oxfordshire Lewis brought news that things were not so bad. Eggs were plentiful if one had the hens; vegetables abounded if one had a victory garden; beer seemed to be flowing uninterruptedly from every tap in the shire. But Mrs Moore could still get a no from the shopkeeper when she asked for 'breakfast cereals, tinned jellies, biscuits, lemons, lime juice, honey, chocolate, and macaroni.'

'I've never been hungry yet — in fact, the only way it affects me is to plunge me back into the pleasures of early boyhood,' wrote Lewis to Greeves; 'I mean, food is a subject infinitely interesting, and every meal a highlight.'

∽

When he arrived at the BBC studios on 20 August, he handed Fenn the typescript of his talk. Pointing to the top of the first page, he whispered that the censor had better take a look. 'I must begin by apologizing for my voice,' the handwriting read. 'Since we last met, I've managed to catch an absolute corker of a cold.' When the light flashed, however, and the hand cue was given, he read without noticeable interruption for fifteen minutes, developing the reality he found behind the law of nature.

'Going back is the quickest way on,' he said in his fourth and final talk. It was 27 August; he was pointing out to an audience estimated at 600,000 people why he and they had cause to be uneasy. If they looked at the present state of the world, they would conclude that humanity was making 'some big mistake.' In this broadcast he was still on the prowl. He wasn't using the Bible or the churches to help him in his search; he was trying under his own steam to discover the somebody or something that was behind the universe, and the moral law that was in men's minds. From the latter he grew to conclude that someone or something was interested in decent behaviour and might in that sense be called good.

In September the British public felt they were being manipulated. What the press and radio were telling them to think was quite different from what they were really thinking about such topics as Churchill's secret meeting in the Atlantic with Roosevelt, Russia's chances against Germany, even food rationing and the rationing of clothes.

With regard to the last, the BBC did some propagandizing for the government. One announcer, a young woman, played stooge to another announcer. She affected to be a pretty housewife who wanted to buy bathing suits and other skimpy things instead of sturdier clothing with her sixty-six coupons per annum. Light-headed creature that she was, she would even forget the old ration book when it came time to apply for a new one. Exasperated but avuncular, the male announcer would chide her with such remarks as 'Cut your cloth according to your coupons' and, 'Never coupon today what you can put off till tomorrow.'

Of the audience who listened to Lewis' 'Right and Wrong' broadcasts in August, a goodly number took exception to some of the extraordinary claims he made about the natural law; they made their complaints known by writing to the BBC. Lewis answered them all by hand, except the one that began, 'Dear Mr Lewis, I was married at the age of 20 to a man I didn't love,' and the one that was signed 'Jehovah.' Somewhat alarmed but mostly delighted, Welch invited Lewis to respond on the air on Wednesday, 3 September, in the same time slot.

In the autumn of 1941 Lewis was listed as a lay lecturer on the staff of the chaplain's department of the RAF; as such he was available on weekends. The Rev. Stuart Barton Babbage wrote to invite him to travel to Norfolk, where he was chaplain of an aerodrome. Bomber squadrons took off nightly from the base to pound German forti-fications on the continent. An ordinary tour of duty consisted of thirty missions; thirteen was the sad average before a man was posted as killed or missing. He, the chaplain, could do with some help. Lewis replied by return, on a scrap of paper, that he would go the following weekend.

Babbage met him at the station that Saturday. They had supper in the officers' mess. Bomber crews were briefed. In the lull before taking off, some talked of death and what difference, if any, Christianity meant at the moment of death. Babbage encouraged those who sought him to think that Christianity gave 'a sense of inner peace, of confident trust, of quiet assurance.' Lewis, on the other hand, decided not to disagree with the men who felt that death was dreadful and that they had a right to fear it.

Early on Sunday morning Babbage officiated at Holy Communion; Lewis attended. After breakfast Babbage introduced the lay lecturer at a parade service. Lewis repeated his talk at another parade service held two miles away at a satellite station. Babbage was in cassock and surplice, scarf and hood; Lewis was in a suit, rumpled and wrinkled. He seemed puffy of face, pudgy of form, but when he spoke, he used no notes, and there was no amplification; his voice was lean and spare; he seemed to hold their attention.

After supper Babbage led Lewis to a recently constructed chapel. It had been donated by the manufacturer of aircraft turrets; its vaulted and timbered ceiling had a beautiful austerity about it; the king had dedicated it just a few months before. Pews filled; by the time the service began, the loft above the door, which had to be reached by ladder, was overflowing. Babbage presided at the lectern, which contained German shrapnel, the result of Luftwaffe strafing during the Battle of Britain. After the hymns, which were as interminable as they were bad, Lewis made the sign of the cross and gave as his text, 'If any man will come after me, let him deny himself, and take up his cross, and follow me.'

It was a hard text for men about to die. Lewis laid out what Jesus himself had undergone on the officers' behalf — 'misunderstanding and loneliness and finally betrayal and death' — and encouraged the men to think what they should do on Jesus' behalf. Whatever it would be, it would have to be costly. He went on to say how costly it had been for him to become a Christian. Oxford had tolerated his intellectual interest in Christianity, but when he showed signs of becoming a practising Christian, he lost friends and indeed suffered some measure of ostracism. At the end of the talk he returned to 'the calamities and indignities Christ endured' and how the soldiers had shouted 'Hypocrite!' 'Serves him right!' 'That's what he deserves!' 'Dirty traitor!'

∽

At the beginning of Michaelmas term, Magdalen found itself short of administrative talent. Paper had to flow; people had to be met if the college were to operate with any efficiency. Lewis was somehow drafted into becoming vice-president. He accepted reluctantly, and soon his worst fears were realized: 'committees, telephone calls, and interviews innumerable.' Then there was the correspondence. At least there was a secretary at the ready with a shorthand pad and sharpened pencils. Soon he tested the sweet delight of dictating ten letters in the time it took to write one by hand. But when the president fell ill in the middle of the term, the administrative load doubled.

∽

Lewis had deliberately ended *Out of the Silent Planet* in ambiguity, but he had kept his characters alive. When he began earlier in the year to make notes towards a sequel, he decided to revive some of them. There was Elwin Ransom, the Cambridge philologist, a seeker after truth. There was Weston, the mad scientist, drunk with the latest philosophical theories. There was himself, the Oxford literary critic and historian, physically inept, but intellectually adept enough to assist the narration of the story.

The plot would begin on earth, or Thulcandra, the silent planet; it would still be a bad planet, ruled by the Bent One. Ransom would be propelled — not without some flak from the Dark Lord, the Depraved Oyarsa of Tellus — by means of a celestial coffin. Destination would be Venus, or Perelandra, as it was known in Old Solar. That would be the first chapter. Ransom would return in the second chapter and be attended by a physician named Humphrey. By the third chapter Lewis would be narrating Ransom's adventures as if they were told to him.

∽

Defending the faith was taking its toll. The more he described belief and how it worked, the less he seemed to believe. There were no intellectual difficulties to speak of, but continuing belief seemed to demand too much spiritual energy. 'I think what really worries me is the feeling (often on waking in the morning) that there is really nothing I *dislike* so much as religion — that it's all against the grain, and I wonder if I can really stand it. Have you ever had this?' he asked Sister Penelope.

∽

Fenn had the scripts of Lewis' new series of radio talks, entitled 'What Christians Believe,' in his hands by the first of December; by the 5th he was able to reply that they were first class. 'There is a clarity and exorableness about them, which made me positively gasp!' So much for the Presbyterian point of view; he had sent copies of these talks to, and was still waiting to hear from, Bede Griffiths, a Catholic priest, and Joseph Dowell, an RAF chaplain who was a Methodist.

~

'This club is long overdue!' wrote Lewis with enthusiasm to Stella Aldwinckle, who served in a pastoral capacity at Somerville, one of Oxford's women's colleges. An undergraduate there, Monica Shorten, had asked her one day what the Christian was supposed to respond to the arguments of the atheist and the agnostic. To answer them, said Aldwinckle, one had to meet them head on; she hastened to develop a forum at which Christian might meet non-Christian in discussion and debate. First step had to be approval by the university; that would come only when she had succeeded in cadging the support and indeed the participation of a senior member of the university. *The Problem of Pain* led her to Lewis. 'Come to coffee in my rooms on Tuesday, and we can talk it over.'

By the time she returned her cup and saucer to the tray on Lewis' table, Aldwinckle had convinced him to become president of the new university society, formed a programme committee, and suggested Hilary term next month as the appropriate time for the first meeting. But what should they call the society? There were other clubs in Oxford offering Christian fellowship. There was SCM. There was OUCH. There was OICCU. Why not name it, suggested Lewis, after the ancient Greek who encouraged philosophers to follow an argument wherever it led, Socrates?

~

When invited by the British Academy to give the next Shakespeare lecture in its annual series, Lewis groaned. He was not especially fond of the plays, although he liked the sonnets. He would have to go up to London, which he was already doing too much of. It would be a glittering occasion, but he despised glitter with a passion. The audience? 'They were all the sort of people whom one sees so often getting out of taxis and then going into some big doorway, and wonders who on earth they are — all those beards and double chins and fur collars and lorgnettes.'

He did have a piece on *Hamlet*, though, a lecture he had given at the Examination Schools, one of a weekly series during Michaelmas Term 1938. Dyson and Coghill had also delivered talks in that series, and didn't Lascelles Abercrombie die the night before he was supposed to lecture? Yes, that talk would do; he had until 22 April 1942, to do some reshaping.

He would begin by saying that he was not a Shakespearean

scholar; he wasn't going to 'plunge into some textual or chronological problem in the hope of seeming, for this one hour, more of an expert' than he was; but he would distinguish three main schools of criticism and what each had to say about poor Hamlet hesitating to do the dirty deed . . . And just when the audience was about to nod off into Cloud-Cuckooland, he would throw some glitter onto the argument. He would draw a figure from the world of art and galleries and artists' shows and cocktail parties, a world the audience was certainly familiar with. He would ask them to forget the play, to put the indecisive Hamlet out of their minds, and to imagine instead a framed piece of canvas.

'Let us suppose that a picture which you have not seen is being talked about. The first thing you gather from the vast majority of the speakers — and a majority which includes the best art critics — is that this picture is undoubtedly a very great work.

'The next thing you discover is that hardly any two people in the room agree as to what it is a picture of. Most of them find something curious about the pose, and perhaps even the anatomy, of the central figure.

'One explains it by saying that it is a picture of the raising of Lazarus, and that the painter has cleverly managed to represent the uncertain gait of the body just recovering from the stiffness of death.

'Another, taking the central figure to be Bacchus returning from the conquest of India, says that it reels because it is drunk.

'A third, to whom it is self-evident that he has seen a picture of the death of Nelson, asks with some temper whether you expect a man to look quite normal just after he has been mortally wounded.

'A fourth maintains that such crudely representational canons of criticism will never penetrate so profound a work, and that the peculiarities of the central figure really reflect the content of the painter's subconscious.

'Hardly have you had time to digest these opinions when you run into another group of critics who denounce as a pseudo-problem what the first group has been discussing. According to this second group, there is nothing odd about the central figure. A more natural and self-explanatory pose they never saw; they cannot imagine what all the pother is about.

'At long last you discover — isolated in a corner of the room, somewhat frowned upon by the rest of the company, and including a few reputable connoisseurs in its ranks — a little knot of men who are whispering that the picture is a villainous daub and that the mystery of the central figure results from the fact that it is out of drawing.'

That sort of gossipy approach, thought Lewis, would certainly brighten the audience up and add some glitter of his own to the lecture. Glitter? 'Patines of bright gold!'

✒ 1942 ✑

'I hope these reach you in time,' wrote Lewis to Fenn. 'I could not get to the job at once, and it has proved a tough one.' He had received comments from Dowell, who wanted justification by faith stressed more and the various types of good distinguished the one from the other. He had heard also from Griffiths, who thought the section on atonement needed amplification. Welch, who had read the scripts from the Anglican point of view, saw nothing to change. Additions, deletions, insertions having been made, Lewis sent the packet of paper off to Fenn on 4 January.

✒

'It's not because I'm anybody in particular that I've been asked to tell you what Christians believe,' said Lewis at 4.45 p.m. on Sunday 11 January. He was sitting in front of a BBC microphone, beginning the new series of talks, the first one of which was entitled 'The Rival Concepts of God'. He was a layman and not a parson, and a former atheist. 'So you see, the long and short of it is that I've been selected for this job just because I'm an amateur, not a professional, and a beginner, not an old hand.'

'Enemy-occupied territory — that is what this world is,' said Lewis in his second talk on 18 January. 'Christianity is the story of how a right king has landed, you might say landed in disguise, and is calling us all to take part in a great campaign of sabotage.'

Travelling back to Oxford on the train that Sunday night, Lewis knew in his bones that he would take some flak for introducing into the Christian story a character who was somewhat out of fashion. Did he really believe, someone was sure to ask after hearing tonight's broadcast, in 'the Devil — hoofs and horns and all'? Appearances aside, Lewis did indeed believe in the existence of this creature and in its ability to play on the 'conceit and laziness and intellectual snobbery' of people by preventing them from doing such things as going to church. That power would also, if it had any sense, prevent non-churchgoers as well as churchgoers from entering bookshops to buy *The Screwtape Letters*, copies of which were just being shipped from the publisher.

&

'I am a man, therefore lazy; you are a woman, therefore probably a fidget,' replied Lewis on 20 January to Neylan. 'So it may be good advice to you (though it would be bad to me) not even to try to do in the trough all you can do in the peak.'

In a state of depression, she had written to him as though he were a spiritual director; he responded, not unlike a director, but more like a co-conspirator. He too knew the despair that accompanied attempts to overcome chronic temptations. But he had the wisdom and indeed the reinforcement of his own spiritual director, Walter Adams of the Cowley Fathers, to know that the impatience, the petulance, the anger one felt were the work of Screwtape instead of his opposite number in the angelic host. It was in fact when a person was most dirty that God became most present. '*No amount* of falls will really undo us if we keep on picking ourselves up each time. We shall, of course, be very muddy and tattered children by the time we reach home. But the bathrooms are all ready, the towels put out, and the clean clothes in the airing cupboard.'

&

'It is very fine today,' said Christianity.

'On the contrary,' said Science, 'it is half-past four.'

It was 26 January. The speaker at the first meeting of the Socratic Club was trying to show how Christianity and science were in conflict. Aldwinckle had opened the meeting at Somerville with a welcome to all who came. She explained how the society got its name, that distinguished speakers would be invited to present the case for Christianity and — ahem — against Christianity. Meetings would be held every Monday evening in term, beginning at 8.15 and concluding no later than 10.30. Those present who were not Christians should feel free to join in the discussion after the main address, which that night was entitled 'Won't mankind outgrow the advance of science and modern ideologies?' which was being delivered by that eminent Oxford physician and philosopher, Robert Emlyn Havard.

Ideologies came and went, said Havard. Christianity had been very much out of fashion in the first and third centuries, in the eighteenth and even in the twentieth centuries, but it was the ideologies competing for the minds and souls of man that died, not

Christianity. Ground lost to the sea was generally recovered in the next tide.

❧

Was Jesus a good man and a good moral teacher, even a great one? Or was he, as he claimed, the Son of God? Lewis asked this question in the course of his third BBC talk on 1 February. If Jesus had said the things he was reported to have said, he wouldn't really be a great moral teacher. 'He'd either be a lunatic — on a level with the man who says he's a poached egg — or the Devil of Hell.' People had to make a choice, and that was why he entitled this talk 'The Shocking Alternative.' 'Either this man was, and is, the Son of God: or else a madman: or something worse.'

Jesus Christ was the perfect penitent, said Lewis in the fourth BBC talk, which was broadcast on 8 February. He repented for fallen man who was the imperfect penitent, the rebel, who was well advised to lay down his arms, throw up his arms, and come out of the trenches in surrender. Christians called that process repentance, a 'willing submission and a kind of death.' When Jesus underwent a similar process, it could not be called repentance, for he had nothing to repent of; it was called atonement; humankind was called somehow to join in the process.

'Why is God landing in this enemy-occupied world in disguise and starting a sort of secret society to undermine the Devil?' asked Lewis in the fifth and final BBC talk on 15 February, even as British soldiers were parachuting into France. God could, and would indeed, invade in force. In the meantime, he was accepting volunteers who would meet him when he landed. 'I do not suppose you and I would have thought much of a Frenchman who waited till the allies were marching into Germany and then announced he was on our side.'

❧

On Wednesday 18 February, Fenn wrote to Lewis from the BBC to ask whether he 'would consider a longish series of talks on the Forces Programme, say, something in the autumn?'

No, was Lewis' first reaction; he communicated that to Fenn in a letter the following Monday. The second series of talks, as had the first, swamped him with letters; he spent all day Sunday responding, thirty-five letters; there were more still to open. Not only the time, which he couldn't spare, but also the postage, which he couldn't afford.

No, he wasn't complaining. 'Yes, I'll try to do a series in the autumn if you like, and look forward to seeing you here to discuss it when convenient.'

❧

On 2 March Williams appeared at the Socratic, where he read a paper entitled 'Are there *any* valid objections to free love?' Undergraduates who went to Somerville that night fully expected a barrage of Miltonic objections to be thrown against free love; they were not disappointed. If 'free' meant the freedom to be ruled by the emotions of the moment, and if 'love' meant the relentless and purposeful pursuit of a certain sort of happiness, then free love was neither free nor love. Bedazzling, thought the undergraduates as they headed home to their various colleges, chaste as the icicles that hung on Diana's temple, chaste at least for the rest of that evening.

A species of free love had been offered Williams the year before. Lewis had finished his manuscript on *Paradise Lost* and offered it to Oxford University Press. About to be published in 1942, it now contained an epistle dedicatory to Williams, first as a favourite author of Lewis', then as a friend, finally as a Miltonic scholar of heroic proportion.

༄

'Like everything except God and the Devil, it is better than some things and worse than others.' Lewis was carrying on a hot and heavy correspondence with Harwood's wife Daphne on the subject of falling in love. 'Thus it comes in my scale of values higher than lust, selfishness, or frigidity, but lower than charity or constancy — in fact, about on a level with friendship.'

When a couple met and fell in love, she called it fate.

When a man and woman came together, he called it providence.

Her anthroposophy became entangled with his Christianity.

If only anthroposophy knew what it meant to be a creature! Lewis threw at her.

Back at him she heaved the charge of authoritarianism.

'If that doesn't take the bun. When you have heard half as many sentences beginning "Christianity teaches" from me as I have heard ones beginning "Steiner says" from you and Cecil and Owen and Wof — why then we'll start talking about authoritarianism!'

༄

On 20 April Lewis took the train to Wantage, where he made his way to St Mary's Convent and rang the bell. It was not without trepidation that he did this. A year before Sister Penelope had invited him to the motherhouse of the Congregation of St Mary the Virgin. He had accepted the invitation willingly because he was a friend, but reluctantly because he was a Protestant with an inborn aversion to religious life for women. She swept him into the convent and towards the tea things, where he met Mother Annie Louisa, known behind her back as 'the three-foot cube.' Banter over the biscuits melted centuries of prejudice. Yes, he would spend the night in the gatehouse. No, there was no trapdoor with a drop to the dungeon. No, there were no skeletons in the closet, to speak of. Yes, the outer doors opened outward. In that gatehouse he spent a peaceful night; the following day he lectured the junior sisters on 'The Gospel in Our Generation.' The young women were attentive, appreciative; their questions were intelligent. He even had time before he left to talk of things spiritual with his friend and even to discuss *Perelandra*, the manuscript of which he would be sending her soon for her amusement.

∽

Overhead at night in the spring there was the roar of bombers, British now, hundreds of them, heading for German cities. A year before the roar was from German planes, sometimes as many as four hundred, ready to unload bombs, incendiary devices, and parachute mines, levelling historic as well as commercial and residential architecture.

Now no more than twenty planes with the black and white cross on the wings made it across the Channel each night. They still carried bombs; wherever they dropped them, there were destruction and death. For one of the fatalities, Lewis wrote an epitaph, which appeared in the 6 June issue of *Time and Tide*:

> She was beautifully, delicately made,
> So small, so unafraid,
> Till the bomb came.
> Bombs are the same,
> Beautifully, delicately made.

∽

'A critic who makes no claim to be a true Shakespearian scholar and who has been honoured by an invitation to speak about Shakespeare to such an audience as this, feels rather like a child brought in at dessert to recite his piece before the grown-ups.' It was Wednesday 22 April. Having just arrived in London from Wantage, Lewis was beginning his address to the British Academy, entitled 'Hamlet: The Prince or the Poem?'

At the risk of appearing to be a literary Peter Pan, he was going to inflict on his sophisticated audience the outrageous view that it was better to read Shakespeare like a child than like an adult. He had tried to read Shakespeare in his teens, but his teachers had so belaboured him with historical criticism and character criticism that he lasted only a few scenes before giving up for the boredom. What he really wanted to do was to pay attention to the characters who wore 'rich clothes' and took centre stage and spoke 'golden syllables.'

When Hamlet took centre stage and spoke poetry, he described 'a certain spiritual region through which most of us have passed and anyone in his circumstance might be expected to pass.' He was not a particularized individual, as much of Shakespearian criticism had suggested, but a sort of Everyman. If Beatrice or Falstaff were at a party that very night, Lewis would cross the room to introduce himself. But if Hamlet were at the same party, he would not brave the crowd. He would not have to. He was himself Hamlet.

At this point in the lecture the audience thought that this puckish don from Oxford, who had begun so poorly, was becoming 'sophisticated, abstract, modern.' At this precise moment, playful as a cat, he gave them a jolt. He said his views were just the opposite, 'naive and concrete and archaic.' He was merely trying to get his well-heeled, well-dressed audience to remember when they first read *Hamlet* as children or near-children . . .

'Night, ghosts, a castle, a lobby where a man can walk four hours together, a willow-fringed brook and a sad lady drowned, a graveyard and a terrible cliff above the sea, and amidst all these a pale man in black clothes . . . with his stockings coming down, a dishevelled man whose words make us at once think of loneliness and doubt and dread, of waste and dust and emptiness, and from whose hands, or from our own, we feel the richness of Heaven and earth and the comfort of human affection slipping away.

'In a sense, I have kept my promise of bestowing all my childishness upon you.'

⤳

For each of his BBC talks, Lewis was paid ten guineas and offered vouchers for the train. The vouchers he took; the fees he asked the BBC to send to a number of worthy and needy people. One of these was a Miss Burton, who had read *The Problem of Pain* and found herself in it. She wrote to Lewis to tell him this, and that she was a Christian, had read English at Oxford, and was now living in Buckinghamshire on a very small income. He sent her books from time to time; money from the BBC was posted to her at his instruction.

Now she was being evicted and had nowhere to go. She had somewhere to write, however; when Lewis received her letter, he wrote to Sister Penelope for help. She replied promptly with a number of suggestions and possibilities. 'I have forwarded it to "Stepsister Burton," as I call the hedge-hogged lady,' wrote Lewis in gratitude to Penelope, 'and you may hear from her anytime.'

⤳

Sister Penelope had translated St Athanasius' fourth-century treatise on the incarnation of the Word of God. Such a work was well within her competence, having read theology and medieval studies at Oxford. When she submitted the manuscript to the Society for the Promotion of Christian Knowledge, it aroused the enthusiasm of the editor.

In turn, Lewis sent her a copy of the manuscript of *Perelandra*. He wanted her personal opinion, of course; so favourably impressed was he by the Community of St Mary the Virgin that he wanted to dedicate the work to them. If Mother Superior would approve, he would put on the dedication page 'To some ladies at Wantage.'

Trinity term having ended and examinations having been graded, he sat in Magdalen and wrote furiously on such subjects as how Christianity made a difference and what part pleasure played in the Christian life, on prickly virtues like chastity and humility, on satiny virtues like charity and hope. Emerging from his rooms at intervals, he made friends with a rabbit, one of a colony that had been recently introduced into the deer grove. He would pick leaves from the chestnut tree and offer them to the rabbit, who came timorously up to the human hand and nibbled away. 'Oh! the great lollipop eyes and the twitching velvet nose!'

On 29 July the manuscript for the next series of talks entitled 'Christian Behaviour' was finished; Lewis wrapped the packet and posted it off to the BBC. He should have felt relieved; instead he was drained. Even the cool air in the colonnade of New Buildings didn't help. His rabbit friend had disappeared for days — something must have disturbed the coney's digestion; when he returned, he cut Lewis dead, disdaining even the fattest leaves in the outstretched hand.

The doctrines he had been expounding on paper for the past month had been so palpable, so plausible. Now they seemed so flat, so fantastic, so full of wishful thinking. So much for apologetics, for defending the faith, he thought as he began to scribble what he would eventually entitle 'Apologist's Evening Prayer':

> From all my lame defeats and oh! much more
> From all the victories that I seemed to score;
> From cleverness shot forth on Thy behalf
> At which, while angels weep, the audience laugh;
> From all my proofs of Thy divinity,
> Thou, who wouldst give no sign, deliver me.
>
> Thoughts are but coins. Let me not trust, instead

Of Thee, their thin-word image of Thy head.
From all my thoughts, even from my thoughts of Thee,
O thou fair Silence, fall, and set me free.
Lord of the narrow gate and the needle's eye,
Take from me all my trumpetry lest I die.

～

When a man got £2,003 income, Lewis wanted to know, was it usual that he had to pay £2,003 in taxes? Only when that man had been giving money away without at the same time declaring it as income, said Barfield. Royalties from *Screwtape* were rolling in, the book having been reprinted six times since publication in February. If Lewis wanted to continue making donations to the Home for Retired Professors of Ichthyosophy and not be taxed for them, he would need some legal instruments. There would have to be a draft of covenant by which Lewis covenanted to pay to Barfield & Barfield, Solicitors, all royalties. There would have to be a trust deed by which Barfield & Barfield declared that it would hold in trust money received from Lewis under the deed of covenant, and would use, firstly, to pay the costs of such trust deed, and, secondly, to apply it to such charitable purposes as Lewis might from time to time direct. That was precisely what Lewis wanted; he named it the Agape Fund. Barfield then made arrangements with Lewis' bank concerning tax withholdings from his account; then he opened an account for the trust; finally he was ready to write cheques for Lewis' charities and send them off with gracious letters.

～

The 'Christian Behaviour' talks for the BBC were to be delivered on Sunday afternoons from September to November. He had posted the scripts to Fenn at the end of July; Fenn had read them; censors had approved them; secretaries had typed them; but it was 15 September before Fenn realized that they were too long. Lewis had thought that they should run, like the previous ones, for fifteen minutes. Now he had to cut five minutes from each one; rather than edit the typescripts prepared by the BBC, he rewrote by hand; but he was ready for the microphone by 2.50 p.m. on 20 September with 'The Three Parts of Morality'.

～

'Imagine three men who go to war. One has the ordinary natural fear of danger that every man has, and he subdues it by moral effort and becomes a brave man . . .' Lewis was reading the third BBC talk on 4 October; in it he was trying to show that Christian morality had little to do with psychoanalytical theory by instancing three soldiers. The first one was normal. 'Let us suppose that the other two have, as a result of things in their subconsciousness, exaggerated, irrational fears, which no amount of moral effort can do anything about. Now suppose a psychoanalyst comes along and cures these two: that is, he puts them both back in the position of the first man.' At that precise moment, Lewis pointed out, the psychoanalytical problem ended and the moral problem began.

Enemy aircraft were spotted over Oxford. Nothing was dropped, neither bombs nor parachutists, but the city was shut down until the following morning, trapping a host of military and academic personnel without lodging. There was a knock on the oak of room 3. Lewis answered. It was Fryer in uniform. He begged lodging for the night. Lewis ushered him in and rang for his scout to make up a bed on the floor of his study.

'You're a sergeant, I see. I'll bet you terrify them.'

'I don't know about that,' said Fryer, 'but at all events I'm just about to become a warrant officer. How do you think I shall be then?'

'I think you'll be a perfect bastard!'

If Lewis in British uniform and a German in military uniform had killed each other simultaneously in the Great War and found themselves together a moment after death, would they have resented each other? Would they have been embarrassed? asked Lewis in the fifth talk of the BBC series, which was broadcast on 18 October. 'I think we might have laughed over it.'

Not everyone in the radio audience approached war with the gaiety of a crusader riding off to defend a good cause. Forgiveness, for that was the subject of the talk, was more difficult in World War II. 'I wonder how you'd feel about forgiving the Gestapo if you were a Pole or a Jew?' But forgive, the Christian was bade, and he should forgive as he would expect to be forgiven. It was possible, said Lewis. 'One might start with forgiving one's husband or wife, or parents or children, or the nearest NCO, for something they have done or said in the last week.'

The last talk was broadcast on 8 November and in the corridors of Broadcasting House Fenn heard only good news. On the stalls of Fleet Street, he wrote on 10 November to Lewis, he had seen unlikely newspapers like the *Daily Mirror* and unsympathetic magazines like the *Freethinker* give more than a passing mention to the series and the burgeoning apologist.

There must have been much that Lewis could take pride in as he left Magdalen on the evening of 16 November and turned up the

High. Bles had put the first two series of BBC talks into one volume and published it under the title *Broadcast Talks; The Problem of Pain* had been reprinted eight times. He turned right at Carfax and headed up the Corn, Woolworth's on the left where late the Clarendon Hotel had stood, past Mary Magdalene's on the right, the Randolph Hotel on the left. *The Screwtape Letters* had been reprinted eight times; Macmillan in New York would publish the American edition in the new year. He went along St Giles' and the beginning of Woodstock Road. Oxford University Press had published *A Preface to 'Paradise Lost'* and had also reprinted the British Academy lecture entitled 'Hamlet: The Prince or the Poem?' Such success as he had achieved, he noted prayerfully as he passed St Aloysius' Roman Catholic Church, were not due to himself alone.

At the entrance to Somerville, he turned left into the quadrangle. He was the featured speaker at the Socratic that night. 'Christianity and Aesthetics' was the title he had given Aldwinckle; he would iterate some of his thoughts on Christianity and culture, which he had formulated several years before in *Theology*; his catchy subtitle — 'The Company Accepts No Liability' — would help fill the room to overflowing.

∽

'I have known only one person in my life who claimed to have seen a ghost. It was a woman; and the interesting thing is that she disbelieved in the immortality of the soul before seeing the ghost and still disbelieves after having seen it. She thinks it was a hallucination. In other words, seeing is not believing.'

It was 26 November. Lewis was preaching in St Jude on the Hill Church, London, on a most unfashionable topic, miracles. Sophisticated moderns, he said, had an almost aesthetic dislike of miracles, whereas educated people often confused the laws of nature with the laws of thought, and considered the suspension of the one a sort of contradiction of the other.

Repeating church teaching for centuries, and with many references to Athanasius as translated by Penelope, Lewis laid down two conditions for a miracle: the law of nature had to be stable, and beyond nature there had to be some higher reality. These established, he showed how God the creator, operating at a slow speed and on a large scale, turned water into wine and a little corn into a lot of corn each and every agricultural year. These very same miracles, the Son of God performed, albeit at a quicker speed and on a smaller scale, at the wedding feast of Cana and for the thousands who came to hear him speak.

But what about the virgin birth, which seemed to be such a

stumbling block to the modern believer? The answer went the same way. What God the creator did with all the spermatozoa from the beginning of life, he did 'directly, instantaneously; with a spermatozoon, without the millennia of organic history behind the spermatozoon.'

These were not arbitrary or meaningless miracles, said Lewis by way of conclusion. 'When I open Ovid or Grimm, I find the sort of miracles which really would be arbitrary. Trees talk, houses turn into trees, magic rings raise tables richly spread with food in lonely places, ships become goddesses, and men are changed into snakes or birds or bears. It is fun to read about; the least suspicion that it had really happened would turn that fun into a nightmare. You find no miracles of that kind in the gospels.'

As Michaelmas term ended and Christmas approached, Lewis became run down. He had had rheumatism for the last year, he wrote to Greeves on 10 December, which prevented him from sleeping on his right side. He now had what was being diagnosed as neuralgia, and Minto was limping about with varicose ulcers. By 22 December he had sinusitis. 'I have to sit for twenty minutes every evening with my face in a jug of Friar's Balsam, like a horse with a nosebag,' he wrote to Sister Penelope, 'and the family say all sorts of things, and I *can't* answer.'

✑ 1943 ✑

'Writing, writing, writing — letters, notes, exam papers, books, lectures.' Between Michaelmas and Hilary terms, Lewis was complaining to Greeves how little leisure time he had. Minto was suffering from ulcers and limping about. Warnie was losing weight, his face emerging like a parcel from its wrappings. He felt himself overweight and over-tired. But when Neylan wrote to him, complaining of feeling 'weak and listless', he had to admit that there was much that was agreeable about sickness. 'To lie in bed — to find one's eyes filling with facile tears at the least hint of pathos in one's book — to let the book drop from one's hand as one sinks deeper into reverie —

to forget what you were thinking about a moment ago and *not to mind* — and then be roused by the unexpected discovery that it is already tea time — all this I do *not* find disagreeable.'

∽

Either Christian ethics was a great obstacle to human progress, or it was the saviour of civilization: that was the argument in wartime England. As 'a Christian, and even a dogmatic Christian untinged with modernist reservations and committed to supernaturalism in its full vigour,' Lewis might have been expected to take up the cudgel for Christianity. Instead, he argued against it. That Christianity promulgated a moral discovery, was a mistake. 'It is addressed only to penitents, only to those who admit their disobedience to the known moral law. It offers forgiveness for having broken, and supernatural help toward keeping, that law and by doing so reaffirms it.'

This and similar remarks, which he had made to some society or other the year before, Lewis polished up for publication and sent off to a quarterly entitled *Religion in Life*. But the ideas contained in the talk-now-essay he really wanted to explore further. He had committed himself to deliver an address at the Socratic Club on Monday 8 February; this would give him the podium he needed.

He would list 'precepts from Greek, Roman, Chinese, Babylonian, ancient Egyptian, and Old Norse sources' and from them demonstrate that there was a 'massive and immemorial agreement about moral law' even though there was a 'massive and immemorial inability to obey it.' In the process, just for fun, he could paddle the Epicureans, the Communists, and H. G. Wells, but he would bring the argument one step further. He would entitle the talk 'If we have Christ's ethics, does the rest of the Christian faith matter?' He would conclude that Christ ended the necessity to discourse about ethics and offered means for carrying out the ethics already known.

∽

In the autumn he had read a novel entitled *The Worm Ouroboros* with much relish, and wrote a letter of appreciation to the author. E. R. Eddison responded; a lively correspondence developed between the two men in a species of Old English. Lewis did not like his next romance, *Mistress of Mistresses*, and complained to the author about the 'hyperuranian whores and transcendental trulls.' Eddison charged Lewis with misogyny.

'It is a thing openlie manifeste to all but disards and verie goosecaps,' countered Lewis on 29 December, that feminitee is to itself an imperfection, being placed by the Pythagoreans in the sinister column with matter and mortalitie.' He then invited Eddison to a dinner party at Magdalen on Wednesday 17 February where he would enjoy the society of such men as Tolkien, Williams, Warren Lewis, and himself.

~~~

On Tuesday 23 February, Lewis and his brother caught a train at Oxford and headed north. They passed through the cathedral town of York, where the station and part of the right of way had sustained recent hits from the Luftwaffe. Further northward in the night they passed through Darlington, bringing back sad memories to Warren, who had arrived at the very station in September 1939 on his way to the RASC encampment at nearby Catterick. The following morning the train pulled into Durham.

As they stepped down onto the platform, both of them were surprised by the scene that greeted them. Crossing a vaulted stone bridge hundreds of feet over the River Wear, they entered a picturesque city, with castle, university, cathedral, and bishop's palace encircled within ancient walls. Especially pleasing to Warren was the cathedral, begun in the eleventh century in honey-coloured stone, with ribbed vaults, transverse arches, and zig-zag markings on the sustaining pillars. When they arrived at the university, they were told that the three Riddell Memorial Lectures, which Lewis had been invited to deliver, would be given in Newcastle upon Tyne.

Sometime in 1940 Lewis had received in the post a copy of *The Control of Language*. He had thumbed through it. It was a textbook for the teaching of English in the upper forms of preparatory schools. Some of the examples he found alarming, not only literarily but also philosophically. Alec King and Martin Ketley, the authors, introduced subjectivity as the norm of observation and expression and ignored the objectivity of such observation and the number of conclusions that might be drawn from it. He put the book onto a shelf in his study.

When he was invited to give the Riddell Lectures, he remembered the book and thought that it would be the perfect illustration of what was wrong with contemporary education. He had received the book from the publisher who had hoped that Lewis would respond with a quotable quote; now that he was about to trounce the work in a public forum, he decided that he would refer to it as *The Green Book* and to its authors as Gaius and Titius.

In the first lecture, on the evening of the 24th, he took an example from the book. A waterfall could be described as sublime, but where did the sublimity reside? Was it in the waterfall itself, or was it in the feelings of the one observing the waterfall? In the former, Gaius and Titius had said. In the latter, Lewis would say, for the emotion of the observer was not trivial or subjective; rather it was important and objective and indeed related to an organized system of values and value judgments. The head could be educated, the belly could be satiated, he said in conclusion, but the 'trousered ape' and the 'urban blockhead' who had learned English from *The Green Book* would be 'men without chests' if they didn't also have emotions trained and disciplined into virtues like fortitude, patriotism, magnanimity.

In the second lecture, on the evening of the 25th, he accused Gaius and Titius of being the products of a 'whole system of values which happened to be in vogue among moderately educated young men of the professional classes during the period between the two wars.' Against their philosophy of subjectivity, he pointed to the existence of the *Tao*, the treasury of moral thought that various nations and civilizations had contributed to since the beginning of the world. They were 'not one among a series of possible systems of value,' he said, but 'the sole source of all value judgments'. 'Only those who are practising the *Tao* will understand it. It is the well-nurtured man, the *cuor gentil*, he alone, who can recognize reason when it comes. It is Paul, the Pharisee, the man "perfect as touching the law" who learns where and how that law was deficient.'

In the third lecture, on the evening of the 26th, he imagined a dominant age, perhaps the hundredth century AD, 'which resists all previous ages most successfully and dominates all subsequent ages most irresistibly, and thus is the real master of the human species.' Nature would appear to have been conquered by such inventions as the aeroplane, the wireless, and the contraceptive. But even such power as these innovations gave mankind over nature was limited, diminishing steadily as the end of the world approached.

Abroad in the dominant age, and indeed partly responsible for it, were the Conditioners who attempted to control nature rather than to obey it, and to construct an artificial *Tao* out of such innovations as the aeroplane, the wireless, and the contraceptive. 'Stepping outside the *Tao*, they have stepped into the void. Nor are their subjects necessarily unhappy men. They are not men at all: they are artefacts. Man's final conquest has proved to be the abolition of man.'

∽

As astronomers discovered that the universe was approaching the infinite in size, they began to charge that Christianity had arrived at the disappearing point. Lewis felt he had to address this charge and accordingly wrote an essay, which was published by *The Guardian* in two parts, 'Dogma and the Universe' in the 19 March issue and 'Dogma and Science' in the 26 March issue.

The larger the universe was, or so the argument went, the smaller the earth was, and the more infinitesimal man became, soon arriving at a point where he was not worth redeeming. To Lewis the argument from size had no meaning, for he respected the five-foot man as much as the man who was five foot three-and-a-half. Indeed man's lengthening shadow in the universe seemed to instil in him awe and a sense of the sublime. 'I should be suffocated in a universe that I could see the end of.' Wasn't it really the human eye that conferred on the nebula in Andromeda something like greatness?

Modern philosophers like Bergson and Whitehead, playwrights like Shaw and Sartre, even novelists like Lewis himself, had begun providing theories to accompany a universe in change or process or supercharged with some sort of force. But these visualizations affected, not the substance or dogmas of Christianity, but only the shadows. 'What God is in himself, how he is to be conceived by philosophers, retreats continually from our knowledge,' he concluded. 'The elaborate world-pictures which accompany religion and which look each so solid while they last, turn out to be only shadows. It is religion itself — prayer and sacrament and repentance and adoration — which is here, in the long run, our sole avenue to the real.'

∽

In February Sister Penelope wrote to tell Lewis that the publications committee of SPCK had not approved her translation of Athanasius's *De Incarnatione*. It was too literary, they said, but publication might be possible if she would make the translation a little more literal; theology students and seminarians could then be encouraged to use it as a crib.

On no account, he advised her, should she give in to such an unreasonable demand. She should write a preface explaining why she did what she did. He would write an introduction providing a rationale for reading a fourth-century theological work in the twentieth century. Then she should send the whole thing off to Geoffrey Bles, Ltd., and he gave her Anthony Sampson's name.

Sentence structure had been simplified, wrote Penelope in the translator's preface; English simplicity had been substituted for Greek verbosity, and there were no footnotes; all this had been done to make the work more appealing to the modern reader. After all, Athanasius himself was modern in many ways. 'Thrilled as he was with the reputed properties of asbestos, what lovely analogies would he not draw from such discoveries of our modern science as wireless and the invisible rays, and with what merciless logic yet unfailing charity would he not expose the weakness of modern unbelief!'

It was April now; Lewis had been labouring over the introduction. 'If you join at eleven o'clock a conversation which began at eight, you will often not see the real bearing of what is said.' By this he meant that it was better to read old books before new books in an area where one is an amateur. This was especially true in theology. Otherwise, how would one know what the controversies were? 'The only safety is to have a standard of plain, central Christianity ("mere Christianity" as Baxter called it) which puts the controversies of the moment in their proper perspective. Such a standard can be acquired from the old books.'

∾

Christian Behaviour was published in book form by Bles in April. Tolkien bought a copy at Blackwell's and saw that the book included the eight talks Lewis had delivered on BBC radio. He saw also that Lewis had added, as he said he would, four new chapters, some of which he had discussed at length with Tolkien.

The first was 'The Cardinal Virtues,' dealing with prudence, temperance, justice, and fortitude; Tolkien was pleased to note that Mohammedanism, not Christianity, was 'the teetotal religion'. The second was 'Charity', the sort of practical charity that meant one had to act as if he loved his neighbour, not wait until he actually liked his neighbour. The third was 'Hope,' the theological virtue that responded to humankind's want for heaven. The fourth was 'Christian Marriage.' Lewis pointed out that Christian marriage was for life, that sexual intercourse outside of marriage was monstrous, that divorce was 'like cutting up a live body . . . a kind of surgical operation,' that wives should be submissive. He also distinguished two kinds of marriage, 'one governed by the state with rules enforced on all citizens, the other governed by the church with rules enforced by her on her own members.'

What Lewis had to say troubled Tolkien enough that he began to make notes towards a reply. The last Christian marriage he had attended turned out to be a double marriage, which he found highly alarming. The first took place in a church; the priest used a formula that included the couple's promising fidelity for life, the woman promising obedience. The couple then went to an office where before 'a registrar, and in this case — adding in my view to the impropriety — a woman,' the couple pronounced another set of vows that made no mention of fidelity or obedience. The latter service, he wrote down, was 'a piece of propaganda, a counter-homily delivered to young Christians fresh from the solemn words of the Christian minister . . .'

Tolkien would write to Lewis more about this when he had the time. For the moment, he folded his notes and inserted them in the pages of the book.

∾

'Pray for me, Sister,' Lewis wrote on 10 April to Penelope. Between Hilary and Trinity terms he was spending most of his time at the Kilns. Minto's ulcer wept without stop. Muriel, a lady gardener, went into hysterical rages, putting off an operation she surely ought to have. Margaret, a mentally deficient young girl who had been hired as a maid, was subject to fits of anger and misery. 'There is never any time when *all* three women are in good temper. When A is in, B is out; and when C has just got over her resentment at B's last rage and is ready to forgive, B is just ripe for her next, and so on. But out of the evil comes good. From praying anxiously for a little of God's peace to communicate to *them*, I have been given more of it myself than I ever had before . . .' That was before the flu struck.

'Very sorry to hear you are laid low,' wrote Tolkien on 20 April, 'and with no U.Q. [Useless Quack, as the Inklings called Havard] to suggest that it might be your last illness! You must be very disconsolate. I begin to think that for us to meet on Wednesdays is a duty: there seem to be so many obstacles and fiendish devices to prevent it.' He was urging a swift recovery so that Lewis could join him and one other in teaching forces cadets who were taking wartime short courses at the university. Of twenty-two cadets tested, not one of them was able to define words like 'apposite, reverend, venal, choric, secular.'

Low spirits swirled around the bedridden Lewis. *Perelandra* had been reviewed in the Sunday papers. 'As an interplanetary novelist, he should read more Verne and less Aquinas,' said *The Observer*. *The Sunday Times* was more generous, allowing an idea behind even the most extravagant of Lewis' fantasies. Barfield had already pointed out that when Lewis should have said something once, he said it twice. Lewis had already written perhaps three hundred pages of a sequel to *Perelandra*; when he gave it a feverish reading, he came to the conclusion that it was 'bosh', as he wrote to Barfield; 'rubbish', as he wrote to Eddison. 'Has this ever happened to you?' he went on to ask on 29 April of Eddison. 'A nauseous moment — when the thought of trying to mend it, and of abandoning it, seem equally unbearable.'

❧

'There aren't any up-to-date books on miracles. People have stopped arguing about them. Why?' asked Dorothy L. Sayers in a letter dated 13 May. He was pleased to hear from her. He had read her *Mind of the Maker*, an examination of the factuality of certain statements in the Christian creeds, which had been published in 1941. This book led him to *Gaudy Night*, her novel in which Harriet Vane, returning to her Oxford college to solve a mystery, eventually needed the help of Lord Peter Wimsey. *Non placet*, said Lewis to that one, for he really didn't like detective stories. *Placet* indeed was the word for *The Man Born to Be King*, a series of radio plays on the life of Christ, which had been broadcast over the BBC in 1942 and was just published in book form in early 1943; characters speaking realistic dialogue instead of orating the Authorized Version were especially pleasing. 'Has physics sold the pass? Or is it merely that everybody is thinking in terms of sociology and international ethics?' Perhaps he should write the book on miracles, he thought as he put her letter down; he had written about everything else.

∽

'The decay of *friendship*, owing to the endless presence of women everywhere,' he wrote on 26 May to Griffiths, 'is a thing I'm rather afraid of.'

∽

Macmillan, New York, had published *The Screwtape Letters* on 16 February; only now were reviews trickling back to Oxford. 'The author exhibits a remarkable knowledge of human nature,' said *Commonweal* in March. 'Entertaining, witty, illuminating,' said *The Catholic World* in April. 'There is a spectacular and satisfactory nova in the bleak sky of satire,' said the *Saturday Review of Literature*. 'The sharpest religio-psychological writing of the season,' said *Time*. The publisher, or so said R. L. De Wilton, assistant editor-in-chief at Macmillan, was selling an average of 1,500 copies a week.

At the beginning of June Bles telephoned Lewis from London. He had just received a cable from Macmillan. It seemed that Edward A. Golden Productions of New York was considering making a film of *Screwtape*. The production company was offering $500 for a six-month option, $500 for another six-month option, and an additional $4,000 if the movie was actually made, all of which was to be considered as an advance against 5 per cent of the profits of the film. Lewis could think of no over-riding objection. Bles cabled approval to Macmillan, who for acting as agent in the transaction would get 10 per cent of the author's proceeds.

∽

On 11 June Fenn wrote to Lewis about the possibility of another 'series of talks which would take some of the more obstruse [sic] theological doctrines and show what sort of difference they make both to thought and to conduct.'

On the 16th Lewis replied on the first scrap of paper that came to hand that he could talk on such topics as the Trinity, creation, incarnation, the two natures of Christ, resurrection, and ascension.

'If I may say so,' replied Fenn on the 18th, 'your passion for paper economy exceeds anything my imagination can grasp,' having had to read Lewis' response with a magnifying glass. He went on to invite Lewis to be a guest on a forthcoming BBC programme.

Only 1 July Lewis wrote a long paragraph in tiny writing on the back of a BBC letter. He would go to London on the 19th and perhaps before the programme, they could discuss the next series of talks. 'P.S. You may use the margin of this letter for any purpose you like.'

∽

'Good evening, listeners. This is the Anvil in session again, with two old friends, Canon Cockin of St Paul's Cathedral and Father Andrew Beck, a Roman Catholic priest . . .' It was 19 July. The Rev. J. W. Welch, Anglican clergyman and director of the BBC's religious broadcasting department, had just begun a programme, which was being recorded for broadcast on 22 July. 'And we welcome tonight the Rev. Dorothy Wilson, who has been minister-in-charge of the Muswell Hill Congregational Church, and also Mr C. S. Lewis, known to many of you through his broadcasts and his books.'

The Anvil was a sort of Christian brains trust to which listeners could write the sort of questions they felt reluctant to ask the clergy. This particular night, Welch had four questions. That it was more important to meet God after death than loved ones, Lewis agreed with Cockin. That a soldier had to be a Christian before he could be brave, Lewis said was bosh, lots of Nazis, even lots of animals, being capable of extraordinary courage. That God allowed suffering appeared to him to have come from evil wills, devils if you like, but certainly from wickedness in the long run.

That the Bible was partly fiction and that when a person picked up the Bible, he didn't know what to believe, Lewis replied that he didn't know this to be true, but of course, he wasn't a biblical scholar. 'All I am in private life is a literary critic and historian; that's my job. And I'm prepared to say on that basis if anyone thinks the gospels are either legends or novels, then that person is simply showing his incompetence as a literary critic. I've read a great many novels, and I know a fair amount about legends that grew up among early people, and I know perfectly well the gospels are not that kind of stuff. They're absolutely full of the sort of things that don't come into legends.'

∽

In the morning mail he found a letter-cum-manuscript from J. B. Phillips, vicar of the Church of the Good Shepherd in London. He didn't know the man, but the vicar said some nice things about his books and broadcasts. As for the enclosed manuscript, well, with bombs falling and sirens wailing and buildings collapsing all about,

London was not unlike first-century Rome, at least for Christians. Paul's epistles seemed right to the point. Trouble was, however, that the young people in his parish could not understand the Authorized Version. What they needed was something just a little easier to read. Hence, his own attempt at Colossians. What did Lewis think?

He immediately put the translation to the test. 'Beware lest any man spoil you through philosophy and vain deceit, after the tradition of men, after the rudiments of the world, and not after Christ,' read the eighth verse of the second chapter in the Authorized Version.

'Be careful that nobody spoils your faith through intellectualism or high-sounding nonsense,' read Phillips' version of the same passage. 'Such stuff is at best founded on men's idea of the nature of the world, and disregards Christ!'

Lewis thought he knew Colossians pretty well, but the paraphrase, for that was what it was, seemed to hit it right on the nail. He then read the Phillips version from beginning to end. 'It was like seeing a familiar picture after it's been cleaned,' he wrote on 3 August to Phillips, and he encouraged the vicar to continue his work through the rest of the epistles and to ignore the attacks that would be sure to come from 'the "cultured" asses who say you're only spoiling "the beauty" of AV — all the people who objected to *Green Pastures* and *The Man Born to Be King* and who are always waffling about reverence. But we must kill that!'

⁂

He woke with a start. Perhaps the flu was coming; perhaps it was something he ate; perhaps he had corrected too many examination papers the day before; whatever it was had caused him to dream something phantasmagoric. Instead of putting his head back on the pillow, he decided to go down and look for something distracting. As he descended the stairs at the Kilns, the Lord Chancellor's nightmare in *Iolanthe* came into his mind, and soon the patter-song was tripping off his lips:

> When you're lying awake with a dismal
>   headache, and repose is taboo'd by anxiety,
> I conceive you may use any language you
>   choose to indulge in, without
>   impropriety . . .

By the time he arrived in the study, he reached for his pen, searched for some paper, and began to scribble what he would eventually call 'An Examiner's Nightmare':

I stood in the gloom of a spurious room
   Where I listened for hours (on and off)
To a terrible bore with a beard like a snore
   And a heavy rectangular cough,
Who discoursed on the habits of orchids and rabbits
   And how an electron behaves
And a way to cure croup with solidified soup
   In a pattern of circular waves . . .

Grubbing about the garden the following afternoon, he saw a car drive up to the Kilns. A cheery American got out. Edward Weeks, he introduced himself; he was editor of *The Atlantic Monthly*, a magazine published in Boston but circulated throughout the United States. He was in England for a vacation of sorts; he was a Cambridge man himself; but he was also on a sort of literary pub crawl, looking for publishable material.

'Stand by for a moment while I finish this job,' said Lewis. 'Then we'll have a cup of tea.'

The magazine, said Weeks a short time later inside the Kilns, had featured British poets from time to time; Masefield; the Sitwells; that sort of thing. *The Problem of Pain, The Screwtape Letters, The Case for Christianity, Christian Behaviour,* and *Out of the Silent Planet* had all just been or were about to be published in New York by the Macmillan Company and, quite frankly, he wanted to know what Lewis was up to at the moment. 'Is that yours?' he asked pointing to the paper on Lewis' desk.

'Do read it.'

Then, I hardly knew how (we were swimming by now),
   The sea got all covered with scum
Made of publishers' blurbs and irregular verbs
   Of the kind which have datives in *-um;*

Weeks bought it and knew as he did so that he would probably have to change the title and some of the references before he could print it. As he got into the car, he made Lewis promise to send him some short, article-length chapters from his next book. Lewis smiled as the car disappeared down the drive; the poem might never leave the country, so full of topical, even political references that the parody might seem to British custom officials a coded message.

⟳

He believed in the old authority where kings, priests, husbands, or fathers held sway, he wrote in an essay published in the 27 August issue of *The Spectator*, but he could live with the new equality found in some democracies and indeed among some democrats. But the root of democracy was not to be found in the wonderfulness of man, as Rousseau had suggested; rather it was rooted in the fall of man, no man being 'trusted with unchecked power over his fellows'. After all, most people were temperamentally unfit to rule their fellows. 'I don't deserve a share in governing a hen-roost, much less a nation.'

༼ ༽

Jill Flewett decided to stay on at the Kilns. She had taken the entrance examination at the Royal Academy of Dramatic Art in London. Mrs Moore had invited her to await the results at the Kilns. There she spent the summer, helping with the shopping and the housekeeping and with the rabbits and hens in hutches about the garden. The sixteen-year-old girl charmed Warren, who conducted the symphony every Sunday night in his study. And she enjoyed Jack, as he insisted she call him. He would talk to her of books, lend her some in his study, and encourage her to visit Blackwell's and charge whatever she wanted to his account. When word came in September of her acceptance at the Royal Academy, she was reluctant to leave. It was a happy household, safe from the dangers of the war that still bedevilled London. Mrs Moore was bedded by her ulcer; Michaelmas term beckoned to Jack; Warren was unreliable. She decided to postpone at least for now her dramatic debut.

༼ ༽

'Poor dear "Muriel," after putting off her operation indefinitely, went completely off the deep end,' wrote Lewis on 5 October to Sister Penelope. A doctor was brought in; he recommended a psychoanalyst; he wanted the Lewis household to sign a document admitting Muriel to a mental hospital. Mrs Moore rose to the occasion and blew the doctor from the house. She sat Muriel down for a cup of tea and a little straight talk. Assured that her part of the garden would be cared for and her chores would be taken up by someone else, the young lady quietened down and agreed to go to the ordinary hospital and have the operation. 'It was a bad time, but I almost venture to say I felt Christ in the house as I have never done before,' wrote Lewis, now signing himself to his spiritual confidante as Brother Ass, 'but alas, such a house for him to visit!'

After dinner of an autumn evening at the Kilns, Lewis would spend some time with Jill and Warnie. Then he would fill a hot water bottle and put it in Mrs Moore's bed, give her a hot drink, and pause for a few moments' conversation. She could say anything she wanted to Jack, but when she was harsh about Warnie, he hushed her up and tucked her in.

Downstairs he would spend some time with the young man sent to the Kilns as a general helper by the Social Services Department for a few months' refuge. He was supposed to have the mentality of a child of eight. Lewis sat him down, drew some pictures, made cards with letters of the alphabet on them, shuffled them about, and tried to teach him simple words. Like the gentle Margaret who had been with the family in the spring, he was humble and attentive for a while; then he would erupt, intellectual things being too hot to grasp.

Back at the desk in his study, Lewis found facing him a manuscript. It was the first six chapters of a book on miracles. Why was it so hard to begin the seventh? Perhaps he was guilty of *accidia*, sloth slowly overcoming him at last.

∽

'I quite agree that most scientifiction is at the level of cowboy boys' stories. But I think the fundamental moral assumptions in popular fiction are a very important symptom.' He was responding to Arthur C. Clarke, who had written him a cantankerous letter about the character of Weston in both *Out of The Silent Planet* and *Perelandra*. Weston, as described by Lewis, had been travelling about the country, proselytizing 'in obscure works of "scientifiction," in little interplanetary societies and rocketry clubs,' making converts to the idea that humankind should explore the universe, populate or colonize other planets, thus bringing the bad news from the earth. Clarke had been doing just that, but not with the intention of morally polluting the universe; he was offended not only on his own behalf but also on behalf of all the other scientists with interplanetary longings. 'I don't, of course, think at the moment many scientists are believing Westons,' said Lewis in his reply of 7 December, 'but I do think (hang it all, I *live* among scientists!) that a point of view not unlike Weston's is on the way.'

∽

'Things are pretty bad here,' he wrote to Greeves in his holiday letter. Mrs Moore's ulcer got only worse; domestic help was harder to come by; continued interruption caused him great unhappiness. What he was calling interruption, however, or so he learned from prayer and counsel, was very often 'one's real life — the life God is sending one day by day; what one calls one's "real life" is a phantom of one's own imagination. This at least is what I see at moments of insight; but it's hard to remember all the time . . .'

The good news was that he had finished the first draft of his third excursionary novel into space, and was thinking of dedicating it to Jane McNeill, a family friend in Belfast with whom he had been in continuous correspondence since he left home.

∽

By 10 December Lewis had finished writing seven ten-minute talks for the new series that would be broadcast over the BBC early in the new year. He entitled them 'Beyond Personality, or First Steps in the Doctrine of the Trinity.' When he could not find a typist available in Oxford, he sent the longhand script to London by way of a friend.

'I like them immensely,' wrote Fenn on 22 December, 'and think that, as usual, you have achieved a quite astonishing degree of clarity in a very difficult subject.' He went on to say that the talks, tentatively entitled 'Beyond Personality', were scheduled for fifteen minutes; Lewis could add perhaps as many as six hundred words to each talk. He had some comments on the contents of the talks, but they would be forthcoming; he sent them to Lewis on 29 December.

Replying on the eve of the new year, Lewis said that he had already expanded the first talk, but that it wasn't going to be so easy with the others. 'Don't be disappointed if I don't adopt all your suggestions . . . But I'll peg away.'

1944

'Mr C. S. Lewis will *answer* Dr Joad,' bellowed Aldwinckle. The crop-haired woman had jumped to her feet even as C. E. M. Joad was finishing his address to the Socratic on 24 January.

'*Open the discussion,* I think, is the formula,' said Lewis quietly.

Joad taught philosophy at the University of London. His reputation as an outspoken atheist was well known, but he was beginning to turn; his book *The Recovery of Belief* had recently been published. It was mauled by the religious press and, peeved at the poor reception, he gladly accepted an invitation from the Socratic to speak 'On Being Reviewed by Christians.' The night was bitterly cold, but the steam was whistling inside Lady Margaret Hall. Two hundred and fifty people had packed the room. As the heat of argument rose, Joad asked if he might remove his jacket. That the atheist might not have the advantage, Aldwinckle asked Lewis to remove his. He couldn't, he said; he had a large hole in his shirt and would have to sweat it through to the dripping end.

The scripts of the new series of talks for the BBC, entitled 'Beyond Personality, or First Steps in the Doctrine of the Trinity,' he had lengthened by five minutes each. Now, in a note dated 8 February, Fenn told him that there would be a new broadcast time, 10.20 p.m. He couldn't spend Tuesday nights in London, replied Lewis on the 10th; a 10.20 talk meant catching the train for Oxford at midnight and not getting to bed before 3.00 a.m. 'If you know the address of any reliable firm of assassins, nose-slitters, garotters, and poisoners,' he concluded in exasperation, 'I should be grateful to have it.' But he did deliver the seven talks, some live, some pre-recorded, beginning on 22 February.

∽

In January Bles got a letter dated 29 December from Macmillan, New York, to the effect that Golden Productions had been unsuccessful 'in trying to find a basis for a treatment of a screenplay' for *The Screwtape Letters*. Rather than renew the option for another six months, Golden proposed 'to reshuffle the deal.' He offered to purchase the rights, with no time limit, by paying an additional $1,000 now and, at such time as the film was made, a final payment of $3,500. 'I have been in touch Mr C. S. Lewis,' wrote Bles on 14 February to De Wilton, 'and I'm afraid we do not feel inclined to agree with Mr Golden's proposal.'

∽

'Ascetic Mr Lewis!' shouted Tolkien as Lewis ordered another pint, echoing the words of *The Daily Telegraph* of 22 February. He was 'going short for Lent,' said Lewis, as he downed his third pint of the session.

∽

'Dear Mr Eliot,' wrote Lewis on 23 February, which was also Ash Wednesday, 'I'm not sure that we are still not a little at cross purposes . . .'

∽

Texts of the talks Lewis gave on the radio were published in *The Listener*. Very soon after the series began, BBC research discovered that the people who were listening to the talks fell clearly into two categories. 'They obviously either regard you as "the cat's whiskers", wrote Fenn to Lewis on 23 March, 'or as beneath contempt.' The research ought to be illuminating to the BBC, but Fenn couldn't think how.

'Thanks for the suitable Lenten reading, which I return,' wrote Lewis in reply on 25 March. 'The two reviews you report . . . aren't very illuminating about *me* perhaps; about my subject matter, it is an old story, isn't it? They love, or hate.'

∽

The report entitled *Curriculum and Examination in Secondary Schools*, which had been published in 1941, encouraged the Parthenon, thought Lewis, when it should have been inculcating the optative. It fostered appreciation of things classical when it should have been drilling declensions and conjugations. Those who had undergone the latter sort of education passed or failed the entrance examination to college with good conscience; the former faced it with horror and generally failed. What the report advocated was a new type of examination that would treat literature as a 'sensitive and elusive thing' and that would accept appreciative commentary from the students. That, said Lewis, putting his thoughts into an article, produced not appreciation but gush.

Could the old examinations, he asked, and the studying for these examinations really spoil something like the appreciation of poetry? It was possible, he had to admit, theoretically possible. These people might be saints by now, he theorized, if they hadn't been examined at an early age in Scripture. They might even be war heroes, except that they had been put into the school OTC. 'It may be so,' he concluded in the article that appeared in the 11 March issue of *Time and Tide*, 'but why should we believe that it is? We have only their word for it; and how do *they* know?'

Evolution took a funny turn, said Lewis in the seventh and final talk of the BBC series, which was broadcast on 4 April. He didn't say he believed in evolution or knew it to be a fact, but it was a working theory that proved a point. That the great armoured creatures dragging around in prehistory did not prevail, he thought rather odd. Odder still was the fact that they were succeeded as rulers of the world by 'little naked, unarmoured' creatures with better brains. At that moment, unrecorded history took a sharp turn.

Such a sharp turn occurred again, this time in recorded history. It was not just a next step but a new step, 'not merely difference but a new kind of difference', 'not merely change but a new method of producing the change.' He was, of course, referring to the incarnation and its inevitable result of Christ making new, if smaller, models of himself.

These new men, as he called them, in the first two thousand years of Christianity, which was only a wink in the history of creation, were already dotting the earth. Some were easy to spot; others were hard to identify; but every now and then there was one standing right in front of you. 'Their very voices and faces are different from ours; stronger, quieter, happier, more radiant.' If people had trouble recognizing them at first, they recognized one another 'immediately and infallibly, across every barrier of colour, sex, class, age, and even of creeds. In that way, to become holy is rather like joining a secret society. To put it at the very lowest, it must be great *fun*.'

These new men were not all alike, yet they resembled each other. They had no personalities of their own, yet their personalities had something of the godlike about them. That was due to the fact that they had abandoned their own personalities, and in return Christ gave them the real personality. 'Look for yourself, and you will find in the long run only hatred, loneliness, despair, rage, ruin, and decay,' he concluded in a barrage of paradox. 'But look for Christ, and you will find Him, and with Him everything else thrown in.'

∽

On arriving at Paddington Station on Tuesday 18 April, Lewis walked to the spot between the entrance to the Underground and the entrance to the Paddington Hotel. 'I am tall, fat, cleanshaven, don't wear eyeglasses, and shall be in corduroy trousers, probably with a walking stick,' he had written to John Ensor of the Electric and Musical Industries Christian Fellowship. Having introduced himself to a number of fawn-coloured raincoats, Ensor finally found him.

From Paddington they drove fifteen miles to Hayes, Middlesex. There Lewis was escorted into the head office of the Gramophone Co., Ltd. Tea was waiting as well as the outstretched hands of the president and other executives. He was told as he sipped that factory workers had come from the district as well as from Wembley and Wimbledon. Some of the local clergy were in attendance; perhaps as many as two hundred were awaiting him in the hall.

'Let's now carry on with the questions,' he said after a few introductory remarks. How can a factory worker find God? What did he think about raffles in the plant? Should the Bible be reinterpreted and rewritten? Why is Christianity such a pain in the neck to most people? How did he explain the Church of England's silence about venereal disease?

A week later Ensor wrote to thank Lewis and to enclose a cheque. The questions and answers had been taken down in shorthand and were in the process of being typed. Would he have any objection to their being published as a pamphlet? None at all, replied Lewis, if he could see the typescript first; and no, he didn't accept fees for doing something at which he was an amateur.

∽

A woodcut of Lewis surrounded by Venusian creatures and objects appeared on the cover of the 8 April issue of *Saturday Review*. Perusing *Perelandra*, Leonard Bacon found Lewis 'beyond question one of the most exciting and satisfactory writers who has come to the surface out of the maelstrom of these turbulent times.' The fact that the reviewer did not share many of Lewis' fundamental beliefs, 'whether by ill fortune or because of the direct interference of "Our Father Below",' did not seem to prevent him from appreciating 'the poetic imagination in full blast.' Indeed, he was most interested when least in agreement with the author's premises.

Wars spawned quack religions and messiahs, wrote Alistair Cooke in the 24 April issue of *The New Republic*; Lewis was one of them, and *Christian Behaviour* was a case in point. He conceded that Lewis was not 'a statesman or editorial writer merely wiring his normal writing style for sound'; rather he was 'a real radio talent,' labouring, like any sweating gag-writer, to find a common and simple idiom for the masses. After all, he had tackled 'about the toughest assignment ever known to radio,' explaining the beatitudes in words of one syllable. The result was 'a persuasive pseudo-simplicity.' As for *Perelandra*, 'the natural and arid counterpart' of *Christian Behaviour*, 'it is a fantasy compensation for Mr Lewis' deep dissatisfaction with mankind and the world he inhabits. It would make a magnificent analytic sourcebook . . .'

&

If Blake could write about the marriage of Heaven and Hell, asked Lewis of Tolkien one spring morning in a pub, why couldn't he write about the divorce that would be sure to follow? The basis for the fictional work he had in mind was the *refrigerium*, a pleasant doctrine emanating from Prudentius in the fourth century and Jeremy Taylor in the seventeenth to the effect that the damned in Hell had holidays of sorts and could take excursions.

Where would they go and what would they do? That depended on the imaginations of the ghostly. Some would take trips to earth where they could haunt houses, spy on their children, play tricks on poor daft women who called themselves mediums. Others, while on earth, literary ghosts, would hang about public libraries to see if anyone was still reading their books. A few would queue up at a bus stop and take the omnibus up to the other place.

The beginning was good, said Tolkien, but he wasn't so sure about the ending. What was Lewis going to call it?

Who Goes Home?

&

'In the church to which I belong, this day is set apart for commemorating the descent of the Holy Ghost upon the first Christians shortly after the ascension.' Lewis was in the chapel pulpit of Mansfield College, a Congregational institution not many streets from Magdalen. Listening was a varied audience, some in elaborately carved stalls, others in simple pews, mostly ordinands and seminary students. It was Whit Sunday, 28 May.

Glossolalia, speaking in tongues that the disciples were reported to have done, was an appropriate, if difficult, subject for Lewis. Indeed, for modern Christians, it was embarrassing. Ninety-nine cases might be interpreted as gibberish, said Lewis, but he undertook to defend the hundredth, for what was at stake, he thought, was the objective existence of the spiritual life. Against the life of the spirit, the modern materialist had made many objections. Wasn't the spiritual life a mirage, a projection of certain odds and ends of the natural life?

To answer this objection Lewis developed a theory called transposition, which meant an 'adaptation of a richer to a poorer medium.' *Glossolalia* was an instance of transposition, but it could be viewed in two ways. If one looked at the phenomenon from below, then one would be fully justified in concluding that this variety of religious experience was merely an involuntary discharge of nervous excitement. If, however, one looked at the phenomenon from above, then one could conclude that the Holy Ghost was moving among men. From there, with the help of logic, he made an elaborate defence of the existence of the spiritual life, claiming transpositions in intellect, emotion, and imagination.

'In a way the claim we are making is not a very startling one. We are only claiming to know that our apparent devotion, whatever else it may have been, was not simply erotic, or that our apparent desire for Heaven, whatever else it may have been, was not simply a desire for longevity or jewellery or social splendours. Perhaps we have never really attained at all to what St Paul would describe as spiritual life. But at the very least we know, in some dim and confused way, that we are trying to use natural acts and images and language with a new value, have at least desired a repentance which was not merely prudential and a love which was not self-centred. At the worst, we know enough of the spiritual to know that we have fallen short of it . . . I'm sorry.'

His voice quavering, he disappeared from the pulpit. Nathaniel Micklem, principal of Mansfield, who had invited him to speak, went to his assistance. The chaplain signalled to the organist; the choir began a hymn. Oliver Cromwell and Peter Abelard, St Chrysostom and Dr Livingstone — these and dozens of other figures Lewis saw as he looked from one stained glass window to another. The hymn finished, his composure returned, he ascended the pulpit and resumed the sermon.

'That is quite, quite out of the question. I should not dream of staying if I'm expected to meet Robert. I am ready to forgive him, of course. But anything more is quite impossible. How he comes to be here . . . but that is your affair . . .'

It was Thursday night in term time. Lewis was reading a new chapter of *Who Goes Home?* to the Inklings. A female ghost who had made the excursion from Hell was talking about her husband to one of the Bright Women, Hilda by name, on the plains of Heaven.

'You always thought Robert could do no wrong. *I* know. Please don't interrupt for *one* moment. You haven't the faintest conception of what I went through with your dear Robert! The ingratitude! It was I who made a man of him! Sacrificed my whole life to him! And what was my reward? Absolute, utter selfishness . . .'

Warren was acting as host, passing the liquid refreshment. Tolkien and Williams were there as well as David Cecil and Dyson. Each was hoping that it was not their wife Lewis was characterizing.

'No, but listen. He was pottering along on about six hundred a year when I married him. And mark my words, Hilda, he'd have been in that position to the day of his death if it hadn't been for me! It was I who had to drive him every step of the way. He hadn't a spark of ambition. It was like trying to lift a sack of coal. I had to positively nag him to take on that extra work in the other department, though it was really the beginning of everything for him. The laziness of men! He said, if you please, he couldn't work more than thirteen hours a day . . .'

Havard, the Useless Quack, had rejoined the Inklings. He was in naval uniform and sported a red beard. He had been summoned from the Far East back to Oxford to do research on malaria. There were tears of laughter in his eyes as Lewis continued.

'I used to spend simply *hours* arranging flowers to make that poky little house nice, and instead of thanking me, what do you think he said? Said he wished I wouldn't fill up the writing desk with them when he wanted to use it; and there was a perfectly frightful fuss one evening because I'd spilled one of the vases over some papers of his. It was all nonsense really because they weren't anything to do with his work. He had some silly idea of writing a book in those days . . . as if he could. I cured him of that in the end . . .'

Of all the men in the room, only Lewis and his brother were unmarried; he seemed to be able nonetheless to capture the exquisite agony of the educated man's being married to an indefatigable and light-headed woman.

'I believe I have changed my mind. I'll make them a fair offer, Hilda. I will *not* meet him if it means just meeting him and no more.

But if I'm given a free hand, I'll take charge of him again. I will take up my burden once more. But I must have a free hand. With all the time one would have here, I believe I could make something of him . . .'

Hugo Dyson rose to prevent Lewis from giving poor Robert back to the hag he had so mercifully escaped by death. Instead of calling it *Who Goes Home?* shouted Tolkien over the laughter, why not call it *Hugo's Home!*

∽

'While feeling that I was *born* a member of your society, I am nevertheless honoured to receive the outward seal of membership.' Lewis was writing in May to the Society for the Prevention of Progress of Walnut Creek, California. 'I shall hope by continued orthodoxy and the unremitting practice of reaction, obstruction, and stagnation to give you no reason for repenting your favour.'

∽

Arriving at Cambridge by train, Lewis walked from the station to Magdalene College, where he was met by Gilmore, the chaplain who had got him started speaking to the RAF back in 1941. He was commandant of the chaplains' school now; he thanked Lewis for coming. He explained that the chaplains he was going to speak to were civilians in uniform, not military professionals; they ranged in age from twenty-six to forty-six; they had been a mixed lot before ordination with perhaps twenty pilots, a doctor, a few journalists and bankers, some university and theological college graduates. This was the last day of their refresher course. They were a good audience but a tough one. They counselled pilots off on a bombing mission one day; when the pilots didn't return, they consoled their relatives on the next day. A parson who had tried to give them stock answers to their tough questions, they had almost hooted out of the room. A certain rugged spirituality was what whetted their appetites. And what did Lewis propose to talk about? 'Linguistic analysis in Pauline soteriology.' Gilmore wished him luck.

When Lewis began he seemed to have trouble choosing his words. Already some of the chaplains yawned; others coughed; a few reached for the crossword. Gilmore himself grew pleasantly drowsy, but when he and the others in the room heard prostitutes and pawnbrokers being 'pardoned by Heaven, the first by the throne', they brightened considerably. Redemption on the hoof was meat and drink to them.

Lewis stayed the night. The following morning, as he was doing his devotions in the fellows' garden, he was joined by Gilmore. He too had a few minutes before leaving for the Air Ministry in London.

He put his briefcase down on the garden bench. Mustn't get too far from that, he explained to Lewis; it contained a bottle of whisky, and whisky these days was a 'virtuous wife whose price was above rubies.'

'I don't think that to be a safe remark,' said Lewis. 'We are alone in this garden; I am bigger than you; and the inference is appalling!'

∽

As August turned into September, the Kilns was converted into a hospital. The piece of shell that had entered Lewis' body in April 1918 was surgically removed in August. Mrs Moore had a stroke, albeit a mild one, but the prognosis was for a full recovery. Jill Flewett, now seventeen years old, struggled valiantly on as the household searched for more domestic help.

'The world has changed since you and I last met,' wrote Lewis on 6 September to Sister Penelope; 'one finds it difficult to keep pace in the almost miraculous mercies we are receiving as a nation. I never in my most sanguine moment dreamed that the invasion of Europe would go quite so well.'

∽

They weren't Christians: of that Lewis was quite sure.

How could he say that? asked an adversary. Had he been able to read their hearts?

By the word *Christians*, Lewis had meant 'persons who profess belief in the specific doctrines of Christianity.'

The word should be used, countered his adversary, only in 'a far deeper sense.'

Wasn't that a sense so deep, replied Lewis in the 22 September issue of *The Spectator*, that no human observer could tell to whom it applied? And wasn't that just killing the word, albeit with kindness, destroying its denotation, allowing only a connotation to survive?

∽

'What period would you have liked to live in, Miss B?' Lewis was telling a story about an elderly lady he knew, an admirer of the works of Sir Walter Raleigh, who had had an exasperating experience when undergoing an oral examination as an undergraduate.

'In the fifteenth century.'

'Oh come, Miss B, wouldn't you have liked to meet the lake poets?'

'No, sir, I prefer the society of gentlemen.'

Warren, Tolkien, and Williams laughed as the oral examiners must have done decades ago. It was Tuesday noon, 3 October; they were sitting in the back room of the 'Bird and Baby' (The Eagle and Child); they ordered another round of beer, which was again in plentiful supply in Oxford.

Laughing with them was a gaunt man in mufti, sporting a South African hat on his head and a hooked nose on his face. He made some remark about Wordsworth. He was then recognized as the author of *Flaming Terrapin* and *Flowering Rifle*, Roy Campbell. Martin D'Arcy, the Jesuit priest, philosopher, principal of Campion Hall, and frequenter of the Socratic, had recommended that he look Tolkien and Lewis up. Lewis, he heard, had roasted him in poetic form. The press-cutters for his publisher had sent him something, but he couldn't quite remember. He would refresh his memory, said Lewis, if he would come to Magdalen for a literary and social gathering that Thursday night.

∽

The Magdalen tower tolled eight; it was a brisk October morning; the fire crackled in the senior common room as Lewis entered. He ladled himself a dish of porridge and sat down at the mahogany table, which had been set for ten. The first to arrive, he dipped his spoon into the steaming cereal and plunged into a copy of *Punch*.

The door opened, and in stepped a man in uniform; he had to be one of the University Naval Division now quartered at Magdalen. He approached the sideboard, used the ladle in the tureen, and brought his bowl to the table.

'I say,' said Lewis, lowering his *Punch*, 'do you talk at breakfast?'

'By training, no,' said James Dundas-Grant, introducing himself; 'by nature, yes.'

'Oh, good,' said Lewis, laying the magazine on the table. 'I'm Lewis.'

'Not Screwtape?'

'I'm afraid so; yes.'

The door to the room opened again, and a gaunt figure strode in. Lewis raised his *Punch* in self-defence. When the don sat down, he opened his copy of *The Times*, leaving Dundas-Grant staring out of the tall windows to the small cloister beyond.

∽

If she ate too many aspirin tablets, a mother told her daughter, she would die.

'But why?' asked the child. 'If you squash them, you don't find any horrid red things inside them.'

This Lewis gave as an example of how one could imagine something that was in error but at the same time think something that was truth. Imagining was not thinking, he concluded in 'Horrid Red Things', which was published in the 6 October issue of *The Church of England Newspaper*.

The question at issue was, how could the ordinary man of the twentieth century accept as literal fact everything the New Testament said about Jesus. An early peasant Christian might have delighted at the prospect of God the Father and God the Son sitting on two chairs of state in some sort of sky-palace, but at such a picture, enlightened in some measure by scientific education, a modern Christian could only scoff and claim that it was untrue. As a picture it was less than true, conceded Lewis, but as a concept it was wholly true.

Why then should imagery be used at all when dealing with things theological if it was going to be misleading? One could avoid images when dealing with objects of sense, replied Lewis, but with everything else one had to speak with myriad images. When one spoke of the activities of God the Father and God the Holy Ghost, one had to use imagery if one were to speak at all. But when one spoke of God the Son's life on earth, and the incidents and episodes involved objects of sense, then one was describing fact and had no need to resort to image.

'If Christ turned water into wine, and we had been present, we could have seen, smelled, and tasted. The story that he did so is not of the same order as his "sitting at the right hand of the Father".'

'It is either fact, or legend, or lie,' said Lewis in a conclusion that was as inevitable as it was awkward. 'You must take it or leave it.'

∽

'Obviously one ought never to thank a critic for praise, but perhaps one can congratulate a fellow scholar on the thoroughness of his work,' wrote Lewis on 29 October to Charles Andrew Brady, professor of English at Canisius College, Buffalo, who had written an appreciation of Lewis' recently published works for *America*, a weekly magazine published by the Jesuit fathers. 'You are the first of my critics so far who has really read and understood all my books and "made up" the subject in a way that makes you an authority.'

∽

One morning in November, at breakfast, Dundas-Grant, talking quickly before someone else came into the room, explained to Lewis that he and four other officers were instructing cadets in basic naval training while the young men were cramming academic courses. Wasn't it a shame, he complained, that he and his officers couldn't avail themselves of the same educational opportunity? Lewis agreed and asked him to pick a subject they would like to study. Philosophy, said Dundas-Grant, but they would need a tutor. 'I'm your man,' said Lewis. Shortly thereafter, the naval officers were meeting in Lewis' room one day a week, preparing their readings, submitting their essays, every tutorial seeming a Trafalgar.

∽

'Is theology poetry?' The question had been asked by Stella Aldwinckle. 'If theology is poetry,' answered Lewis at the 11 November meeting of the Socratic Club, 'it is not very good poetry.' The doctrine of the trinity, for example, had neither the solitary grandeur of monotheism nor the varied richness of polytheism. The one was satisfying; the other was delicious; but Christianity seemed to fall somewhere between the two.

An idea, he went on to say, had a way of seeming like poetry. One felt cool towards an idea he did not believe in, but he felt quite warm towards the idea he did believe in. In that sense Christianity, Life-Force-Worship, Marxism, Freudianism had all become poetry to their own believers. In that sense, because he believed in Christian theology and felt comfortable with it, he could say that theology was poetry.

Perhaps the question before the Socratic should have been, is Christianity mythology? If it were, said Lewis, he would still like 'Greek mythology much better, Irish mythology better still, Norse best of all.' And, in the face of the scientific outlook and Wellsianity, he went on to spin Christianity as the grandest myth of all.

෴

On 24 November Lewis delivered to the English Association an essay entitled 'Kipling's World.' Rudyard Kipling had written about work and workers in a way that no one before him had; discipline of one sort or another seemed to be the theme that invigorated his writing. Lewis had been reading Kipling with great relish at every stage of his life. But lately, each time he picked up a volume, he found himself reading fewer pages at a sitting. That was what he wanted to explore in this essay.

Did the doctrine of work and discipline, so pleasing at the periphery, hide at the centre 'a terrible vagueness, a frivolity, or scepticism?' At that centre Lewis perceived a master passion. What seemed to live in Kipling's prose and poetry was 'an intimacy within a closed circle.' Earlier writers had tried that sort of thing, but it always came out as snobbery. The magic of the inner ring, however, Kipling seemed to portray with brilliance. But why, Lewis was driven to ask, had Kipling never stood outside the ring to criticize its obvious limitations? Snugness, after all, could quickly lead to smugness in the Kipling canon, even in the face of justice and other virtues. Wasn't Kipling really the slave of the inner ring? Was this what Lewis found so cloying?

෴

Lewis was invited to give the annual commemoration oration at King's College, London, on Thursday 14 December. His reputation as a middle-aged moralist had preceded him; he proceeded to do some middle-aged moralizing. He could say some things about the Devil, with whom he was now closely associated in the popular imagination, or about the flesh, of which the undergraduates knew about as much as he. Instead he decided to give advice and issue warnings about the world of which he knew considerably more than his audience.

In the world there were two systems or hierarchies; one was printed, the other wasn't; one was formal, the other very informal; it was the latter system he wanted to talk about. People inside that system used words like 'we,' 'you and Tony and I,' and 'all the sensible people at this place.' People outside that system used words like 'they,' 'that gang,' 'the inner ring.' Inner ring it was then; it had as many layers as an onion had skin.

The desire to be included in any of the inner rings, and the terror of being left outside, were desires that assailed every normal adult. Exclusion was the controlling principle; secrecy seemed to grow up around it. The inner ring itself was not an evil, but the desire to be included in it had broken many a heart and turned some good men into scoundrels. 'Unless you conquer the fear of being an outsider, an outsider you will remain.'

Conquer the temptation to do anything to break into the inner ring, and Lewis promised that something pleasant would result. A person doing fine work would soon find other persons doing similar work just as well. Inclusion seemed to be the principle of this ring. Such secrecy as there was was accidental; such exclusiveness, incidental; and no one was lured by the odd or esoteric. 'It is only four or five people who like one another meeting to do things that they like,' he said in conclusion, with perhaps the Inklings in mind. 'This is friendship. Aristotle placed it among the virtues. It causes perhaps half of the happiness in the world, and no inner ringer can ever have it.'

1945

On 3 January Jill Flewett left for London where, at last, she would enter the School of Dramatic Art. At the leavetaking Lewis gave 'dear Juin', as he called her, a copy of *The Screwtape Letters* to remember the Kilns by, and when she asked him to write something in the front of it, he penned:

> Beauty and brains and virtue never dwell
> Together in one place, the critics say.
> Yet we have known a case —
> You must not ask her name —
> But seek it 'twixt July and May.

Warren said goodbye to her after walking the new dog, an Irish setter named Bruce. She had to go, he knew that; in his diary he wrote that she was such a nice girl, such a lovely Christian, such a clever person. With her gone and Jack often away, he would have no one to talk to at the Kilns.

'Pray for us always,' wrote Lewis to Sister Penelope that night; 'we are not a very happy house.' Mrs Moore was ailing, perhaps no worse in body, but in mind she was deteriorating. Her spirits brightened considerably at 5.00 p.m. on 8 January; Maureen gave birth to Richard Francis Blake at the nearby Radcliffe Infirmary.

On 30 January, a cold and windy Tuesday, Tolkien visited Magdalen, where he and Lewis tried to get two logs to burn in the fireplace. Concluding that elm didn't burn and that the college bursar had been bilked into buying it, they retired to the Mitre, where there was cheering fire and warming beer. Tolkien plotted how he could escape from Pembroke where he was wretched to Merton where he could be happy in the Merton Chair of English Language and Literature. Merton had another English chair. Wouldn't Lewis be happy there too?

༄

'You see this book?' asked Lewis. 'Ptolemy's *Almagest*. You know what it is?'

'Yes,' said the Atheist. 'It's the standard astronomical handbook used all through the Middle Ages.'

'Well, just read that,' said Lewis, pointing to Book I, chapter 5.

'The earth,' read out his atheistical friend, hesitating a bit as he translated the Latin, 'the earth, in relation to the distance of the fixed stars, has no appreciable size and must be treated as a mathematical point!' There was a moment's silence. 'Did they really know that *then*? But, none of the histories of science, none of the modern encyclopedias, even mentioned the fact.'

'Exactly,' said Lewis. 'I'll leave you to think out the reason. It almost looks as if someone was anxious to hush it up, doesn't it? I wonder why.'

He left no one wondering why in 'Religion and Science,' an imaginary dialogue that appeared in the 3 January issue of the *Coventry Evening Telegraph*, for he went on to point out that the immensity of the universe and the smallness of the earth had been known for centuries and could not be trotted out, as it had been for the last hundred years, as an argument against Christianity.

'Don't you think,' asked Lewis in conclusion, 'that all you atheists are strangely unsuspicious people?'

～

On 10 February, a Saturday, at the invitation of Anne Spalding, a friend of Williams', Lewis addressed the Society of St Alban and St Sergius in Oxford with a paper entitled 'Membership.'

Religion was being defined recently as what a man did with his solitude. Such a definition was gaining popularity, for it seemed to fly in the face of the collectivism that was encroaching on so much of public and personal life. It was even paradoxical in that the world was starved 'for solitude, silence, and privacy' but starved also for 'meditation and true friendship.' Vogueish as it was, however, it was a dangerous definition and indeed part of the strategy of the Enemy, for it had as its purpose to divorce the Christian from the church. The Christian was called 'not to individualism but to membership in the mystical body.' There the Christian was promised that he could handle serpents and drink deadly things and yet live.

～

Williams had been threatening for some time to introduce two of his friends to each other. Eliot and Lewis had corresponded, but Eliot never liked the sort of essay Lewis submitted for publication. Eliot's views of *Paradise Lost* he had savaged in the Ballard Matthews Lectures in 1941 and in the book that resulted. Eliot's notion that only poets were capable of judging poetry he had reduced to the absurd. So severe had his criticism been that he felt it necessary to send a note of tentative apology to the captain of contemporary literature. As he saw Williams with Eliot in tow striding across the lobby of the Mitre Hotel, his heart sank.

'Mr Lewis,' said Eliot with a smile, 'you are a much older man than you appear in photographs.'

In meeting an attack, Lewis remembered saying to Eliot in the epistle apologetical, one aims at the officers first.

'I must tell you, Mr Lewis,' said Eliot, trying again, 'that I consider your *Preface to "Paradise Lost"* your best book.'

Tea was poured, and biscuits served. Lewis grimaced, and Eliot squirmed. Williams enjoyed his cigarette immensely.

〰️

Shortly after Easter, between the spring and summer terms, Lewis went by train to Carmarthen. He had been invited — and he dared not refuse — to address a conference of youth leaders and junior clergy of the Anglican Church in Wales. It was not without reluctance that he did so, for he was a layman addressing professionals, but the subject was something he knew about, 'Christian apologetics.'

Another reason for his reluctance was that his portraits of the Anglican clergy — Mr Broad in *The Pilgrim's Regress* and Fr Spike in *The Screwtape Letters* — were most unflattering. And in *Who Goes Home?* he had just sent an Anglican bishop to Hell. The reason he did so was that the fat man with cultured voice and clerical smile didn't believe in a literal Heaven or Hell; matters like that, thought the bishop, ought to be discussed 'simply, seriously, and reverently', but they did not have to be believed. When the doctrine of the resurrection ceased to commend itself to the critical faculties, he denounced it from the pulpit; and he had no hesitation about accepting a bishopric when it was offered. For him God was the spirit of sweetness and light and tolerance and — er — service. Alas, back to Hell he went, where he would read papers at the weekly meetings of the theological society.

But that really was the point. Lewis had heard Anglican priests preaching doctrine that was not Anglican Christianity; what they were saying was either Roman or so broad, liberal, modern that it excluded the supernatural and thus ceased to be Christian. Boundary lines had to be drawn; priests who went to either extreme, however honestly they arrived there, should abandon their Anglican ministry.

From there, he laid down some practical principles for defending the faith. First, tell people about Christianity because it was true, not because it was likeable or good for society. Second, tell people that they had to face up to all of the elements of original Christianity, even the obscure and repulsive ones; 'do not attempt to water Christianity down.' Third, keep up private reading, always testing contemporary thought against the standard of permanent Christianity. Fourth, talk to the people in their own idiom, if he had learned anything from his years of lecturing to the RAF, it was that the ordinary Englishman was uneducated. Fifth, preach the divinity of Christ even before going into the existence of God; 'the number of clear and determined atheists is apparently not very large.'

'One last word. I have found that nothing is more dangerous to one's own faith than the work of an apologist. No doctrine of that faith seems to me so spectral, so unreal as one that I have just successfully defended in a public debate . . . We apologists take our lives in our hands and can be saved only by falling back continually from . . . Christian apologetics into Christ himself. That is also why we need one another's continual help — *oremus pro invicem.*'

〜

On Friday 13 April, the last of twenty-three weekly instalments of *Who Goes Home?* appeared in *The Guardian*. Sampson of Bles had contracted to publish the work in August under the Centenary Press imprint. Another title was needed, Lewis' having already been used before for a book; they quickly settled on *The Great Divorce: A Dream*. Lewis dedicated the book to Barbara Wall, who had typed the manuscript; after acknowledging a debt to a piece of American scientification whose title he could not remember, he put the finishing touch to the preface. 'I beg readers to remember that this is a fantasy. It has of course — or I intended it to have — a moral. But the transmortal conditions are only an imaginative supposal; they are not even a guess or a speculation at what may actually await us. The last thing I wish is to arouse factual curiosity about the details of the afterworld.'

〜

'And how did *you* feel on V-Day?' asked Lewis of Griffiths on 10 May, the day after the German surrender went into effect. 'I find it impossible to feel either so much sympathy with the people or so much gratitude to God as the occasion demanded.'

There was a wildness in England, Lewis felt; for all the orderliness during the war, peacetime would mean new orders and new reforms; the effect would be stifling.

> A new scent troubles the air — to you, friendly perhaps —
> But we with animal wisdom have understood that smell.
> To all our kind its message is guns, ferrets, and traps,
> And a ministry gassing the little holes in which we dwell.

〜

'If the Christ appeared and disappeared and yet was possessed of a natural body, then a new mode of being had appeared in the universe,' Lewis was recorded as having said at the 14 May meeting of the Socratic. 'Then the ascension, the going up of the body . . . was an essential part of the same story . . .' His paper was entitled 'Resurrection'; he was exploring the possibility of new modes of being resulting from the resurrection and ascension. 'Heaven is not merely a state of the spirit, but a state of the body . . .'

∽

When Warren arrived at Magdalen on Tuesday 15 May, Lewis told him that Williams was ill, or so he had heard; something to do with the intestines. He was leaving early for the Bird and Baby, hoping first to visit Williams in the hospital and lend him a book. Warren said he planned to spend the morning with Louis XIV. When Lewis arrived at the Radcliffe Infirmary, he learned that Williams had been operated on, that he had never recovered consciousness, indeed that he had just died. It was a spring day, with a splendid sky, but Lewis brought winter back with him on the short walk to the Bird and Baby. He walked through the door, past the bar, and out into the garden. Tolkien and a few others were there. He half expected to see Williams in his blue suit, sitting on one of the wire-backed chairs, his legs crossed, his trembling fingers tamping a cigarette. He announced the fact that Charles was no more.

∽

The grief Lewis felt he let flow through his pen.

'We all know that your marriage was one in a thousand,' he wrote to Michal, Charles' wife who lived in London. 'I think you will not be offended if I tell you this: that whenever Charles disagreed with anything we had said about women in general, it was a common turn of raillery to reply, "Oh Charles! — Of course he's in love, so his opinions are worthless!" '

'It has been, and is, a great loss,' he wrote to Sister Penelope. 'But not at all a dejecting one. It has greatly increased my faith.'

'To put it in a nutshell,' he wrote to Barfield; 'what the idea of death has done to him is nothing to what he has done to the idea of death. Hit it for six; yet it used to rank as a fast bowler!'

∽

Weeding a field was not unlike praying for a good harvest, wrote Lewis in 'Work and Prayer,' which was published in the 28 May edition of the *Coventry Evening Telegraph*. One certain difference, though, was that when one pulled a weed, the field was one weed short. But when one prayed, one did not know whether at the end of the season God would grant a full harvest. In answering prayers of petition, it seemed, God retained some measure of discretion. Perhaps he was like the headmaster at a boys' school. 'Such and such things you may do according to the fixed rules of this school. But such and such other things are too dangerous to be left to general rules. If you want to do them, you must come and make a request and talk over the whole matter with me in my study. And then — we'll see.'

∽

He wrote a ten-line poem entitled 'On the Death of Charles Williams' and sent it off to *Britain Today*, which promised publication in its August issue. But he felt a more substantial literary effort was required to commemorate his friend; perhaps a volume of essays. Tolkien, Gervase, Matthew, and Barfield said they would contribute. He would write a piece himself; Warren said he would try his hand. Lewis sent inquiries to Sayers and Eliot. She promised something on the *Divine Comedy*; he had things to say about Williams' plays. At Eliot's suggestion Lewis contacted Humphrey Milford at Oxford University Press. He got back to Lewis with 'terms and prices'. Lewis had not expected to subsidize the volume; he thought it could pay its own way; he wanted to offer the royalties to Mrs Williams. When he pointed this out to the publisher, Sir Humphrey said, 'Good gracious, no!' Of course, what he meant was, the press would publish at its own expense.

∽

Standing in a toolshed, Lewis saw flecks of dust dancing in a sunbeam. Moving closer, he looked right up the beam through the crack at the top of the closed door to some leaves beyond and, ninety million miles or so away, the sun. Looking along the beam, he observed, was quite a different experience from looking at the beam. For the last fifty years, he thought as he pottered about the Kilns that day, certain scientists had been looking *at* experience. Anthropologists had been analysing religion; psychologists had been dissecting sexual love; sociologists were generating theories about medieval chivalry. The result was that the people who looked *along* experience — the religious, the lovers, the literary critics, and historians — and saw, albeit at a far distance, the source of the experience were being either ignored or laughed at. Was looking *at* or looking *along* the more correct account? Were both accounts equally correct? Maybe they were both equally wrong. 'We just have to find out,' he concluded in 'Meditation in a Toolshed,' which was published in the 17 July edition of the *Coventry Evening Telegraph*. 'But the period of browbeating has got to end.'

∽

On Monday 6 August, over Hiroshima, one atomic bomb was exploded. On Thursday 9 August, over Nagasaki, another was dropped. Not long thereafter he began what he called a 'metrical experiment', a poem of seven stanzas, twenty-eight lines:

. . . Nor hope that this last blunder
Will end our woes by rending
Tellus herself asunder —
All gone in one bright flash like dryest tinder.

As if your puny gadget
Could dodge the terrible logic
Of history! No; the tragic
Road will go on, new generations trudge it.

Narrow and long it stretches,
Wretched for one who marches
Eyes front. He never catches
A glimpse of the fields each side, the happy orchards.

✎

'This used to be a God-fearing village with a God-fearing parson who visited and ran the Scouts ("Lovely troop we 'ad. *And* you should have 'eard our choir of a Sunday," says my bricklayer host).' This letter, an imaginary one from an invalid lady in a village, Lewis sent to *The Guardian* as an answer to the gentleman who took exception to Lewis' remark, in one of the BBC talks, that one couldn't get eternal life just by feeling the presence of God in flowers and music. 'The young were polished up and sent to Sunday school, their parents filled the church to the brim. *Now* they have an octogenarian. No harm in that! My late uncle — at that age was going as strong as most two-year-olds. But this one — I noted for myself, seeing him pass — has been dead for years . . . He does not visit the sick, even if asked. He does nothing. And — listen — he stuck up a notice in the church: *No children admitted without their parents or an adult.* The village . . . went instantly Pagan. I must get away from it. Never before but in the vile pagan West Indies have I been without so much as an *extorted* Holy Sacrament. (*Can* one forbid the church to a Crissom child? — legally, I mean? Pass me a Bishop.)'

✎

Lewis visited Campion Hall on occasion. He had only to walk up the High, turn left at Carfax, and stroll down St Aldate's to the small building with the red roof, the last college before Folly Bridge. A private hall for the members of the Society of Jesus who were matriculating at the university, it was named after Edmund Campion, a young man of brilliance and a fellow of St John's College, who in the sixteenth century, when forced to choose, chose the Church of Rome over the Church of England; he fled to the continent, where he became a Jesuit and a priest, returned to England as a missionary, and in 1581 was put to death, a traitor against England and its new church, but a martyr in the eyes of the Church of Rome.

Lewis was guest of Martin Cyril D'Arcy, the principal. Lewis had recruited him for the Socratic; in 1943 he had spoken on proving the existence of God; in 1944 he had delivered an address on the rational and the irrational. One night in the senior common room, Lewis made the point that what was needed in England was, not more little books about Christianity, but more books of whatever size by Christians on any subject whatsoever. That would speak to Screwtape in the only language he understood. That would be truly diabolical, wouldn't it? Diabolical? asked D'Arcy with a twinkle. That would be jesuitical!

∽

'For God's sake, stay to lunch if they ask you,' begged the vicar's daughter. 'It's always a little less frightful when there's a visitor.' Lewis stayed and lunched with the vicar and his wife, their son who was in the RAF, and their daughter who was in the ATS. The 'bright patter of trivial conversation' quickly disintegrated, the vicar changing subjects and interrupting, the mother complaining too much about a neighbour, the son trying to correct the father, the daughter failing to sympathize with the mother. All that might not have been so bad if the vicar later that day hadn't preached that 'the home must be the foundation of our national life.' Everyone under thirty must have gone to sleep during the sermon, thought Lewis, for family life differed so much from precept to practice. In the 21 September issue of *The Church of England Newspaper*, in an article entitled 'The Sermon and the Lunch', he urged vicars 'to stop telling lies about home life and to substitute realistic teaching.'

∽

The Christian family, such as it was at the Kilns, was being severely tested. Minto, the farther she was from her son Paddy's death, the farther also she was from the Christianity of her youth. Ulcerous and ailing still from a stroke, she was confined to bed until noon each day. She smoked a lot, the ash falling where it might, igniting whatever paper there was in the vicinity. Others doing the housework, when she saw them, filled her with what Lewis felt was unpardoning envy but might have been only frustration. Her mind meandered, but when it was still, she managed to peruse, not without interest, *War and Peace*.

∽

On 27 September Lewis wrote a letter of recommendation for George Sayer, asking at the same time if he should put in a good word with D'Arcy at Campion Hall who would know of jobs at

Catholic schools. On the same day Warren, who was now handling his brother's general correspondence, typed the three-hundred-and-thirty-seventh letter since the beginning of the year; it was to Brewer who had had to leave Magdalen for the war; 'I'm delighted to hear that you are coming back.' On 12 October he wrote by hand to Blamires who had asked him to read a manuscript of his, rehabilitating the sagging reputation of Scott; 'I think you have struck gold and made a real critical advance.'

⌘

He addressed the first Socratic in Michaelmas, meeting on 15 October in St Hilda's, just down the Cherwell from Magdalen. When the audience filled the double junior common room, he began to talk on the nature of reason. He dealt with the is-ness and is-not-ness of the language of observation and progressed to the must-ness and must-not-ness of the language of reason. Along the way, he gave examples from geometry, history, and natural science. In the discussion that followed, the name Einstein came up. The theoretical physicist was rapidly approaching deification. His theory of relativity seemed to disprove normal logic and suggested thought on a higher plane by faculties not as yet developed by humankind. When it was suggested that, by refusing 'rational proofs of unreason as well as irrational,' Lewis 'took too safe a position', he seemed to the recording secretary of the Socratic 'pleased rather than dismayed.'

⌘

He was cold when he arrived shortly after 8 p.m. at Musgrave House, a gathering place for the women of St Anne's Society, students who lived at home or with relatives but who attended the university. The first week of November had been particularly brisk; the walk from Magdalen was a long one. Coffee was being served in the lounge. This night's meeting was under the sponsorship of the Aquinas Society, who had invited him to speak on a topic of his choosing. 'Religious Imagery' was his choice; he felt he could test one of the themes he was developing for a book that would eventually be entitled *Miracles*.

The lounge could hold perhaps forty people with comfort. Perhaps as many as one hundred showed up. Some stood, some sat on chairs, some flopped on the floor, male as well as female students and not a few clergy. After speaking for an hour, Lewis glided to a halt. His audience gasped for fresh air and gossiped for a few minutes. When they returned to the lounge, Lewis fielded questions from the floor until 10.30. Were the images of Heaven and Hell faulty? Perhaps so, but the ideas behind them were sound. Weren't all imagery and picture-making, as the modernists claim, absurd?

Man cannot talk or think at all, replied Lewis, without using images.

〰

'I am hoping to try the microphone again in the next few years,' wrote Lewis to Welch at the BBC on 24 November; he had asked Lewis about the possibility of his doing a new series of talks. 'But this year and the next, work will be so fast and furious at Oxford (the full tide of the demobbed pupils is now upon us) that nothing can be done.'

〰

To celebrate England's recent victories on the battlefields of the world, the Inklings planned a winter hike based at Fairford, some thirty miles west of Oxford. Reconnoitring the place with a two-day holiday in September, the Lewises had found 'one of the loveliest of small towns', Georgian and Queen Anne predominating, every house a gem. The food was good at the Bull; the beds were excellent.

On Tuesday 11 December Warren and Tolkien set out for Fairford by train and arrived before noon. Jack materialized the following morning, but without Barfield, who had promised to come. Havard showed up at noon. For the next few days they walked, they argued, they were 'courteous but by no means obsequious.' They enjoyed 'a fine English winter beauty of plough and haystack and stubble and bare trees and roads and dry stone walls and white skies.' They visited an Anglican church where, much to the edification of the Anglicans, the Catholics said prayers. They discovered the Pig and Whistle, where the landlady gave them homemade gingersnaps to dip into their bitter.

On Friday afternoon it was back to Oxford. The brothers Lewis dined at the Royal Oxford with Christopher, Tolkien's son just back from the service. Then they took a cab up to the Kilns.

〰 **1946** 〰

'So you think Milton was an ascetic, do you? Ho, ho! You are quite wrong there!'

Why did Lewis, reputed to be the most eminent English scholar at Oxford, look — and indeed sound — so much like Friar Tuck?

asked George Bailey to himself, an American who had the temerity to apply for entrance to Magdalen.

Wasn't he a bit long in the tooth to be beginning university studies? asked Lewis.

No older really than any of the other men in the forces who were trying to pick up their education where they left off.

Was his background in English literature sufficient? asked Lewis. Perhaps he should take the alternative course, the one that emphasized language and etymology.

He preferred literature, said Bailey; Lewis agreed to take him on.

'Are you aware, sir, that your fly is open?' asked Lewis as the American headed for the door.

'If I had been, sir, I should never admit it.'

〜

It was the fourth Sunday of Lent, 31 March. Lewis was preaching at evensong at Holy Trinity, Headington, clarifying some phrases in the general confession, which was made at Holy Communion. There, the burden of sins was described as 'intolerable.' Warren, who was in the congregation, always left this phrase out, for he didn't find his emotions exercised by the burden of sins. 'Unbearable' would be a better choice of words, said Lewis, if one were writing the Prayer Book today. It was not so much that the burden of sins was emotionally unbearable as that the burden was like a heavily laden truck about to cross a fragile bridge. Cross it, and the bridge, instead of bearing the load, would collapse into rubble below. 'I wonder if this is what the Prayer Book means; that . . . there is on each of us a load which, if nothing is done about it, will in fact break us, will send us from this world to what ever happens afterward, not as souls but as broken souls.'

〜

'Give me a number from one to forty,' said Lewis to Kenneth Tynan, an undergraduate he had invited to his rooms after dinner.

'Th-Th-Th-Thirty,' stuttered Tynan.

'Right. Go to the thirtieth shelf,' said Lewis, pouring some beer for them both. 'Give me another number from one to twenty.'

'F-F-Fourteen.'

'Right. Get the fourteenth book off the shelf.' Lewis dropped back into an armchair by the fireplace. 'Now let's have a number from one to one hundred.'

'F-Forty-six.'

'Now turn to page 46. Pick a number from one to twenty-five for the line of the page.'

'Six,' said Tynan, relaxing with the beer.

'So, read me the line.'

To Lewis' astonishment, Tynan read the line without stammering; to Tynan's astonishment Lewis recognized, from that one line, not only the title of the book but also was able to continue the quotation for lines.

∽

'I wonder, would I be safe in guessing that every second person has in his life a terrible problem conditioned by some other person . . .' It was the fifth Sunday of Lent, 7 April. He was preaching in St Matthew's Church, Northampton. That other person had a 'fatal flaw,' which seemed to wreck all those who tried to reach it. But one had only to look within his or her own life to discover the presence of such a flaw. Once discovered, what should one do about it? One good method, he suggested, was confession to a priest, which an Anglican was free to do or not. If not to a priest, then one 'should at least make a list on a piece of paper, and make a serious act of penance about each one of them. There is something about the mere words, you know, provided you avoid two dangers, either of sensational exaggeration — trying to work things up and make melodramatic sins out of small matters — or the opposite danger of slurring things over.' If one did that, wouldn't morbidity or gloominess result? 'It is the reverse of morbid. It is not even, in the long run, very gloomy. A serious attempt to repent and really to know one's own sins is in the long run a lightening and relieving process.'

∽

'I think it unlikely that if other books as generally entertaining as *The Great Divorce* appear this year, they will be as generally instructive, and vice versa,' wrote Auden in the 13 April issue of *The Saturday Review*, 'so that it seems ungracious to ask for more, but I cannot help wishing Mr Lewis were a little less energetic or a little less patient. He might then give us fewer books, which would be a pity, but our satisfaction in the books he did write might be more lasting and complete. Thus, there are a number of little points in his latest volume which I am sure he would have modified if he had taken more time . . .'

∽

When invited by undergraduates and if he had the time, Lewis would go to a pub, drink beer, and discuss poetry until closing time. But when invited to dinner by a bore, he refused, pleading a glandular condition that during digestion would become acute and unsightly. He didn't have the disease, he was quick to say when sympathy was offered; he just had all the symptoms.

∽

'In making this collection, I was discharging a debt of justice,' wrote Lewis in the preface to an anthology of the writings of George MacDonald, which Bles published in the spring. 'I have never concealed the fact that I regarded him as my master; indeed I fancy I have never written a book in which I did not quote from him.' MacDonald in 1850, at the age of twenty-six, was minister to a dissenting chapel in Scotland for three years and for the next fifty-three he preached, tutored, wrote prose and poetry. More than one hundred volumes bore his name as author or editor. As a model for the anthology, Lewis used MacDonald's *Diary of an Old Soul*, which contained 365 seven-line poems, each one containing a devotional reflection. He too picked 365 passages from novels like *Lilith* and *Phantastes*, the reading of which some thirty years before Lewis felt had baptized his imagination; from children's stories like *The Princess and the Goblin* and *The Princess and Curdie*; and from three volumes entitled *Unspoken Sermons*. To the last he was especially in debt; he always suggested them to people inquiring about Christianity; he had recommended them to Neylan, and it was to her that he dedicated the anthology. 'I dare not say he is never in error,' he wrote near the end of the preface; 'but to speak plainly, I know hardly any other writer who seems to be closer, or more continually close, to the spirit of Christ himself.'

༄

Angelic minds, they say, by simple intelligence
Behold the forms of nature . . .

Essences they perceived, admitted Lewis, who was now irrevocably associated with angels of one sort or another, but they had no skin, no nose, no nerves. They could never feel hot sun turning into cool shadow, smell mown fields or wood smoke, taste porridge or oranges. Far richer these angels might be, he concluded in 'On Being Human', which was published in the 8 May issue of *Punch*:

Yet here, within this tiny charm'd interior,
This parlour of the brain, their Maker, shares
With living men some secrets in a privacy
Forever ours, not theirs.

༄

'My dear — —,' he wrote on 25 May and 28 May to Barfield in London. On 25 May he directed that £20 be sent to a librarian. On 28 May he asked that £75 be sent to 'a poor gentlewoman forced to move.'

༄

On Wednesday 26 June the brothers Lewis took an afternoon train from Oxford to London, the first lap of a journey to St Andrew's, Scotland, where, at St Mary's College, he would receive an honorary doctor of divinity degree. They had dinner in London. Before the sun set, they strolled around the neighbourhood of Euston Station. Buildings had been razed by the bombings; of the local church nothing remained but 'a fine Norman doorway.' The ruins might be sad for an adult in the neighbourhood, but for the child, observed Jack, they would be a paradise.

As darkness fell, they returned to the station, crowded now, 'hot and airless,' and boarded the train for Scotland. They each had 'a single berth room elaborately fitted with lights, fans, etc.' As the train lumbered northward during the night, they slept well. In the morning, eating 'real porridge . . . plenty of butter, edible sausages, toast, marmalade, coffee,' they could see from one window 'trim little stone towns by a calm sea' and from the other 'swelling country . . . grey stone walls, distant hills.' On arrival they went straight for the shore where along the high watermark ran 'a line of rather blackguardly-looking crows'; Jack supposed that they had been ordered by their doctors to take the sea air.

After breakfast on Friday they brought their bags to the station and deposited them there. Then they strolled towards St Mary's. Academic types were now entering the college grounds; they were wearing white collars and ties, Jack noticed. With haste they retreated to Fudyce the draper who fitted Jack out with a white collar and tie; they promised to pay him by mail just as soon as they returned to Oxford. In the college grounds Jack disappeared in one direction; Warren entered Young Hall. The undergraduates were already there, looking pretty, Warren thought, in their red gowns with fur trimmings. As the academic procession entered the hall, he couldn't believe his ears; the girls struck up 'The animals came in two by two.' Jack was at the end of the procession, clad in black cassock with scarlet buttons.

Baccalaureate degrees were conferred on seventy, perhaps eighty girls; Warren having lost count. Then came the honorary degrees. The dean of faculty eulogized each recipient and gave him or her a tubular case containing the parchment. Jack was last. At the moment the vice-chancellor apologized for not consuming more time reading his address, the hall applauded. Under cover of the noise, Warren absented himself from the gathering. There was going to be a meal; he wasn't invited. What he wanted right then was a pint of bitter and perhaps a bit more sightseeing.

At 4.55 p.m. Warren returned to St Mary's in a taxi and picked up

Jack as he emerged from a doorway; they went to the station just in time to catch the 5.20 northward. At Dundee they found the station master, who assigned them berths on the train southward. In the time that remained, they found a hotel, had beer in a comfortable bar, and dined in a splendid room. Back at the station, the London overnight express was crammed with undergraduates going down. They were even standing in the corridors. Warren was indignant. Jack was indignant too, but now that he was a doctor of divinity, he knew that if he expressed his indignation, he would reveal only his lack of virtue under stress.

∽

'God bless you,' read Lewis, as he opened the first piece of mail on Saturday 13 July. The correspondent thanked Lewis for his writings. They had friends in common; the poet Herbert Palmer, for example. She herself was a poet, with several published volumes; she asked if a meeting at Magdalen was out of the question. A sensitive nobody approaching a greatly gifted person — that was the tone of her letter: how could he refuse her? 'Would Wednesday 17 July suit?' he wrote to Ruth Pitter. 'I shall be here all morning.'

∽

'Recently in a party of six people, I found that all without exception would like *fewer* hymns,' he wrote on 16 July to Erik Routley who had asked him, on behalf of the Hymn Society of Great Britain and Ireland, to join a panel assessing the value of new hymns. 'Naturally, one holding this view can't help you.' Warren shared his brother's view, but as he was getting his hair cut a month later, he had to modify it. Victor Drew, the barber, a troubled man in the best of times, confided that he found great comfort in the hymns he sang in church of a Sunday; as his scissors flashed, he began to quote couplets that were so banal that Warren blushed. Never, vowed Warren as he went under the steaming towel, would he be dogmatic about how everyone hated hymns.

∽

'I am primarily an arguer, not an exhorter, and my target is the frankly irreligious audience,' wrote Lewis on Tuesday 16 July to the Rev. T. Wilkinson Riddle who had invited him to speak; 'nor do I ever speak my best in a very large hall with an atmosphere of enthusiasm in it.'

∽

'Do you realize that you almost blinded my baby?' It was a lazy Sunday afternoon; visitors were strolling about Magdalen; but one of them bounded up staircase 3 and burst into Lewis' rooms, accusing him of emptying his loaded pipe out of the window onto the walk below.

'No,' said Lewis with some equanimity. 'I didn't even know you were married.'

∾

On the morning of 17 July he sported the oak for Ruth Pitter. She was about his age, he was relieved to see; no chance of her seducing him. She was much moved by his radio talks, she said; they and the books that followed had touched her life; she was now approaching Christianity in a more positive way. They talked about poetry for a while. Before she left, she gave him copies of her own stuff. The door closed, he had the distinct impression that he had made an ass of himself.

The next day, when he dipped into her poems, it was like gliding into a deep pool. 'A Trophy of Arms' was mystical, classical. 'Turn not aside, Shepherd' was beautifully middle-aged. 'Caged Lions' and 'A Solemn Meditation' were his favourites. She was unusually good with metres, especially Sapphics, which he had never liked in English. Only one poem did he dislike, 'The Flower Piece.'

'I meant to send you something of mine, but I shan't. It all sounds like a brass band after yours,' he wrote to her on 19 July. 'Why wasn't I told you were as good as this?'

An exchange of letters followed. With his of 24 July he enclosed 'The Birth of Language,' 'To Charles Williams,' 'On Being Human,' 'Solomon,' and 'Some Believe.'

> Some believe the slumber
> Of trees is in December
> When timber's naked under the sky
> And squirrel keeps his chamber.
>
> But I believe their fibres
> Awake to life and labour
> When turbulence comes roaring up
> The land in loud October,
>
> And plunders woods and sunders
> And sends the leaves to wander
> And undisguises prickly shapes
> Beneath the golden spendour.
>
> Then form returns. In warmer,
> Seductive days, disarming
> Its former will, the wood grew soft,
> And put forth dreams to murmur.

Into earnest winter,
Awaked and hard, it enters.
The hunter Frost and the keen winds
Have quelled the green enchanter.

'I know (or think) that some of these contain important thoughts and very great metrical ingenuity. That isn't what I'm worrying about. But are they real poems, or do the content and the form remain inseparable — fitted together only by force?'

&

Mrs Dyson was still attractive, thought Warren, as he and his brother were greeted. Dyson had recently been named to the Merton faculty and moved from Reading to Oxford. A tour of the house was followed by dinner. The linen was crisp, the table silver gleamed, the crystal was sparkling with hock; the fish salad, sweet, and savoury were a delight to the palate. After dinner Gervase Mathew, a Dominican priest and lecturer on several of the university faculties, dropped in, and later two women who were tutors. The conversation was pleasant; the whisky and sodas were refreshing until 10.30 p.m., when it was time to leave. Returning through the deer grove, Warren couldn't help remarking how slatternly the Kilns was in comparison to the house on Holywell Street, and how the meals up on Shotover had 'the air of being a perpetual *picnic.*'

&

'I see your point only too well. I also am haunted at times by the feeling that I oughtn't to be doing this kind of thing,' he wrote on 29 July to Sayers. He had invited her to write a booklet-length piece on some aspect of Christian knowledge for young people in top forms at school. Not wanting to do it, she questioned at length whether it would be an honest piece of work for a writer such as her to do or a dishonest piece. Lewis had another sort of uneasiness about the project; it could be yet another danger to his faith. 'Anyway, thanks for an intensely interesting letter.' Honest or dishonest, he went on to write two thousand words; he entitled it 'Man or Rabbit?' and sent it off to the Student Christian Movement in Schools; it was just the sort of four-page pamphlet they wanted.

&

'This is more than driving a bird to a gun,' wrote Lewis to Pitter on 28 August. An acquaintance of hers had joined the RCs as a result of reading his books. 'It is more like introducing a phoenix to a fire. Congratulations (and condolences). Of course, in any shoot the beater's role is a very humble one.'

&

Lewis often wondered what he was about, writing and speaking for the faith. Now, in the September issue of *The Atlantic Monthly*, an American told him. He was an 'apostle to the sceptics'; he was 'in the thirteenth year of his one-man campaign to convert the world to Christianity'; he was 'systematically waging private war against the religious scepticism of the English-reading world.' Chad Walsh was the author, an agreeable young man with whom he had been in correspondence. He seemed to have read his way from atheism at the University of Virginia to theism at the University of Michigan where Auden upheld the fantastic doctrine of original sin; to the divinity of Christ in Washington, D.C., where he read the New Testament and Lewis' radio talks; to the rest of the basic Christian dogmas at Beloit, Wisconsin, where he was received into the Episcopal Church, baptized, and confirmed. The magazine article was articulate and comprehensive, but why did it have to end with such an impossible and embarrassing sentence? 'If Christianity revives in England and America, the odds are that it may bear strong traces of the gospel according to C. S. Lewis.'

∿

'Can't we devise something that will get her to Oxford?' asked Dyson at the height of the luncheon. He was speaking of Ruth Pitter, whose poetry he held almost in awe. Lewis was the host of the luncheon, which was being served in the New Room at Magdalen on Wednesday 9 October. The Cecils were there and Warren too. Feeling her chronic Jude-the-Obscure syndrome receding for the moment, she engaged in lively conversation with the man next to her, Warren, telling him how she had met the famous AE (George William Russell) in Galway and how she had tried to lure her into a secret society by means of a gold ring.

∿

No, he would not give a lecture to the British Interplanetary Society, Lewis had written to Arthur C. Clarke on 14 September.

'Yes, it is only too true,' he wrote to Sister Penelope on 21 October about the rumours that travel in space was imminent. 'I begin to be afraid that the villains will really contaminate the moon.'

∿

'I love the monotonies of life — getting up and going to bed — looking out at the same view and meeting the same people at the same times every day. I never "want things to happen." They're always happening; and I'd rather they happened in the right order than in the wrong order. I don't like interferences in the normal order of events; and to me the most disagreeable experience would be one that suspended normality.'

Lewis was being interviewed by Ashley Sampson for *The Church of England Newspaper*, which was beginning a series of word-portraits of interesting and indeed living Anglicans.

'But what about pleasant surprises?' asked Sampson. 'They aren't in your catalogue of monotonies.'

'No — and, of course, one is delighted at them; but there's a rich variety of surprises within the content of one's daily doings. For instance, when I walk across from these rooms to breakfast every morning, the view is precisely the same; but the sky is a different texture nearly every day. The trees vary from month to month; and even the angle of the sun makes a difference. I welcome changes.'

Unwelcome, though, and embarrassing were the headlines in the 4 October issue: on the front page, 'Christian Commando Campaign'; on page 7, 'The Crusading Intellect.'

⁓

At dinner on Monday 14 October Warren was driven to indigestion by Minto. Vera the new maid, she said, had attempted to murder a woman in Oxford by throwing her out of a second-storey window; the victim escaped with a broken rib; the whole matter was hushed up. Vera would surely strike again, this time at the Kilns, and Minto would be her victim.

He couldn't believe his ears at first, but then it seemed to fit a pattern. Burning within the old woman was a flame he diagnosed as 'greed and hate,' but which might in reality have been only the flutterings of an imagination that was expiring. As he went to bed that night, he could hear Dyson in the dining hall at Merton, warbling a piece of Shakespeare that seemed to epitomize Jack's predicament at the Kilns: 'O cursed spite that gave thee to the Moor!'

⁓

Americans appeared regularly in Lewis' mail. Sister Madeleva, whom he had met in 1934, thanked him for his books, wished for unity between Rome and Canterbury, and invited him to South Bend, Indiana, where she was now president of St Mary's College. Warfield Firor admired Lewis' works, especially his latest, *The Great Divorce*, sent him gifts of stationery and dried fruits, and invited him to Baltimore. That Americans liked his books was pleasing to Lewis; that American reviewers read the books before writing their critiques was often more than British reviewers did.

This Tuesday morning, 29 October, a photographer from an American magazine came to call. Hans Wild was his name. *Life* had commissioned him to shoot a roll or two of the Oxford don. He asked Lewis to relax, sit behind his desk, and talk. The photographs, Lewis expressed the hope, would be better than that woodcut in the *Saturday*

Review a few years ago. Wild chatted amiably as he moved about the room, snapping Lewis puffing on a cigarette, trying to capture in black-and-white the starched white shirt, the dark tie with stripe, the sweater, the tweed jacket straining at two buttons, then at one.

Lewis rushed to his own defence in the autumn issue of *The Modern Quarterly*. In a previous issue of that journal, biologist J. B. S. Haldane reviewed Lewis' works of science fiction and levelled heavy charges against them. Referring to these three works as romances, Lewis reduced Haldane's charges to three. That his science was usually wrong, Lewis readily admitted, but he pointed out that Haldane's science was not always right. That he traduced scientists, Lewis claimed was inaccurate; what he seduced was scientism. That he was attacking scientific planning, that the application of science to human affairs led only to Hell, Lewis turned the other way around. 'Any effective invitation to Hell will certainly appear in the guise of scientific theory — as Hitler's regime in fact did.'

'Is progress possible without religion?' That was the announced topic of the Socratic on 4 November. The meeting was sponsored by four undergraduate societies, and hence had to be held in the large debating hall of the Oxford Union. Speaking first, Arnold Lunn identified himself as a Roman Catholic and a liberal. That Nazism and Communism, both of which promised progress, had failed miserably, was his point. He was witty and humorous at first, but his presentation against religionless ideologies 'deteriorated into a political invective.' Members of the Rationalist Society and the Socialist Club, who were co-sponsoring the event with the Socratic, began to heckle. Responding, J. D. Bernal, who described himself as a dialectical materialist, had a sunnier interpretation of history. He claimed that the years since the revolution had produced both change and progress in Russia and that in England it was a socialist, G. B. Shaw, who had championed most of the progressive causes. Members of the Student Christian Movement as well as the Socratic hooted at that. Chairing the meeting was Lewis, who had to remind the audience several times that catcalls and rude remarks were not in the spirit of rational exchange. At the end, in an attempt to draw some clarity, he defined progress and religion to the satisfaction of neither speaker.

Chesterton was dated, said an article in the 17 October issue of *The Listener*; in the 9 November issue of *Time and Tide* Lewis rushed to his defence. A writer could be dated in a negative sense, he suggested, when he wrote poems in the shapes of altars and crosses simply because it was the vogueish thing to do; such poetry quickly passed out of vogue. But a writer could be dated in a positive sense when he wrote of 'matters of permanent interest' in the conventions of his particular age. 'The "Prelude" smells of its age. "The Waste Land" has twenties stamped on every line. Even Isaiah will reveal to a careful student that it was not composed at the court of Louis XIV nor in modern Chicago.'

Chesterton's journalism was certainly dated in the negative sense, as were his little books of essays. Certain aspects of the 'Ballad of the White Horse' appeared silly and transitory after several decades, but surely its theme — the message Alfred received from the Virgin — embodied the feeling that almost-defeated men of every age have just before they fought the final battle and won. 'Hence, in those quaking days after the fall of France, a young friend of mine, just about to enter the RAF, and I found ourselves quoting to one another stanza after stanza of the "Ballad." There was nothing else to say.'

❦

In the hope of cadging a preface from Lewis, Bles sent him a copy of the manuscript of *How Heathen Is Britain?* Quite by accident, it seemed to Lewis as he read, the author B. G. Sandhurst had discovered during his wartime work something that corresponded with Lewis' experience with the RAF, that when young men were schoolboys, they had not been presented with 'the content of, and the case for, Christianity,' and that when they did learn about it they were impressed. If they appeared unchristian today, it was only that their teachers had been 'unwilling or unable' to pass the good word on. Religion had not declined so much as it had not been taught.

'After that discovery we should turn a deaf ear to people who offered explanations of a vaguer and larger kind,' wrote Lewis enthusiastically in his preface, 'people who said that the influence of Einstein had sapped the ancestral belief in fixed numerical relations, or that gangster films had undermined the desire to get right answers, or that the evolution of consciousness was now entering on its post-arithmetical phase.'

❦

'Reason can see truth in sleep with three kinds of clarity . . .' Lewis was at the rostrum in the Schools building; he was at that point in his lecture, one of the series introducing medieval and Renaissance literature, when he checked to see if his audience was asleep. 'In the oracle kind (*oraculum*), some venerable person — an ancestor, wise man, parent, or *even a tutor* . . .' They must have been awake; they laughed.

〰

The chapels in Oxford were full in 1900 but empty in 1946; more than one person concluded that religion was in decline. What was in decline, wrote Lewis in the 29 November issue of *The Cherwell*, was not Christianity but 'a vague theism with a strong and virile ethical code, which, far from standing over against the "world", was absorbed into the whole fabric of English institutions and sentiment and therefore demanded church-going as (at best) a part of loyalty and good manners as (at worst) a proof of respectability.' The decline of that sort of religion was clearly a blessing. Chapel was mandatory in 1900 but not in 1946. The modern undergraduate was free to attend, free to choose Christ, and able to consider Christianity as one of the intellectual options. Writers and lecturers who presented the Christian viewpoint were proliferating to the point where they could howl against 'the highbrow Christian racket.'

〰

So he was a foe of humanism, was he? Looking through the 25 December issue of *The Christian Century*, he came across an article entitled 'C. S. Lewis: Foe of Humanism.' He remembered the author, the Rev. George C. Anderson, who had tramped through the rain and mud one morning not many months past to New Buildings. Lewis took his dripping hat and mackintosh and ushered him towards the Georgian chair by the fireplace. Auden, it seemed, was a parishioner of Anderson's at his parish in Swarthmore, Pennsylvania; indeed Auden had introduced him to Lewis' works. So much for the small talk. Anderson was full of questions, and Lewis would have to do his best. Kierkegaard he thought was 'sawdust'; Niebuhr he thought was difficult; he was unfamiliar with Barth and ignorant of existentialism, but modernism was 'a bucketful of bubbles.' And so the hour was over, and Anderson trooped out into the rain. In the article that resulted, he seemed to have got everything right, but still Lewis felt a twinge. Why did he have to say that Lewis' voice was almost as familiar to the British people as the tones of Big Ben? D'Arcy, Sayers, and Knox had done as much religious broadcasting. And wasn't it hyperbole of an unpardonable sort to conclude that 'in the years to come Lewis will be recognized as England's foremost champion of Christianity during those dark times that cried for a voice to reassure the people of the faith of the fathers'?

〰

'We must, if it so happens, give our own lives for others,' he wrote on 20 December to Griffiths, trying to dissolve the Benedictine's disillusionment over the state of the world, 'but even while we're doing it, I think we're meant to enjoy our Lord, and, in him, our friends, our food, our sleep, our jokes, and the birds and the frosty sunrise.'

ᥴᥴᥴ 1947 ᥴᥴᥴ

'I've just had a poem (but then I never was a poet like you) refused by *The Spectator* for the first time — I mean, the first time since I was a youngster,' he wrote on 4 January to Pitter. 'Very tonic; I'd forgotten the taste of that little printed slip. What one suffers between the ages of seventeen and twenty-two!'

Mrs McNeill had died in Ireland, and Lewis wrote a letter of condolence to Janie. Forrest Reid had died also, and on 5 January Lewis wrote to Greeves. He inquired after Arthur's mother, who now required a 'nurse companion', something he could wish for Minto if only she would allow it. He talked about growing old. The pupils at Oxford seemed never to have had a youth such as the one he and his friend enjoyed in the environs of Belfast. They did seem to have read all the important books, but never to have had 'private and erratic imaginative adventures of their own. I suppose the explanation is that I am the last person who is likely to hear of such things even when they exist. I mean, with me they're all talking "grown-up" as hard as they can. Yet I don't know: the modern world is so desperately serious.'

ᥴᥴ

> I dreamt that all the planning of peremptory humanity
> > Had crushed nature finally beneath the foot of man;
> Birth control and merriment, earth completely sterilized,
> > Bungalow and fun-fair, had fulfilled our plan;
> But the lion and the unicorn were sighing at the funeral,
> > Crying at the funeral,
> > Sobbing at the funeral of the god Pan.

'Pan's Purge' was the title of the poem, which combined serious-ness and silliness to such an extraordinary degree that *Punch* published it in the 15 January issue; Lewis had to warn his friends to look for the poem, for he signed it with the initials N.W.

∽

'I'm a tethered man,' he wrote to a correspondent on 11 March. Minto had pneumonia with fever raging and lungs wheezing. The doctor was summoned, a nurse was hired, and Warren, giving his dislike of the woman a respite, prayed for her recovery. Maureen arrived at the Kilns. As her mother recovered, she convinced her that Jack and Warnie needed a holiday. She would return to the Kilns on 4 April and stay until the 15th; during that time Jack and Warnie could stay at her house in Malvern. 'A diplomatist of the first order,' wrote Warren of Maureen in his diary of that night, 17 March.

∽

The floppy package from Oxford University Press contained galley proofs of the essays in memory of Charles Williams; it would be dedicated to his widow, and such income as it earned would go to her. Lewis tore the package open, read the letter accompanying it, and unfurled the galleys on his cluttered desk.

About to begin proof-reading, pencil poised for correction, there was a knock at the door. It was a photographer, Arthur P. Strong. Lewis was expecting him, and he wished him all speed with the camera. Strong asked Lewis what he was doing; Lewis explained about the proof; Strong immediately sat him down at his desk. It couldn't have been more pleasantly disarrayed — pipes and pencils, matches and ink bottles, galley proofs and a small globe — if the photographer had arranged it himself. Then he asked Lewis to go to the window of the sitting-room and gaze contemplatively out at the deer park. Then, if he would, still standing at the window, turn back towards the camera . . . Then, if he would lean against a bookcase and perhaps explain the picture on the wall . . .

The thick wool jacket and the baggy corduroy trousers were perfect. The white-panelled walls and the strong floral print of the fabric in the draperies and sofa would reproduce well on black and white film. Good face, thought Strong, good rolling features; white starched shirt collar points akimbo, tie with argyle design: perfect.

When Lewis finally ushered the congenial, ever-snapping photographer from the room, he went back to his desk and began to read the galleys of his contribution to the Williams work, 'On Stories.'

∽

Lewis loved 'the cut and parry of prolonged, fierce, masculine argument,' but when it came from a pupil, he could be exasperated. One of them — he could not remember in his fury whether it was George Bailey the American or Geoffrey Dutton the Australian —

had just said that he could not bring himself to read 'Sohrab and Rustum.' If he wouldn't read it, then Lewis would recite it, beginning to chant the climactic scene where Rustum, champion of the Persian armies, was meeting in single combat Sohrab, champion of the Tartar armies, who was his unknown son. Even under the force of Lewis' dramatic baritone, the pupil refused to admit that the narrative poem had any redeeming qualities, Matthew Arnold's iambic pentameter sounding like so much caparisoned clopping.

'The sword must settle it!' shouted Lewis. He plucked a broadsword from the corner of his room — he might have been Beowulf with Naegling, Unferth with Hrunting — and lofted a rapier to the pupil. They started whanging each other about the room. Lewis drew first blood; the pupil scrambled through the oak, down the staircase, and out into the colonnade, glad to be alive.

∽

On Good Friday, 4 April, Maureen and her son went to the Kilns, her husband having gone on a business trip; the Lewises motored to her home in Malvern. Winter had yet to leave central England; but spring would arrive while they were there. They discovered an excellent pub, the Unicorn, and a horrid bar in the Foley Arms. They performed their Easter duty with propriety at a nearby priory. During the days they walked, and during the evenings they read. They were even visited for a short time by Dyson; he took to the hiking more than a sedentary man might be expected to; in the evenings his intellectual hyperactivity, accelerated by distilled spirits, led to barrack-room ballads, Folies Bergères kicks, and Tararaboomdyay!

'The sound of lambs, the clean air, the vast landscape, the springy turf,' thought Warren as he flopped at the top of a hill, falling back in memory some thirty-five years. Refreshed, exhilarated at first, he was then flung back into the present by having to return after ten days of vacation to that 'horrid house' in Headington. The Kilns must still have had some beauty about it, but because of Minto he loathed 'every stick and stone and sound of it.'

∽

On Monday 19 May a Lewis addressed the Socratic Club and a Lewis responded. H. D. Lewis, a philosopher, read a paper entitled 'Belief and Conduct,' in which 'he attacked what he called the "perverted" and "villainous" doctrine of original sin. To blame yourself for what happens independent of your own will is an irrational state of mind that only a psychiatrist can explain. From St Augustine onward, this doctrine had been an excuse for disregarding the rigorous and exacting ethical principles of Jesus.'

So wrote Frank Goodridge, a pupil at Magdalen and secretary of the Socratic. He recorded his tutor C. S. Lewis as replying to H. D. Lewis that 'he accepted the doctrine of original sin because St Augustine and St Paul taught it, and to reject St Paul meant rejecting the canon and so casting doubt on even the sayings of Jesus.'

～

In a dark garden, by a dreadful tree,
The Druid Toms were met. They numbered three,
Tab Tiger, Demon Black, and Ginger Hate.
Their forms were tense, their eyes were full of fate;
Save the involuntary caudal thrill,
The horror was that they should sit so still . . .

Pitter had sent Lewis her poem entitled 'Quorum Porum,' the first word of the title meaning a competent number, the second being the genitive plural of the Latin word for puss. 'A very cheerful and companionable work,' he replied, and not long thereafter he sent her a leporine epigram:

Call *him* a Fascist! Thus the rabbit,
Oblivious of their varying merits,
Takes all, who share the simple habit
Of eating rabbit pie, for ferrets.

～

Reading the *Morte D'Arthur* for the first time had opened a new world to Lewis. 'The very names of the chapters, as they spring to meet the eye, bear with them a fresh, sweet breath from the old-time fairy world,' he wrote in 1915 to Greeves. How could a reader resist chapters entitled 'How Launcelot in the Chapel Perilous gat a cloth from a Dead corpse' and 'How Pellinore found a damosel by a Fountain and of the Jousts in the Castle of the Four stones'? In 1934 Malory scholarship came to an almost complete halt when a manuscript of his Arthurian romances was found in the library of Winchester College. Working for more than a decade, Eugene Vinaver produced a definitive work, which was published in 1947 by the Clarendon Press. The *Times Literary Supplement* sent the three volumes to Lewis for an evaluation. He had reservations, but in general he was enthusiastic. 'It is a very great work,' he wrote in an unsigned review, which appeared in the 7 June issue, 'and a work which hardly any other man in England was qualified to perform.'

Vinaver had entitled his opus *The Works* of Malory because the manuscript contained eight separate romances. These had been rendered into a seemingly cohesive whole by editor-publisher-printer William Caxton at the end of the fifteenth century. Now in the twentieth century readers had these two versions of Malory's works to choose between. 'We should approach [the *Morte D'Arthur*] not as we approach Liverpool Cathedral, but as we approach Wells Cathedral,' he wrote near the end of his review. 'At Liverpool [which was built in the 20th century] we see what a particular artist invented. At Wells [which was begun in the 12th century] we see something on which many generations laboured, which occupies a position halfway between the works of art and those of nature.'

On the publication of *The Works*, the character of Sir Thomas Malory took a dreadful dip. Vinaver had succeeded in showing that Malory had been convicted of 'cattle-lifting, theft, extortion, sacrilegious robbery, attempted murder, and rape.' Lewis explained these charges as best he could by saying that they represented only what partisan lawyers had put down on the record. 'The record tells us nothing more than we might expect such records to tell of a man on the locally unpopular side who attempted on the whole to live as a good knight should.' After all, what would happen 'if we imagine the life of Sir Tristram as it would be presented to us by King Mark's solicitors'? Having read that last sentence in the *TLS*, Barfield felt obliged to respond.

'We act for H. M. King Mark I of Cornwall, who has recently consulted us in the matter of the behaviour of your client, Sir Tristram,' read the letter from Barfield & Barfield, Solicitors, dated 11 June 503. 'It appears that while your client was, at our client's expense and as his confidential agent, escorting our client's then fiancée across the Irish Channel, he took advantage of those very circumstances to seduce this unfortunate lady and has, both before and since her marriage to our client, been carrying on a criminal conversation with her as and when opportunity offered, at Tintagel and elsewhere. We regret to say that the evidence in our possession removes all doubt of the authenticity of these disgusting allegations . . .'

'[Mr Lewis], under the guise of a book on miracles, offers a rational justification both of theism and of doctrinal Christianity,' read the unsigned review of *Miracles* in the 14 June edition of *The Times Literary Supplement*. 'In so discursive a treatment some points are overlooked which would have found a place in a more analytic account. Especially we want to know how a miraculous event is to be discerned . . .'

On Saturday 21 June, Lewis got a wire from a Dr Costello; his brother was in the hospital, sick, perhaps unto death. Warren had left on vacation for Ireland ten days before, but how did he get to Drogheda, Jack asked himself as he rummaged around Magdalen for clothes and money. Arranging things as best he could at the Kilns, he left for Ireland the following morning, hardly knowing whether he should ferry to Belfast and drive south along the coast of the Irish Sea, or ferry to Dublin and motor northward. It was Monday morning when he arrived travel-stained at Drogheda. He asked directions to the Convent Hospital of Our Lady of Lourdes. Having got Warren's room number from the front desk, he walked down the corridor, dreading what he would find. Warren smiled as his brother turned into the private room.

After a few moments of reassurance, Jack left the room and sought out one of the nuns. Mother Mary Martin told him that Warren had arrived at the hospital last Friday night; he was suffering from severe intoxication; he had been drinking, or so he admitted, for ten days. Over and above that, the gin served in Dunany had been extended by the addition of methylated spirits. It was a wonder, said Lewis, that his brother was still alive. It was a wonder, said Mother Mary Martin, that he suffered no internal or cerebral damage. Jack expressed his gratitude to her for taking his brother in and asked where he might stay and where he might get some money.

Having cashed a cheque at the hospital and checked in at the White Horse, Jack freshened himself up and returned to visit Warren at tea time. His brother was feeling better; he was able to tell Jack that the cottage he had rented in Dunany was a bust; the stove didn't work, and water had to be fetched from a well a mile off; he sought the company of the locals and drank too much, which might not have been so bad if the gin they served hadn't been laced with wood alcohol. And, he confessed, he had succumbed to despondency and depression.

It was a joyful place, the hospital. One of the sisters tucked him in at night with 'God be with you', said Warren; another of the sisters woke him up in the morning with 'It's a fine day, thanks be to God.' The nuns were Catholics, but all that Protestant propaganda about their being 'sad-faced women gliding about noiselessly, rarely speaking and never smiling, spying and being spied upon' was a lot of rubbish. Mother Mary Martin was a saintly type, very efficient as an administrator, and always had time for a gossip. He was being spiritually refreshed as he recovered physically; the hospital was a 'little fortress of happy, valiant Christianity.'

With the tea came Fr. Quin, the chaplain. He had heard that Warren was not Church of Rome, and would he perhaps be taking the opportunity God and sickness had provided him of reconsidering the eternal verities in general and a change of denomination in particular? He talked without stop, his argument streaming with mariology, in a way that seemed like a set-piece oration in school, and in an Ulster accent. Had he the tongue of an angel, said Warren to Jack when the chaplain left, an Ulster Catholic could never convert an Ulster Protestant to the Church of Rome!

Jack saw Mother Mary Martin again, and again expressed his gratitude to her and his admiration for her cheerful and holy staff. The Medical Missionaries of Mary they were called. She had founded them ten years before; her main purpose in doing so was to staff mission hospitals in tropical Africa. The sisters he saw in the hospital were training to become nurses, technicians, and doctors. It was a shame, said Lewis, that word about her group had not got around so that others might join. If he should write about them, she said in riposte, the word would indeed get around. Of course, he would write something about them. Perhaps a pamphlet celebrating their tenth anniversary? He would begin that very night.

'At first sight nothing seems more obvious than that religious persons should care for the sick,' he wrote by lamplight at the White Horse; 'no Christian building, except perhaps a church, is more self-explanatory than a Christian hospital. Yet on further consideration the thing is really connected with the undying paradox, the blessedly two-edged character of Christianity. And if any of us were now encountering Christianity for the first time, he would be vividly aware of this paradox . . .'

On Wednesday Warren was able to get out of bed; he was so wobbly that he was glad to return to it some minutes later. On Thursday he got dressed and was able to leave the hospital with his brother for a walk 'into the quiet green countryside.' On Friday Jack took a taxi to Dunany to pick up Warren's things and bring them back to Drogheda; in the evening the brothers went for a walk even as the rain began to fall. On Saturday it was pouring as Warren signed out of the hospital and into the White Horse, 'arriving just in time for a bottle of Guinness before a most substantial midday dinner.'

Warren would stay at the inn for another four weeks, continuing his recuperation on an out-patient basis; Jack had to leave for Oxford at 4.45. As his brother receded into the distance, Warren was overcome with depression. Suppose Jack were to die before him? he thought as he sipped a glass of sherry before bedtime. 'A sheer wave of animal panic' spread over him 'at the prospect of the empty years . . .'

'It is possible that the reader who opens this volume on the counter of a bookshop may ask himself why we need a new translation of any part of the Bible . . .' In 1943 the Rev. J. B. Phillips had sent Lewis a translation into modern, colloquial English of Paul's letter to the Colossians. Lewis responded so favourably that he encouraged the London vicar to do the same with the rest of the epistles. Phillips sent him each one as he finished it. Once the twenty-one epistles were completed, Lewis suggested a title for the work, *Letters to Young Churches*, and cadged Geoffrey Bles into publishing the work by offering to write an introduction.

༄

'You know what awful things Americans ask one to do?' wrote Lewis to Pitter on 9 August. 'I have a letter from a lady in dear old Kentucky, asking me to look in the London directory for the address of FERNANDRO LORRAINE who lives at Harrow on the Hill and is described as a "professor" of mathematics. This is accompanied by butter (praise) and jam (parcel), so I feel I cannot neglect it . . .' Pitter looked the address up and sent it to Lewis, who on 19 August was able to forward it, together with a thank-you note for the parcel, to Mr and Mrs E. L. Baxter of Versailles, Kentucky.

༄

Fr. Patrick Irwin asked Lewis to write something about forgiveness, which he might include in the parish magazine for St Mary's, Sawston, Cambridgeshire. Lewis did not respond right away. Then it occurred to him that he might say something about the hard reality of having to forgive the sins of others before one could expect one's own sins to be forgiven by God.

To forgive a single, horrible offence was easier in some ways than forgiving over and over again 'the bossy mother-in-law, the bullying husband, the nagging wife, the selfish daughter, the deceitful son.' But if one expected mercy from God, one had to offer mercy to others. 'There is no hint of exceptions,' he wrote in the last sentence, hastening to catch the post on 28 August, 'and God means what he says.'

༄

Christianity could cost one his career, Lewis had said on more than one occasion. Hot gospelling, as he was now somewhat ruefully calling his efforts at evangelizing, certainly seemed to have turned the electors of the Merton Professorship of English Literature against him; his name had not been mentioned last year in connection with the foundation of a new chair of literature. He had been careful never to mention religion in lectures or tutorials, nor did he ever proselytize in his professional publications. But the Socratic had won him enemies, and the spectre of Screwtape bedevilled him right from the moment of creation.

Now, as he looked at the 8 September issue of *Time* magazine, he wondered how much more his feeble commitment to Christianity would cost him. He was on the cover. Not a bad portrait actually, although rather idealized, he thought, with angel wing on one side and Screwtape on the other, by someone with the unlikely name of Artzybasheff. 'Oxford's C. S. Lewis — His heresy: Christianity' read the caption; the cover story was to be found, not in the education section, but in the religion section.

'Don v. Devil' was the title of the story; it began on page 65 and ran, interspersed with ads for products like Polident and Tampax and for a movie starring Alan Ladd and Dorothy Lamour, to page 74. 'I like monotony,' the anonymous magazine writer quoted him as saying; at least the magazine got that right. And he was included with a growing band of heretics — Eliot and Auden, Dorothy L. Sayers and Graham Greene — intellectuals who believed in God; not a bad paradox. There were generous quotations from the *Broadcast Talks*, *The Pilgrim's Regress* and *The Screwtape Letters*. The influence of George MacDonald and Charles Williams was acknowledged. And mention of the publication by the American Macmillan of the MacDonald anthology in the spring and *Miracles* in the fall was welcome.

'One of Lewis' severest critics insists that his works of scholarship, *The Allegory of Love* (on Spenser), and *A Preface to Paradise Lost*, are "miles ahead" of any other literary criticism in England.' This was the paragraph that gave Lewis pause. 'But Lewis' Christianity, says his critic, has brought him more money than it ever brought Joan of Arc, and a lot more publicity than she enjoyed in her lifetime.' How much more, O Lord? prayed Lewis as he continued to read slowly. 'In contrast to his tight scholarly writing (says this critic), Lewis' Christian propaganda is cheap sophism: having lured his reader onto the straight highway of logic, Lewis then inveigles him down the garden path to orthodox theology.'

∽

On Thursday 25 September the Inklings met at Magdalen shortly after nine. Colin Hardie and Christopher Tolkien showed up, Dyson and Warren and Lewis' guest for the evening, George Sayer from Malvern. A bottle of Cyprian wine materialized; the assembly pronounced it 'very sweet and smooth.' Sweet and smooth too was Lewis' reading of a poem by Eliot, which, suddenly, he broke off, declaring it to be bilge. Sayer came to his master's support. Dyson and the younger Tolkien defended the poem, at least on the ground that Eliot did not have to be another Masefield, another Auden.

∽

The scout brought yet another parcel from America up staircase 3 to Lewis' door. 'Johns Hopkins Hospital, Baltimore, Maryland' on the label meant that the package was from Warfield Firor. Once in July and twice in September Lewis had to fire off notes of thanks to the surgeon. The parcels meant having ' "something nice" over and above the monotonous scanty ration,' he wrote on 13 September, Minto being the special beneficiary of them. But when he opened the large package that arrived on 1 October, he was overcome. 'A ham such as you sent lifts me up into our millionaire class,' he wrote in thanks. 'Such a thing couldn't be got on this side unless one was very deep in the black market, and it would probably set one back about £12-0-0. And as for the cheese I found I'd almost forgotten what real cheese tastes like.'

‿

'D. G.!' hailed Lewis. I've got a rather nice ham in my room.' Dundas-Grant, now retired from the navy, ran a Catholic hostel for Oxford Students. 'Would you care to come up tonight and have some?' From that moment on, D. G. was an Inkling and appeared regularly on Thursday evenings in college rooms and Tuesday mornings at various pubs.

‿

'His face we thought ugly; I am not sure that the word "monkey" has not been murmured in this context,' wrote Lewis in the preface to *Essays Presented to Charles Williams*, which was published in November. 'But the moment he spoke, it became, as was also said, like the face of an angel — not a feminine angel in the debased tradition of some religious art, but a masculine angel, a spirit burning with intelligence and charity.' For the touching memoir of her husband, Michal thanked Lewis; he pointed out that the book was dedicated to her, although Oxford University Press had forgotten the dedication page.

‿

'To die without having read the *Symposium* would be ridiculous,' said Lewis in lecture; undergraduates would echo the sentiment in pubs, vulgarizing it only at the end; 'it would be like never having bathed in the sea, never having drunk wine, never having been in love.'

‿

A brilliant atheist, Jean-Paul Sartre, but he probably had a bad liver, said Lewis to his pupil Frank Goodridge. It was wintry and dark on the night of 3 November. They were walking through the gardens of Somerville College and fell into a ditch. These Monday night walks to the Socratic, said Lewis, springing up and brushing himself off, were a really odyssey. He was to speak that night on Sartre's new book, which he had read in French. Existentialism was a sort of humanism, argued Sartre; humanism was to be a tool of social struggle. That he should construe goodness as conformity, Lewis took particular exception to, insisting that conformity was only an accident of goodness and that there could even be 'a measure of inventiveness and freedom in some moral actions.' Replying, the Rev. E. L. Mascall found, in Sartre's notion of the absurdity of the world, some relation to the Christian doctrine of the contingency of the world, implying as it did some reference to a transcendental end. 'Sartre underwent various transformations and was chased into many tight corners,' recorded Goodridge that evening in his capacity as secretary of the Socratic. 'If, as it might have appeared, the president had only set fire to a man of straw, yet the effigy kept appearing and being reburnt.'

╰∽╮

'H-H-He is e-t-t-ternally tr-tr-trotting out his d-d-damned f-f-figures in tutor-r-rials,' railed Tynan. ' "N-N-Now if you h-h-have th-th-three apples, and I h-h-have f-f-five banan-n-nas . . ." ' Stammering like King George VI, the flamboyant undergraduate was filling the coffee house with mirth. 'It's always th-th-three apples and f-f-five banan-n-nas and n-n-no cigar. He's c-c-casuistic!'

╰∽╮

'A staggering blow in the papers this morning: potatoes are put "on rations" on a scale of 3 pounds per week for the bourgeois,' wrote Warren on 10 November in his diary. 'And so the last "filler" food disappears from the diet, and the days of real hunger are upon us.'

'In sending to those behind Mr Attlee's Iron Curtain,' wrote Lewis on 24 November to Vera Mathews of Beverly Hills, California, who had already sent some admirable parcels, 'you can never go wrong with MEAT, TEA, and SOAP — soap for washing clothes, that is . . .'

In November the domestic situation at the Kilns seemed to improve. There was a cook now, and there was a new maid, who had brought along her child. Lewis always knew where the little girl was because she emitted 'a noise like the whistle of a railway engine nearly all day.' But Mrs Moore did not improve, old age pressing hard upon her. 'I am tighter tied every month,' he wrote on 21 November.

In December things got worse. Warren had absented himself from the Kilns; the burden of correspondence — sometimes as many as twenty pieces a day — fell entirely on Lewis. 'Of course, the real trouble is within,' he wrote on 16 December to Barfield. 'All things would be bearable if I were delivered from this internal storm . . . of self-pity, rage, envy, terror, and general bilge!'

Maureen came to the rescue. She insisted on coming to the Kilns for Christmas and sending the Lewises to Malvern. There, with her husband Leonard and her son Richard, they had a fine Christmas feast, Warren catering 'soup, turkey, boiled potatoes and sprouts, pudding.' There were seasonal toasts, Leonard producing gin, Warren vermouth, Jack burgundy.

∽

'Keep your conscience bright and your brain clear,' wrote Lewis on the last day of the year to Rhona Bodle, a New Zealander who had come to England to teach and was struggling with faith, 'and believe that you are in good hands.'

∽ 1948 ∽

Revising and expanding the Clark Lectures, which he had given at Trinity College, Cambridge, in 1944, and which would form Volume III of the *Oxford History of English Literature*, was a slow and gruelling affair for Lewis. From time to time he gave a chapter to a friend for comment or commentary. He had given 'The Close of the Middle Ages in Scotland' to John Wain, a former pupil now teaching in the university; he had given another to Tolkien. Wain returned his without comment, but Tolkien, in a sort of *furor scribendi*, responded at length and with heat, in prose and in verse. Lewis was offended and replied, he hoped coolly, to the criticisms. 'I regret causing pain, even if and insofar as I had the right,' wrote Tolkien on 25 January, 'and I am very sorry indeed still for having caused it quite excessively and unnecessarily.' He held the longish letter for a week before sending it the short distance from Merton to Magdalen. 'Do me the great generosity of making me a present of the pains I have caused,' he concluded, knowing that Lewis would not be resentful and that he would offer them to the Lord, 'so that I may share in the good you put them to.'

∽

Naturalism was not self-refuting, maintained the speaker at the 2 February meeting of the Socratic. G. E. M. Anscombe was philosophy tutor at Somerville; she was taking exception to arguments Lewis had used at previous meetings of the Socratic and also in his newly published book entitled *Miracles*. In the third chapter, she said, he had used, with less than precision, words like 'rational' and 'irrational' causes, 'valid' and 'invalid' reasonings, the 'cause' of a conclusion and the 'ground' of a conclusion. Replying, Lewis 'agreed that the words "cause" and "ground" were far from synonymous,' wrote Goodridge, the recording secretary, 'but said that the recognition of a ground could be the cause of assent, and that the assent was only rational when such was its cause.' Lewis had misunderstood her, she claimed. The word 'valid' had been an unfortunate one in the context, he admitted. Her dichotomy of 'having reasoned' and 'having reasons' he hadn't even noticed. That was not a dichotomy, he countered; that was a tetrachotomy! Some at the Socratic rose to his defence; others rallied around her. He didn't think he had lost. Blowing a smoke ring from her cigar, she thought she had won.

Two nights later Lewis had dinner with some tutors and undergraduates. The horror of what had happened on Monday still clung to him. 'His imagery was all of the fog of war,' wrote Brewer in his diary that night, 'the retreat of infantry thrown back under heavy attack.' Why had Betty attacked so relentlessly something so central to his intellectual defence of Christianity? After all, she wasn't an atheist; she was a Roman Catholic. Now that he had lost everything, said Dyson, trying to find a bright side for Lewis, he was brought to the foot of the cross. Ribaldry rose around, but Lewis went home earlier than usual. His wounds would heal soon at a dinner that Havard would host and to which Anscombe would also be invited.

༜

'Clara Boot Lace?' asked Lewis incredulously.

Last September, acting as agent for Lewis, Bles had entered into an option agreement with Twentieth Century-Fox Film Company. Clare Boothe Luce, a playwright, scenarist, and recent convert to Catholicism, was signed to adapt 'the novel about Hell' to the screen. She began in November, but in a month or two she had to give up. By March Christopher Morley was again inquiring if his screenplay, done in 1943, might not be acceptable.

༜

'The route you are following seems to be the right one,' wrote Lewis on 10 February to Bodle, who now seemed to rely on him as her spiritual director.

'I prefer sometime in the early evening, before one has got sleepy,' he wrote to her on 3 March about prayer, 'but of course it depends on how your day is mapped out.'

           ∽

On Thursday 11 March, around a ham from America, Lewis gave a dinner for the Inklings. The kitchen at Magdalen warmed the joint and prepared soup, fillet of sole, and a paté savoury, and served the menu in New Room. Lewis sat at the head of the table, Hardie at the foot; on one side were Havard and the two Tolkiens; on the other were Dyson, Cecil, and Warren. Lewis had provided the preprandial sherry. Hardie carved the ham. The burgundy, four bottles of it, were the contribution of the elder Tolkien and Dyson. The dinner was modest by pre-war standards, but in post-war England it was sumptuous.

After dinner the Inklings retired to Lewis' rooms, where the postprandial port — two bottles of it from Cecil — were poured. The climax of the evening was the great American tuxedo raffle, a suit having been sent by Allen of Massachusetts. Squabbling like Cinderella's sisters, they drew lots. Hardie won it, but only Christopher Tolkien could fit into it. Before they departed, they wrote, with some ceremony, each giving his college affiliation or occupation and former military service, that the undersigned had dined on Firor's ham and had drunk to his health.

           ∽

The Inklings did not meet on 25 March; it was Maundy Thursday. Having worked all day at the college, Jack and Warren dined in the hall; after coffee, they decided to walk to the Kilns. The Passover moon was shining; the walking was pleasant across the deer grove and through the fellows' gardens. Autobiography was inevitable, said Jack, so many people wanting to know the details of his passage from atheism to Christianity. As the brothers climbed Cuckoo Lane, they talked of the old days, of their parents and nurses, of the Belfast Lough and the Holywood Hills, of Jack's Animal Land and Warren's India. In Headington they stopped for a pint at the Mason Arms — a contest of skill in bar billiards was in progress — and then they ambled up to the Kilns for night prayers and bed.

           ∽

'Pretty grim' and 'somewhat drab' were the most cheerful adjectives the Lewises could use in letters to their American friends, describing conditions in England; the cheese ration had just been lowered from two ounces per person a week to one-and-a-half. But help was on the way and in the air. The European Recovery Act, first proposed by George C. Marshall in the commencement address at

Harvard University on 5 June of the preceding year, hit Magdalen and the Kilns with full force on 29 March. On that day three 'admirable' and 'excellent' parcels arrived from America; Jack hastened to draft, and Warren to type, the letters of thanks.

The first was to Vera Mathews of California, who had been sending bacon, tea, shortening, eggs, and butter. The second was to Allen of Massachusetts, who had sent not only food — 'Not one person in a thousand would have thought of the tin of lemon juice!' — but also a dinner jacket, which Warren could wear so long as he didn't sit down, and silk socks of which Jack figured there were not a dozen pairs in the university. The third was to Firor, the surgeon from Maryland, who, in addition to hams, which seemed to be arriving on a monthly basis, had sent, since the beginning of the year, plum pudding, chocolates, jelly, chicken, sardines, lard, syrup, and butter. As to what Firor might send in future parcels, the brothers Lewis had a suggestion: 'Put yourself and a ham in the stateroom of an eastbound liner, and come and eat it with us at Magdalen.'

〰

'I accept, with surprise and very cordial thanks, the very kind offer of the Council of the Royal Society of Literature,' wrote Lewis on 19 March when he was informed of his election. 'Please convey to the Council my vivid sense of the honour they have done me.' Certification of fellowship was signed by F. S. Boas on 14 April and sent to Lewis on 15 April. On the 17 April he sent a cheque for five guineas as the annual contribution to the society.

〰

'P-P-Please,' asked Tynan, 'can I postpone the examinations until the winter?'

'Why?' asked Lewis.

Tynan explained how he had been brought low by his bronchial condition and also by a girl who had promised to marry him; they had even got the wedding license before she decided to bolt.

'Not only do I want to p-p-postpone them, I really don't see any reason for l-l-living — at least not now.'

'Tynan,' said Lewis sucking on his pipe, 'am I right in thinking that you once told me that during the war, when you were about twelve years of age, living in Birmingham, there was an air raid on the town?'

'Yes.'

'Didn't you tell me that one plane dropped a land mine by parachute and that it nearly blew up your house, missing it only by inches?'

'Yes.'

CLIVE STAPLES LEWIS

'Now, if the wind had blown that bomb a few inches nearer your house, you would be dead. So ever since then — and that was seven years ago — all the time you have lived has been a bonus. It is a gift. It is a fantastic present you have been given. And now you are talking about giving up this incredible gift, and you could have been dead for eight years. You have had eight years of life that you had no reason to expect. How can you be so ungrateful?'

Tynan left Lewis, thoughtfully, having got the help he needed but didn't know how to ask for directly.

⁂

'I knew in a general way, of course, that very very large quantities of gift food, clothing, etc., were coming into Britain,' wrote the Lewises to Allen on 29 May in thanks for his thirty-first parcel, 'but I was nonetheless surprised to read in a recent debate in the House of Lords that every household in the kingdom benefits by American aid to the tune of £1.0.0 a week, and has done so for the past *two years*.'

⁂

'Welcome home! and thank you for writing to tell me,' responded Lewis on 24 June to Bodle on the occasion of her baptism. 'This has been a wonderful week, for I have just heard that my oldest friend is to be baptized on Saturday.'

⁂

'Don't print the letter I sent you this morning,' he wrote on 27 July to the Rev. Alexander Vidler, editor of *Theology*. 'I don't think it unjust, but I am sure it is uncharitable.'

⁂

It was summer. Lewis wanted to spend mornings in the Bodleian, working on his never-ending opus in the Oxford History of English Literature series. But this particular morning he had promised to devote to an American. Chad Walsh had insisted on travelling from Wisconsin to Oxford, not just to visit, which would have been welcome, but to gather material for a scholarly study of Lewis' works. Lewis had tried to dissuade him, arguing that critics should deal only with writers who were safely dead.

Walsh, when he arrived in Oxford, checked into the King's Arms and contacted Lewis. Lewis met him there; remembering recent photographs of Lewis in American magazines and newspapers, Walsh noted to himself that the don had grown a moustache; they agreed on a place and a time when they could talk at some leisure. On that day Walsh was astonished to find that the moustached Lewis he had met at the pub was not the Lewis standing in front of him. It seemed that Jack had sent Warren to check the American out, but that Warren had not revealed his own identity.

Once seated, Walsh rehearsed the part Lewis' books had played in his conversion to Christianity. He insisted that America needed to know more about him and his books. What he proposed to do was a study that would analyze all of Lewis' works published to date and provide some accurate and responsible biographical data at the front. Lewis found Walsh amiable, affable, and stopped resisting the project; he even agreed to be photographed.

Lewis was not what some people had led Walsh to expect, 'a Welsh farmer', 'a benign Anglican bishop', 'the avatar of Dr Johnson.' Nor did his face as it appeared in the viewfinder resemble the stone-like photograph circulated by Macmillan for publicity purposes, which also must have been the inspiration for the woodcut commissioned by the *Saturday Review* in 1943. When Walsh said cheese, all Lewis did was freeze, petrified, like a frightened stag at the dawn of photography. His ruddiness, his sparkling eyes, his animated personality were not captured on the film; there was only a death-mask stillness on the prints.

Between the two men there was more than one conversation. Walsh mentioned writers who were alive; Lewis responded with candour sometimes, sometimes with 'I don't know enough to have an opinion.' No, he didn't keep reviews of his books; he would be hard put to lay hands on every book of his that had been published. Yes, he did have an opinion of Surrealist art; it was not a favourable one. As for biographical dates and bibliographical data, Walsh could consult *Who's Who*.

He walked with Walsh through the parks around Magdalen — 'This looks like my hat,' said Lewis, plucking a tan fisherman's hat from a bush and trying it on; 'this must be my hat!' — and he invited him to the Bird and Baby on Tuesday mornings. He would invite Walsh to the Socratic if he stayed on till term time; there had been too many pro-Christian papers read in recent terms, said Lewis; 'we have discovered there was an undersupply of atheists willing to speak without pay.'

Where were the women in Lewis' life? Walsh knew that he was a bachelor, but what about the rumour, a persistent one, that Lewis locked himself into his room every time a woman approached. 'Pure bosh,' said Lewis; 'I've taken female pupils of all ages, shapes, sizes, and complexions for about twenty years.' If indeed he had ever locked one out, it was because she was a bore, or perhaps the fifteenth visitor on a busy day.

Walsh left Magdalen to see if he could find Lewis elsewhere in Oxford. Lewis' books were not in the windows of Blackwell's or the other bookshops. The scholarly titles were often out of stock, so great was the demand, said one shop assistant; the theological titles were never quite as popular here as in the rest of England, Oxford being already a Christian city.

An editor at Oxford University Press said that *The Allegory of Love* and *Preface to 'Paradise Lost'* had brought Lewis to the heights, but that the theological books were just 'one long decline and fall.' He also complained that Lewis' friend Tolkien was wasting his time on those bloody little creatures with hair on their feet instead of writing something definitive about Old Norse or Anglo-Saxon.

The Anglican clergy Walsh spoke with about Lewis were enthusiastic, some of them, but others wished he wouldn't describe dogmas and doctrines in such an either-or fashion; and he would do well not to preach in Congregational churches in Oxford at the very same time that high mass was being celebrated in Anglican churches; he had done that on at least two, highly publicised occasions.

On his way to London to consult Lewis' publishers and to look through their review files, Walsh now had a picture of Lewis as a 'relaxed and active' fellow, 'a close friend to a few, a famous name to many', moving among 'the familiar scenes of Oxford with the ease of long habit and the sureness of a man who knows what he is doing, whether walking to the pub, the lecture hall, or church.'

∽

'The Sailing of the Ark' was published in the 11 August issue of *Punch*. It was a humorous poem in sixteen couplets about the sons of Noah, who, ready to unmoor the ark, did not let one last creature in. As the waters rose and the ark rocked, Noah looked out of a porthole to see scampering off, 'noble and unmated', the unicorn, who would return again 'to stable and to manger' only ages hence.

On 13 August, to satisfy their appetite for dressed animals, the Lewises went to the cinema to see *Bambi*. The Disney film had been released in the United States in 1942, but it was only now getting its first showing in England. Warren liked the colouring of the seasons and Thumper's fooling and Bambi's feeling 'kinda wobbly' on the ice; the forest fire was full of authentic animal terror. Especially pleasing to the brothers was 'the prince of the deer, who, without caricature, was given more than brutish dignity and majesty.'

∽

In 'A Petition to the Lambeth Conference', which appeared in the 10 July issue of *Time and Tide*, Lady Nunburnholme claimed that the equality of men and women was a Christian principle, that men and women were in fact interchangeable, and that the Church of England would be well advised to declare women capable of ordination to the priesthood. 'To take such a revolutionary step at the present moment, to cut ourselves off from the Christian past and to widen the division between ourselves and other churches by establishing an order of priestesses in our midst,' wrote Lewis in the 14 August issue, 'would be a most wanton degree of imprudence.'

There was indeed a shortage of priests, it could readily be admitted, and women could do pastorally what men did. Everything, that is to say, except be symbols. For Lewis a priest was a representative of God to man and hence had to be masculine. God taught men to speak of him in the Scriptures as masculine; hence, to say that the masculine imagery of the Scriptures was human in origin and not divine was 'arbitrary' and 'unessential' and indeed 'intolerable.' A priest was another Christ; as such, he was a representative of men to God and of God to men; hence, he had to be masculine. Moreover, the sexes were vital and relevant not only to the natural life but also to the supernatural life; hence, role-reversal as proposed by the innovators would destroy the images of Church as bride and Christ as bridegroom and would generate such monsters of prayerful expression as 'Our Mother, who art in Heaven.'

❧

'We don't like rationing which is imposed on us, but I suggest one form of rationing which we ought to impose on ourselves,' wrote Lewis in concluding 'The Trouble with "X" ', an article that appeared in the August issue of the *Bristol Diocesan Gazette*. 'Abstain from all thinking about other people's faults unless your duties as a teacher or parent make it necessary to think about them. Whenever the thoughts come unnecessarily into one's mind, why not simply shove them away? And think of one's own faults instead? For there, with God's help, one *can* do something.'

❧

From 16 August to the 31st, the Lewises and the Blakes exchanged houses. At least, Maureen went to the Kilns; Jack and Warnie went to 4, The Leas, Malvern, where they were greeted by Leonard and little Richard. The three-and-a-half-year-old behaved very well during the vacation. Warren shared the domestic work with Leonard; Leonard talked interestingly about music and hymns; he even played some of his own for the edification of the older men. Warren read a good Beatrix Potter and some bad science fiction. There was good cider at the Unicorn, and there was plenty of hiking; but Jack seemed to go out a good deal by himself. 'Everything horrid that ever happened to me was in August,' he wrote to Pitter, when he arrived back in Oxford on the 31st.

❧

In Michaelmas term in 1945, not many months after Williams had died, Lewis lectured on his friend's Arthuriana. Available to the pupils at the time were two cycles of lyric poems, *Taliessin through Logres*, published in 1938 by Oxford University Press, and *The Region of the Summer Stars*, published in 1944 by Editions Poetry London. Enthusiasm enough was aroused by the lectures that Lewis decided, with the permission of Williams' wife, Michal, to put into one book, a prose work entitled *The Figure of Arthur*, which Williams had read to him and Tolkien on sunny mornings in vacation time, and his own commentary entitled *Arthurian Torso*; and he dedicated the one-volume work, which had just been published by Oxford University Press, to Michal, 'Hector's Andromache'.

'It is in one way a wholly modern work,' Lewis wrote in conclusion, 'but it has grown spontaneously out of Malory, and if the king and the Grail and the begetting of Galahad still serve, and serve perfectly, to carry the twentieth-century poet's meaning, that is because he has penetrated more deeply than the old writers themselves into what they also, half consciously, meant and found its significance unchangeable as long as there remains on earth any attempt to unite Christianity and civilization.'

∞

Michaelmas term had just begun, Lewis had a cold, and another American was rattling the gates. Nathan C. Starr had written to him a year before; he had responded with warmth, inviting Starr to visit when next in England. But Lewis was so overwhelmed with papers and dogged with the flu that he declined the pleasure of a visit. Starr took another tack. He put into a package some tins of edibles brought from America and appended the following:

> And now, with sorwe, at his beddes heed,
> Displacying twenty bokes in blake and reed,
> An heep of boteles, whose bitre bote
> Constreyneth hym to wisshe a shorter throte.
> A curssed tyme, O wikke aspect grym
> Of Saturn whose forlevying rageth hym.

Whether it was the Chaucerian verse or the baconian package that did the trick, Lewis issued an invitation forthwith.

When they met, the conversation was easy. Starr learned that when he was at Christ Church in 1918, Lewis was at Univ. Arthurian studies interested him; he would probably put the fruits of his research into a book. The Arthurian story, Lewis explained, he first met in Twain's *A Yankee at the Court of King Arthur*; he read it before he was ten years old, which meant that he liked it before the critics would tell him that it was an inferior piece of work. Starr liked the Arthurian aspect of Williams' *War in Heaven*, and the conversation turned towards the appreciation of Charles Williams' novels.

❧

'Pish! There's nothing to be proud about. The whole situation is that of being lent a dignity that doesn't belong to us — the child being allowed to give the penny to the bus conductor, the dog being given the newspaper to carry home,' he wrote to Bodle on 24 October about intercessory prayer. 'Or, look at it another way. The really efficacious intercession is Christ's, and yours is *in* this, as you are *in* him, since you became part of this "body", the Church.'

❧

'Thanks for long letter from lady I don't know about a poem I haven't seen whose subject as stated in your letter I can't read,' he wrote on 1 November to Barfield. 'But she sounds a good object for £100 from [the Agape Fund], and if you think proper, will you send it?'

❧

On 9 November he got an invitation to address the Dante Society. He had lectured them once before on the similes in the *Divina Commedia*; perhaps now he would analyze the metaphors, using the methodology of Caroline F. E. Spurgeon. In *Shakespeare's Imagery, and What It Tells Us*, which was published by Cambridge University Press in 1935, she catalogued the images and categorized them and was able to conclude that Shakespeare had five outstanding qualities: 'sensitiveness, poise, courage, humour, and wholesomeness.' But where she was interested in Shakespeare's psychology, Lewis was interested in Dante's poetry. Of the hundred cantos in the *Commedia*, he took the last eleven of the *Paradiso* and counted the images, concentrating only on the metaphors. Among many others, he found two each of smell and sea and student's life; nine each of astronomical, military, clothes and attire, and binding as with cords; twenty-five each of light/heat and horticultural/agricultural; twenty-six of technical. 'The curiousness, the almost sensuous intensity about things not sensuous,' that was one thing this preliminary analysis revealed to Lewis. Then there was 'Dante in the garden, and Dante in the streets, his feeling for the silent growing life, and his cheerful, spontaneous interest in the state and courtesies, the trades and skills, of men.' All this had to do with Heaven, or Dante's conception of it: fields ploughed, workshops resonating, it made 'very few concessions to the natural man.'

❧

Christians were often thrown to the lions in the first few centuries of the new era, much to the delight of pagan audiences. Much to the delight of a Christian audience, a pagan agreed to enter the arena of the Socratic. J. B. S. Haldane would deliver a paper entitled 'Atheism.' A college hall would be too small for the expected crowd; Aldwinckle arranged the meeting at the Taylorian near the Randolph Hotel.

On 15 November a flotilla of bicycles rode at anchor outside the building, the undergraduates expecting a dramatic confrontation between the great atheist and the great theist. Lewis had used Haldane, everyone was convinced, as the remote inspiration for the character of Weston, the mad but loquacious scientist in *Out of the Silent Planet* and *Perelandra*. These two and *That Hideous Strength* Haldane had thrashed in 'Auld Hornie,' an article that appeared in the autumn 1946 issue of *Modern Quarterly*. It would be a contest of giants this November night; one of them would have to emerge the victor.

Haldane appeared at ease on the stage of the lecture room, which was large enough to be a small theatre. Atheism, he said, was the only intellectually honest position to take. Theism, he was sure they would have to agree, was founded on insufficient evidence. The existence of evil could never be reconciled with the concept of a good god. Religious people — a statistical study could easily verify this — led worse lives than non-religious people. In fact, by a happy sort of inverse ratio, the closer one got to the pope, the worse one's life seemed to grow.

Lewis could hardly contain himself. He was president of the club and could, of course, speak whenever he wanted, but he had to let Ian Crombie, philosophy tutor at Wadham College, give the official reply. 'Atheism may encounter fewer intellectual difficulties,' said Crombie, 'but that is because it is not a hypothesis but a refusal to look for explanations of a certain type.'

Commenting briefly on the reply, and sensing that the audience was lusting for his blood, Haldane did not wait for the questions from the floor. Edging from the podium, he made 'an impressive running panegyric of atheism,' his last words being spoken as he went off the stage and out of the building.

 ∽

How could anyone as nice as Mr Lewis have become the slave of such a detestable woman? asked Vera. Warren had just arrived back at the Kilns and was having his cocktail when the maid burst in to complain of Minto's meanness. She didn't even ask the question because Warren cut her short. If he had an answer, he would give it.

'When I reply, perfectly truthfully, that I don't know, and that J and I never discuss this side of his life,' he wrote in his diary later that night, 'I always see that I am suspected of an honourable reticence.'

⁊

'Judging from the label (all that I've yet seen),' wrote Lewis on 6 December to Allen, 'there are enough good things here to provide a Christmas dinner and then a New Year party on top of that.'

⁊ **1949** ⁊

Parcels from America continued to rain on Oxford and its environs. There was one from South Carolina and another from California. There was a third from Massachusetts; it was marked 'Package no. 54'; in the note that accompanied it, Allen figured he had spent in 1949, doing up packages for Lewis and others abroad, 230 hours. There was a parcel stamped 'Hercules,' which signified to the knowing eye that it was a huge ham sent air express from Maryland.

⁊

'Thanks mainly to you, we are in a position to be able, not only to face quite a bit of austerity ourselves, but to help less fortunately placed neighbours,' wrote Lewis on 5 January to Firor. The surgeon was not the first to invite him to America. To be away from the Kilns even for an afternoon, explained Lewis on the 22nd, one had to plan carefully ahead; to visit another continent, however, was about as possible as a visit to the moon. 'O what a pity! To think that I might as your guest have seen bears, beavers, Indians, mountains.'

⁊

'Poor Mrs Greeves: she was always kind to me.' Arthur had yet to write to Lewis about his mother's death: he had heard it from others; but it had taken him almost two weeks to gather his thoughts. 'God bless you, my oldest friend; you and she will be in my prayers.'

⁊

On 28 January Warren walked into the Kilns, wearing a new suit. It wasn't really new; Chad Walsh had contributed it to the household; Warren commissioned a Headington tailor to reconstruct it around his own frame. It looked like new, said the cook and the maid, but they wanted to talk to him about something else. Mrs Moore had been at it again. This time she had ordered the study fire put out that afternoon and the one in the dining-room to be lit, thus forcing Dr Lewis to take his book from the study to the dining-room.

Why should she do a thing like that? asked Warren.

'To save fuel,' said Vera.

'But where is the saving of fuel?'

'There isn't any,' said the maid, 'but she can worry the unfortunate man easier if he's in the dining-room.'

～

'As to the next move, I never, in my own frequent early disappointments, hit upon any subtler plan than flinging the manuscript at one publisher after another, and was always too ignorant to select the publishers except by fancy and rumour.' Sister Penelope had written to Lewis for help, and he was replying on 31 January. 'In other words, a large supply of sealing wax, brown paper, and fortitude is called for.'

～

On 11 February Lewis travelled to London where, at the BBC studios, on the Third Programme, he delivered a talk on the novels of Charles Williams. He thought they were not sufficiently appreciated, and such further appreciation as his talk might engender would help not only the memory of Charles but also the coffers of Michal. Trouble was that Williams mixed the realistic and the fantastic in the same story. Many readers found that repugnant; for them he distinguished several kinds of novels. There was straight fiction, the classical sort of novel which had come from the pens of Fielding and Galsworthy. Then there was pure fantasy such as one found in works like *The Wind in the Willows*. But there had to be a third kind of novel, the kind of novel that Williams wrote, in which the novelist asked his readers to skip from the probable to the marvellous and back again. 'Let us suppose that this everyday world were, at some point, invaded by the marvellous,' was the sort of supposition Williams began with. 'Let us, in fact, suppose a violation of the frontier.' He went on to illustrate the third kind of novel by reference to the brothers Grimm and Edith Nesbit, to *Dr Jekyll and Mr Hyde*, and *Gulliver's Travels* and several of Williams' novels. The point was that Williams shed light on both sides of the frontier, on both the ordinary world and the fantastic world. 'His writing, so to speak, brings me where I have never gone on my own sail or steam; and yet that strange place is so attached to realms we do know that I cannot believe it is mere dreamland.'

～

How long did he propose to stay cured this time? asked Minto without mercy. It was Friday 4 March; Warren had just been released from 'the warm, cosy Acland', an Oxford nursing home, and returned to the refrigerated, ever-frosty Kilns. The illness he had diagnosed as resulting from insomnia and depression, which then led him to the consumption of alcohol, too much of it. His brother, however, had diagnosed it the other way round; it was too much alcohol that produced the insomnia and the depression. 'His kindness remains unabated,' wrote Warren in his diary that night, 'and what more can I want?'

∽

'Not with brogans, please,' said Lewis to a pupil who had just read his essay. 'Slippers are in order when you proceed to make a literary point.'

∽

'Once there were four children whose names were Peter, Susan, Edmund, and Lucy. This story is about something that happened to them when they were sent away from London during the war because of air-raids. They were sent to the house of an old professor who lived in the heart of the country, ten miles from the nearest railway station and two miles from the nearest post office. He had no wife, and he lived in a very large house with a housekeeper called Mrs Macready and three servants. (Their names were Ivy, Margaret, and Betty, but they do not come into the story much.) He himself was a very old man with shaggy white hair, which grew over most of his face as well as on his head, and they liked him almost at once; but on the first evening when he came out to meet them at the front door, he was so odd-looking that Lucy (who was the youngest) was a little afraid him, and Edmund (who was the next youngest) wanted to laugh and had to keep on pretending he was blowing his nose to hide it . . .'

It was the evening of 10 March; Lewis was reading from the first chapter of a story he had written for the children of Roger Lancelyn Green, a former pupil whom he had invited to dinner. The picture of a faun carrying an umbrella and an armful of parcels in a snowy wood, explained Lewis, had been with him since he was sixteen, but he didn't try to put it down on paper until sometime at the beginning of the war when he took in at the Kilns some schoolgirls fleeing from the blitz in London. He wrote some chapters last summer and read them to Tolkien who, flushed with the publication of his own *Farmer Giles of Ham*, thought them dreadful. Now, what Lewis wanted to know from Green was if they were any good.

∽

'The welcome we look forward to giving you,' wrote Lewis on 22 March to Firor, who might be visiting Oxford in the next few months, 'will probably be a slice of Spam and a glass of port.'

As editor of *English Church Music*, Blake got Lewis to write, for the April issue, how music appeared to the person in the pew. 'Fewer, better, and shorter hymns,' wrote Lewis candidly; 'especially fewer.' Of course, he had to admit that he had had no musical education, nor could he claim a lifelong attendance at a hymn-singing church. Although he was a layperson and not a member of the clergy, he could still admit the basic idea behind music in church: 'it glorifies God by being excellent in its own kind; almost as the birds and flowers and the heavens themselves glorify him.' In every church, however, there were highbrows and lowbrows. The priest or the organist was generally the highbrow, a person of 'trained and delicate taste,' who revelled in Palestrina. The lowbrow was the 'stupid and unmusical' layperson, who at best could carry a tune in a taproom. If the former could tone down his aesthetic appetite, and if the latter could believe that the music he didn't appreciate in church did indeed give glory to God, then perhaps there would be hope.

'I am sorry to say that I don't think I shall be able to be at your confirmation on Saturday,' wrote Lewis to his godchild Sarah Neylan on 3 April. 'For most men Saturday afternoon is a free time, but I have an invalid old lady to look after and the weekend is the time when I have no freedom at all, and have to try to be nurse, kennel-maid, wood-cutter, butler, housemaid, and secretary all in one.'

'I hear you've been reading Jack's children's story. It really won't do, you know!' Tolkien had met young Green on the street and was giving his vehement opinion firsthand. 'I mean to say, *Nymphs and Their Ways, The Love Life of a Faun*. Doesn't he know what he's talking about?'

Only a few days before, Lewis had given Green the completed manuscript, nineteen chapters; he was reading them avidly. The main fault he found was in the introduction of the character of Father Christmas in the tenth chapter. The giving of gifts — a sewing machine to Mrs Beaver; a dam and a sluice gate to Mr Beaver; a shield and a sword to Peter; a horn and a bow with arrows to Susan; a dagger and a little bottle of cordial whose drops would heal — these broke the magic of the narrative, Green felt. On the whole, however, the story was far better than Tolkien thought.

'An English edition of a book so essentially addressed to an overseas public would not in the long run have done credit to you or him,' wrote Lewis on 16 April to R. L. De Wilton, assistant editor-in-chief of Macmillan, New York; such an edition of Chad Walsh's *Apostle to the Skeptics* Lewis felt would cause himself embarrassment if not much worse. 'This conviction, however, by no means alters the great gratitude I feel for the self-restraint and delicacy that you have exercised. I am most deeply in your debt.'

∽

An article in the 6 May issue of the *Church Times* to the effect that the liturgy might conveniently be lengthened for such things as 'devotions to the Mother of God and to the host of heaven' upset Lewis. He decided to write a response, which appeared in the 20 May issue. To lengthen a service by as much as ten minutes could throw out of line the whole congregation's order of the day. As for the devotions, they were not so much a matter of liturgiology as of doctrine; hence, they should be debated and accepted before being slipped in without notice.

∽

'My mother says I have waited too long to thank you for having turned me into a reasoning and fairly lovable Christian,' wrote Vera Mathews on 10 May to Lewis. 'It seems I was quite the simpering little demon before reading *Screwtape*, etc., and she wants you to know how grateful she is to you for having taken me off her hands (spiritually speaking). She claims you accomplished this by speaking to my sense of humour (the logical approach to most young demons, I tell her) and that, with your help, I literally laughed my way out of the darkness (which is better, I feel, than groping around in the cloisters with God in a knapsack on one's back, and a look of smug piety on one's face).'

∽

'Warnie is now definitely better as far as this bout is concerned,' wrote Lewis to Greeves on 7 June, 'but we dare not assume that it is the last.' The same combination of symptoms that drove Warren to the hospital in March brought him to the doorstep of the Acland again in mid-April. 'As long as there was no one but him to leave in charge at the Kilns and as long as he is a dipsomaniac, it *seems* impossible for me to get away for more than a very few days,' sighed Lewis, seeing his vacation in Ireland about to evanesce; 'but I don't doubt at all that if it is good for us both (I mean, you and me) to meet and have some happiness together, it will all be arranged in ways we can't now foresee.'

∽

It was mid-morning on Monday 13 June. Having spent a pleasant weekend with George and Moira Sayer in Malvern, Warren had just walked up to Magdalen from the station. When he learned from the porter that Jack had not been in college that morning, he rushed to the Kilns. There he found Jack being carried to an ambulance. Warren boarded it too and rode into Oxford, Jack telling him on the way that his head ached with fever, that his throat was sore, that the glands in his neck were swollen. Havard met them at the Acland Nursing Home and would tell Warren only that it was 'a serious illness for a man of fifty.' Warren walked slowly back to Magdalen where he went through his brother's mail. Slipping a sheet of paper into the Hammond, he typed at the top 'Ref. 284/49.'

On Tuesday Warren visited the Acland and found Jack still in pain. He had a streptococcus infection, said Havard, and he was receiving an injection of penicillin every three hours. If he hadn't been so exhausted, he might have been able to fight off the germ. When he recovered, he had two choices, either to take a long vacation or to get another doctor. Back to the Kilns stormed Warren, where he gave her ladyship what for, extracting from her a promise that Jack could take a month's vacation when he got better.

On Wednesday Warren found his brother feeling much better, and broke the news that he would have to take a vacation and that Minto had already agreed to it. On Thursday Warren found him sitting up and reading *Captain Margaret*, a novel by Masefield, and chattering about its good and bad points. Warren walked back to Magdalen in high spirits, where he transacted Jack's university business and attended to the mail, even rejecting an invitation to a garden party at Buckingham Palace.

The better Lewis felt, the more bad-tempered he grew with the hospital; as he lay awake when he wanted to sleep he couldn't help remembering an epitaph he composed the year before:

> From end to end of the bright airy ward,
> From end to end of each delirious day,
> The wireless gibbered, hammered, squealed, and roared;
> That was the pain no drugs could drive away.
> I asked for an hour of silence — half an hour —
> Ten minutes — to die sane. It wasn't granted.
> Why should one prig, one highbrow, have the power
> To stop what all those honest fellows wanted?
> Therefore, oh God, if Heaven, as they tell,
> Is full of music, yet in mercy save
> For me one nook of silence even in Hell,

And therefore, stranger, tiptoe past this grave;
And let posterity know this of me —
I died both for, and of, democracy.

∽

'I have been ill and am ordered a real change,' he wrote on 21 June to Greeves. 'I'm coming home (Belfast) for a month.' The next day Warren started drinking uncontrollably. By Sunday Lewis and the doctor were trying to get him to enter the hospital for a few days until he straightened out. On Friday 1 July, they took him by force to the Acland; the following morning the hospital called to say that Warren was uncontrollable and would have to leave. A psychiatrist would be seeing him and, if lucky, he could be transferred to the Warneford Hospital where the surroundings were more secure. 'Naturally, there is no question of a later Irish jaunt for me this year,' wrote Lewis on 2 July to Greeves. 'Don't imagine I doubt for a moment that what God sends us must be sent in love and will all be for the best if we have grace to use it so. My *mind* doesn't waver on that point; my *feelings* sometimes do.'

∽

'I am humbled (I think that is the right word) by your great news,' he wrote on 23 June to Barfield, who was about to be baptized. 'I wish I could be with you. Welcome and welcome and welcome.'

∽

On 27 July he wrote to Greeves that he might be able to take that Irish vacation after all. Warren was still sober, but he was beginning to show symptoms of drinking again. Two days later he wrote to Greeves to forgo the second attempt to get to County Down. Warren had a holiday coming up, and Jack would have to be on duty at the Kilns. Warren still hadn't touched a drop; Havard was suggesting that the drinking problem was more a medical than a moral one.

∽

'I am a man in chains, especially at this time of year,' he wrote on Sunday 14 August to a friend who had sent him a book. Oxford was enveloped 'in a drought and heatwave.'

My garden's spoiled, my holidays are cancelled,
    the omens harden;
The plann'd and unplann'd miseries deepen;
    the knots draw tight.
Reason kept telling me all day my mood was
    out of season.
It was, too. In the dark ahead the breakers
    only are white.

Warren, shaky from his recent enforced stay in hospital, and rueful for having made Jack cancel his holiday, sallied forth for a holiday of his own before he had a chance to see Jack's poem in the 17 August issue of *Punch*.

> Yet I — I could have kissed the very scullery
>   taps. The colour of
> My day was like a peacock's chest. In at each
>   sense there stole
> Ripplings and dewy sprinkles of delight that
>   with them drew
> Fine threads of memory through the vibrant
>   thickness of the soul . . .

∾

'He is certainly a fool and perhaps a lunatic, but he seems very miserable.' It was 22 August; Lewis was forwarding to Barfield a letter from P. G. R. Baker or Baller or Batler who might be a candidate for the Agape Fund. 'I *think* he means he is poor.'

∾

On Tuesday 20 September, Lewis boarded the eleven o'clock train for London. At Paddington he was met by Barfield; they proceeded by taxi to Chelsea. Ruth Pitter had invited them to lunch. Lewis introduced Barfield as his oldest and best friend in England, a solicitor in London, and an author to boot. Pitter introduced Kathleen O'Hara, her friend and business associate since 1930. It was a leisurely lunch, during which they talked of conversion and poetry and painted trays. The two women, in the depth of the depression, with no more than £600, had started a business by painting decorations onto things until they had a thriving business employing as many as fourteen people and producing enough income to buy this handsome house. The blitz came and drew all their employees off to the war effort. They too went to work in a factory that was dark and grim. After the war they resumed their decorative craft, but on a smaller scale; they now worked at home.

After lunch, Pitter served grapes grown in the vineyard of her country home in Essex. At the insistence of her guests she read some of her poems, Lewis trying to make friends with Blitzekatze, a puss Pitter and O'Hara had found wandering around some ruins after an air raid. When it was time for Lewis and Barfield to leave, she spread out on the floor a number of trays and asked each to pick one. When they both admired the artistry, she said that people did not tend to use them; they stood them on end as decorations instead. When

Lewis' tray arrived by post two days later, he had trouble opening the package, it was wrapped so well; but once opened, it created delight in all the Kilns. 'The only snag,' he wrote to her that very day, 'is that I detect already a tendency to call it "the good tray" and prevent its ever being used.'

✎

In August a woman had written to Lewis in such anguish that he brought her problem up with Adams, his own spiritual adviser. The woman's husband, it seemed, had taken on a mistress and was proposing a living style that would make his wife an accessory after the fact. Without knowing the parties involved, said his adviser, it would be difficult to prescribe, but generally speaking, Lewis might tell her that she could do one of two things: either have no intercourse with her husband and ignore the mistress; or the husband should refrain from mentioning the mistress at any time in his own household. 'I can't myself quite see the point of no. 2,' wrote Lewis on 2 September to her, 'and I take it that anyway it is impracticable.'

Overcoming a sense of disloyalty, the woman sought help from an elderly priest, who suggested that she make a distinction between enduring a situation which was someone else's fault and sanctioning it in a way that made her an accessory. She thought the advice was dishonest, but Lewis disagreed. 'After all, your husband has no duty (or right) to make him feel as if he had. It would do him no harm to realize that this affair is *just as much* adultery as if it were "furtive visits to a prostitute".' As September wore on she felt that her husband would turn their children against her and that she was fast losing her faith. Lewis was sympathetic and told her not to be alarmed. Nothing seemed to make faith go faster than trying to find out if it was truly there.

✎

'I have taken the liberty of readdressing it,' he wrote to Vera Mathews on 1 October on the arrival of a parcel of fresh meat from California, 'and — I admit not without a sigh — have sent it to a lady in London who does not find it easy to make both ends meet and to whom it will be a real godsend.'

✎

One of the worst by-products of a bad habit is the nervous expectations and infuriating vigilance it creates in the sufferer's family,' wrote Lewis to Greeves on 12 October, 'and also in him, if he's trying to fight it.'

Warren had arrived home from Ireland on 27 September. He was drinking again, but in moderation. On the passage from England to Ireland at the beginning of his holiday, he had taken a large whisky and soda and found that he could be content with one. Ever since he had been drinking sensibly, praying to God that this was 'the prelude to complete victory.'

&

'There is a good deal in what you say,' said Lewis to the pupil whose essay was appealing. 'There is something in what you say,' said Lewis to the pupil whose essay was middling. 'There may be something in what you say,' said Lewis to the pupil whose essay was appalling.

&

'You'll get all the "sidelights" you can want on me in Chad Walsh's *C. S. Lewis: Apostle to the Skeptics*,' he wrote on 25 October. The American's book had just been published by the Macmillan Company in New York; Lewis was recommending it to the Rev. Edward T. Dell, who was working on graduate degrees in theology and history at Eastern Nazarene College, Wollaston, Massachusetts.

&

'You have got (what you most desired) the quality of an exciting story,' he wrote on 11 November to Sayers. 'On that side you may record almost complete success.' Her translation of the *Inferno* had just been published, the fruit of six years' effort that had begun during an air-raid. V-1 rockets were whistling over London; her husband grabbed her, she grabbed the book Charles Williams had been urging on her and both ran for the cellar of their house. When the all-clear sounded, she had read enough of the *Divina Commedia* in medieval Italian to know that she wanted to translate it into modern English. 'I think the metrical audacities are nearly all effective in their places, i.e. as things in *your* poem . . . They have on me the effect of making Dante rather like Browning. That is certainly better than making him like Milton.'

&

Letters to Firor deepened from thank-you notes for food parcels to ruminations of substance. On 17 August Lewis went on at some length to distinguish glorifying, magnifying, and exalting. On 15 October, still a month from his fifty-first birthday, he felt old age fast advancing on him; the particular corner he was about to turn was 'the sharp realization that I shall be compulsorily "retired" in 1959, and the infernal nuisance (to put it no higher) of patching up some sort of life somewhere . . .' On 15 December he noted again the passing of years, sometimes longed for, other times begrudged, and meditated on the resurrection. 'At any moment something may sink an artesian well right down into one's past self, and old joy, even old power, may come rushing up. That is why I think that *resurrection* (whatever it exactly means) is so much profounder an idea than mere immortality. I am sure we don't just 'go on.' We really die and are really . . . up again.'

᠃

'No, I don't think I have a favourite cake,' scribbled one Lewis as a reply to the latest from Mathews; 'but the whisky one sounds most exciting,' added the other Lewis as he typed the letter on 30 November, 'and if your efforts to bake the perfect whisky cake should be crowned with success — !'

᠃

On Saturday 31 December, after a strenuous morning discussing the possibility of priestesses in the Church of England, Lewis hosted a luncheon in the Wilde Room at Magdalen. He welcomed Pitter, Barfield, Green, and a few others. Straggling and appearing somewhat out of place was a young illustrator from London, Pauline Baynes. Lewis introduced her around the table as they sat down. She had done the illustrations in *Farmer Giles of Ham*, Tolkien's story published earlier in the year; and she was to do the drawings for his own children's story, *The Lion, the Witch, and the Wardrobe*, which would be published next year. In fact, he had seen them already in Bles' office earlier in the month and found them 'really excellent.' The lunch was a rollicking affair, just what Lewis had intended, a distraction from the preposterousness of the morning conference. By the time the lunch drew to a close, he had put Baynes totally at ease; she watched with fascination as the great Dr Lewis, saying it was a pity to waste them, fished chestnuts out of the dish of Brussels sprouts.

 **1950**

In the morning mail Lewis sent off a poem in English Alcaics to *Punch*, 'As One Oldster to Another.'

> Well, yes the old bones ache. There were easier
> Beds thirty years back. Sleep, then importunate,
>   Now with reserve doles out her favours;
>   Food disagrees; there are draughts in houses.

Headlong, the down night train rushes on with us,
Screams through the stations . . . how many more? Is it
Time soon to think of taking down one's
Case from the rack? Are we nearly there now . . .

And in the morning mail, he got letters from America, one of them from a new correspondent, Joy Davidman Gresham.

⁓

'I just must tell you what I saw in a field,' wrote Lewis on 9 January to his godchild Sarah, 'one young pig cross the field with a great bundle of hay in its mouth and deliberately lay it down at the feet of an old pig. I could hardly believe my eyes. I'm sorry to say that the old pig didn't take the slightest notice. Perhaps *it* couldn't believe *its* eyes either.'

⁓

'Pray for me,' he wrote on 12 January to Sister Penelope. 'I am suffering incessant temptations to uncharitable thoughts at present; one of those black moods in which nearly all one's friends seem to be selfish or even false. And how terrible that there should be even a kind of *pleasure* in thinking evil . . .'

⁓

'Bruce is dead and buried,' announced Lewis to his brother. It was late in the afternoon of Tuesday 17 January; Warren, who was heading back up to the Kilns, rejoiced. For too many years now that Irish setter had been the agent of so many of Minto's petty tyrannies. She had coddled the dog as though his health were frail and announced, quite arbitrarily, any number of times in a single day, that he needed a walk. Anyone within earshot would then have to trot the poor creature outside. Too often it was Warren who had to do the honours; on more than one day Bruce had been forced to lift his leg as many as three times in one hour. Ahhh well, sighed Warren as he walked up Cuckoo Lane, he's gone to the land of his fathers. Only one obstacle remained now before Jack would be freed from his prison.

⁓

'Crocus, primrose, daffodil have all appeared now; almond blossom and catkins too; but no leaves on trees yet,' wrote Lewis on 12 March to Firor in thanks for the latest *Hercules* to arrive in Oxford. 'And there's a Firor ham in the refrigerator — I've never spelled that word before and have my doubts. God bless you.'

⁓

The literary impact of the Authorized Version was the subject Lewis chose for the Ethel M. Wood lecture at the University of

London on 20 March. He was at great pains to distinguish the Bible as a book from the translation known as the Authorized Version, and also to distinguish between the one as source and the other as influence. In the end, having traversed the history of the Scriptures and rehearsed the works of any number of English writers, he concluded, perhaps to the surprise of his audience, that the literary impact, such as it was, was less than expected.

There were several reasons why this was so. The AV gave great pleasure in most centuries, but its excessive popularity, instanced by constant quotation, gave it a certain superficiality and prevented it from truly sinking into the consciousness of the average writer. Nowadays the Bible was no longer being spoken of as a sacred book; it no longer housed God's communications with humankind; rather it hoarded the golden treasures of sixteenth-century English prose. 'But I cannot help suspecting, if I may make an Irish bull, that those who read the Bible as literature do not read the Bible.'

If this was true, another question loomed on the horizon. Would the Bible return as a book? Not unless as a sacred book, was the only answer he could make. 'For the Bible, whether in the Authorized or in any other version, I foresee only two possibilities: either to return as a sacred book or to follow the classics, if not quite into oblivion, yet into the ghost-life of the museum and the specialist's study. Except, of course, among the believing minority who read it to be instructed and get literary enjoyment as a by-product.'

∽

'If I can succeed in getting just over a fortnight away this summer (as I was prevented from doing last summer) . . .' wrote Lewis on 14 April to Firor; he made tentative plans with Greeves for a vacation in Ireland.

∽

There had to be a map of Narnia, the publishers said; Lewis hastened to draw a sketch that he would send to Baynes for the official piece of cartography. Narnia would be in the centre; to the north would be the Wild Lands; to the south, Archenland. Cair Paravel was by the sea; the Beaver's dam was up the Great River. 'Major woods' he indicated as well as 'moderate hills' and 'real mountains.'

∽

Early on Saturday morning, 29 April, Mrs Moore fell out of bed three times. With the help of the maid, Lewis got her back into bed; in the morning he called the doctor. When he arrived he examined her, found her childish and incoherent, and said that the time was come. He telephoned the Restholme, which was not far from Somerville College; yes, there was an opening; they brought Mrs Moore there. Her language was harsh; she made it known that she considered her new residence a hell. Ten guineas a week was the tariff, learned Lewis in the front office; that meant £560 a year, which he could barely afford now, but what would happen in nine years' time when he had to retire? 'I hardly know how I *feel* — relief, pity, hope, terror, and bewilderment have me in a whirl,' he wrote on 2 May to Greeves, cancelling whatever plans there were for the summer. 'I have the jitters! God bless you. Pray for me.'

&

You said 'The world is going back to Paganism.' Oh bright
Vision! I saw our dynasty in the bar of the House
Spill from their tumblers a libation to the Erinyes,
And Leavis with Lord Russell wreathed in flowers, heralded
   with flutes,
Leading white bulls to the cathedral of the solemn Muses
To pay where due the glory of their latest theorem . . .

Lewis did not often attack publicly those who held theological opinions different from his own, but F. R. Leavis, the much-published Cambridge don, and Bertrand Russell, just announced as this year's Nobel laureate for literature, were exceptions; they appeared in his poem 'A Cliché Came Out of Its Cage,' which was published in the May issue of *Nine: A Magazine of Poetry and Criticism*.

. . . Heathendom came again, the circumspection and the
holy
   fears . . .
You said it. Did you mean it? Oh, inordinate liar, stop.

&

'Go quickly,' read Dyson aloud. 'Summon all our people to meet me here as speedily as they can,' he read, now standing up, the better to be heard at the Bird and Baby. 'Call out the giants and the werewolves and the spirits of those trees who are on our side.' It was Thursday morning, 22 June; Inklings were assembling for a morning pint and an hour's conversation. 'Call the Ghouls and the Boggles, the Ogres and the Minotaurs!' Lewis had brought with him the first proofs of *The Lion, the Witch, and the Wardrobe*; from the parcel Dyson had snatched a galley and was orating the White Witch's call for help before finally confronting the golden lion. 'Call the Cruels, the Hags, the Spectres, and the people of the Toadstools! We will fight! What?' The noontime regulars were beginning to arrive at their local and looked towards the hub-bub in the back parlour. 'Have I not still my wand? Will not their ranks turn into stone even as they come on?' Someone pulled Dyson back into his seat and pushed a glass into his hand. 'Be off quickly! I have a little thing to finish here while you are away.'

An allegory, said an Inkling; the story was an allegory.

Of course, it wasn't an allegory, said Lewis with a smile; it was just a story for children.

This was not the first time the Inklings had heard the story. The manuscript had been read to them in the past months, but as they perused one galley or another, they looked beyond the details of the narrative to its meaning. Aslan had to be a Christ-figure in lion's clothing. Edmund was obviously a young Adam who erred, betrayed his primal trust. That White Witch, insisted Dyson, had to be Screwtape, but in alarming costume with ghastly cosmetic. Deep magic was original sin and its human consequences. The deeper magic was the redemption by, and the resurrection of, the golden-maned character. The lion's visiting the witch's castle at the end to revivify the petrified figures was nothing else than the harrowing of Hell.

Smuggling theology was one thing Lewis did well.

∽

'What are we to make of Jesus Christ?' Lewis was asked to write some paragraphs on this subject for a book entitled *Asking Them Questions*. He had to admit the question had its comic aspects. It was something like asking a fly to comment on the elephant it was buzzing about. The one recurring answer, and the favourite one of non-Christians, was that Jesus was a moral teacher par excellence. The other, rather alarming answer was that Jesus made claims no moral teacher had ever made — not Buddha, not Socrates, not Allah, not Confucius; these were the claims either of a megalomaniac like Hitler or of the son of God himself.

'If you had gone to Buddha and asked him "Are you the son of Bramah?" he would have said "My son, you are still in the vale of illusion." If you had gone to Socrates and asked "Are you Zeus?" he would have laughed at you. If you had gone to Mohammed and asked "Are you Allah?" he would first have rent his clothes and then cut your head off. If you had asked Confucius "Are you Heaven?" I think he would probably have replied "Remarks which are not in accordance with nature are in bad taste." The idea of a great moral teacher saying what Christ said is out of the question. In my opinion, the only person who can say that sort of thing is either God or a complete lunatic suffering from that form of delusion which undermines the whole mind of man.'

∽

'Very bad news: killed,' sobbed Mrs Moore, handing a letter to Warren, who had just entered her room at Restholme. He tore the letter open and found only a brief, cheery note from Maureen. He was truly alarmed and exasperated and considered it yet another shameful attempt on her part to dominate those around her.

Lewis visited her every day; it didn't make him feel the cheerier, but as June became July his visits seemed to be cheering to her. 'She was for many years of a worrying and, to speak frankly, a jealous, exacting, and angry disposition,' he wrote on 28 July to Firor. 'She now gets gentler — I dare to hope not only through weakness. Certainly, I think she is a little happier, or a little less unhappy, than she was in health.'

The summer mornings he spent in the Bodleian, working on his volume in the OHEL series. Reviewing periodicals relating to the English literature of the sixteenth century seemed to reveal mostly rubbish. In the afternoons, before or after his visit to Restholme, he stopped at Parson's Pleasure, where, suitless, he plunged into the shady but tepid Cherwell.

༄

Peter Bide was ordained to the priesthood in the Church of England, Lewis learned from the morning mail. He remembered Bide well. He was a Communist in his undergraduate days; that is, until Molotov and Ribentropp signed a Russian-German allegiance in August 1939; on that day, his idealism in tatters, he tore up his membership card. He had even tried, totally without success, to convince Lewis of the excellence of Eliot as a poet, having prepared an elaborate choral reading of *The Waste Land*.

Since the war Bide had visited Oxford several times and brought Lewis up to date on his life. He had been at the debacle of Dakar. He had seen men die and had given some thought to the meaning of life. He met Teresa of Avila in Vita Sackville-West's *The Eagle and the Dove*; he had even carried around with him, in the British campaigns through France, Teresa's complete works in the Peers translation.

'Home on Monday — married on Saturday,' Bide had telegraphed to his bride-to-be as the war ended. But that Monday, when he arrived, he learned, to his horror, that she had engaged the local parish church. He was not yet a believer; he fled to the Book of Common Prayer and read the marriage ceremony. He had no trouble with marriage as a lifelong commitment; if he sort of put the God bits to one side, he could get through the vows comparatively undamaged.

A job at the War Office was waiting for him. The woman he married turned out to be not only the occasion for his confronting Christianity but also the cause of his deepening commitment to it.

One thing led to another. Conversion led to commitment. Confirmation was soon followed by theological studies, which were consummated in ordination. Will wonders never cease? thought Lewis as he put the letter down.

∽

'I reckon these [*expletive deleted*] Russians are going the same [*expletive deleted*] way as 'Itler did!' The Lewises were standing in a pub with a pint as the talk among the working-class men, who were old enough to have known two wars and young enough to have fought in one, turned to the war in Korea. 'We don't want no bloody appeasement *this* time!' The Lewises looked at each other in mild surprise, having expected that for these men three wars in one lifetime would be too much. 'The sooner they're taught a lesson, the better!'

∽

The September sun was setting; the heat was beginning to lift at the Kilns when Warren arrived back from London. He had represented the Lewises — Jack had been too sick to go — at the wedding of Jill Flewett to, of all people, a grandson of Freud's, Clement. As he had sat at the back of St James's Church and watched the guests sauntering down the aisle, he cooled off. But when the bride floated through the church door on her father's arm, he felt possessive. At the reception that followed, he was cordially received by Mrs Flewett, who thanked him once again for all the favours to her daughter during the war. The heat was oppressive, rendering limp all of his best clothes, but kissing the bride, which she specially requested, was most refreshing indeed.

∽

'I should need to be either of angelic humility or diabolical pride not to be pleased at all the things you say about my books,' wrote Lewis on 26 October to Mary Willis Shelburne. She lived in Washington, D.C., and was a widow; although she was once financially independent, she had fallen on hard times. 'May I assure you of my deep sympathy in all the very grievous troubles that you have had. May God continue to support you; that He has done so till now, is apparent from the fact that you are not warped or embittered. I will have you in my prayers.'

∽

'You should buy yourself an enormous fur coat, fill the pockets with brandy and aspirin,' wrote the Lewises on 8 November to Mathews, enclosing a copy of *The Lion, the Witch, and the Wardrobe*, which had just been published, 'and come over here to see how the poor live, on the fringes of civilization!'

∽

'Tell me, Professor Lewis, what do you think of the use of four-letter words in literature?'

'I find them objectionable because they are not erotic enough.'

Tynan smiled. He was preparing for presentation on British television a programme entitled 'Eros and the Arts'; he had suggested to the interviewer that Lewis would uphold the traditional point of view but probably for a non-traditional reason.

'What do you mean?' asked the interviewer.

'Well, if you look at the ancient poets, you will find that when they are describing the act of love, they never use four-letter words because four-letter words do not arouse the senses. They always use images and metaphors and similes. You will find that in ancient literature four-letter words are confined to scurrility and abuse.'

The interviewer asked the camera to be turned off while he thought how to elicit from Lewis something stale and tired that might be used to counterpoint the fresh, modern point of view; but when the red light went on again, he fared no better.

'If you wished to describe the act of love in detail, you are restricted to the language of the nursery, the language of the operating theatre, or the language of the gutter, and you may not wish to bring in any of these.'

'But surely,' said the interviewer, 'it is possible to describe the physical activities in words?'

'Can you describe to me, sir, how a pair of scissors works?'

'Well, it is a piece of steel that has little . . .'

'If you can't describe a pair of scissors, how can you describe the act of love?'

⁓

What most people who talk about reunion don't realize,' wrote Lewis on 13 November to Griffiths, 'is that *continental* Protestantism regards the C. of E. as still theologically 'unreformed' and the Lutheran-Anglican gap is really at present at least as wide as the Anglican-Roman. It is thus a three-cornered affair.'

⁓

'I never read the paper and would not have known anything about [the high cost of holiday turkey], except for my brother, who kindly reads me out the more cheerful extracts at breakfast,' wrote Lewis to Mathews on 20 November, commemorating the arrival of nine pounds fourteen ounces of comfort and cheer from Beverly Hills. 'However, I am grateful to him for one excerpt from yesterday's paper — a delicious printer's error in a description of a revivalist meeting in the Midlands: — "At the conclusion of the exercises, a large crow remained in the hall, singing *Abide with Me*".'

Why did photographers always seat him at his desk? asked Lewis on Saturday 25 November. Because, said John Chillingsworth of the *Radio Times*, they like to situate an animal, especially a large carnivorous one, in its lair. Going on a photographic shoot, he continued as he snapped Lewis from every angle, catching the litter on the desk in front of him and registering noon on the mantelpiece clock, was not unlike going on safari. It was, however, less dangerous.

Why did photographers always come in the winter when he was wearing flannel shirts and woollen sweaters and tweed jackets and once even a dressing gown? In the summer he shed all that wool and became what some people considered slightly svelte. Perhaps, suggested Chillingsworth, it was that he resembled Father Christmas.

~

'I have been regaling myself on *Tom Sawyer* and *Huckleberry Finn*,' wrote Lewis on 6 December to Firor, who had sent another parcel. 'I wonder why that man never wrote anything else on the same level? The scene in which Huck decides to be 'good' by betraying Jim, and then finds he can't and concludes that he is a reprobate, is unparalleled in humour, pathos, and tenderness. And it goes down to the very depth of all moral problems.'

~

'I cannot quite understand why the errors of Rome occupy your mind so much,' wrote Lewis on 7 December to Mrs Frank J. Jones of Darien, Connecticut, a sender of parcels. 'Have you asked yourself what exactly is your motive for dwelling on the matter so much? Are you defending some particular person from joining the R.C.s? Are you hoping to convert some R.C. to Protestantism?

'One wants to be very careful, you know! The Devil loves drawing our attention away from our own duties and our own sins into the evil pleasure of working on some traditional enemy — the pope, the Communists, the Fascists. He hopes to produce in us all the worst pleasures — the pleasures of hatred and self-righteousness . . .

'I don't say this is your case (I know it has often been mine), but I do say "Take care." Your enemy is very old and very clever. And he has many assistants — in the newspaper, in the popular gossip, in the traditions of the society one lives in.'

~

Lewis had just received a letter from Sheldon Vanauken, an American, who was doing some research work at Jesus College. He and his wife Davy were not Christians, but since arriving in Oxford at the beginning of Michaelmas term they had met charming and intelligent people who were Christians. He had just read Lewis' science fiction romances; she had just read *The Screwtape Letters*;

they were beginning to feel that if Lewis and the others believed in Christianity, perhaps they could also.

But, wrote Vanauken, he just couldn't bring himself to believe. If he had been an apostle or a disciple, he would, of course, have found it easy to believe in Jesus. But he lived 'in a "real world" of red busses and nylon stockings and atomic bombs.' He just couldn't cross the threshold, but he could write to someone like Lewis to explain where he stood.

'My own position at the threshold of Christianity,' replied Lewis promptly on 14 December, 'was exactly the opposite of yours. You wish it were true; I strongly hoped it was *not*.' Lewis went on to disagree with Vanauken's picture of the history of religions. He encouraged him to read Chesterton and to attempt to practise the Tao. 'I don't know if any of this is the least use,' he wrote in conclusion. 'Be sure to write again, or call, if you think I can be of any help.'

❧

'Here is beauty from CARE just come in in nice time for Christmas,' typed Warren to Mrs Jones, who had sent two large food parcels, 'and we are all grateful to you for [them].'

'I am not a mathematician enough to calculate how many months of confectionary the boxes would represent on our scale,' typed Warren to Harold S. Latham, vice-president of Macmillan, New York, 'but I should think something far into 1952.'

❧

'There is nothing in Christianity which is so repugnant to me as humility — the bent knee,' wrote Vanauken to Lewis. 'The bad part of wishing it were true is that any impulse I feel towards belief is regarded with suspicion as stemming from the wish; the good part is that the wish leads on. And I shall go on; I must go on, as far as I can go.'

'I think you are already in the meshes of the net!' replied Lewis on 23 December. 'The Holy Spirit is after you. I doubt if you'll get away!'

❧

'Our domestic life is both more physically comfortable and more psychologically harmonious for Mrs Moore's absence,' wrote Lewis on 30 December to Sister Penelope. Warren had moved from the first floor to Maureen's room on the second floor where it was warmer in winter and without mosquitoes in summer. But Mrs Moore's descent into senility was inevitable, if gradual, and it was not without its moments of loveliness. The weekly expense worried Lewis, but he would rather have some worries than no worries at all. 'I have been feeling that very much lately: that *cheerful insecurity* is what our Lord asks of us.'

⤞ 1951 ⤝

'Why should one read authors one doesn't like because they happen to be alive at the same time as oneself?' wrote Lewis on 6 January to Pitter. 'One might as well read everyone who had the same job or the same colour hair, or the same income, or the same chest measurements, as far as I can see.'

⤝

Beginning to feel that when he came to believe, he would have to choose some theological career, Vanauken wrote to Lewis again.

'I think there is a great deal to be said for having one's deepest spiritual interest distinct from one's ordinary duty as a student or professional man,' replied Lewis on 5 January, pointing out that Paul had been a tent-maker by profession. 'When the two coincide, I should have thought there was a danger lest the natural interest in one's job and the pleasures of gratified ambition might be mistaken for spiritual progress and spiritual consolation; and I think clergymen sometimes fall into this trap.'

Vanauken replied instantly and achingly, asking just how one should bring God into one's own work. On 8 January Lewis wrote among other things that if Vanauken was thinking of changing career, he had also to think of time. 'If you can get an extra year, it would be another matter. I was not at all meaning that 'intellectual history' involving theology would *in itself* be academically a bad field of research.'

⤝

'I doubt if there is a man in America besides yourself,' wrote the Lewises on 8 January to Allen, 'who would have seriously contemplated sending a private gift of coal to this country.'

⤝

When Mrs Moore breathed her last — the clock read 5.00 p.m.; the day was Friday; the date was 12 January — Lewis was with her in Restholme. Senility had long ago claimed her mind; influenza had just claimed her body; but what about her soul? he thought as he walked slowly along Woodstock Road. She seemed so unmoved, so untouched by Christianity. Monthly, sometimes even weekly, he got news from correspondents who had been moved by his books or broadcasts to undergo the conversion experience. Though he lived with Minto for thirty years, did housework, washed dishes, took the dog for a trot, all the while talking with her about one thing or another, he seemed not to have touched her soul. That no man was a prophet in his own country offered little consolation.

She could be harsh, and for that he had nailed her in *The Screwtape Letters*. She was the inspiration for the young man's mother, 'the sharp-tongued old lady at the breakfast table.' Glubose was assigned to bedevil her, and he was to develop what was already well-advanced, a 'domestic hatred' that expressed itself by saying 'things which would appear quite harmless on paper, but in such a voice, or at such a moment, that they are not far short of a blow in the face.' Ask her what time dinner would be, and she might fly off into a tantrum. Perhaps all that would have been bearable if only she had not been so jealous of the place religion had in her son's life.

But there was another side to Mrs Moore, and Lewis put that into *The Lion, the Witch, and the Wardrobe*. Mrs Beaver was a Minto-like character at its best. Trout hissing in the pan; potatoes boiling in a pot; a jug of creamy milk for the children; a jug of beer for the grown-ups; and in the middle of the table, 'a great big lump of deep yellow butter.' Nothing, said Mrs Beaver who had to be echoing Mrs Moore, could beat 'freshwater fish if you eat it when it has been alive half an hour ago and has come out of the pan half a minute ago.' Except perhaps 'a great and gloriously sticky marmalade roll, steaming hot,' which had just come out of the oven. 'And when each person had got his (or her) cup of tea, each person shoved back his (or her) stool so as to be able to lean against the wall and gave a long sigh of contentment.'

Lewis sighed, but not with contentment, as he trudged up Headington Hill. It was something else. He had made a promise to Paddy Moore that long-ago day in 1917, and only God knew how well he had tried to keep it.

⌘

Mrs Moore was laid to rest in Holy Trinity churchyard in Headington Quarry on Monday 15 January. Warren was not able to attend, having been struck down by the same strain of virus that had done Minto in. By Wednesday he was well enough to sit up and write down his thoughts on her passing. She had enslaved his brother, he wrote, raped his life, robbed him of his holidays, prevented his concentration for more than a half-hour at a time, and presumably 'rescued him from the twin evils of bachelordom and matrimony at one fell swoop!' She and Maureen had stretched his annual income of £210 from Magdalen beyond its endurance. If it hadn't been for the royalties and the gifts from America and such help as he, Warren, had been able to offer, the household would have fallen apart years ago. Whatever her faults, though, she never succeeded in turning Jack against him, and she put up with his own 'debaucheries in a way in which a better woman would not have done.' If she sinned, perhaps she didn't know it, so innocent was she of her own imperfections. 'I add [all this as] a biographical note,' he wrote at the end of the longish entry, 'for the benefit of the yet unborn author of J's biography, who has my fullest permission to use it as "thickening".'

∽

The Oxford Professorship of Poetry was a position, founded in 1708 by Henry Birkenhead, that offered a stipend for lecturing. By the 1950s that stipend was £250 a year, for which the chair holder would have to deliver three lectures, judge the final entries for two annual university prizes, and every other year orate in Latin at the Encaenia ceremony. Cecil Maurice Bowra would conclude his five-year term in February. To succeed him, candidates were nominated, and campaigning by supporters was allowed. All the masters of arts of the university were eligible to vote, perhaps as many as thirty thousand of them; only a few would make the trip to Oxford for the actual voting on 8 February.

The paper nominating Lewis was signed by most of the faculty at Magdalen and by most of the heads of the other colleges. But the cry went up that a poet, not a critic, should hold the chair this time. The names of Edmund Blunden and Cecil Day-Lewis were also put into nomination.

Campaigning for Day-Lewis, and indeed the one who encouraged him to stand for nomination, was a don who loathed Lewis. During the month of January, wearing jackets and slacks in shades of red and blue, Enid Starkie of Somerville College pedalled about Oxford, gathering support for her candidate. She even encouraged Blunden to withdraw on the ground that he would split the vote for a poet. He did so, much to the amazement of Day-Lewis.

Campaigning for Lewis was Dyson. He walked through every open door in Oxford and opened not a few doors that were closed. 'If they offered you sherry, you're done; they won't vote for you,' he reported to the Inklings on Tuesday 30 January; 'I had lots of sherry,' he said sadly, and more than one person told him that he would not vote for C. Screwtape-Lewis. By month's end Starkie had been able to erode Lewis' early lead, and the outcome of the election was a toss-up.

∽

On Thursday 8 February the MAs in the colleges voted clearly and easily for their choice as the next Oxford Professor of Poetry, but the MAs who journeyed to Oxford that day to cast their votes were confronted with a ballot on which the candidates' names were, but for one letter, identical; the telltale hyphen was missing; some of them just had to guess which name was their candidate. By nightfall 194 had voted for C. D. Lewis, and 173 for C. S. Lewis.

The atheist-Communist bloc voted him down, blustered Warren that night. He and Jack, together with Havard, Cecil, Dyson, and J. A. W. Bennett, a fellow and tutor at Magdalen, were about to dine at the Royal Oxford Hotel when the news arrived. So much for publishing all those poems in *Punch* under the initials N. W., said somebody. One consolation, said somebody else, was that all the best people voted for Jack and only the 'pentecostal sweepings bearing all sorts of Slav and Balkan names' voted for the other fellow. If only Day-Lewis didn't look like 'an ageing old-time musical comedy star,' said Warren, 'off the stage, same soigné appearance, and same ravaged grey face.' Perhaps Jack should challenge Day-Lewis to a public poetry competition, the winner to take the chair fair and square. It was simple, said Jack; there were political issues on both sides, and the greater number of votes won. 'In spite of our defeat,' wrote Warren in his diary that night, 'we had a merry dinner.'

੭

A vacation in Ireland now seemed possible to Lewis; he wrote to Greeves that he would arrive on Saturday 31 March, and would leave on Monday 16 April. 'I'm off to Northern Ireland after Easter to try my native air,' he wrote on Palm Sunday to Ruth Pitter, 'half-frightened at the thought.' 'Looking forward! — yes, I can't keep the feeling within bounds,' he wrote on Good Friday to Greeves. 'I know now how a bottle of champagne feels while the wire is being taken off the cork.'

੭

As part of his Easter duty and in preparation for his jaunt to Ireland, he went for a haircut. He picked up some recently delivered parcels from America and lugged them to Headington. The March Hare was it? asked Victor Drew as Lewis barged into his shop, or was it the Easter Hare? Both, said Lewis; he explained that the parcels had come from California and were meant to give Easter cheer to the recipients. He had more than enough cheer for this Easter; he hoped Drew and his wife would gratefully accept these gifts as coming not only from himself and his brother but also from one Vera Mathews. His wife had been ill, said Drew, as he tucked Lewis into the chair and spun him about. Yes, she'd been ill, but she was well now; she'd welcome whatever cheer she could get, especially if it came from the Kilns and from America. A lover speaking of his beloved, thought Lewis as he watched in the mirror 'the queer little pot-bellied, grey-headed, unfathomably respectable' barber dancing about. 'She looks so pretty, sir,' said Drew of his wife, 'so pretty, but terribly frail.'

〰

'May I book 10 May, 1.15?' wrote Lewis on 26 March to Pitter. It was the day after Easter; he invited her not only to lunch at Magdalen but also to pick up a spectacles case she must have left behind on a previous visit and he had only just found down the side of an old armchair, 'a place which rivals the seabed for lost treasure.' She accepted the invitation and chastised him for his housekeeping. 'I didn't know armchairs were ever cleaned,' he replied in all innocence. 'Should they be?'

〰

'I have hardly ever had so much happiness as during our late holiday,' he wrote on returning from Ireland to Greeves. 'God bless you — and the Unbelievable,' which was Greeves' dog. In gratitude he sent a huge Firorian ham to his friend and promised to visit him again in August.

Back at Magdalen, he was faced with a month's worth of letters. Some containing regular business Warren had been able to transact and send off. Others requiring personal answers he had to contend with himself.

'I cannot oblige the Society,' he wrote to the Royal Society of Literature, which had asked him to deliver an address on a subject of his choice. 'I expect to be in Cornwall or the Scilly Islands on 26 June.'

'There has been nothing like it before,' he wrote to Sister Madeleva in Indiana, who had sent him a copy of her latest book, *Lost Language*, 'and it emphasizes a side of Chaucer too often neglected.'

'Many religious people, I'm told, have physical symptoms like the "prickles" in the shoulder,' he wrote to a woman he had been counselling by post. 'But the best mystics set no value on that sort of thing, and do not set much on visions either.'

'I feel,' he wrote to Firor, 'twice the man I have been for the last ten years.'

〰

'My prayers are answered,' he wrote to Vanauken on 17 April. They had corresponded so frequently and so intimately during the past few months that Lewis dropped the honorifics; Vanauken couldn't drop the 'Mr,' at least not yet. He and his wife, it now seemed, had some vision, not much, perhaps three feet in front of them, but that was enough to decide that they could believe in God. Soon, Lewis promised them, they would see the horizon. Soon also the Enemy would counter-attack, trying to reclaim what he had so ingloriously lost. Hence, he urged them, since they had been baptized in youth, to pray, to choose a denomination, and to be confirmed. 'Blessings on you and a hundred thousand welcomes,' he wrote in conclusion. 'Make use of me in any way you please; and let us pray for each other always.'

⚬⚬⚬

'Mr Schofield?' asked Lewis as though he were about to identify Dr Livingstone. He ushered his guest into the hall at Magdalen and sat him at a table for two. Stephen Schofield was his name; he was a Canadian journalist cycling through England in search of stories and personalities. He had just come from London where he had heard, in the House of Commons, Churchill rise to eulogize Douglas MacArthur, who had just been dismissed from his command in Korea. Lewis was attentive, Schofield found; when he explained that he was deaf, Lewis leaned even closer.

After lunch, as they both settled down in leather chairs in the common room, Schofield asked if he could light up. Lewis nodded, pulling out a pack of Gold Flake cigarettes; as Schofield stoked his bowl and lit the pile, he wished he had prepared a list of questions and submitted them beforehand. The chatting, however, was easy. Did Lewis like walking? Yes. Did he climb with ropes? No. Did he care for American writers? Robert Frost and Ralph Waldo Emerson. Had he read Thomas Wolfe? No. With an appreciative smile, Lewis rose from the chair and shook Schofield's hand warmly, saying goodbye loudly, and wishing him well on his peregrinations around the island.

⚬⚬⚬

'I . . . come to the matter fighting on another front, against atheists who say (I have seen it in print) "Christians believe in a God who committed adultery with a carpenter's wife," ' he wrote on 23 May to Peter Milward. He was a Jesuit who in the course of preparation for the priesthood was reading English at Campion Hall. At a meeting of the Socratic, he had taken a position counter to Lewis', expressed it forcefully, but wrote a letter apologizing for what might have appeared to be rudeness. 'You use language which could have been interpreted as an agreement with *them*. Naturally there is no disagreement between us on that point.'

⚬⚬⚬

On Thursday 31 May Roger Lancelyn Green dined with Lewis at Magdalen and afterward strolled the gardens and walks. When darkness fell, they climbed staircase 3 and entered room 3, where they talked into the night of gods and mythologies, of Smyrnaeus and Shakespeare, of Jeanne d'Arc and Samuel Johnson, of biography in general. Would he, asked Lewis, ushering him out at 11.45 p.m., like to write his biography? That is, assuming Green survived him?

❧

On Friday 1 June the Lewises were to be the guests of Gervase Mathew. It was a warm, if blustery, day as they set off up the High, then right along the Corn and on into St Giles'. I thought he was a Benedictine, said Warren. No, he was a Dominican, said Jack; Griffiths was the Benedictine. Well, what was the difference? About seven hundred years. Halfway up St Giles', they turned left into Blackfriars. Other Dominicans of the community had invited guests also; perhaps as many as fifty assembled 'in a low and beautiful upper room full of cool, grey light.' When it was time for lunch, friars and guests went downstairs, and in a long corridor grace was said. Then they filed into the refectory, a squarish room, where they stationed themselves at tables. Their backs were to the wall; they faced a friar, sitting at a small table in the middle of the room. When he had read a passage in Latin from the Vulgate Bible of St Jerome, they all sat down. In honour of the distinguished guests, the prior tinkled his bell, dispensing the community from silence. 'Cream soup, fried fish with vegetables, a sweet, Gorgonzola, biscuits and butter, bottled beer' were served; the conversation was as abundant and filling as the fare. At the end of the meal, grace was chanted, and the entourage returned to the upper room for coffee. 'Peace, light, simplicity were the dominating tones,' wrote Warren in his diary that night; 'the beauty of austerity everywhere, nothing of that tinselly effect which R. C. interiors are so apt to have.'

❧

'I specially need your prayers because I am (like the pilgrim in Bunyan) travelling across "a plain called Ease,"' wrote Lewis to Penelope on 5 June. 'Everything without, and many things within, are marvellously well at present.'

❧

Are you pregnant? asked Havard as his fingers felt the tenderness just in front of and slightly below the ears. Mumps! he shouted. Lewis was not amused; he was uncomfortable. The fever had come, beaching him not unpleasantly on a bed with a book, but now his jowls felt inflamed; he was not encouraged to learn that there was no antidote to the disease, that it would have to run its course. Would he live? That, said Havard, depended on a number of circumstances, not all of which were in his control. Would Lewis like him to read a little something to ease his misery? Havard went to the bookcase and pulled out a slender volume. Opening it as though it were the *Aeneid* and looking for some oracular passage, he picked a random page and let his finger run half way down. 'To surrender a self-will inflamed and swollen with years of usurpation is a kind of death . . .' He had picked out *The Problem of Pain*; that sentence was in one of the chapters on human pain. 'Hence the necessity to die daily . . .' From a desire to live expressed only a few moments ago, Lewis quickly passed to the urge to kill. 'That this process cannot be without pain,' droned Havard out of reach of the bedstead, 'is sufficiently witnessed by the very history of the word "mortification" . . .'

&

'Your letter,' wrote Lewis on 12 September to Pitter, 'is a bright spot in a hailstorm of correspondence in arrears, which I find awaiting me on my return from Ireland today.'

'I stayed for a fortnight in a bungalow which none of the peasants will approach at night because the desolate coast on which it stands is haunted by "the good people," ' he wrote to Mathews. 'There is also a ghost but (and this is interesting) they don't seem to mind *him*; the faeries are a more serious danger . . .'

&

> Hard light bathed them — a whole nation of eyeless men,
> Dark bipeds not aware how they were maimed. A long
> Process, clearly, a slow curse,
> Drained through centuries, left them thus.

Lewis was putting into poetry a sentiment he had expressed many times in prose, that there was an original sin and that it had filtered down the centuries into modern times. A nation of men, he supposed, had been blinded by the guns of Heaven. Some with their inner eyes were able to see reflections of divine truth in reason. But others, using imagery they could no longer sense and had only heard about from their ancestors, painted word pictures of reality that were surreal.

> Do you think this a far-fetched
>   Picture? Go then among
>
> Men how famous; attempt speech on the truths that once,
> Opaque, carved in divine forms, irremovable,
>   Dread but dear as a mountain-
>   Mass, stood plain to the inward eye.

'The Country of the Blind,' as Lewis entitled the poem, appeared in the 12 September issue of *Punch*.

'It has gone to a particularly hardhit member of the most unfortunate class in this country,' wrote Lewis on 18 October to Mathews about her latest parcel; 'an elderly lady (65), who has always had to struggle to make ends meet, and who, owing to a failure of dividends, is now on the verge of actual want.'

∽

H. H. Price had skirmished before with Lewis; in Michaelmas term they met again at the Socratic. Price delivered a paper entitled 'Is Theism Important?' In it he discussed various philosophical and theological approaches to God, finding that the former were not very convincing and that the latter often seemed more persuasive. All men had an 'awareness of God'; a reading of ancient literature seemed to indicate that; the Scriptures certainly demonstrated it. Indeed, the ancient pagans were not so very far off.

Replying, Lewis distinguished two kinds of faith, 'a settled intellectual assent' and 'a trust or confidence.' The former was often found in the pagan who philosophized. The latter, however, did not necessarily flow from the former, and in most cases existed without it. As for the ancient pagan, Lewis too had a warm spot in his heart for him because he was 'a man eminently convertible to Christianity', 'essentially the pre-Christian, or sub-Christian, religious man', who was as different from the modern pagan — the post-Christian pagan, the kind of pagan who wrote for the *New Statesman* — as a virgin from a divorcee.

∽

'I feel greatly obliged to the prime minister, and so far as my personal feelings are concerned, this honour would be highly agreeable,' wrote Lewis on 3 December. Churchill's secretary had written to offer him the title of Commander of the British Empire. 'There are always, however, knaves who say, and fools who believe, that my religious writings are full of covert anti-leftist propaganda, and my appearance on the honours list would, of course, strengthen their hands. It is, therefore, better that I should not appear there. I am sure the prime minister will understand my reason, and that my gratitude is and will be nonetheless cordial.'

∽

'The book really begins to look as if it might be finished in 1952,' wrote Lewis on 20 December to Firor about *English Literature in the Sixteenth Century, Excluding Drama*, 'and I am, between ourselves, pleased with the manner of it — but afraid of hidden errors.'

∽

'*Porcus sum*,' he wrote on 29 December to Pitter. 'I am a pig: *porcissimus*.' She had sent him a book. A long time passed. She asked for the book back. He couldn't read it, he said, but then again he couldn't read Newton's *Principia*, Byron's *Childe Harold*, or Dreiser's *American Tragedy*. But he could read her poems. 'I blame myself for not reading them oftener.'

⤳ 1952 ⤳

'I can't *bear* the least suggestion (however sportive) of love affairs between different species or even between children,' wrote Lewis on 8 January to Pitter. 'That is one of the many things which for me sinks *Tom Sawyer* so immeasurably below the divine *Huckleberry*.'

⤳

Differences in the Church of England between the Evangelicals and the Anglo-Catholics could only be squabbles, thought Lewis on reading a letter in the 1 February issue of *The Church Times*. What was important, he decided to write to the *Times*, which published the letter in its 8 February issue, was that both groups present a unified front against the onslaught of the liberals or modernists; to that end they needed a common name. Low Church or High Church just wouldn't do. 'May I suggest "Deep Church"; or, if that fails in humility, Baxter's "mere Christians"?'

⤳

Forewarned that he did not teach modern literature and that the short story was a form he wasn't fond of, Mathews had sent him 'Nabub'. His critique, four pages long, ran towards the negative. 'Are we still friends?' he wrote on 17 February. 'I hope so.'

⤳

'Apropos of horrid little fat baby "cherubs," ' he wrote on 31 March to Shelburne, 'did I mention that Hebrew *Kherub* is from the same root as *Gryphon*? That shows what they're really like!'

⤳

Easter fell on 13 April; right after that Lewis boarded the train at Oxford and headed for Malvern, where he was met by Sayer. The following day they were driven a day's march from Malvern and let out. They began to climb the hills, switching the pack every half-hour or so, Sayer doing the timing, Lewis not comfortable with a timepiece. They walked and rested periodically, flopping down on the turf for a soak — a term from Lewis' childhood meaning a moment when one could rest and be thoughtful — and for a cigarette. Up again, they moved along the ridge; they talked, Lewis quite frankly and easily about his spiritual difficulties and personal temptations and about Warren's increasing dependency on alcohol. When it was time for lunch, they opened the pack and fell upon the sandwiches made by Mrs Sayer. After another rest and another cigarette, they continued homeward. Not much talk now, Lewis reflecting that the trek had a poetic, even an anagogical, significance.

> By now I should be entering on the supreme stage
> Of the whole walk, reserved for the late afternoon.
> The heat was to be over now; the anxious mountains,
> The airless valleys and the sunbaked rocks, behind me . . .
>
> Now, or soon now, if all is well, come the majestic
> Rivers of foamless charity that glide beneath
> Forests of contemplation. In the grassy clearings
> Humility with liquid eyes and damp, cool nose
> Should come, half-tame, to eat bread from my hermit hand.
> If storms arose, then in my tower of fortitude —
> It ought to have been in sight by this — I would take refuge;
> But I expected rather a pale mackerel sky,
> Feather-like, perhaps shaking from a lower cloud
> Light drops of silver temperance, and clovery earth
> Sending up mists of chastity, a country smell,
> Till earnest stars blaze out in the established sky
> Rigid with justice; the streams audible; my rest secure.
>
> I can see nothing like all this. Was the map wrong?
> Maps can be wrong. But the experienced walker knows
> That the other explanation is more often true.

ಉ

'I expect there *is* a photo of me somewhere, but my brother, who knows where things are, is away, and I couldn't find it today,' wrote Lewis to Mary Shelburne on 17 April. 'Ask me again at a more favourable hour! — if you still have the fancy for this very undecorative object.'

ಉ

Lewis sent her a ticket, although Pitter would have bought her own, to his British Academy lecture in London. Arriving early, she took a seat in the middle and watched the seats fill up. Some retired lady dons tottered down the aisle to the front rows and began adjusting their hearing aids. Surrounding them soon were some fashionable figures with flagrant companions. Behind these and around Pitter sat rather more modestly dressed people, who were somewhat bewildered by the largeness of the hall, but were nonetheless beaming in anticipation; these she figured were Christians. Over the edge of the gallery, peeping from time to time, were some authors she recognized. Who but Lewis, she thought to herself as he strode onto the stage, could have drawn such a heterogeneous audience? As the applause lessened, he bowed and began 'Hero and Leander', the Wharton lecture in English poetry.

⟡

'I loathe prunes,' said Lewis once in a hotel dining-room.

'So do I,' came the immediate but unexpected response from a six-year-old at the next table.

This, said Lewis in an address to the Bournemouth Conference of the Library Association, meeting from 29 April to 2 May, was the sort of instantaneous and immediate communication an author of a good book had with a child. 'On Three Ways of Writing for Children' was the subject of the address. The first was to put into a story what the market seemed to want, which at the time seemed to be realism instead of magic. The second, which was the way of Lewis Carroll, Kenneth Grahame, and J. R. R. Tolkien, was that the story should be composed for, and told to, one specific child and that the oral tale would grow into a finished form suitable for the printed page. The third, which Lewis said was his way, was to write a children's story because a children's story was the best art form for something he had to say; he did not have to instance *The Lion, the Witch, and the Wardrobe* as an example of what he meant. He peppered his address with paradoxes — 'A children's story which is enjoyed only by children is a bad children's story' — and he even eulogized 'that extraordinary amalgam of high rank, coarse manners, gruffness, shyness, and goodness' who was Mr Badger in *The Wind in the Willows*. 'The child who has once met Mr Badger has ever afterward, in its bones, a knowledge of humanity and of English social history which it could not get in any other way.' He closed his address with a defence of the fairy tale against those who in every age would rise up to ban it. Against the charge that it gave a false impression, he argued that it was the realistic stories that deceived. Against the charge that it was a form of escapism, a subtler charge, he argued that it gave a new dimension of depth to the reader. Against the charge that it frightened a child, he argued that books rarely produced phobias and that 'to keep out of his mind the knowledge that he is born into a world of death, violence, wounds, adventure, heroism and cowardice, good and evil,' would be a disservice.

〰

'When are you going to pay Mrs Hooker's bill?' asked the voice at the other end of the telephone.

'Who is Mrs Hooker,' asked Lewis, 'and why should I pay her bill?'

'She's your wife!'

Larceny it was; on Wednesday 7 May he boarded the train for Paddington, travelled by Underground to Waterloo, where he emerged to take the train, with changes, for Ramsgate. It was the worst possible time to leave Oxford, Trinity term having just begun, but he was looking forward to meeting his wife. Apparently this woman had been, for at least a year, advertising herself as his wife, running up bills in resorts along the south coast, and even borrowing money on the strength of his name. He arrived after dinner, was met by Nell and Alan Berners-Price, and enjoyed the hospitality of their inn, the Court Stairs. The following morning they went to the police court. There she was, Mrs Hooker, also known as Mrs Lewis. She was 'an animal at bay', he found to his horror, 'surrounded by its enemies,' and justice did its work swiftly on her. 'But . . . what I really remember most,' he wrote his hostess of 9 May, 'is a delightful visit to very nice people in a charming house.'

〰

'I believe that you are free as a Christian woman to divorce him especially since the refusal to do so does some harm to the innocent children of his mistress,' he wrote on 13 May to the woman who had first written to him for advice last September; 'but that you must (or should) regard yourself as no more free to marry another man than if you had not divorced him. But remember, I'm no authority on such matters, and I hope you will ask the advice of one or two sensible clergymen of our own church.'

〰

'Very hearty congratulations,' he wrote by hand on 23 May to Vera Mathews now Gebbert. She had just announced her marriage and sent photographs of the honeymoon in Sun Valley, Idaho. In some of them there were antelope; he told her of the deer herd at Magdalen and how in palmier days they were often fed with bread soaked in port. About the only thing that did not win his praise were the sunglasses, which he supposed were, like civilization and everything else, a necessary evil. 'I hope you will both live happily ever after,' he closed in blessing, 'and tell stories to your great-grandchildren, travelling in donkey carriages along the mountain roads with hairs as white as the snow. God bless you both.'

✍

'My old *directeur*, Fr. Walter Adams, of the Cowley Fathers, died a few weeks ago,' he wrote on 17 May to Griffiths. 'He died suddenly while celebrating, and his last words were "I am coming, Lord Jesus." I owed him a great deal. Everything he ever said to me was so simple that you might have thought it childish, but it was always what was needed.'

✍

'They are alien equally to our goodness and our badness. They ought to be repulsive and boring. How is it that they are in fact *shatteringly* beautiful?' Lewis had to read through, with the help of a translation, the fragments of Sappho and wrote his impression to Griffiths on 28 May. 'Does the quenching of even the natural light in ancient Lesbos produce, across this gulf of time, an effect that superficially resembles innocence? Very queer.'

✍

'What if this present were the world's last night?' Quoting John Donne, he was writing about the second coming of Christ for a quarterly entitled *Religion in Life*. It was an unpopular doctrine with contemporary theologians. To them it seemed the product of first-century Palestine and would be better forgotten than remembered. It was the twentieth century; doctrines like Darwinism and its off-spring evolutionism were helpful, stating that the universe was making progress, growing towards perfection. Christian apocalyp-ticism, on the other hand, foretold 'a sudden, violent end imposed from without; an extinguisher popped onto a candle, a brick flung at the gramophone, a curtain rung down on the play — "Halt!"'

To Lewis all Christian doctrines had to be faced squarely, whether likeable or unlikeable. The second coming was clearly one of the unlikeable ones. He didn't think about the Son of God coming on the clouds or about physical catastrophe in the material universe. What he thought about was judgment. Each soul will be on trial. Each soul will be, like Mrs Hooker, a defendant. And the judgment, when it comes, will be infallible. 'If it is favourable, we shall have no fear; if unfavourable, no hope that it is wrong. We shall not only believe, we shall know, know beyond doubt in every fibre of our appalled or delighted being, that as the judge has said, so we are: neither more nor less nor other.'

✍

'You can trust Steiner about fertilizers,' wrote Lewis on 10 June to Miss Marg-Riette Montgomery of San Antonio, Texas, who had inquired about anthroposophy, 'but not about the nature of Jesus Christ.'

✎

'One of the things that make it easier to believe in providence is the fact that in all trains, hotels, restaurants, and other public places,' wrote Lewis on 16 June to Mary Shelburne, 'I have only *once* seen a stranger reading a book of mine, though my friends encounter this phenomenon fairly often. Things are really very well arranged.'

✎

Mrs Joan B. Pile, an acquaintance of Lewis', stood accused of slander; she was going to fight back. She asked him to testify as to her good character if the court proceedings required it. He agreed and offered her some money for the coming legal expenses. She would accept it as a loan. He insisted that it was a gift from the Agape Fund, but that it would not run to ' "several" hundred pounds, for that would be unfair to other claimants.'

✎

Late on the morning of Wednesday 24 September he strolled up the High to arrive at noon at the Mitre Hotel, where he had been invited to lunch by two married women, Phyllis Williams, a friend who lived in London, and Joy Gresham, an American who was staying with her and who had been corresponding with him since January 1950.

They had a friend in common, said Gresham, Chad Walsh; and they had a publisher in common, Macmillan. She thanked him for his books and also for the invigorating replies to her letters questioning the faith. He had been of immeasurable help on her pilgrimage, which was perhaps as wild as the one in *The Pilgrim's Regress*. She had been born into a Jewish family in New York City; Judaism wasn't practised; after reading Wells' *Outline of History* at the age of eight, she became an atheist; in the thirties she joined the Communist Party and studied Marxist theory; by the end of the war and with the coming of her marriage, her interest lessened in Marxism; one night in 1948, having learned that her husband had had a nervous breakdown in his New York City office and was nowhere to be found, she encountered, for the first time in her life, such loneliness and anxiety that 'God came in.' She found herself on her knees, praying at one moment, at another reflecting that she had to be 'the world's most surprised atheist.' The feeling as she remembered it in the Mitre Hotel was one of 'terror and ecstasy, repentance and rebirth.'

What was she doing in England? he asked. She was on a sort of sabbatical. Her doctor had recommended a change of climate; she wanted to finish a book. Her husband was at home in Staatsburg, New York; her cousin Renée was taking care of her two children, David, who was eight last 27 March and Douglas, who would be seven on 10 November. The lunch passed almost too quickly; he promised that the next time, which had to be soon, he would be the host, and the place would be Magdalen College.

∽

'Certainly come this weekend,' wired Lewis on Tuesday 14 October, to the Gebberts, who had just arrived at the Berkeley Hotel, London; 'will meet you at college entrance 1.10 Saturday.'

Before they left their hotel on Saturday morning, however, the Gebberts got a telegram from Lewis saying that he and his brother had been felled by the flu.

∽

It was just as well, he wrote on Monday to the Gebberts who were now in Munich, because Vera Henry, the housekeeper at the Kilns who would have been pressed into service as hostess, had also come down with the flu. On Tuesday a parcel arrived from the Gebberts, and Vera Henry was removed to the hospital with pneumonia. 'Yes, indeed, the whole parcel arrived intact, and I'm sorry that I did not make it clear that we got your beautiful scarves (and the cigarettes) as well as the whisky,' he wrote on 28 October to the Konigshof Hotel; 'and when the two latter gifts are, alas, nothing but a fragrant memory, we shall still be enjoying the scarves — which can be used with comfort for about nine months of the English year, as you can well imagine . . .'

∽

Warren bowed out of the luncheon Lewis had arranged at Magdalen for Phyllis Williams and Joy Gresham; at the last moment he had to ask Sayer to come from Malvern to step in. Salmon mousse was served as the main course; the conversation was as sparkling as the wine. Sayer found the American not that loud and indeed rather tastefully dressed. When asked her impressions of England, she responded promptly and wittily. Countering, Lewis said that the Renaissance, whose literature and history were his specialities, had produced three disasters. What were they? The invention of gunpowder, the invention of printing, and the discovery of America!

After lunch there was a tour of the college, Sayer falling in with Williams, Lewis leading the way with Gresham. When he asked about her education, she replied that she had been something of a prodigy, learning to read before she was three. She had an IQ that was astronomic, and her memory seemed photographic. She entered Hunter College in New York City at the age of fifteen, was graduated at the age of nineteen, and acquired a master's degree in English from Columbia University at the age of twenty-one. She must meet his brother Warren, he said; he promised to invite her, if she would come, to lunch at Magdalen again soon.

❧

'Thousands of members of the Church of England doubt whether *dulia* is lawful,' he wrote to *The Church Times*, which published the letter in its 17 October issue. Someone in the preceding week's issue had proposed that *dulia*, the veneration Romans paid to the saints and angels, might also be accorded by Anglicans to their holiest of happy memory. Canonization had even been mentioned. Alarmed at yet another Romeward drift by certain members of the Church of England, he took immediate exception and expressed the hope that the archbishops would explain what was going on. 'Does anyone maintain that it is necessary to salvation?' asked Lewis, fearing that schism would be the only result if the Romish practice were introduced. 'If not, whence comes our obligation to run such frightful risks?'

❧

Gresham once again was invited to a luncheon at Magdalen. Lewis introduced her to his brother and several other guests. She has spent some time in Hollywood, said Lewis as they sat down; he proceeded to tell a tale of the American West that he had heard in the twenties and felt sure had been made into a film by this time. It seemed that a man had been hanged before his innocence was proved. Who would tell the widow? It had to be someone who would reveal the mistake not too suddenly, for that would be brutal, but rather with some refinement. At last the sheriff was chosen to wait upon the lady. 'Say, ma'am,' said the sheriff, hemming and hawing, 'I guess you've got the laugh on us this time.'

Metro-Goldwyn-Mayer periodically scouted eastern colleges, looking for promising young script-writers. Yale University had already published her poems entitled *Letter to a Comrade*, and Macmillan had accepted for publication her novel entitled *Anya*; hence, she was picked. Once there in Hollywood, she wrote four screenplays. M-G-M didn't like them; after six months she returned to New York.

What year was that? asked Warren.

That was 1939, said Gresham.

I missed you by nine years, said Warren, expanding on his tour of Los Angeles. He had seen the set of *The Taming of the Shrew*, which had been produced in 1929, starring Douglas Fairbanks as Petruchio and Mary Pickford as Katharina. And the houses: they were enormous, lawns yawning all the way to the street. Swimming pools. Pegged wooden floors. Raftered ceilings. The glorious marble bathrooms . . .

'Is there anywhere in this monastic establishment,' asked Gresham, 'where a lady can relieve herself?'

❧

On 3 November D. E. Harding delivered to the Socratic a paper entitled 'The Living Universe', the substance of which was contained in his newly-published work entitled *The Hierarchy of Heaven and Earth: A New Diagram of Man in the Universe*. Lewis responded to the talk as he had written the preface to the book. It was a first step, he said, in the direction opposite to which philosophy had been travelling for centuries. The movement had been from a rich and genial universe packed with will, intelligence, life, and other positive qualities, in which every tree was a nymph and every planet a god, to a universe emptied first of its gods and then of its colours, smells, sounds, and tastes. The movement had been from object to subject, from animism to the brink of nihilism, where even man himself was now being considered a symbol, a personification. Harding's book, he said, was a first step back from the void and gave him a 'bracing and satisfying experience.'

❧

'I believe we are very near to one another, but not because I am at all on the Romeward frontier of my own communion,' he wrote on 10 November to Shelburne, who had just left the Church of England in America to join the Church of Rome. 'I believe that, in the present divided state of Christendom, those who are at the heart of each division are all closer to one another than those who are at the fringes.'

❧

'I shan't say goodbye,' said Lewis to Vanauken as they emerged from the Eastgate Hotel where they had had lunch. 'We'll meet again,' said Lewis, shaking hands and wading into the traffic. It was Vanauken's last day in Oxford; tomorrow he and his wife would take a train for London, where they would have lunch in a club; thence to Liverpool, where they would board a liner bound for the United States. 'Besides,' bellowed Lewis, beached safely on the other side of the swiftly flowing High, 'Christians *never* say goodbye!'

❧

'How very kind of you to sweeten my Christmas with the cake, which arrived this morning,' typed Warren on 22 December to Mrs Roderick Watson of Ridge Spring, South Carolina; 'externally in good condition, and before the day is out I shall be examining the internal condition of the parcel.'

✍

Knowing that Gresham had to board ship on 3 January for New York City, the Lewises invited her to spend some time at the Kilns, preferably the weeks after the end of Michaelmas term; she accepted. When she arrived, she joined in whenever she was invited and whenever she could.

Lewis had begun a book on prayer; 'it's going to be a wonder', she wrote to Walsh. He began proofing the galleys of *English Literature in the Sixteenth Century*; 'it's full of controversial stuff and reversals of conventional judgments.' He offered her his poetry; 'it's quite new and strange and unfashionable.' She showed him *Letter to a Comrade*; he found much to his liking. She presented to him the manuscript — 50,000 words or so, but still unfinished — of her work on the Ten Commandments tentatively entitled *Decalogue*.

There was walking and hiking in the rain and drinking at the pubs. The three even went to a Christmas pantomine, where they laughed at the oldest jokes and joined — especially Jack — in the choruses of the songs:

Am I going to be a bad boy? No, no, no!
Am I going to be awful? No, no, no!
I promise not to put some crumbs in Aunt Fanny's bed,
I promise not to put gravy over the baby's head . . .

There was sky-watching in the evenings. For two or three successive nights around the 25th, Venus and Jove were blazing at each other; on one night the moon was directly between them: 'majesty and love linked by virginity.'

On Christmas Day, Lewis gave her a copy of *Diary of an Old Soul*, which MacDonald had inscribed on 27 April 1885; he further inscribed it 'from C. S. Lewis to Joy Davidman, Christmas, 1952.' In return, she promised to dedicate her Decalogue book to him. And the Christmas dinner she prepared was sumptuous, an enormous turkey with trimmings, enlivened by bottles of burgundy from the Magdalen cellar. She might have been three thousand miles from Staatsburg, New York, but nonetheless she seemed to feel at home.

Darkening the holiday was a four-page, typewritten, single-spaced letter from her husband Bill. In her absence, he had fallen in love with Renée. Two writers in one family meant a dusty house and dirty dishes. Renée was not a writer and could therefore devote herself to the full-time job of being a wife. He still had 'tremendous affection' for her, wrote Bill, but he felt that she should marry 'some really swell guy' and live near him and Renée 'so that the Gresham kids could have a mommy and daddy on hand.'

Gresham showed the letter to Lewis and revealed more of her past life than perhaps she had originally intended. Her husband had been and still was a victim of alcoholism; he had been unable to sustain his writing career; he had the strong urge, which he seldom seemed able to resist, to sleep with willing females. He too had been converted from Communism to Christianity; he too had embraced the Presbyterian Church; but even to that commitment he was unfaithful; he was espousing dianetics as it was being expounded by L. Ron Hubbard. When she asked Lewis what she should do, he talked; the more he talked, the more divorce looked like the practical alternative.

Having to return to New York with such a prospect disheartened her. For her to return to America, whose sins she had written about in the Decalogue book, distressed Lewis. But Warren, not knowing the full details of her domestic condition, revelled in the merry days they had together and bade her farewell, sincerely hoping that he would see her again.

❧ 1953 ❧

'I don't wonder that you got fogged in *Pilgrim's Regress*,' wrote Lewis on 19 January to Allen's mother. 'It was my first religious book, and I didn't then know how to make things easy.'

❧

'Our Christmas was conditioned by having a visitor for nearly three weeks,' he wrote on 26 January to Sarah Neylan; 'a very nice one but one can't feel quite free.'

❧

Anthony Boucher, editor of *The Magazine of Fantasy and Science Fiction*, which was published in New York, wrote to Lewis, introducing himself and asking Lewis if he would like to contribute something to the pages of the magazine. Lewis declined. All of his energy was going into children's stories; if and when he did write another fantasy story for adults, it would probably be 'too quiet or leisurely' for the readers of the magazine. Most science fiction writers, Boucher and Ray Bradbury excepted, he went on to say, were bogus, merely transplanting the gangster story from this planet to another; they, however, were 'the *real* thing.' 'If you are ever in England or I in the U.S.A.,' he concluded his letter of 5 February, 'we must certainly meet and split a CH_3CH_2OH together.'

❦

'Probably the whole thing is only a plan for kidnapping me and marooning me on an asteroid!' he wrote on 14 February, declining an invitation to speak extended by Clarke.

'I confess that the kidnapping plan had not occurred to me,' wrote Clarke on the 16th, 'and I promise you that if we do have an opportunity of marooning you on an asteroid, we will give you time to pack your winter woollies!'

❦

There was this young Catholic boy who lay dying of poliomyelitis, said Bide on a visit to Lewis, telling his old tutor an unusual story of his first year of ministry in Brighton. Michael was the boy's name; and he was flat on his back when Bide visited him in the isolation ward of the children's hospital, convulsing and foaming at the mouth and rolling his eyes so that only the whites were visible. The boy's mother had asked him to go, hoping against hope for a miracle. Grounded as he was with an education heavy in science and the laws of science, Bide did not expect a miracle. He simply knelt down on the floor by the bed, put his hand on the boy, and said something like, 'Look down, O Lord, on this thy child, and if it be thy gracious will, restore him to his family. For the sake of Jesus Christ, our Lord. Amen.' But he had gone further in the prayer than he intended; he was amazed when he said to the nurse as he rose from the floor, 'I hope he'll be all right'; she looked at the priest as though he had lost his mind.

Back to the boy's family Bide went and told them that Michael was in the hands of God and that they should pray. Then he went to the saintliest spinster in his parish and asked her to pray for Michael until she fell asleep that night. Then he went to the neighbouring parish where he was giving a weekly Lenten discourse on the gospel of St Mark. The previous week, in connection with the raising of Jairus' daughter, he had explained the relationship between healing and the faith of the community. Well, that very night, he told the congregation, they had a chance to put that relationship to the test. Everything they had ever learned from the church, the Bible, the sacrament of the altar, he asked them to offer up to God, to ask God to use them for Michael so that he could be given back to his father and mother. 'If you do this,' Bide was astonished to hear himself say, 'he'll get better.' The following morning, when the senior physician telephoned the hospital to learn the results of the post-mortem, he was told that the boy was sitting up and eating breakfast. Obviously, said Lewis, deeply moved, your prayer and the prayers of the community were answered.

On 18 March Vera Mathews Gebbert wrote to Lewis that the seasickness, bouts of which had been recurring since her return to Beverly Hills, was not *mal de mer* at all but morning sickness. She was pregnant, said her doctor, and was probably in her seventh month. Lewis had not regarded her 'frightful illness as a joke' when he wrote to her on 9 December. When he wrote to her on 23 March, he put the phenomenon into perspective. 'I am sure you feel as I did when I heard my first bullet, "This is war: this is what Homer wrote about." '

'It's fun laying out all my books as a cathedral,' wrote Lewis on 28 March to William L. Kintner of Muhlenberg College, Allentown, Pennsylvania. 'I'd make *Miracles* and the other "treatises" the cathedral school. My children's stories are the real side-chapels, each with its own little altar.'

'The quite enormous advantage of coming really to believe in forgiveness is well worth the horrors (I agree that they *are* horrors) of a first confession,' wrote Lewis on 6 and 7 April to a woman whom he was counselling by post. She had undergone conversion; in her zeal she was thinking of joining a religious order. 'Also,' continued Lewis, 'there is the gain in self-knowledge; most of us have never really faced the facts about ourselves until we uttered them aloud in plain words, calling a spade a spade. I certainly feel that I have profited enormously by the practice.'

In April Vanauken wrote from Virginia, where he was teaching at Lynchburg College, to thank Lewis once again for the part he had played in the conversion process. 'My feeling . . . is always mixed with awe and fear,' replied Lewis on 22 April; 'such as a boy might feel on first being allowed to fire a rifle. The disproportion between his puny finger on the trigger and the thunder and lightning which follow is alarming.'

'The young gentleman looks already, as he should, fathomlessly American,' wrote Lewis on 20 July after having received a photograph of the newly born Charles Marion Gebbert; 'not so much the current model as the heavy millionaire of earlier fiction and film (you'd hardly remember) who was always bringing his clenched fist down on the desk and raging "We gotta smash the Medicine Hat Toothbrush Combine!" '

〰️

'You are quite right,' wrote Lewis to Mary Shelburne, admitting that he did not go to the coronation of Queen Elizabeth on 22 June. 'I approve of all that sort of thing immensely, and I was deeply moved by all I heard of it; but I'm not a man for crowds and best clothes. The weather was frightful.'

'The pressing of that huge, heavy crown on that small young head becomes a sort of symbol of the situation of *humanity* itself,' he wrote to Shelburne again; 'humanity called by God to be his vice-gerent and high priest on earth . . .'

〰️

The Lewises were with book as Trinity term came to an end in the middle of June. Warren had just received galley proofs of *The Splendid Century: Some Aspects of French Life in the Reign of Louis XIV*; it was the fruit of eleven years' work; Eyre and Spottiswoode planned to publish it in the autumn. Jack was going over proofs of the text of his volume in the OHEL series. He was also spending a considerable amount of time in the Bodleian, standing at the card catalogue in the Duke Humfrey, rummaging through trays of index cards, verifying titles and editions of books that he was including in his bibliography. 'I'd sooner walk *ten* miles,' he said to his brother intoning the Irish saw, 'than *stand* one.'

〰️

Coronation, pageantry, Narnia were all swirling in Lewis' mind, and he began to write a 'Narnian Suite.' The first part would be a 'march for strings, kettledrums, and sixty-three dwarfs.'

> With plucking pizzicato and the prattle of the kettledrum
> We're trotting into battle mid a clatter of accoutrement;
> Our beards are big as periwigs and trickle with opopanax,
> And trinketry and treasure twinkle out on every part of us —
>   (Scrape! Tap! The fiddle and the kettledrum) . . .

〰️

'I wish your *bad* poets weren't so exportable!' he wrote on 27 June to Firor. 'You send us Eliot in the flesh and Pound in the spirit.'

〰️

The second part of 'Narnian Suite' was coming to him now, a 'march for drum, trumpet, and twenty-one giants.'

With stumping stride in pomp and pride
We come to thump and floor ye;
We'll bump your lumpish heads today
And tramp your ramparts into clay,
And as we stamp and romp and play
Our trump'll blow before us —
Oh tramp it, tramp it, tramp it, trumpet, trumpet blow
    before us! . . .

～

The tap on the door had to be — Lewis looked at the letter on his desk — Clyde S. Kilby from Wheaton College, wherever that was. Welcoming him by name, Lewis ushered him into the room and installed him on the sofa. He himself plunked down on his desk chair and swivelled to face the American.

Wheaton, Kilby explained as he watched the famous Christian light up his pipe, was a small Protestant liberal arts college not far from Chicago, where the gangsters came from. Neither fundamentalist on the one hand nor liberal on the other, it was properly described as evangelical. He first met Lewis, he said, in the college bookstore in 1943 when he picked up a copy of *The Case for Christianity*. Then came the novels, around which he had managed to organize a course. Would Lewis agree, he asked, that a novel was, as some critic had proposed, a well-told lie? Sometimes there was more truth in a novel, replied Lewis, than in the daily newspaper. What was the relationship, asked Kilby, between Christianity and art? About the same, replied Lewis, as between Christianity and carpentry. His wife sent her regards, said Kilby, rising to leave. Lewis returned the sentiment, asking where she was. Waiting, said Kilby; he would have brought her in if he had known beforehand that Lewis received women in his rooms.

～

'Look,' wrote Lewis to Green in July, 'I think I must abandon the idea of an expedition on my way back from Ireland, for *this* year. It is becoming clear that I shan't finish the proofs and horrible bibliography of my OHEL volume before we sail on August 11th. That being so, every day between our return and the beginning of Michaelmas term becomes precious as gold; for if the job drags on into another term, I don't know what will become of me.'

～

'Yes, I too think there is lots to be said for being no longer young,' he wrote on 1 August to Shelburne; 'and I do most heartily agree that it is just as well to be past the age when one expects or desires to attract the other sex.'

'Dear Ruth,' wrote Lewis on 1 October to Pitter. She had known him for seven years and suggested that perhaps first names might now be allowed. Men of his generation, he countered, had been taught that a woman must ask first. 'Yours in all service,' he signed off; 'Jack.'

∽

For perhaps a year he had been trying to write a book on prayer, but he always hit a snag. He had been advised in prayer by several Cowley Fathers; he had read about prayer in John Jewel, Lancelot Andrewes, and Richard Hooker; and indeed he had passed on the rudiments of instruction to those correspondents who asked. But what exactly happened when a Christian asked for something in prayer and the request was not granted troubled him greatly. Hence, when he was invited to address the Oxford Clerical Society, he felt he could put the whole problem to them.

There were at least two patterns of petitionary prayer; they seemed the one to exclude the other. Pattern A was characterized by submission to God's will. One could ask for something in prayer and know that its granting was conditional on the will of God. Jesus encouraged this pattern when he said on the hillside that one of the petitions in the perfect prayer was 'Thy will be done.' That very same petition Jesus himself used in the garden when he prayed 'not my will but thine.'

Opposed to pattern A was pattern B. If someone prayed for something and indeed had faith in Jesus, then he or she would be like the centurion and a host of others; the prayer would be answered. If that person prayed with one or two others, then that *ecclesia*, that gathering, might be considered a church, and when the church, believing as it did in Jesus Christ, would pray with one voice, then its prayer would surely be answered.

Trouble was, he pointed out, and the clerics knew it better than he, was that most prayers seemed to go unanswered. Jesus' prayer in the garden seemed to have fallen on a deaf ear; at least twice in the twentieth century the church — composed of, among others, the 'Anglicans in Cambridge, Congregationalists in Liverpool, Salvationists in East London' — had prayed for peace, and the petition was not granted.

What pattern of prayer, then, did the church use when it failed? What pattern should the individual Christian use that would succeed? Lewis wanted to know, for he prayed daily for others, whose names he kept on a list, and he asked others to pray for him and his intentions. 'I come to you, reverend fathers, for guidance,' he said in conclusion. 'How am I to pray this very night?'

'I have to thank the master and fellows of Trinity College, Cambridge, for allowing me to use this book, in an embryonic state, as the Clark Lectures (1944),' wrote Lewis on 7 October in preface to *English Literature in the Sixteenth Century, Excluding Drama*; he went on to thank 'Professor F. P. Wilson for such painstaking and skilled help as few authors have ever had from their friends; Mr Dowling for much help with my bibliography, and Professor Douglas Bush for submitting to certain petty pilferings from his; Mr R. E. Alton for guidance through the labyrinth of our faculty library; Dr J. A. W. Bennett and Mr H. V. D. Dyson for advice and criticism; and Miss Joy Davidman for help with the proofs.'

∽

'Of course I have been praying for you daily, as always,' wrote Lewis on 6 November to Shelburne, who had lost her job some months before and found herself financially dependent on her daughter and son-in-law, 'but latterly have found myself do so with much more concern and especially about two nights ago, with such a strong feeling how very nice it would be, if God willed, to get a letter from you with good news. And then, as if by magic (indeed it is the whitest magic in the world) the letter comes today.'

∽

'What I want to see there,' wrote Lewis on 7 November to Gebbert about an invitation he wouldn't be able to accept, 'is yourself and three or four other good friends, after New England, the Rip Van Winkle Mountains, Nantucket, the Huckleberry Finn country, the Rockies, Yellowstone Park, and a sub-Arctic winter.'

∽

Now that Gresham was back in England, the Lewises invited her to come for a weekend visit. David was nine-and-a-half, she said, introducing her sons on Friday 18 December, and Douglas celebrated his eighth birthday on 10 November in the middle of the Atlantic. The boys she had already enrolled in Dane Court, a boarding school in Surrey, about an hour's train from London. She herself had taken a two-room apartment in the annexe to the Avoca House Hotel in Hampstead, London, which was not too far from Phyllis Williams.

The reason she had fled the United States, she told the Lewises when the boys were out of earshot, was that divorce from her husband Bill was imminent. He had knocked her about when she returned to New York last January, choking her and punching her; he was drinking heavily again. He planned to marry her cousin Renée as soon as he could; Renée had already divorced her husband in Miami; Bill planned to file for divorce from Joy in Miami on the mutually agreed grounds of desertion and incompatibility. But it would be the middle of the new year before that divorce was final. In the meantime, with the blessing of the British Home Office, she had a temporary visa. When that ran out, she didn't know what she was going to do.

One of the first things they did do at the Kilns was to set out for a hike through the woods. Warren and Joy walked at a good pace, but Jack and the boys plunged ahead, thrashing their way through thickets, stomping across patches of mud, scampering up steep rises. Back at the Kilns the Lewises taught David to play chess. Douglas sawed wood for the fireplaces and tended the coals in the grates, rousing the grey lumps to glowing red by means of an instrument new to him, called the bellows.

Strolling down Headington Hill towards Oxford, the boys kept a sharp lookout for bobbies, policemen with funny domed helmets. At the college, Lewis gave them a tour. They stalked the deer in the park; no reindeer these; these were tiny and nervously trotted away as the boys approached. Lewis introduced them to the grotesques — the werewolf, the hyena, the panther, the griffin — carved stone figures perched on top of the buttresses of the fifteenth-century cloister.

As the Greshams were leaving on Monday 21 December Lewis asked the boys to call him Jack and gave them a typescript of *The Horse and His Boy*. It was the fifth book in the Narnia series. He had dedicated each book to a select group of young friends. The first was dedicated to Lucy Barfield; the second, to Mary Clare Havard; the third, to Geoffrey Barfield; the fourth, to Nicholas Hardie. If the boys had a good opinion of the fifth, he would dedicate it to them.

∽

'Welcome to what Tolkien calls the Little Kingdom, at least to the marches of it,' he wrote the same day to Pitter. She had divested herself of the family cottage in Essex with its lovely vineyard; she and Kathleen O'Hara had sold their house in Chelsea, London, and bought a plain solid brick house, only forty years old, set on two-and-a-half acres of garden and orchard in the picturesque village of Long Crendon, about fifteen miles east of Oxford. 'It will be interesting to see how soon you rusticate — grow slow-witted like us and believe that the streets of Thame (now your metropolis) are paved with gold and shiver delightfully at the thought of its mingled wickedness and splendour.' He was still frazzled, he said, from the just concluded visit with Mrs Gresham and her boys. Had she ever heard of the American — she was published under the name Joy Davidman — and did she know her poetry?

∽

'Twenty years ago I felt no doubt that I should live to see it all break up and great literature return,' he wrote to Gresham the day after she returned to London; she had left behind a tattered paperback copy of *Childhood's End* by Arthur C. Clarke; the science fiction work he found full of emotion and mythopoeia; in fact, he was bowled over by it, beating as it did the realistic drivel being published nowadays about neurotics living in London flats. 'But here I am, losing teeth and hair, and still no break in the clouds.'

୰

'Thank heavens!' said Warren to his brother as he waded through the mail on the morning of 23 December; 'here's something like a *real* present at last.' There were dozens of Christmas cards and some parcels, one of them a monster from Gebbert in California. Warren immediately sat down and typed a letter of thanks, adding that although they had removed the outer wrappings, 'like good little boys', they would not open the parcel itself until the morning of the twenty-fifth.

୰ 1954 ୰

'Thanks for your letter of the 28th, to which I'm afraid I can manage only a very small answer, for Christmas mails have "got me down," ' wrote Lewis on 1 January to Mary Shelburne. 'This season is to me mainly hard, gruelling work — write, write, write, till I wickedly say that if there were less *good will* (going through the post) there would be more *peace on earth.*'

୰

'I've been having a sebaceous (no, not herbaceous) cyst lanced on the back of my neck,' he wrote on 16 January to his godchild Sarah; 'the most serious result is that I can never at present get my whole head and shoulders under water in my bath. (I like getting down like a hippo with only my nostrils out.)'

୰

'We had a very odd few days this vacation: a lady and her sons (ages 9½ and 8) staying with us,' wrote Lewis on 18 January to Gebbert. 'A tough "assignment" — I talk American like a native, don't I? — for two old bachelors. Phew!'

୰

'Are you ever in this city?' asked Lewis on 20 January of Arthur C.

Clarke, who had just sent Lewis a copy of his latest book, a collection of short stories entitled *Expedition to Earth*. 'If so, be sure to let me know, and we will make a tryst. I know where the best beer and the best cider and the only draught stout are.'

⁓

'Thanks enormously for all the intense work you have put into them all,' wrote Lewis on 21 January to Baynes. He had had lunch with Bles the day before, during which they both pored over the fifteen drawings she had done, one for each chapter in *The Horse and His Boy*. Lasaraleen was 'a rich feast of line and of fantastic-satiric imagination.' Rabadash was 'the best comedy you've done yet.' Tisroc was 'superb.' 'And more power to your elbow: congratulations.'

⁓

'Dear Hugh, Anne, Noelie (There is a name I never heard before; what language is it, and does it rhyme with *oily* or *mealy* or *Kelly* or *early* or *truly*?), Nicholas, Martin, Rosamund, Matthew, and Miriam,' he wrote on 24 January to the Kilmer family who called Shelburne Aunt Mary Willis. 'Thank you very much for all the lovely letters and pictures.'

⁓

Contemporary poets were very much on his mind at the end of January. Two of his unfavourites — Dylan Thomas and Ezra Pound — he railed against in a letter to Clarke. Two of his favourites — Ruth Pitter and Joy Gresham — he invited to lunch at the Eastgate on Monday 1 February. After the lunch, however, despite Lewis' best attempts, British poetry was no closer to, perhaps even farther away from, poetry in America.

⁓

'I have had to abandon the book on prayer,' he wrote on 15 February to Sister Penelope; 'it was clearly not for me.'

⁓

Tolkien had something on his mind — it wasn't the impending publication of *The Lord of the Rings* — and he wanted to talk to Lewis. Cambridge University, he told his friend over a glass, was setting up a professorship of medieval and Renaissance studies. A board of electors was about to begin a search for the appropriate person to fill the chair. He, Tolkien, was one of the electors; he was empowered to ask Lewis if he would accept the professorship. He was the unanimous choice of the electors, said Tolkien before Lewis could say no. That *The Allegory of Love* had been a critical success and that Lewis had been delivering prolegomena lectures to medieval and Renaissance literature for decades qualified him for the chair better than anyone else who could be imagined. It would mean the end of tutorials, which dreary job he had been doing for almost thirty years; and it would mean a substantial increase in income. The professorship was attractive, Lewis had to admit, but his roots were in Oxonia, not Cantabrigia.

∽

'The typescript of *your* book went off to the publisher last week, though it won't be out till next year,' he wrote on 19 March to the Kilmer children, to whom he was dedicating the next Narnia novel. 'It is called *The Magician's Nephew*.'

∽

'I happen to have copies of this ugly book in which you may find some of the articles worth reading,' wrote Lewis on 25 March to Greeves; with the letter he enclosed a copy of *These Found the Way: Thirteen Converts to Protestant Christianity*. 'Joy Davidman's is the best, I think.'

∽

On Friday 9 April the Lewises and the Greshams drove to Whipsnade, where they visited the zoo. Warren walked ahead with the boys, pointing out the general layout and the best way to attack the exhibits and habitats. The boys seemed to be happy, said Joy, but she was not. Her husband had promised, when they separated, to send $60 a month for the support of the boys. Most months the money didn't arrive; now the spring-term fees and tuitions were due at Dane Court. The Agape Fund would take care of that, said Jack as they arrived at the bears. There, two mothers were nursing three woolly cubs; almost nose to nose, they were sharing the joys of lactation. Further on, there was a tigress, who was separated from the tigers by metal bars; her large brown eyes were sad and seemed to say there was no joy in celibacy.

∽

At the insistence of Gresham, Lewis read — and in some cases reread — the works of American poets like Robert Frost and Edgar Lee Masters, Robinson Jeffers and Stephen Vincent Benét. They all seemed to have something to say, he was able to report to Pitter and Griffiths; not a few of them said it artfully; all of them said it unboringly. Contemporary British poets, on the other hand, with rare exceptions like Pitter, bored him beyond belief. But perhaps he was wrong. He examined his conscience. The result was a sort of critical confession, which he sprinkled, if not with humility, then with a little humour:

> I am so coarse, the things the poets see
> Are obstinately invisible to me.

For twenty years I've stared my level best
To see if evening — any evening — would suggest
A patient etherized upon a table;
In vain. I simply wasn't able.
To me each evening looked far more
Like the departure from a silent, yet a crowded shore
Of a ship whose freight was everything, leaving behind
Gracefully, finally, without farewells, marooned mankind . . .

He might not be the best of contemporary poets, he thought to himself, but he could still get his stuff published in *Punch*, *The Spectator*, and *The Times Literary Supplement*.

࿓

'Only a scrap, for everyone writes to me at Easter, so that what ought to be a bright spot in the year threatens to become for me a very dark one,' wrote Lewis on 17 April, which was Holy Saturday, to Shelburne, whom he now addressed as Mary. 'Will you, please, always avoid "holiday" periods in writing to me?'

࿓

At seven sharp on Thursday 22 April, in the smoking room at Magdalen, Lewis greeted Blamires; after a sherry they proceeded to dinner. Lewis had liked *The Devil's Hunting Ground*, a novel his former student had sent him in manuscript. If it could find a publisher and an audience, it would be the first of a trilogy in which a man, accompanied only by an angel, would make a pilgrimage from Hell through Purgatory to Heaven. When writing Screwtape's correspondence with Wormwood, Lewis revealed, he had thought of running a parallel correspondence from an archangel to a guardian angel. After dinner they retired to New Buildings, where Lewis showed him the latest issue of *The Month*, which contained his blast against contemporary poetry. From there the conversation turned to theology.

'We're troubled with a bad crop of clergy,' said Lewis. 'And it isn't just the Church of England. I'm told the Romans have the same problem.'

When Blamires mentioned high church and low church, Lewis said he preferred the term 'deep churchman.'

'I think the Anglo-Catholics are the only Evangelicals left,' offered Blamires.

'Oh no,' said Lewis with a twinkle, 'there are still just a few of us here and there.'

'Queueing up to kiss the crucifix goes against the grain,' said

Blamires, citing the Good Friday practice as one high-church custom he found difficult.

'Oh, but it shouldn't, you know. The body must offer its homage.'

❧

Early in May Tolkien made sure that Lewis heard the new Cambridge professorship was being offered to Helen Gardner. She was ten years younger than Lewis, had written a book on the art of T. S. Eliot, and had just edited the divine poems of John Donne. She hesitated to accept, however, because she had just been appointed to the readership in Renaissance English Literature at Oxford and because the professorship seemed so clearly to have been created for Lewis. Tolkien urged Lewis to reconsider. Permanent residence in or near Cambridge was not mandatory. During the week he would live at Magdalene College. Weekends and vacations he could still spend at the Kilns. 'Come to Macedonia and help us!' hallooed Basil Willey, professor of English literature at Cambridge. Better to be where he was wanted, Lewis was beginning to think. Medieval and Renaissance studies were slipping in importance at Oxford; the nineteenth and part of the twentieth centuries were about to be added to the literature curriculum, at the expense no doubt of the Middle Ages. Yes, he would go to Cambridge; it was nice that he would have the same collegiate patroness, but was he really leaving Athens for Macedonia?

❧

'To face anew those shelves in the Bodleian, full of the brown-and-gold meditations of our ancestors — on hunting, poetry, bishops, love, diet, Arthur of Britain, the returns of the electors, Greek pronunciation, import of wines, the soil of Derbyshire, Petrarch's metres, saving grace, a hue-and-cry in Norwich — and to set all that in order,' wrote Millar MacLure in *Canadian Forum*, reviewing *English Literature in the Sixteenth Century, Excluding Drama*. 'Mr Lewis has earned his new chair at Cambridge.'

❧

In May Lewis got a letter from Vanauken in Virginia. Both he and his wife, much to their surprise, had been asked by several members of their Christian group what was wrong with homosexuality. The Vanaukens replied as best they could; he wrote to Lewis for further opinion. Lewis replied at length, admitting first of all that he had seen all too little of it, but what he had seen was too much.

Vanauken also asked him about petitionary prayer. 'I presume God grants prayers when granting would be good for the petitioner and others,' replied Lewis on 14 May, 'and denies them when it would not.' He then went on to distinguish the worthiness from the unworthiness of the one praying and the possible goodness from the possible badness of the thing prayed for. 'All very crude,' he wrote in conclusion. 'The point is that worthiness might easily be taken into account, though not in the way of direct *earning* and *reward*.'

❧

'I am tall, fat, rather bald, red-faced, double-chinned, black-haired, have a deep voice, and wear glasses for reading,' he wrote on 29 May to a class of fifth-graders in Rockville, Maryland, who had written about his Narnia books. 'Best love to you all. When you say your prayers, sometimes ask God to bless me.'

❧

On Saturday 12 June the Lewises were picked up by the Cecils, David and Rachel, and driven the fifteen miles to Long Crendon, where they had been invited for a visit by Ruth Pitter. How delightful she had found *The Lion, the Witch, and the Wardrobe*, she said during lunch, the serving of which was assisted by her friend O'Hara. The logic of the story, however, had several lapses in it. That the truth might appear, Lewis encouraged her to try to prove her point.

'The Witch makes it always winter and never summer?' asked Pitter.

'She does,' embaritoned Lewis.

'Does she allow any foreign trade?'

'She does not.'

'Am I allowed to postulate a *deus ex machina* perhaps on the lines of Santa Claus with the tea tray?'

'You are not.'

'Then how could the Beavers have put on that splendid lunch?'

'They caught the fish through holes in the ice.'

'Quite so,' twinkled Pitter, 'but the dripping to fry them?' O'Hara began to grin. 'The potatoes, a plant that perishes at a touch of frost?' The Cecils smiled. 'The oranges and sugar and suet and flour for the lovely surprise marmalade roll?' Warren was about to whoop. 'The malt and hops for Mr Beaver's beer?'

'I must refer you to . . .'

'The milk for the children?'

'To a further study of the text,' ahemmed Lewis.

'Nonsense, Jack!' roared Warren. 'You're stumped, and you know it.'

❧

'I'm on the eve of a great adventure,' wrote Lewis on 6 June to Delmore H. Banner, 'having accepted the new chair of medieval and Renaissance English at Cambridge.'

'My address will be Magdalene, so I remain under the same patronness,' he wrote on 30 July to Sister Penelope. 'This is nice because it saves "admin." readjustments in Heaven.'

∽

August brought divorce to two of the women in Lewis' life. In Miami the process had just ended for Joy Davidman Gresham. In Los Angeles it was barely begun for Vera Mathews Gebbert.

∽

Lewis was examining without respite during the month of July. At the beginning of August, Warren had to leave the Kilns for the hospital, having drunk himself into a stupor, and the Greshams arrived at the Kilns for a visit. Her financial plight was as severe as ever. She had been working for *European Press*, but she didn't think the magazine would survive the year. She shouldn't worry, said Jack; the Agape Fund would pay the boys' fees and tuitions at Dane Court.

When Warren emerged from the hospital, he was chastened and charming and greeted the Greshams warmly. Joy he immediately put to gainful employment, doing research for his next book. In Jack's rooms at Magdalen he introduced her to a pile of books, some from his own collection, others from libraries in Oxford; he explained what he wanted her to look for. She was grateful for the funds and indeed for the month in the country with her boys. On 16 August the Lewises left Oxford for a vacation in Ireland. The first two weeks they would spend in the south. Then Warren would return; Jack would venture northward to spend two weeks with Greeves.

There was a knock at the door of room 3. Gresham put a bookmark into Mme. de Maintenon. When she opened the door, she startled two women. They looked like tourists to her, but she didn't look like Lewis to them, even though his name was above the door and the figure in front of them was trousered. No, he was away on vacation, said Gresham. As the women walked down staircase 3, she hollered after them that they should have telephoned from the porter's lodge and not just barged in.

∽

'Learned, vivacious, individual, this nine-years-pondered handbook is a notable performance,' wrote the anonymous writer in *The Times Literary Supplement* of 17 September, reviewing *English Literature in the Sixteenth Century, Excluding Drama*. 'Few critics of recent years have brought to the study of English literature so wide a knowledge both of the classical literatures and of French and Italian literature (to say nothing of the "Scots"). And Mr Lewis, be it said, knows how to make his learning felt — you feel, reading him, that he has read what he is talking about. Even so, what is best in this book, perhaps, is the lively, individual quality of it.'

∽

Lewis began to put down on paper some thoughts for his inaugural address at Cambridge, which he learned would take place in November. Much of what he had already said about the Middle Ages and Renaissance was well known in Oxford, and in due course would become better known in Cambridge. What perhaps he should describe was where he stood as a critic of the literature of those periods. That would involve some history.

'I know nothing of the future, not even whether there will be any future,' he wrote in an attempt to disclaim any expertise in the philosophy of history. 'I don't know whether past history has been necessary or contingent. I don't know whether the human tragi-comedy is now in Act I or Act V; whether our present disorders are those of infancy or old age. I am merely considering how we should arrange or schematize those facts — ludicrously few in comparison with the totality — which survive to us (often by accident) from the past. I am less like a botanist in a forest than a woman arranging a few cut flowers for the drawing room.'

A woman indeed, snorted Gresham when she read what he wrote.

∽

'I say! You *have* learned something about animals in the last few months: where did you do it?' wrote Lewis on 2 October to Baynes. He had just seen the fifteen illustrations for *The Magician's Nephew*, the sixth book in the Narnian series. The elephant, which would appear at the beginning of chapter eleven, was 'the real thing,' as was the winged horse, which would appear at the beginning of chapter twelve.

∽

'On 31 December I have to move all my goods and chattels out of these rooms,' wrote Lewis from Magdalen on 26 October to Gebbert, 'and distribute them between Cambridge and the Kilns . . .'

'I think I shall like Magdalene better than Magdalen,' he wrote on 1 November to Shelburne. 'It's a tiny college (a perfect cameo architecturally), and they're all so old fashioned, and pious, and gentle, and conservative — unlike this leftist, atheist, cynical, hardboiled, huge Magdalen.

'Has any theologian (perhaps dozens) allegorized St Mary Magdalene's act in the following way, which came to me like a flash of lightning the other day!' he wrote on 1 November to Griffiths. 'The precious alabaster box which we have to *break* over the holy feet is our *heart*. It seems so obvious, once one has thought of it.'

❧

It was tea-time at the Picadilly Hotel. Lewis walked through the lobby briskly, looking about. Gresham spotted him and hailed him into the dining room. There she introduced him to Jeannette Davidman, her mother, and Joseph Davidman, her father. Jen and Joe, please — and Jack, of course. When Lewis had heard they were going to be in London, he certainly wanted to meet them. Yes, they were just passing through on their way to the continent, where they would spend six weeks. It was the vacation they had dreamed of all of those years, working in the New York City public school system. Never missed a pay cheque, said Joe, not even in the darkest years of the Great Depression. But things weren't all that bad. Even Prohibition proved to be a blessing.

'One day when I was twelve,' interrupted Joy, 'I found a bottle of my father's apricot brandy and poured it down the sink.'

'And I walloped her for it too,' said Joe; 'I had it for perfectly justifiable reasons.'

'Our *own* case is always different, isn't it?' bristled Lewis.

'You're doing wonderfully,' whispered Joy to Jack near the end of the tea.

'I'm doing my best!' he said woefully.

That evening he did better. He was participating in a debate with Sayers and someone else. The Davidmans thought she had considerable wit and a massive intellect, but she was fat, dressed in a tent, and simply brushed her hair back on her head like a man. 'If brains made a woman look like that,' said Jen, who was wearing a black suit with rhinestone buttons, pink blouse, shocking pink hat, and pearls at wrist, throat, and ears, 'then I'm glad I'm not an intellectual.'

❧

'Your book came at the moment of low spiritual temper, external worry, and (mild) physical pain,' wrote Lewis on 1 November to Griffiths. 'I had prayed hard a couple of nights before that my faith might be strengthened. The response was immediate, and your book gave the finishing touch.' The book he was referring to was *The Golden String*, Griffiths' spiritual autobiography which had just been published. Lewis himself was a character in it, appearing as the author's tutor in the late twenties when both of them were unbelievers already on the long intellectual pilgrimage towards belief.

❧

'Miss Margaret Radcliffe (Tree Top, Hindhead, Surrey) has had an operation and been in hospital for weeks at £4-4-1 a week,' wrote Lewis on 8 November to Barfield; 'and you know her income. Could you send her £21?'

❦

'The sins of Americans (for whom, in the first instance, the book was written) are doubtless not exactly the same as our own.' Lewis was writing a foreword to the British edition of *Smoke on the Mountain: The Ten Commandments in Terms of Today*, Gresham's book which would be published by Hodder & Stoughton in the spring of 1955. 'Many of their sins, indeed, we are now hardly in a position to commit. Hence, inevitably, there are passages in this book which English readers may make bad use of, reading them with complacent self-congratulation. But in the main it is a true bill against all western civilization.'

❦

'It is a long time since you wrote and told me of your wife's grave illness,' he wrote on 23 November to Vanauken in Virginia. 'You asked my prayers and of course have had them: not only daily, for I never wake in the night without remembering you both before God . . . I liked you both so well: never two young people more.'

❦

'Speaking from a newly-founded chair,' Lewis began his inaugural lecture at Cambridge. It was Monday 29 November. The hall was full of caps and gowns. The podium was draped with microphone cords and recording apparatus. He was following quick upon the kind introduction of G. M. Trevelyan, author, historian, and master of Trinity College, who said that in his long experience of university elections, Lewis' was the only unanimous one.

Ranged about the dais 'like a *sceldtruma* or shield wall resolved to defend their liege lord' was a platoon of Oxonians who had driven eastward to Cambridge to hear their former tutor speak and found nowhere else to sit. Tweaked in the back they soon felt when Lewis mentioned that some tainted theory has 'survived . . . if not (let us hope) at Cambridge, yet certainly in the *western* darkness from which you have so lately bidden me emerge.'

At Oxford, among his peers, Lewis had come to be thought of as an old fogey, a defender of the past; at Cambridge he knew he could become an *enfant terrible* simply by choosing an appropriate metaphor. Better make a virtue of necessity, though, and he decided to take his stand just short of the twentieth century. He would represent what he called old European, or old western, culture. He was a native of that world, for better or worse; indeed his appearance at Cambridge, a university that excelled in the sciences, was not unlike that of a dinosaur dragging its slow length into the laboratory. A frightening figure from the past, but even as the undergraduates fled, would they not look back to see 'how it really moved and looked and smelled and what noises it made'?

'It is my settled conviction that in order to read old western literature aright, you must suspend most of the responses and unlearn most of the habits you have acquired in reading modern literature,' he said in peroration. 'And because this is the judgment of a native, I claim that, even if the defence of my conviction is weak, the fact of my conviction is a historical datum to which you should give full weight. That way, where I fail as a critic, I may yet be useful as a specimen. I would even dare to go further. Speaking not only for myself but for all other old western men whom you may meet, I would say, use your specimens while you can. There are not going to be many more dinosaurs.'

⌒

Oxford was ending even as Cambridge had begun. At ten minutes to one on Friday 3 December, Lewis finished his last tutorial. Slips of paper saying that all further correspondence should be sent, not to Magdalen College in Oxford, but to the Kilns in Headington, Warren typed as fast as his index fingers allowed. The English faculty sported a farewell party at Merton College. The two Tolkiens were there, Cecil and Coghill, Hugo and Humphrey, Wilson of Merton and Bennett of Magdalen, and, of course, Warren, who pronounced the dinner, which included turtle soup and bottles of delicious hock, 'excellent.'

The Florio Society at Magdalen, named after a sixteenth-century graduate of the college, also paid their respects at a dinner in the oldest part of the college. Lewis sat at one end of the table; Bennett at the other. In between, on both sides, sat the undergraduate members of the literary society. After the savoury but before the port, someone asked Lewis what would come after the OHEL volume. Lewis didn't reveal what he was writing; he did say that he was having a problem with style; his paragraphs tended to end an iambic pentameter.

'If you *will* end your paragraphs in iambic pentameter,' commented Richard Selig, a Rhodes scholar, 'why do you grumble about it, sir?'

'As usual, Selig, you missed the point,' said Lewis. 'The difficulty is that I remember everything I ever read, and bits of it pop up uninvited.'

'Surely not *everything* you've ever read, Mr Lewis?'

'Yes, everything, Selig, even the most boring texts.'

'What about Lydgate's "Siege of Thebes," Mr Lewis?'

'Give me a line,' said Lewis, sipping his port; 'you'll have to start me.'

Selig excused himself and ran to the college library, snatched the book from the shelf, and retraced his steps to the small dining-room where he calmly opened the volume at random and began reading.

'Stop!' shouted Lewis, as he raised his eyes towards the ceiling and continued the passage from memory.

When his eyes again met Selig's, the American closed the book slowly and sat down.

⚜

He didn't see how she could do it, the American who was sitting on the sofa in his rooms. Jane Douglass was an actress and a playwright; she wanted to dramatize *The Lion, the Witch, and the Wardrobe.* 'Aslan is a divine figure,' he had written on 19 June to discourage her, 'and anything remotely approaching the comic (anything in the Disney line) would be to me simple blasphemy.' But here she was, at noon on Wednesday 15 December, trying to talk him into something that caused him only horror.

There were so many cheap programmes for children on the radio, she began; and she wanted to do something with quality for them, even something with a Christian message.

'Of course, if I should agree to what you want, I should more than ever be accused of making propaganda for Christianity.'

'Well, with the world in the state it's in,' countered Douglass, 'could that do any harm?'

'I know next to nothing about the drama,' said Lewis, unable to sit down for the discomfort the conversation was causing him. 'I believe that plays should be plays; poems, poems; novels, novels; stories, stories; and certainly the book you mention is pure narrative.'

'If that is the case, what are you going to do about *Romeo and Juliet*?'

'Well, you have me there,' he said, finally igniting the tobacco in his pipe. 'Now you see how little I know about these things.'

⚜

On 18 December Warren typed a note of thanks to Mrs Watson of South Carolina, who once again remembered the Lewises with a Christmas cake; the bachelors were especially grateful because in a day or two they would be entertaining a brace of schoolboys.

The holiday and holy day fast approaching was not a pleasant one for Lewis. The 4 December issue of *Time and Tide* printed what he had submitted as 'a lost chapter from Herodotus.' It was as though that ancient Greek historian had come across Niatirb, a backward island in many ways, whose strange inhabitants celebrated a great festival they called Exmas. They commemorated the holiday by sending square pieces of hard paper stamped with pictures of birds

335

sitting on branches or ancestors riding in coaches or roofs covered with snow; they expected to receive in return similar square pieces. They gave gifts and expected gifts of equal value in return. On the day of the festival itself, exhausted from the rush of preparation, they slept late. When they did awake, they over-ate and over-drank and tried to calculate how much they had overspent.

❧

'Thank you for the card,' wrote Lewis by hand on 22 December to Idrisyn O. Evans; 'as a logician, if for nothing else, I like them to have some connection with Christmas! — and for the cheery book of verses.'

❧ 1955 ❧

'Oh what a fool I am!' said Lewis, grimacing and pacing about in his empty rooms at Magdalene. 'I had a good home, and I left!' All his things were out of place because they had not yet been put into place. He had asked Gresham to come to Cambridge over the New Year not only to see his new collegiate home but also to help him put it into shape. She unpacked; she dusted books and put them on the shelves; she went out to buy sheets. It was rather like a boy leaving a warm little school to enter a cold stone institution, he said. It was rather like getting a divorce, she said.

❧

> Now you go to England's other Eye
> Take with you, Sir, your pupils' love.

Lewis was reading a poem of valediction sent to him by Selig.

> May th' other college of the tearful Mary
> Be twin, in youths' love, to this you leave
> Whose eye you opened year by year to see:
> The Past can change but changeless is its glory.
>   The hour when you departure take
>   Let Oxford weep and Cambridge wake.

❧

An adaptation of George Orwell's novel *1984* had been broadcast by BBC television on 12 December, causing considerable critical ruckus and prompting Lewis to wonder why this novel was so much more popular than the same author's *Animal Farm*. He weighed one book against the other in the 8 January issue of *Time and Tide*; one was short, the other long; both had the same theme; both expressed disillusionment. Except for its 'magnificent and fortunately detachable' appendix on Newspeak, however, *1984* was thoroughly disappointing.

Animal Farm, on the other hand, 'is formally almost perfect; light, strong, balanced. There is not a sentence that does not contribute to the whole. The myth says all the author wants it to say and (equally important) it doesn't say anything else. Here is an *objet d'art* as durably satisfying as an Horatian ode or a Chippendale chair.'

∽

January was bitterly cold in Cambridge; it snowed much of the month. Pipes not embedded in the fifteenth-and sixteenth-century stone and brick froze, burst, sprayed, and froze again, much to the discomfiture of Magdalene College. Lewis rose early in the morning and attended matins at 8.00 a.m. in the chilly chapel; then it was to breakfast at 8.30, followed by correspondence and the preparation of a lecture series.

The senior common room after dinner was warm. As port was being poured for him, he learned that it was the custom at Magdalene for the junior member present in the room to do the pouring. He leaped to the task and decanted with panache. When he rose to refill, he was politely refused, learning later that where Magdalen served three glasses of port of an evening, Magdalene served only one.

He commuted several times between Oxford and Cambridge, the train being a slow one that allowed him to read a book or say some prayers or both. By the third week of January he had been visited by a virus at the Kilns and was confined to bed where fever made his days delirious, and he was unable to read. By month's end he was up and about and able to correspond.

∽

'What strange optimism led you to suppose that I could ever write an ecclesiastical history?' wrote Lewis on 3 February to J. Randall Williams of Macmillan, New York. 'Not at all up my street. And I'm not sure that I think it a good subject for young readers anyway.'

∽

'I am most distressed to find that my answer to your previous letter has never reached you,' he wrote on 10 February to Vanauken.

Davy, as the young American called his wife Jean, had died of an undiagnosed and irreversible disease; he wrote to ask if Lewis would scatter some of her ashes at the church in Binsey by St Margaret's well. Lewis was particularly distressed, he replied, 'since its miscarriage has left you in doubt whether I would have liked to do (if you can understand) for the very reasons that I would not have liked doing it, since a deep spiritual *gaucherie* makes [me] uneasy in any ceremonial act.' He encouraged the young man to look after his own health, promised him continued remembrance in prayers, and signed off 'under the omnipotence.'

෴

'I'm not a fundamentalist in the direct sense: one who starts out by saying, "Everything we read is literal fact." The presence of an allegorical or mystical element in Genesis was recognized by St Jerome. Origen held Job to be moral fable, not a history. There is nothing new about such interpretation.' It was 28 February; Lewis was writing in reply to a letter by Joseph M. Canfield of Deerfield, Illinois. 'But I often agree with the fundamentalists about particular passages whose literal truth is rejected by many moderns. I reject nothing on the grounds of its being miraculous. I accept the story of the fall, and I don't see what the findings of the scientists can say either for or against it.'

෴

'I say, your children are dreadfully behind-hand with their Narnian history!' wrote Lewis on 3 March to Philip. The South African had congratulated Lewis on his Cambridge appointment and said how much his children had enjoyed reading *The Lion, The Witch, and the Wardrobe*. Lewis pointed out that four more Narnian books had since been published. 'Call yourself a father and let them grow up in such ignorance! All good wishes.'

෴

'I think I can understand that feeling about a housewife's work being like that of Sisyphus (who was the stone-rolling gentleman),' wrote Lewis on 16 March to Mrs W. W. Johnson of Hawthorne, California. 'But it is surely in reality the most important work in the world. What do ships, railways, mines, cars, governments, etc., exist for except that people may be fed, warmed and safe in their own homes?'

෴

In the latter half of March, after Hilary term had ended at Cambridge and before Trinity term began, the Lewises invited Gresham to spend a week with them at the Kilns. It was a quiet time: she was writing; Warren was writing on the house of Gramont from 1604 to

1678; but Jack was not even 'with poem.' How ironic it was that now, with tutoring a thing of the past, he had more time to write but nothing to say. *Surprised by Joy* was at the typist's and would be sent to Bles forthwith; he was expecting proofs of *The Last Battle* and Baynes' drawings that would illustrate it; but in the meantime . . .

Complaining loudly and at length one evening, emboldened by a whisky, he sat Joy down. She had been more than helpful with her remarks on his autobiography. Surely she would listen to the things he could possibly write about. Cupid and Psyche had always interested him. At least twice, many years before, he had tried to rewrite the myth. Both times he had used verse; perhaps now he should try it as a novel. The bare bones of the story had been ingeniously told by Apuleius, a second-century Roman writer, in *The Golden Ass*. Perhaps he could retell the story with a few new twists of his own. She poured another whisky for herself and him and made some comments; he made some improvements; by evening's end he knew what he would be writing on the morrow.

'I am old now and have not much to fear from the anger of the gods,' he scribbled. 'I have no husband nor child, nor hardly a friend, through whom they can hurt me. My body, this lean carrion that still has to be washed and fed and have clothes hung about it daily with so many changes, they may kill as soon as they please. The succession is provided for. My crown passes to my nephew.'

Gresham wanted to interrupt, but if she did, he said, he wouldn't dedicate the work to her. So she left him in the study and went to breakfast. Comment she would on the paragraphs later in the morning. He would revise them after that and plunge onward into the novel he would entitle *Bareface*.

〰️

'It is delicious,' he wrote on 19 March to Pitter, having sunk his teeth into her 'gold and amber gift', a jar of homemade marmalade; 'a proper gift from a poetess, to show that you can imprison sunlight in other snares than words.'

〰️

When Pitter learned that Lewis was going to Cambridge, she asked what he was going to do to atheists at that university. There they called themselves humanists, he replied; he anxiously awaited what they were going to do to him. But when he, reading an issue of *The Twentieth Century* magazine devoted to Cambridge, came across a writer who called for a 'retreat from the faith in culture,' he decided to make the first move. 'I don't want retreat; I want attack or, if you prefer the word, rebellion. I write in the hope of rousing others to rebel. So far as I can see, the question has nothing to do with the difference between Christians and those who (unfortunately, since the word has long borne a useful, and wholly different, meaning) have been called "humanists." I hope that red herring will not be brought in. I would gladly believe that many atheists and agnostics care for the things I care for. It is for them I have written. To them I say: the "faith in culture" is going to strangle all those things unless we can strangle it first. And there is no time to spare.'

~

'I heard *Time* had been at me (Time, in another sense always is!)' he wrote on 14 May to Shelburne, 'but didn't see it.' Soon a copy of the 2 May issue was sent to him; he found that the magazine had rendered an account, indeed had condensed, the argument of his inaugural lecture under the title 'The Greatest Divide.' At least it was in the education section, not the religion section, but why did they have to identify him as the author of *The Screwtape Letters* instead of *The Allegory of Love* or *English Literature in the Sixteenth Century*?

Accompanying the article was a photograph of Lewis taken in 1946 by *Life* photographer Hans Wild. Fine photo Gebbert thought it, but Lewis thought it 'a hair shirt.' At least it was animated; the photograph commissioned by the National Portrait Gallery to commemorate the Cambridge appointment and taken by Walter Stoneman was lapidary.

~

'Can we expect men to work efficiently on Mars for five years without women?' asked Robert Richardson, astronomer at the Mount Wilson and Palomar Observatories and member of the International Mars Committee, in the 28 May issue of *The Saturday Review*. Barely a month before, the Soviet Union announced that the basic studies for space travel had been completed; all that remained was application and engineering. In a year or two there would be trips to the moon; before too much longer there would be trips to other planets. What sort of human society would men have to develop on a far planet to survive? 'To put it bluntly,' asked Richardson at the close of his article, 'may it not be necessary to send some nice girls to Mars at regular intervals to relieve tensions and promote morale?'

The question Lewis found irresistible and immediately sat down to write an answer, which he felt might better be put into fictional form. There would be a space station on Mars, populated by characters like Monk who doubled as a meteorologist, Botanist, Captain, and two young technicians. As the story opened, they had already completed three years on the fourth planet, and had only six months to go before relief would be sent; an unexpected spaceship would arrive.

Emerging from the craft and soon entering the airlocks of the space station, came a captain named Ferguson, two crewmen, and two others who had been sent as ministering angels. The Thin Woman, a trained psychologist from a red-brick university, tried to explain her mission in the technical language of her profession. 'She means you're to have tarts, duckie,' said the Fat Woman in the language of the oldest profession. What a pleasant surprise, said the young technicians. When they inquired as to the whereabouts of the tarts, and when they learned that the Thin Woman and the Fat Woman comprised the total first shipment from earth, they were ready for mutiny.

'We cannot indeed claim,' said the Thin Woman by way of explanation, 'that the response to our appeal was such as we had hoped. The personnel of the first unit of Woman's Higher Aphrodisio-Therapeutic Human Organization (abbreviated WHAT-HO) is not perhaps . . . well. Many excellent women, university colleagues of my own, even senior colleagues, to whom I applied, showed themselves curiously conventional. But at least a start has been made. And here . . . we are.'

Who on the advisory council had recommended this course of action?

'Och, a pack of daft auld women (in trousers for the maist part) who like onything sexy, and onything scientific, and onything that makes them feel important,' replied Ferguson. 'And this gives them all three pleasures at once, ye ken.'

❧

The bad news, said Gresham, was that child-support payments from her husband came so irregularly as to be invisible in the family budget. Equally bad were the reports that *Smoke* had sold only one thousand copies in the United States and only three thousand in England. The good news was that her mother and father, passing through London on their way home to New York, bought clothes for her and the boys and told her that they had perhaps as much as $25,000 in savings accounts and insurance policies; she could draw on these resources, but only in the direst emergency.

How would the Greshams like to live in Oxford or thereabouts? asked Lewis. He enjoyed their company; they seemed to enjoy his. He and his brother could provide some measure of employment for Joy. The Agape Fund could still pay the fees and tuitions at Dane Court. There were plenty of houses in Headington that wanted tenants; he felt sure that rents were not higher in the country than in the city.

Gresham was uncertain. Debt deepening into dependency made the smoothest skin raw. The one soothing thing was that the dependency seemed to have a psychological dimension. Lewis really wanted them to forsake London and move to Oxford.

❧

The Walshes from Wisconsin, most of them, showed up in London in June. They visited the Greshams; one day with Joy they took the train to Oxford. Lewis met them at Magdalen. Walsh introduced his wife Eva and their daughters Damaris, who was sixteen, and Madeleine, who was fourteen. They toured the college, walked in the meadows, lay back in the grass, and recited Shakespeare. Before returning to London, they sought refreshment in a pub. He had been terrified of the American girls at first, Lewis had to admit, but he was delighted to find out that Damaris and Madeleine were just like English girls.

❧

As August began Sayer drove down from Malvern to Oxford where, among other things, he visited Lewis. On an impulse both of them drove to Long Crendon where they expected to surprise Pitter. They were met instead by O'Hara, who was wearing, of all things, breeches. 'The only female trousers I can't bear are the modern American like this,' wrote Lewis the next day to Pitter and drew a picture, 'a truncated image being always a mean shape, and none the better for being inverted.' He was sorry to have missed her, hoped her trip to London had been a success, and said how much he and George had enjoyed their visit with Miss O'Hara.

❧

How could Lewis know that 10, Old High Street, Headington, resembled the Gresham Farmhouse in upstate New York? Well, not exactly. It was not made of wood; the bricks must surely have been fired at the Kilns when it was a working factory. It didn't have columns or a verandah with chairs for lazy rocking, but it did have a generous-sized garden where vegetables and flowers were thriving in the August sunshine.

The Greshams had just supervised the unloading of the removals van that brought them and their possessions and a cat named Sambo from London. The furniture, which had so crowded their flat, now seemed sparse in the semi-detached two-storey house. There were a sitting-room, a dining-room, and a kitchen on the ground floor; there were three bedrooms and a bath on the first floor. Not only was the square-footage larger, the rent was larger also; Lewis said he would take care of that.

Gresham plunged into domesticity, planting bulbs, harvesting the garden, making jams. Douglas explored the neighbourhood, investing ten shillings in a budgerigar with cage. David, with Lewis' encouragement, went to Blackwell's, where he was allowed to charge whatever he wanted to the Lewis account. Before leaving on 1 September for a three-week vacation in Ireland, Lewis once again tendered the funds for the fees and tuitions.

∽

A former pupil with a young woman in tow was visiting him at Magdalene. He was 'a decent enough fellow', but as he droned on, Lewis looked at her. Her lips were rather thin, her teeth irregular, her complexion rough, her figure less than ample. She was a far cry from the creature modern advertising encouraged her to be. What an interesting story Peggy would make, for that was what he called her; the kind he could send with confidence to *The Magazine of Fantasy and Science Fiction*, especially if he wrote it in a 'stream of consciousness' style.

Daydreaming, the professorial central character found himself in another world. One shop window displayed gems, brooches, tiaras in tasteful configuration. A second shop presented frocks. A third dandled shoes, 'the toe-pinching and very high-heeled sort.' But what kind of world was he wandering around in? 'Trees no good; grass no good; sky no good; flowers no good, except the daffodils; people no good; shops first class.' Everything real was shoddy; everything artificial was shining.

Further on in the daydream, the wandering professor came upon a figure taking the sun on a beach. It was huge, larger than life; if anatomy were any clue, it was a female. Her figure was curvier than Peggy's; her complexion creamier; her lips riper; her teeth whiter. She had to be the new improved Peggy that advertisers and their products had enabled the old Peggy to become.

He followed her into her bedroom, decorated with flamboyant florals, and watched her remove the top and bottom of her beach attire in front of a full-length mirror, a French maid sprinkling salts into the bath that was being run in the room beyond. The young woman seemed to enjoy what she saw, but the middle-aged bachelor didn't. He had half-expected to be aroused by the voluptuousness of the female form, but instead he was repulsed: brownness where sun had baked and sun oil had basted the skin; and whiteness, bands of it like leprosy across her buttocks and her breasts.

'If I had to marry either, I should prefer the old, unimproved Peggy,' thought the professor, about to snap back into reality. 'But even in Hell I hoped it wouldn't come to that.'

⁓

'I wish your project heartily well, but can't write you articles,' he wrote on 28 September to Carl Henry, who was planning the first issue of a magazine called *Christianity Today*. 'My thought and talent (such as they are) now flow in different, though I trust not less Christian, channels, and I do not think I am at all likely to write more *directly* theological pieces.'

⁓

Rarely did the charity one practised coincide with the pleasure one sometimes derived from the very act itself. It was a principle of the spiritual life Lewis had learned early on from the spiritual writers he had read and the spiritual directors he had had; occasionally he passed the lesson on to those who sought his counsel. 'The act which engenders a child ought to be, and usually is, attended by pleasure,' he wrote on 20 February to Shelburne. 'But it is not the pleasure that produces the child. Where there is pleasure, there may be sterility; where there is no pleasure, the act may be fertile.'

The charity he had exercised towards the Greshams was a necessary one, the sort that he had done many times before to others. But unlike these other acts, it was producing more than its share of pleasure. She responded so warmly to his witticisms; he laughed, sometimes uproariously, at her jokes. They had entertained the Walshes in June almost as if they were husband and wife. By October they were walking hand in hand through the heather that covered much of Shotover Hill.

When he was in Ireland in September, he discussed the situation with Greeves. His friend insisted that he was putting himself, or allowing himself to be put, into a compromising situation. Unless, of course, he meant to marry the woman. That would be adultery, replied Lewis. The solution to the problem seemed to be to disclose the financial dependency to as few people as possible, and not to allow the emotional interdependency, which had been growing at a rapid rate, to progress beyond a certain point. Be friends with the woman he would, but marry her he would not. The Church of England forbade that; he needed to think no further.

⁓

'The book is too original and too opulent for any final judgment on a first reading,' wrote Lewis in review of the volume containing Tolkien's *The Two Towers* and *The Return of the King* in the 22 October issue of *Time and Tide*. 'But we know at once that it has done things to us. We are not quite the same men. And though we must ration ourselves in our re-readings, I have little doubt that the book will soon take its place among the indispensables.'

⸎

Before hiking became fashionable, Lewis liked walking great distances; he enjoyed Trollope before reading his novels became popular; and he was a devotee of 'scientifiction' before it became 'science fiction.' The explosion in this species of narrative writing began fifteen or twenty years before; most of it was bad, although some of the ideas were good. Five or six years ago, however, the good stories began to get better and more numerous, he told the Cambridge University English Club, whom he was addressing on 24 November.

Science fiction as he read it had at least five subspecies. The first was the 'fiction of displaced persons', persons whose ordinary love- or crime- or war-story had been transplanted into a planetary, sidereal, or even galactic setting. Second, there was the 'fiction of engineers,' which dealt with the realistic details of the future in space. Third, there was the fiction of the engineers enlivened by speculation — political, social, theological — about what it would be like to live in space. Fourth, there was the fiction of the eschatologists, in which the story was an imaginative vehicle to explore the ultimate destiny of the human species, even as doom approached. Fifth, there was the fiction of the literary artists, whose imagination visited 'strange regions in search of such beauty, awe, or terror as the actual world' did not supply.

He did not think the first subspecies was a legitimate one; the second was certainly legitimate but of no particular interest to him; the third and fourth were interesting, but it was the fifth subspecies that excited him and perhaps himself alone. In it he included such disparate works as *Beowulf* and the *Odyssey*, Irish immram and Arthurian romance, *The Faerie Queene* and *Gulliver's Travels*.

'I am not sure that anyone has satisfactorily explained the keen, lasting, and solemn pleasure which such stories can give,' he said in conclusion. Jung had offered the best, if still somewhat lame, explanation to date. But Lewis knew at least one Jungian who wasn't convinced of the wholesomeness of the phenomenon. She was a psychologist who felt that her world was becoming dreary, that her power to feel emotion was drying up. Trying to be helpful, Lewis asked if she had a taste for fantasies or fairy tales. Muscles tightening, hands clenching, she managed to say, 'I *loathe* them!'

⸎

'I have had some experience of such disappointments myself, first as an unpublished, and then as an unnoticed, author,' he wrote on 12 December to Blamires. He had liked Blamires' novel *The Devil's*

Hunting Ground, which Longmans, Green had published in 1954; he had liked also the second volume of the trilogy, *Cold War in Hell*, which was published in the spring; he liked best of all the third volume, *Highway to Heaven*, which had just been published and which he had just finished. 'It is like a *bereavement*.' He suggested that Blamires treat it like a tribulation and put it before God. 'But, of course, you know all this.'

⚮

'Your card is most interesting as an application of Japanese style to a Christian subject,' he wrote on 17 December to Milward in Tokyo; 'and *me judice* extremely successful.'

'I seem to have been writing Christmas letters most of this day!' he wrote on 19 December to Shelburne. 'I'm afraid I hate the weeks just before Christmas, and so much of the (very commercialized and vulgarized) fuss has nothing to do with the nativity at all.'

'Thank you, thank you (but you really shouldn't) for the beautiful, sleek, shining bottle of sherry,' he wrote on 19 December to Gebbert. 'It's a feast for the eyes; mouth shall have its share on Christmas Day.'

'I write letters all day,' he wrote on 26 December to Teensie, a teenager named Joan Lancaster who lived in New York State; 'it spoils Christmas completely.'

⚮ 1956 ⚮

'To go down to that sea (I think St John of the Cross called God a sea),' said Lewis, describing his endlessly recurring temptation, 'and there neither dive nor swim nor float, but only dabble and splash, careful not to get out of my depth and holding on to the lifeline which connects me with my things temporal.'

It was Sunday 29 January; he had been invited by the chaplain of Magdalene to preach at evensong. More than a hundred people crowded into the tiny chapel, sitting in the choir stalls and on folding chairs, others just standing about in the flickering light of candles. He had begun by saying that not so long ago he made a slip of the tongue in his evening prayer, interchanging the words 'eternal' and 'temporal.' Not all slips were Freudian, but this one surely was. He ended by saying how hard one had to fight to prevent the eternal from becoming hopelessly entangled with the temporal. 'Our morning prayer should be that in the *Imitation*: *"Da hodie perfecte incipere* — grant me to make an unflawed beginning today, for I have done nothing yet."'

∽

'I dreamed that I was presented to the Queen,' he wrote on 31 January to Pitter, who a month or two before had been presented to Her Majesty to receive the gold medal for poetry, 'and found to my horror, halfway through the audience, that I was wearing my hat. At the same moment a lady in waiting approached me from behind with the speed of a roller-skater and snatched it off my head with the words "Don't be a fool!"'

∽

'Yes, I do feel the old Magdalen years to have been a very important period in both our lives,' he wrote on 8 February to Griffiths, who had been pleased to discover that *Surprised by Joy* was dedicated to him. 'More generally, I feel the whole of one's youth to be immensely important and even of immense length. The gradual reading of one's own life, seeing a pattern emerge, is a great illumination at our age.'

∽

The Home Office, said Gresham when Lewis dropped in at 10, Old High Street, was not going to renew her visa. What reason did they give? No reason, she said. Probably because she had once been a Communist, and a loud one at that. She couldn't go back; Bill would try to woo the boys away from her; her parents would never let her forget what a mess she'd made of her life; the United States she had said goodbye to in *Smoke on the Mountain*; what could she possibly do to stay in England? Become a British citizen was the only thing she could think of. But if they were kicking her out because she was once a Communist, then it was not bloody likely they'd allow her to become one of them. The only way she could become a citizen by the end of April, he said, was to marry a British citizen. Was that a proposal? No, no, no, he was too old to propose; besides, if ever she decided to marry again, she should pick a younger man. What he had in mind was a proposition. They would go to the register office in Oxford where they would be married in a civil ceremony; no one would be the wiser, except the Home Office. Barfield could draw up a paper they could both sign that would say the marriage was nothing but a manoeuvre to outwit the government; annulment was hers whenever she wanted it. And life could go on, separate households and all that. But, she asked, wouldn't a civil marriage legally oblige him to support her and the boys? He had felt the full weight of that obligation for some time; he would continue to bear it manfully. But wouldn't such a marriage oblige him to love her as a wife? He was already in love with her, he'd have to admit; he would continue to love her in all ways but one. He'd make her a British citizen; for that she was grateful; but when would he make her an honest woman? He was visiting her so often — and sometimes he left in the middle of the night — that the neighbours were beginning to talk.

∽

'For me the real evil of masturbation would be that it takes an appetite which, in lawful use, leads the individual out of himself to complete (and correct) his own personality in that of another (and finally in children and even grandchildren) and turns it back,' he wrote on 6 March to Keith Masson, 'sends a man back into the person of himself, there to keep a harem of imaginary brides.'

∽

'I've been reading your poems,' he wrote on 11 April to Kathleen Raine, a research fellow at Girton College, Cambridge, whom he had met not long before at a dinner party. 'They are like a combined bathe and drink (you know — all the pores and mouth open at once) that I once had on a walk in the Highlands: cold, bright, and yet with a dash of the dark earth-taste in them. I congratulate you. Philosophically (as you will guess) I am in much disagreement . . .'

∽

'I call upon these persons here present to witness that I, Helen Joy Davidman Gresham, do take thee, Clive Staples Lewis, to be my lawful wedded husband.' It was Monday 23 April; Gresham, limping badly from something Havard diagnosed as fibrositis, and Lewis had come from Headington to the register office in Oxford at 13, St Giles' where they stood before the superintendent registrar, Cecil W. Clifton, and solemnly declared that they knew no lawful impediment to their being joined in matrimony. 'I call upon these persons here present to witness that I, Clive Staples Lewis, do take thee, Helen Joy Davidman Gresham, to be my lawful wedded wife.' Witnessing the ceremony and signing the register were Havard and the Rev. Austin M. Farrer, chaplain of Trinity College.

∽

'Don't get rid of more books than you must,' wrote Lewis on 9 May to Gebbert, who was moving from a house in Carmel, California, to an apartment in New York City. 'I've hardly ever sold a book in my life without finding in the next few weeks that I needed it.'

∽

'No, no, I mustn't,' said Lewis. He and Green were standing at a railway buffet; Green had just offered him a hard-boiled egg. 'It's supposed to be an aphrodisiac. Of course, it's all right for you as a married man — but I have to be careful.' The Cantab crawler pulled into the station, and they boarded the through train to Cambridge. It was Monday afternoon, 28 May; during the leisurely three-hour ride, they talked of mythology. Green had written something called *Helen of Sparta*; Lewis suggested he rename it *Mystery at Mycenae*. *Bareface*, which was now being called *Till We Have Faces*, had been sent to the printer at the end of February, said Lewis, and would be published in September. It was the Cupid and Psyche story, but told through the eyes of one of Psyche's sisters, a middle-aged woman and an ugly one at that. The point of view was entirely Orual's, the sister's; the psychology, or so said Gresham who had edited and typed the manuscript, was entirely feminine. That should make the reviewers sit up and take notice. Another unusual twist was that Orual established a friendship with a man and eventually fell in love with him; he reciprocated the *philia* but did not return the *eros*. Next, he wanted to write something about Helen of Troy . . . .

'I think it would be more use to you to come here,' he wrote on 1 June to Dabney Adams, an American from the University of Wisconsin who was spending a year at the University of London on a Fulbright scholarship. 'It is here that I have two fat envelopes full of old articles, etc.' She was preparing a dissertation on Lewis' literary theory. 'I have two sitting-rooms, so you can have one to yourself and do the job in peace and comfort.'

On Wednesday 6 June at 2.00 she knocked on Lewis' door. He invited her in and placed her on the big sofa facing the fireplace. On the long low coffee table were the two envelopes. He told her to look through them at her leisure. He would be in the other sitting-room. A gift box of chocolates on the table he urged her to finish since he was 'supposed to be slimming.' In the envelopes she found 'scribbled notes, incomplete drafts of poems, offprints of articles, and newspaper clippings.'

'Professor Lewis,' said the young man who had just knocked on the door; he was carrying a parcel wrapped in brown paper; 'the chalice has just come, and I wanted you to be the first to see it,' he said as they disappeared into the other sitting-room.

Adams looked at each of the pieces of paper in the envelopes, but she found little to add to the bibliography of Lewis' writings she had already compiled. When it was 4.00 Lewis put water into an electric kettle. He made the tea in an earthenware pot and with it served 'some delectable cream-filled pastries' he had bought especially for her visit. They talked. She would have liked to discuss his writings.

He asked her if she had read *Band of Angels* by Robert Penn Waren, a novel in which a male writer used a female narrator.

'You had better finish your dissertation promptly,' he said to her as she left to catch the train back to London, 'before I publish something that will invalidate your conclusions.'

※

'If you can persuade any "sucker" (as the Americans say) to buy the manuscript of *Screwtape*,' he wrote on 18 June to Sister Penelope, 'pray do, and use the money for any pious or charitable object you like.' Hidden among her papers for fifteen years, she had just discovered it. He had sent it to her for safekeeping during the war; now, since he refused the return, she asked his permission to sell it to a representative of the Berg Collection in the New York City Public Library; the result she would add to the fund for redoing St Michael's chapel at Wantage. 'Did it ever occur to you that the replacement of the scrawled old manuscript by the clear, printed book in mint condition is a pretty symbol of resurrection?'

※

'It is refreshing,' he wrote on 22 June to H. C. Chang whom he had met in Oxford and who was now teaching in Singapore, 'to know any man who, like myself, cannot drive a car.'

On 9 July he wrote to Pitter, asking if she had been invited to the royal garden party and would she like to go with him. She hadn't; he went alone. But he wasn't alone in the grounds of Buckingham Palace. There were eight thousand other people lounging about, none of whom he knew. A cup of tea would have helped, but the refreshment tables were like Brighton on August bank holiday: swarming. Somewhere in the grounds the Queen was supposed to be greeting people. He would have liked to see her, if not talk with her, he thought as he wandered down by the lakes; he had to settle for a slanging match with metal flamingos. Bronze herons they were, Pitter told him when he wrote on 14 July to complain of the whole experience; they were placed by the water to frighten off real herons who came for the fish. No matter. Lewis finally found a friendly face and went off to a nearby pub for a consoling pint or two before taking the tube for Paddington and the train to Oxford. 'In a word, it was simply ghastly!'

※

'I doubt if you'll find any leprechauns in Eire now,' he wrote on 8 September to Shelburne while on vacation in Donegal. 'The radio has driven them away.'

※

When cobwebs were necklaces, when leaves were scarlet and coppery, when nights were cold almost to the point of frost, people called it St Luke's summer, the apostle's feast day being 18 October. None of this did Lewis see on the following day when he sped, fast as the Cantab crawler could carry him, from Cambridge to Oxford. All he could remember was the ominous telephone call to the effect that Gresham had been rushed to the hospital that very morning in great pain.

When he arrived in Headington and found the Wingfield-Morris Orthopaedic Hospital, which was no more than a quarter-mile from 10, Old High Street, he saw Havard first. Preliminary X-rays revealed that her left thighbone, what was left of it, had been broken; cancer was the culprit, devouring the femur like a starving worm. Did he know she had a lump on her breast? How would he know that? asked Lewis without humour. A biopsy would reveal whether or not it was malignant. And how long had it been since the woman underwent a full-scale gynaecological examination? Husbands were supposed to know things like that.

She seemed in good spirits when he entered her room. He told her what Havard had said. So much for fibrositis and rheumatism, she said wryly; Havard had made a ghastly mistake and would have to be replaced. Whatever she wanted, he said; she proceeded to tell him the most remarkable story. She was in such discomfort the night before — it was late, eleven o'clock or so — and she was walking about the house, wondering whether she should call him in Cambridge, when she tripped on the telephone cord. Trying to keep her balance, she heard something snap, as though she had stepped on a twig, and fell to the floor with a scream. Next thing she knew, she heard Kay Farrer's voice, asking if she were all right. The telephone was sprawled on the floor next to her. Kay had called the very moment she had tripped, fearing that something was wrong with her friend. Now wasn't that a chapter out of *Miracles*?

Havard had already explained everything to her, she said wearily, the pain beginning to return; she hoped the doctor, another doctor, would be able to cure her ills, all of them this time. She was sorry she was such a burden; how was he going to pay for all of this? The hospital would surely bill Mrs Gresham the American, but if she were Mrs C. S. Lewis, the British citizen, the hospital would send the bill to the government. He'd worry about that when the time came. Her medication was about to be renewed; he rose to leave. Would she like something to read? *The Problem of Pain* would be nice, she said with a smile.

'No. It would never do,' wrote Lewis on 26 October. Back in Cambridge, he was replying to Willey of Pembroke, who had suggested that Lewis might want to consider being chairman of the faculty board of English. Memories of his inefficiency as vice-president of Magdalen for a short time and his inability to say no even to the most unusual requests caused him to demur. 'I am both muddlesome and forgetful. Quite objectively, I'd be a disaster. But thank you for your suggestion.'

Critical if not terminal, was the medical prognosis when Lewis arrived at the hospital. The biopsy revealed that the tumour was malignant; it would have to be removed; the surgeon wanted it fully understood that once he made the incision, he would excise the whole breast if necessary. Gynaecological examination indicated that her ovaries were dicey; they would have to be attended to surgically. The femur had been set; the patient's leg and hip had been immobilized in plaster of Paris. The poor woman was in great discomfort; powerful pain-killers were being given to her, but always less than was needed so as to avoid the beginning of addiction.

How long would she be in the hospital? She could go home once the cast was taken off, and if there were no complications from the surgery. Radium therapy had begun and would continue as long as it seemed to help; she could return to the hospital on an out-patient basis for that. But the cancer would run its course; when she got home, she would probably need round-the-clock care until the end came. He couldn't let her go back to 10, Old High Street, thought Lewis, but what else could he do?

'I wish you would pray very hard for a lady called Joy Gresham and me,' he wrote on 14 November to Mrs Johnson, an American he had been counselling for some time by letter. 'I am shortly to be both a bridegroom and a widower, for she has cancer. You need not mention this till the marriage (which will be at a hospital bedside if it occurs) is announced. I'll tell you the whole story some day . . .'

'I must thank you,' wrote Lewis in November from Cambridge, 'for your most kind article on my Narnian works in the copy of *America* which someone has sent me.' In the 27 October issue, Charles A. Brady of Canisius College, Buffalo, who in 1944 had praised the interplanetary romances in the pages of the same magazine, called *The Chronicles of Narnia* the greatest addition to children's literature since *The Jungle Book*. It was 'a nursery *Faerie Queene*,' 'a child's *Nibelungenlied*, and *Divina Commedia* too.' Narnia was 'another world, another mode of being, another *place*.' The seven volumes took their place forever 'beside the jasper-lucent landscapes of Carroll, Andersen, MacDonald, and Kipling.'

∽

With heart in hand, Lewis went to see the bishop of Oxford. He explained to his lordship that he wanted to marry his dying friend so that he could take her without scandal to the Kilns when she was released from the hospital. Problem was, said Lewis, that the woman had been married once before. She had married William Lindsay Gresham, who was already a divorced man, in a civil ceremony; both of them were Communists at the time, and she had been born Jewish to boot. Together they underwent a conversion to Christianity inspired, ironically enough, by reading some of his books. They enrolled in a nearby Presbyterian church, but their marriage was never solemnized or sacramentalized by the Presbyterian pastor. Gresham subsequently committed adultery, divorced Joy, married for a third time, and fell from the faith into something faddist called dianetics. Hence, as Lewis analyzed it, Joy was free to enter into a sacramental marriage. Now he had to admit that he had already married the woman in April in a civil ceremony in order to give her British citizenship; that marriage had never been announced to the public, nor had it been consummated. He didn't intend to consummate the church marriage either. Practical charity was the point of it all; he prayed that his lordship would agree.

He made a good case, conceded the bishop of Oxford, one that might even win annulment of the Gresham marriage in a tribunal of the Church of Rome. The Church of England, however, had no sucn tribunal, nor was it the custom of the Church of England at that time to marry a person or persons who had been previously divorced, no matter what the mitigating circumstances might be. To ease the discomfort he knew Lewis must be feeling, he recommended that he read, as a pastor to one of his flock, the chapter entitled 'Christian Marriage' in that wonderful little book called *Mere Christianity*.

∽

'You are attracted by a girl,' he wrote, trying to describe the desire, the itch, an author all of a sudden feels to write; 'but is she the sort of girl you'd be wise, or right, to marry?'

'The *New York Times Book Review* had asked him, now that *The Chronicles of Narnia* were completed, to say something about fairy tales, whether they were for children or for adults; and what about Christianity? 'Everything began with images,' wrote Lewis; 'a faun carrying an umbrella, a queen on a sledge, a magnificent lion. At first there wasn't anything Christian about them; that element pushed itself in of its own accord. It was part of the bubbling.' As for the form, he needed one that demanded 'no love interest and no close psychology,' and the form that excluded all three was 'the fairy tale.' As a child he himself had found religion inhibiting, indeed paralyzing. He was plagued by oughtness and reverence, by too much stained glass and Sunday school. But could an adult author creep 'past those watchful dragons' to present to children in story form something like the experience of Christianity instead of the doctrines of Christianity nakedly stated? 'I thought one could.'

〰

There was one chance in a hundred that she would be cured, he wrote on 25 November to Greeves; fifty chances in a hundred that she would live as long as a year; seventy-five chances in a hundred that she would die in a few months. When she was discharged from the hospital, he would take her to the Kilns. There, he could supervise the boys, who would be coming home for the holidays and he could see that she was properly taken care of while he was in Cambridge. That the great Christian apologist might not seem to be the scandal of the world, he would soon announce that a marriage had taken place. Warren had already written to the Irish relatives to prepare them for the announcement. Lewis didn't want Arthur to be the last one to know.

〰

'I got back from my Cambridge term today — a great college feast last night with all the good wines and good foods in the world, and no hangover this morning,' wrote Lewis on 10 December to Vera Gebbert. 'Never is if you stick to what you drink at table; it's that silly messing about with spirits afterwards that does the trouble.'

〰

If the cancer didn't kill her, she said as she vomited into the porcelain dish, the radiation treatment would. The pain in her hip — or was it in her thigh? — which had once been tolerable, now lapsed into agony. 'I think I know now how the martyrs felt,' she said to Jack when he visited her on the day before Christmas.

When she was quiet, he produced from his pocket a handful of letters. One was from her brother Howard; it was friendly and solicitous. Another was from her parents; they sent their love and asked what else they could send to help her out. A third was from the relatives in Ireland; they welcomed her to the family and offered to entertain her boys in Eire during the holidays.

What was he, of all people, doing with a newspaper? she asked. He spread *The Times* on her bed and turned the pages as nimbly as his jointless thumbs allowed until he came to page 8; there he pointed to some small type. 'A marriage has taken place,' she read, 'between Professor C. S. Lewis, of Magdalene College, Cambridge, and Mrs Joy Gresham, now a patient in the Churchill Hospital, Oxford.' She squeezed his hand as he read the rest of the announcement. 'It is requested that no letters be sent.'

*

'The boys are, of course, with me, and I'm learning a lot,' he replied on 30 December to Bill Gresham, who wrote to congratulate him and Joy on their wedding. 'They're a nice pair and easy to get on with — if only they got on better with one another; but, of course, they are of very different types and have no tastes or interests in common. According to school reports, both have brains (David more) and are both disinclined to work hard. (Who isn't!)'

*

'I had my brother in bed, two boys in the house, no domestic help, all the chores to do in fact for four people, four geese, ten hens, a cat, and a dog,' he wrote on 31 December to Gebbert; he had sent her *The Last Battle* and *Till We Have Faces* for Christmas; she had sent him and Warren ties. 'Whew, but it has left me tired!'

✑ 1957 *✑*

Back in Cambridge for the beginning of Hilary term, Lewis found once again that the below-freezing temperatures had burst unprotected piping and that both gas and electricity pressure was very low. He too was feeling low. 'I'm in great mental agony,' he said to Richard W. Ladborough, who had asked one evening after dinner at Magdalene if he were tired; 'please pray for us.' When Basil Willey happened upon him and asked after his wife, he tried to reply with nonchalance: 'It's a sword of Damocles, you know.'

*

'Hope is the real torture,' he wrote on 28 January to Pitter. 'I try to hope as little as possible. Have us in your prayers — but I know you do.'

*

'Orual is, not a symbol, but an instance, a "case" of human affection in its natural condition, true, tender, suffering, but in the long run tyranically possessive and ready to turn to hatred when the beloved ceases to be its possession.' He was writing on 10 February to Kilby of Wheaton College who had inquired about the ultimate meaning of *Till We Have Faces*. 'What such love particularly cannot stand is to see the beloved passing into a sphere where it cannot follow.'

∽

Peter, you told me that story, he wrote to Bide, remembering his extraordinary experience of healing a child; will you come up and lay hands on Joy?

∽

'When I see her each weekend,' he wrote on 6 March, which was Ash Wednesday, to Sister Penelope, 'she is, to a layman's eyes (but not to a doctor's knowledge) in full convalescence, better every week.'

∽

He was embarrassed when he saw Bide at the hospital on Wednesday 20 March, but he was also desperate. Doctors and hospital had given up on her; death was imminent; she could be made comfortable with drugs, but even that was no longer entirely possible. Was he looking for a miracle? What happened once might never happen again, warned his former pupil; no one was a greater sceptic than himself. The tutor submitted himself to tutelage, but asked anyway if the priest would pray over the woman. After an introduction and a few pleasantries, which were more than Gresham could endure, Bide laid hands on her and prayed that he might become the instrument of God's holy will. Out in the hallway afterward, he said he would congratulate Lewis on the title that was appearing in all the bookshop windows if it weren't so grotesque; *The Problem of Pain* had just been published in paperback.

∽

'Dear beloved, we are gathered together here in the sight of God, and in the face of this company, to join together this man and this woman in holy matrimony . . .'

It was 11.00 a.m. the next day in the hospital; Bide was reading from 'The Form of the Solemnization of Matrimony.' Joy was in bed. Jack was holding her hand. Warren was standing on one side, a nurse on the other.

'I require and charge you both, as ye will answer at the dreadful day of judgment when the secrets of all hearts shall be disclosed, that if either of you know any impediment in matrimony, ye do now confess it . . .'

Lewis had spent much of the night before telling Bide about the civil marriage and the piece of paper, signed and cosigned, that said the marriage was a fiction to placate the Home Office. He told him also that the bishop of Oxford had refused the solemnization of the marriage on the ground that the Church of England considered Joy's previous marriage valid.

'For be ye well assured, that if any persons are joined together otherwise than as God's word doth allow, their marriage is not lawful . . .'

As a priest in the diocese of Chichester he could not perform a marriage in the diocese of Oxford without specific permission, explained Bide to Lewis the night before, although he had to admit with Lewis that the Church of England's stand on validity was more a custom than a law. The marriage, pleaded Lewis, would last a day, perhaps a week, perhaps as long as a month.

'Wilt thou love her, comfort her, honour, and keep her in sickness and in health; and, forsaking all others, keep thee only unto her, so long as ye both shall live?'

'I will,' said Jack; when the priest repeated the vow, Joy said the same.

'With this ring I thee wed: In the name of the Father, and of the Son, and of the Holy Ghost. Amen.'

Solemnizing the marriage was a difficult act for Bide, but the look on the woman's face was enough. More difficult would be the trip to the episcopal residence, for confess he must to the bishop of Oxford; and he hoped his lordship would see the situation as he, Bide, saw it, an act of practical charity to a dying woman.

'Those whom God hath joined together, let no man put asunder.'

Lewis bent to kiss his bride. She immediately expressed the desire, now that the hospital had given up on her and she had received the sacrament of matrimony, that she have the consolation of dying at the Kilns as Mrs C. S. Lewis.

∽

At the beginning of April Joy was brought by ambulance to the Kilns. With her came a nurse, who moved into one of the guest rooms. A hospital bed had been set up in the common room on the first floor; she was settled into it carefully. Straps hung down so that she might pull herself up, but at the moment she didn't have the strength. When she wanted to eliminate, she had to ring a bell; as many as three people laid hold of her, crying out in pain at the wrench to her frail body, just to ease her onto the bedpan.

∽

On learning that Joy was about to die, Bill Gresham asked for his boys back; if they were not forthcoming, he would take them back by force. Her agony increased. Douglas burst into tears. David wrote a letter renouncing his father. 'You have tortured one who was already on the rack,' wrote Lewis for his wife on 6 April; 'heaped extra weights on one who is being pressed to death.' It was Joy's wish, he went on, that the boys complete their education in England and enjoy whatever psychological security there might be at the Kilns. If Gresham did not relent, indeed if he tried to take the boys against their will, he, Lewis, would take legal action, which he assured Gresham would be long and costly. That was Jack's draft; Joy approved it; Warren typed it.

Later in the day, however, Lewis wrote another letter to Gresham, this one full of his own thoughts. He was sympathetic with Gresham's wanting to support his boys and not always being able to do so, and with wanting to see them again, but it would be premature now. 'The boys remember you as a man who fired rifles through ceilings to relieve his temper, broke up chairs, wept in public, and broke a bottle over Douglas' head.' When the boys had grown up and the scars had healed, that would be time for 'a real, unconfused reconciliation.'

❧

'I lead the life of a hospital orderly,' wrote Lewis on 13 April to Shelburne, 'and have hardly any time to say my prayers or eat my meals.' Pray he did, though, that if only it were God's holy will, he would take on some measure of his wife's heart-rending sufferings. Bide had insisted on prayer; although his laying on of hands and the prayers accompanying it did not immediately bring Joy to a sitting position, hungering for breakfast, at least they were not in vain. Or so Lewis thought. God would answer them, but in a way not yet known.

❧

'How can I thank you?' he wrote on 15 April to Pitter, who had offered a gift of money against his medical expenditures. 'There's a good deal in the kitty still. But thank you again and again.'

❧

On 4 May he described his wife as 'desperately ill' to Baynes. On 8 May he described her as 'a dying woman' to Sister Madeleva and worried what he was going to do with 'two orphan stepsons.' On 12 May he was able to write to Sister Penelope, 'There is little pain, often none; her strength increases; and she eats and sleeps well.' By the end of the month, however, he himself was howling and screaming with pain in his hip. Hastily summoned, the doctor diagnosed rheumatism at the very least, a slipped disc at the very most, and prescribed deep heat and a long rest.

❧

Lead us, Evolution, lead us
  Up the future's endless stair:
Chop us, change us, prod us, weed us,
  For stagnation is despair:
Groping, guessing, yet progressing,
  Lead us nobody knows where.

❧

Lying about, unable to move much, Lewis and his wife let their imaginations gambol. He came up with an idea for a poem, a sort of hymn to evolution, with tongue in cheek, which he would surely submit to *The Cambridge Review*; each successive verse, singable to the melody of 'Lead us, heavenly father, lead us,' sent them further into laughter.

Wrong or justice in the present,
  Joy or sorrow, what are they
While there's always jam tomorrow.
  While we tread the onward way?
Never knowing where we're going,
  We can never go astray . . .

❧

By 18 June the trouble in his back had been reduced to 'a wearisome ache.' By 3 July she was 'in no pain and in wonderful (apparent) health and spirits.' 'It is not all tribulation,' he was able to write on 1 August to Griffiths. 'A new element of beauty as well as of tragedy has entered my life.' But the pain in his back flared up again. The doctor ordered him to the hospital where X-rays were taken, bone marrow sampled, anus and rectum explored. Osteoporosis was revealed, a disease of the bones. It wasn't fatal, but it wasn't curable; it afflicted women mainly and in most cases was the precursor of senility. A board under the mattress was the only prescription and a surgical belt under the shirt. 'The cure, if there is one,' he wrote on 21 August to Greeves, 'depends on getting the system to turn into bone marrow more of the calcium one's ordinary food contains — a question of blood and metabolism.'

❧

Visiting the Kilns for three days in August was Bel Kaufman, a classmate of Joy's from Hunter College. She brought with her gifts and greetings from New York City. Joy may have been dying, she said, but she certainly looked at peace. That was because she was in love, said Joy. Jack was better looking than his photographs, Bel assured her. He was hobbling about and encouraged their guest to take a hike over Shotover Hill but to be sure to return for lunch: pheasant. At tea-time they played Scrabble, allowing words in all languages. On the final day of her visit, Joy bade farewell to Bel as she was being carried to the ambulance that would take her to the hospital for radiation treatment. Love certainly seemed to agree with her, said Bel. 'The movies and the poets are right,' said Joy; '[love] does exist!'

∾

Warren was 'dead drunk' and had been for several days, said the telephone call from Ireland. He couldn't go to pick up his brother, said Lewis, for he was sick himself. Perhaps the caller could admit Warren to the Lourdes Hospital in Drogheda, where his brother was already known. It was a heart complaint, wrote Warren the next day; it would kill him in a year's time. Lewis wrote to Mother Mary Martin for the real story. Nothing to worry about, she replied; there was a heart murmur; it was slight and curable; but it was surely the 'by-product of acute alcoholism and pneumonia.'

∾

'Far less clothes, please! I mean, ordinary clothes,' wrote Lewis on 2 September to Jane Gaskell. Both he and Joy had read her book and found it 'a quite amazing achievement'; in order that her next book might be 'at least twice as good,' he offered her six suggestions, the fifth one of which had to do with clothes. 'If you had given your fairies strange and beautiful clothes and described *them*, there might be something in it. But your heroine's tangerine skirt! For whom do you write? No *man* wants to hear how she was dressed, and the sort of woman who does seldom reads fantasy; if she reads anything, it is more likely to be the women's magazines.'

∾

'My wife's condition has improved,' he wrote on 24 September to Griffiths, 'if not miraculously (but who knows?), at any rate wonderfully.' He went on to describe what was, if not a recovery, at least a reprieve. The relationship with the woman who was his wife was growing too. It 'began in Agape, proceeded to Philia, then became pity, and only after that, Eros. As if the highest of these, Agape, had successively undergone the sweet humiliations of an incarnation.'

∾

'This is not a work of scholarship. I am no Hebraist, no higher critic, no ancient historian, no archaeologist. I write for the unlearned about things in which I am unlearned myself.' He was putting down some introductory comments to a book that he would entitle *Reflections on the Psalms*. 'I write as one amateur to another, talking about the difficulties I have met, or lights I have gained, when reading the

Psalms with the hope that this might at any rate interest, and some-times even help, other inexpert readers.' He would use Coverdale's translation found in the Prayer Book, with a few emendations. This was not an apologetical work, he insisted, although he wrote as a member of the Church of England, differing here from Roman Catholics and there from Fundamentalists. 'I hope I shall not for this forfeit the good will or the prayers of either. Nor do I much fear it. In my experience the bitterest opposition comes neither from them nor from any other thorough-going believers, and not often from the atheists, but from semi-believers of all complexions. There are some enlightened and progressive old gentlemen of this sort whom no courtesy can propitiate and no modesty disarm. But then I daresay I am a much more annoying person than I know. (Shall we, perhaps, in Purgatory, see our own faces and hear our own voices as they really were?)'

By October he could rise by himself in the morning. There was a residue of pain in the lower back. He bathed and shaved; by the time he dressed, the pain had disappeared. At the beginning of Michaelmas term he hired a car to ferry him and his luggage from Oxford to Cambridge with a stop for lunch on the way. After that he was able to commute by train between the two cities. Indeed the corner seat in a railway carriage turned out to be most hospitable to his sacral difficulties.

'You . . . realize the connection, or even the unity, of all the books — scholarly, fantastic, theological,' he wrote on 29 October to Kathryn Stillwell, who had sent him her master's thesis, 'and make me appear a single author, not a man who impersonates half a dozen authors, which is what I seem to most.'

'I was very crippled and had much pain all summer, but am in a good spell now,' he wrote on 6 November to Penelope. 'I was losing calcium just about as fast as Joy was gaining it, a bargain (if it was one) for which I am very thankful.'

As Joy's leg healed, it also grew shorter. An orthopaedic shoe was fitted; with it she was able to limp about the house, even to walk in the garden, with the aid of a stick. With the aid of Paxford, still gardener and general handyman at the Kilns, she was able to achieve some landscaping, transforming the drab and neglected grounds into a place of some order and beauty. When the telephone rang, she went to answer it almost without thinking, something she hadn't been able to do for a year. 'The improvement in my wife's condition,' wrote Lewis on 12 November to Gebbert, 'is, in the proper use of the word, miraculous.'

∽

'There! They're at it again. "Ark, the errol hygel sings." They're knocking louder . . . 'It was the local choir made up of boys who to Lewis' ear had never learned to sing or memorize the words of the carol they were murdering. About the only instruments they could play with conviction were the doorbell and the door knocker, after which they expected a substantial contribution. 'Boxing Day is only two and a half weeks ahead,' he wrote for the 7 December issue of *Time and Tide*; 'then perhaps we shall have a little quiet in which to remember the birth of Christ.'

∽

'There are faint springtime stirrings that suggest my wife . . . may soon begin to write again,' he wrote on 16 December to Gebbert. 'Then all three of us will be at it, and I'll put up a plate at the door reading *Lewis, Lewis, and Lewis, Inc., Book Factory*.'

∽

'The variety of Dorothy Sayers' work makes it impossible to find anyone who can deal properly with it all,' he wrote. His friend had died on 18 December; he had been asked to speak at the memorial service at St Margaret's in London on Wednesday 15 January. He would have to be in Cambridge that day, but he would write something that perhaps someone else could deliver. 'For all she did and was, for delight and instruction, for her militant loyalty as a friend, for courage and honesty, for the richly feminine qualities which showed through a port and manner superficially masculine and even gleefully ogreish,' he wrote in conclusion, 'let us thank the Author who invented her.'

∽ 1958 ∽

On the morning of Tuesday 14 January Lewis watched his luggage being stowed in the boot of the car he had hired to take him to Cambridge for the beginning of Lent term. Joy was sorry to see him go. Suddenly he asked her to come with him for the ride. Bedridden and houseridden for so long, only recently being able to venture forth for a Sunday dinner, she hesitated. But the cancer was gone, said the doctors, or at least it had been arrested; where there had been fragments in the X-rays, there now was solid bone. She decided to go; in a few minutes Clifford Morris was able to enclose the couple in the back seat of his sedan and set off on the eighty-mile journey to Cambridge. For Joy it was like discovering the world all over again. Lunch in Cambridge was delicious; parting was sweet; Morris drove her back to Oxford. Lewis went to his rooms at Magdalene and after unpacking, began to take care of his correspondents, to most of whom he told the wonderful odyssey. 'It sounds like a small thing,' he wrote to Shelburne in the eighth letter of the day, with others still to be answered, 'but it would have been incredible even a month ago.'

∽

'If my wife's recovery *is* due to medical science (and not either to miracle or to the interior natural forces of the body),' he wrote on 6 February to Harold Dawson whose brother had just contracted cancer, 'then testosterone and radio-therapy were the things that did it.'

∽

If the Kilns were a tenement in the Bronx, it would have been torn down a long time ago. Feet had plunged through floorboards; ceilings had crashed onto furniture; walls would surely have caved in long before if it hadn't been for the bookcases all over the house. No wonder his friends called it the Midden, the Dungheap. Repairs had to be made, said Joy, before someone got hurt. There was some logic to that, said Jack, and delegated her for the task. How much should she spend? He made his cheque book available to her. Before she could use it, however, she had to reconcile the account against the bank statements in order to discover the correct balance; that, he assured her, was a process that had been wanting for some time. Credits outweighed debits by thousands of pounds, she discovered; she instructed him to put some of the funds into savings accounts and other banking investments where they would earn interest. With the rest, she budgeted for the repair of the Kilns and the painting, at least, of the interior, Warren excepting his own rooms from all the bother.

From the windows she had torn down the blackout curtains that had been hanging since 1939. Mrs Miller, the daytime housekeeper at the Kilns since 1952, suggested that they be washed, but when they hit the tubs they turned to ink. The carpets were in tatters; some of them she replaced. In danger from eating off chipped dishes and drinking from cracked glasses, she invested in new china and crystal. When Jack asked her how much she had spent, she gave a good round figure. Things had gone up since he last bought anything like this, he admitted, but wasn't there something cheaper on the market? Half that, she told him laughingly, having shopped about to buy as much as she could in the sales. If he was bewildered at the cost of repairing and refurbishing the Kilns, he relished the dinners she served on the tablecloth she had crocheted. Game on china. Wine in crystal. Candles in sconces. Romance.

∽

'I have wondered before now whether the vast astronomical distances may not be God's quarantine precautions,' he wrote in 'Will We Lose God in Outer Space?' which appeared in the April issue of *Christian Herald*. 'They prevent the spiritual infection of a fallen species from spreading.'

∽

Joy was not able to negotiate church on Easter Sunday, 6 April, but she did allow herself to be driven to a country hotel where she and Jack spent a week-long honeymoon. He couldn't help feeling naughty, 'a confirmed old bachelor' sharing a room with a married woman. Joy didn't ease the situation, suggesting as she did that he check the newspapers each morning for report of his scandalous, not to say adulterous, behaviour. For the week her movements were confined to the hotel and its immediate environs. When she returned home, she made her Easter duty, the Rev Ronald Head, vicar of Holy Trinity in Headington, bringing her the sacrament.

∽

'The subject I want to say something about in the near future, in some form or other, is the four loves,' wrote Lewis on 1 May to Bishop Girault M. Jones of the Episcopal Radio-TV Foundation, Inc., of Atlanta, Georgia. 'This seems to bring in nearly the whole of Christian ethics.' The foundation had used the good offices of Walsh to find out if Lewis would be open to another broadcast project. When he said he was, the bishop make a formal approach by letter, even going so far as to suggest that the talks could be recorded in England and that there would be an honorarium. 'I shall be glad to hear from you on the further details.'

'In Greek they have four words for love,' he began to write. '*Storge* means affection, the sort of love there ought to be between relations. *Philia* means friendship. *Eros* is, of course, the love between the sexes. And *agape* is love in the Christian sense, God's love for man and the Christian love for the brethren. I want to talk about all four, and I'll begin with *storge* or affection . . .'

∽

'The Kilns is now a real home, with paint on the walls, ceilings properly repaired, clean sheets on the beds — we can receive and put up several guests,' wrote Joy in May to the Greens, June and Roger. 'We'd love a visit.'

↬

'I am most grateful for your very kind offer to send some stockings,' wrote Lewis on 30 May to Gebbert, who had said that tins of tobacco and fruitcake were already in the mail; 'but I'm given to understand that nylons can now be got over here without any difficulty. But my wife nonetheless appreciates your thoughtfulness.'

↬

'It's only since I've been ill and helpless that I've realized just how good people in general are, when they have a chance,' wrote Joy on 6 June to Shelburne, who had recently been in hospital. Jack would have responded himself if he wasn't involved in the Cambridge tripos examinations. 'So many people have taken trouble over me and gone out of their way to give me pleasure or help! It's very heartwarming — and humbling, for I remember how cynical I used to be about humanity and feel a salutary shame.'

↬

'The moment a man seriously accepts a deity, his interest in "religion" is at an end. He's got something else to think about.' Lewis was writing about the apparent growth of interest in religion in the west, which he planned to submit to *Punch*. 'The ease with which we can now get an audience for a discussion of religion does not prove that more people are becoming religious. What it really proves is the existence of a large "floating vote." Every conversion will reduce this potential audience.'

↬

As the aeroplane gathered speed down the runway, the Lewises thought they had made a dreadful mistake. Travelling to Ireland, they had chosen the plane in preference to the ferry, the ship's rolling being a threat to their bones, but they couldn't turn back now. They grasped the armrests, their knuckles turning white, until the craft became airborne and the vibrations lessened. It was the first time flying for both them; when the plane finally reached cruising altitude, they were able to peer through the port-holes down onto the clouds and see 'a new world of beauty.' Below them was the Irish Sea; when the coastline loomed on the horizon, it looked just as it did on a map, and the headlands, when they were directly below, look 'very dark,' 'like a bit of enamel.'

↬

He was getting used to checking into a hotel with a married

woman on his arm, even though he was the one she was married to, and the July jaunt was meant as the real honeymoon. Greeves joined them with his car and chauffeured them about Louth and Down and Donegal. How could they say he did all the talking? complained Lewis as he kept track of the petrol consumption; Joy and Arthur rarely let him get a word in edgeways. After two weeks, they returned to Oxford 'drunk with blue mountains, yellow beaches, dark fuchsia, breaking waves, braying donkeys, peat-smell, and the heather just beginning to bloom.'

∽

'What comes first is a delighted preoccupation with the beloved in her totality. It hasn't, so to speak, leisure to think of sex. She's primarily a person. Even the fact that she's a woman may seem for a while almost irrelevant. It's far more important that she's herself . . .' Joy was able to sleep late. He used to enjoy sleeping late when he was very young, but the habit of decades woke him at 7.15. He decided to rise and do some work on *eros*, one of the four loves. 'If you asked the lover what he wanted, and if he knew himself well enough to speak the exact truth, I think he'd reply, "I want to go on thinking about her." He's a contemplative. And when, at a later stage, the explicitly sexual element awakes, he won't feel, unless scientific theories are influencing him, that this had all along been the root of the whole matter.'

∽

The happiness that passed him by in his twenties Lewis now had when he was almost sixty: this sentiment he sent to Sister Penelope and other correspondents; and this he voiced after a luncheon he hosted in Oxford at which he introduced his wife to friends, including Coghill and Peter Bayley, a former pupil who was now a tutor. The happiness that had eluded her in her first marriage when she was young and full of health, Joy now had in her second marriage, when she was barely forty-three and recovered from cancer. It was also much in evidence when the Walshes from Wisconsin visited in the first part of August. The parents stayed at the Eastgate; the girls Madeleine, Sarah, and Alison stayed at the Kilns. Only Jack was absent, having business in Cambridge.

∽

'In spite of the unlikely hour (immediately after breakfast),' wrote a special correspondent of *The Times* who was covering the annual conference of the Classical Association at Cambridge on 7 August, 'the hilarity of Professor C. S. Lewis, in his most mischievous mood, proved irresistible this morning when he delivered to the conference of classical teachers a withering attack on modern translations of the classics.'

❧

It was Tuesday 19 August. Lewis was late, two hours late, arriving at Recorded Productions, Ltd, Morris House, 1 Jermyn Street, London. Caroline Rakestraw of the Episcopal Radio-TV Foundation greeted him with relief and introduced him to J. R. Hale, the engineer. He still didn't have a typescript to give her, but, if Mrs Cartwheel . . . Rakestraw, she corrected him. If she didn't mind, he would read from his handwritten manuscript. Rakestraw and Hale adjourned to the control room. Lewis put his homburg and walking stick on the table by the microphone and sat down; at the signal he began to read about the first of the four loves, *storge*.

Hale was picking up extraneous noises. The day before both he and Rakestraw had detected a faint hum; it was coming from a fan somewhere in the Underground; London Transport agreed to turn it off for two days, but only because it was Lewis doing the recording. The noises had to be the manuscript; Hale asked him to stop crinkling it. He was doing the best he could, replied Lewis, but he would stop speaking when he turned from one page to another. Every time he inhaled, Rakestraw noted, he sounded like a bellows being pumped. 'I'm Irish, not English,' said Lewis. 'Did you ever know an Irishman who didn't puff and blow?' After several re-takes, and with Lewis' voice sounding dry and cracking, they gave him the afternoon off.

The following morning, he was on time; he finished recording by noon. Some of the talks were over-long and would have to be cut, said Rakestraw during lunch. He left that to her discretion. Eros was all right, but when he ventured into Venus, she said, the talk got a little too hot, at least for some American Christians. Why did he have to say that some young couples would have to learn about the act of love from textbooks like Freud and Krafft-Ebing? Cut it where she liked, said Lewis. No, he didn't need to hear the revised and edited tapes before they were aired. Would Mrs Cartwheel like to see snapshots of his dog, his wife, his stepsons?

❧

'Rum chaps, those medievals,' he wrote on 30 August to Brewer; 'they actually thought temptations ought to be tempting.' Acting as general editor for a series of medieval and Renaissance English texts, he was commenting on manuscript page 47 of the introduction written by Brewer for his edition of Chaucer's *Parliament of Fowlys*. 'I'll return the text when I've got a large enough envelope. (If only you scholards would use ordinary quarto sheets and *not* enclose your manuscripts in great flapping containers . . .)'

❧

'We must both, I'm afraid, recognize that, as we grow older, we become like old cars — more and more repairs and replacements are necessary,' wrote Lewis on 30 September to Shelburne, who had been complaining in recent letters of earaches and toothaches and the possibility of an operation. 'We must just look forward to the fine new machines (latest resurrection model) which are waiting for us, we hope, in the divine garage.'

∽

Would he care to reply, wrote Harold E. Fey, editor of *The Christian Century*, to the article in the 1 October issue entitled 'Apologists Versus Apologist'?

'He has used his brilliant, not to say coruscating, style to commend a version of Christianity which is often not even "orthodox" (for what that is worth) and which in any event is frequently incredible.' Yes, thought Lewis, he'd want to reply to that.

W. Norman Pittenger was the author of the article. He was identified on the inside front cover as one of the day's outstanding Christian apologists, professor of Christian apologetics at General Theological Seminary in New York City, chairman of the theological commission of the faith and order movement, member of the study commission of the World Council of Churches, and author of the recently published *The Episcopalian Way of Life*.

'Although it seems to be a fashion nowadays to quote Mr Lewis as if he were one of the church fathers, along with Augustine and Chrysostom and Athanasius, I believe he teaches a version of the Christian faith which is not only on occasion dubiously orthodox by the narrowest standards, but is also a kind of uncriticized "traditionalism" which is stated with such eloquence and brilliance that it deceives those who are not instructed and misleads many who are.' *Miracles* Pittenger considered one of the worst books on the subject. He disagreed with Lewis' definition of miracles and his treatment of naturalism and was surprised by Lewis' apparent ignorance of the last hundred years of biblical scholarship. *Mere Christianity* presented a Jesus that was either a God or a madman; Pittenger, on the other hand, interpreted Jesus as 'one in whom God was so active and so present that he may be called "God-man", the incarnate word,' and 'a prophet who announced the coming of God's kingdom and who may even have thought that he himself was to be the anointed one or messiah, who would inaugurate it.' If he had the space, he would treat Lewis' sub-Christian view of sexuality and his callous attitude towards the animal kingdom.

'I rejoice that many have been awakened to interest in Christianity through his writings,' concluded Pittenger. 'I can only hope that they will derive their understanding of what Christianity, in its authentic and reasonable form, actually affirms from somebody else.' Ohhh yes, thought Lewis, he would want to reply to that.

∽

Autumn was delicious; Joy drank it in as she limped about the property surrounding the Kilns. Everywhere she saw signs of trespassing. Some of the neighbours hunted the small game scampering about the grounds; others scavenged live trees for firewood. Even the outbuildings had been violated; old weapons and a telescope had been stolen. The 'no trespassing' signs had been riddled with buckshot, and every so often she let go with a small-bore shotgun, the recoil rattling her frail frame. She was aiming at pigeons, she told Jack, but she hoped she was hitting the consciences of all trespassers within earshot.

Warren informed her that the 'constant theft' of their timber was a little bit of social and economic history. 'Until about a hundred years ago, our garden was the villagers' common, where all had a right to cut their fuel wood, and what is now our reservoir was the village spring. One fine morning [Headington] Quarry woke up to find its common being enclosed for shooting land — stolen from them without compensation, in fact. The story of the theft has been handed down from generation to generation, and the injustice is resented to this day. Taking our wood is the assertion of a right to whose relinquishment they never assented, and the cutting of our wire is a parish duty; there is an old man in the village who keeps a pair of wire cutters for that special purpose!'

∽

'You pay me a wholly undeserved compliment to my erudition by supposing that my debts to modern theologians might be too complicated to sort out!' wrote Lewis on 31 October to Corbin Scott Carnell of the University of Florida at Gainesville. 'Tillich and Brunner I don't know at all. Maritain I tried but did not admire; he seems to say in ten pages of polysyllabic abstraction what Scripture or the old writers would say in a couple of sentences. Kierkegaard still means nothing to me. I read one book of Niebuhr's — I can't remember the title — and, on the whole, reacted against it. I tried Berdyaev, but he seemed to me terribly repetitive; one paragraph would do for what he spins out in a book. I thought Buber made the point well, but with some exaggeration. I never read Marcel but met him and felt him to be venerable; but his message [was] the same as Buber's. Barth I have never read, or not that I remember. Otto's *Das Heilige* I have been deeply influenced by. Nygren's *Eros and Agape* gave me a . . . useful classificating instrument, though I did not think his own use of that instrument is profitable. I liked, but could make no use of, Aulen's *Christus Victor*. I think this is almost all,' he wrote in conclusion. 'You would hardly, among literate people, find a man who is less "in the know" or "up to date" than I am.'

❧

In his rejoinder to Pittenger, Lewis admitted some indelicacies of phrasing, but when it came to *Miracles* he insisted that the theologian had misinterpreted, if not misquoted, him. The real value of his work, and what the good doctor seemed not to realize, was that it had been written for, and indeed spoken to, the person who had trouble believing in God or the divinity of Christ or the validity of Christianity. He was in a very real sense a translator, turning the technical language of the professional theologian into the language of the people in the street. 'If the real theologians had tackled this laborious work of translation about a hundred years ago, when they began to lose touch with the people (for whom Christ died),' he wrote in conclusion, 'there would have been no place for me.'

❧

'Oh Lor'! They bring religion into everything,' said an old woman on a bus when she saw a crib in front of a church. 'Look — they're dragging it even into Christmas now!' Warren had overheard the woman; when he told Jack, his brother put the story into his Christmas correspondence.

Those he didn't write letters to got cards, the first ones to emanate from the Kilns. On the front was an engine with carriages chugging towards picturesque hills; it was identified on the back as the Talyllyn Railway, a narrow-gauge train in Wales; profit from the sales of the cards would go to the preservation of the ninety-seven-year-old line. 'With best wishes for a merry Christmas and a happy New Year,' read the mesage.

❧

Lewis' rejoinder to Pittenger appeared in the 26 November issue of *The Christian Century*. Pittenger wrote a reply, which appeared in the 24 December issue, in which he maintained, courteously enough, that differences still remained between the two apologists. One thing he and Lewis were *ad idem* about was that theology needed translation into the vernacular. Fey, editor of the magazine, airmailed the 24 December issue to Lewis and asked if he might like to write an article on just how the translation into the vernacular might be accomplished. By return airmail Lewis declined, stating that only an American could translate into the American vernacular. One thought did occur to him, though. 'It is absolutely disgraceful that we expect missionaries to the Bantus to learn Bantu but never ask whether our missionaries to the Americans or English can speak American or English.' He proposed that one requirement for ordination should be the successful translation of theological esoterica into exoterica., 'The vernacular is the real test. If you can't turn your faith into it, then either you don't understand it or you don't believe it.'

ᙍᙍ 1959 ᙍᙍ

'I think an anthology of extracts from a living writer would make both him and the collector look rather ridiculous,' wrote Lewis on 20 January to Kilby, who had proposed an anthology, 'and I'm sure publishers would not agree to the plan.'

ᙍᙍ

Relaxing after a substantial dinner at Westcott House, an Anglican college at Cambridge University, many of whose pupils were theological students, Lewis picked up a book entitled *Windsor Sermons* by the Rev. Alexander Vidler. Sipping port and waiting for his host to return, he started to read 'The Sign at Cana.'

What did he think of the book? asked the Rev. Kenneth Carey, principal of Westcott, when he returned to the room.

Wasn't it incredible, said Lewis, that they had to wait nearly two thousand years before a theologian told them that what the church had always regarded as miraculous was in fact a parable?

But that was the course of much New Testament exegesis these days.

Were they denying the historicity of the gospels? Lewis wanted to know.

Of some things, but not of others. For example, they weren't denying the resurrection.

But if they could swallow a camel like the resurrection, why were they gagging on such gnats as the feeding of the multitudes?

Another glass of port; Lewis went on to explain how devastating a church that abandoned the miraculous would be. Told that the position the church had held for almost two thousand years was no longer valid, the uneducated believer would throw the whole thing off and become an atheist. The poor man might just be perverse enough to stay in the old church with the miracles and demand that the theologians stop calling themselves Christians and start looking for new employment.

The educated believer, said Lewis, accepting a third glass of port, who was educated in one way but not in a theological way, was not better off. If the Anglican theologians abandoned the miraculous, he would be forced to leave the Anglican Church and look for a church that still held the miraculous; he would, in fact, have to become a Roman Catholic . . .

Suddenly, he felt he had said too much.

'I wish you would come and say all this to my young men,' said his host.

∽

'American children, as I know from the letters they write me, are just as "Aslan-olatrous" as English ones,' he wrote on 10 March to Patricia Hillis of Austin, Texas. 'The world of fairytale, as the world of Christianity, makes the heart and imagination royalist in a sense which mere politics hardly [touches]. What my stories do is to liberate — to free from inhibitions — a spontaneous impulse to serve and adore, to have a "dearest dread", which the modern world starves, or diverts to film stars, crooners, and athletes.'

∽

'If I may say so, you are the sanest and fairest teetotaller I have met for a long time,' wrote Lewis on 18 April to Allan C. Emery of Boston, Massachusetts. 'I think that if I lived in certain American or Scotch cities, I might feel it my duty to be one too.'

∽

Bide's wife had cancer, read one of the items of mail on the morning of 29 April. 'I wish I could help. Can I? You did so much for me,' replied Lewis immediately. That the cancer was in its beginnings and seemed to be operable was some consolation. But there would be fear and anxiety and the monotony of anxiety, he warned. 'If you find (some do) that mental anguish produces an inclination to eat more — paradoxical but it can — I should jolly well do so.'

As Bide rallied others to pray for the boy Michael and for Joy, so Lewis would enrol his correspondents to pray for Bide and his wife. 'Would you mention him in your prayers?' he asked the next day of Griffiths. 'Will you, of your charity, have him in your prayers?' he wrote on 6 May to Shelburne.

∽

He came as a sheep before the shepherds, he said in addressing the future priests of the Anglican Church who were studying at

Westcott House; he had four chief bleats.

First, the New Testament exegetes, Bultmann among them, might be good biblical critics but they were poor literary critics who didn't know the difference between legend and history, person and personality; he gave a number of examples. What in effect they asked readers to do was read between the lines when they themselves were unable to read the lines themselves. They claimed to see fern seed, which was supposed to render a person invisible, but they couldn't see 'an elephant ten yards away in broad daylight.'

Second, liberal theologians claimed that something had been lost and that they themselves had just recovered it. The real behaviour and purpose and teaching of Jesus Christ had very quickly been misunderstood and misrepresented by his followers in the first few centuries of the Christian era. That was preposterous, he said; he gave examples from literary and philosophical history. 'There is an *a priori* improbability in it which almost no argument and no evidence could counterbalance.'

Third, the theologians stated that the miraculous didn't occur. One could agree with that statement, he countered, only if one held the philosophical position that miracles never occurred, a position no more valid than its contradictory.

Fourth, the theologians attempted to reconstruct the genesis of the texts they studied. The probability of their doing so with any accuracy was almost nil. In support of his position, he cited recent attempts to reconstruct the history of *Piers Plowman* and *The Faerie Queene*. He cited also reviews of his own books and Tolkien's, in which the reviewers made all sorts of impossible assertions. The atom bomb was the inspiration for *The Lord of the Rings*, said some reviewers, but the actual chronology of the composition of that book made that theory impossible. The ultimate trouble with reconstruction and reinterpretation of texts, literary as well as biblical, was that there was no way to check for rightness or wrongness.

'Such are the reactions of one bleating layman to modern theology. It is right you should hear them,' said Lewis in conclusion. 'You will not perhaps hear them very often again. Your parishioners will not often speak to you quite frankly. Once the layman was anxious to hide the fact that he believes so much less than the vicar; he now tends to hide the fact that he believes so much more. Missionary to the priests of one's own church is an embarrassing role; though I have a horrid feeling that if such mission work is not soon undertaken, the future history of the Church of England is likely to be short.'

'To be sure, we had a common point of view, but we had it before we met,' he wrote on 15 May to Charles Moorman, who had undertaken a study of writers like Williams, Tolkien, Sayers, and Lewis. Lewis admitted to influencing, and to having been influenced by Williams. Nobody influenced Tolkien. Sayers lived in London and never met Tolkien; she did know Williams earlier and Lewis later, but it was unlikely that she either influenced, or was influenced by, anybody else in the group of writers mentioned by Moorman. 'It was the cause rather than the result of our friendship.'

∽

Why did you lure us on like this,
Light-year on light-year, through the abyss,
Building (as though we cared for size!)
Empires that cover galaxies . . .

He was expostulating in verse against a certain sort of science fiction.

If at the journey's end we find
The same old stuff we left behind,
Well-worn tellurian stories of
Crooks, spies, conspirators, or love,
Whose setting might as well have been
The Bronx, Montmartre, or Bethnal Green?'

∽

'This book is based on lectures given at Cambridge during the last few years and is primarily addressed to students,' wrote Lewis in June in preface to *Studies in Words*, which would be published by Cambridge University Press. The lectures grew out of a practice which was at first his necessity and later his hobby to fill the margins of texts and the pages of notebooks with the meanings of words. Sandwiched between an introduction and an essay entitled 'At the Fringe of Language' were lecture- or chapter-length treatments of such words as 'nature,' 'sad,' 'wit,' 'free,' 'sense,' 'simple,' 'conscious,' and 'conscience.' One thing the book was not, said Lewis in the preface; it was 'not an essay in the higher linguistics.'

∽

'I can't find the name and address of the secretary of our commission on the Psalms,' he wrote on 14 June to Eliot. 'As you are in London, would you kindly let her know that I have received the use of the inner library at Magdalene for our July session?' He, Eliot, and five others were engaged in revising the wording of the Psalms as they appeared in the Book of Common Prayer. 'My wife and I would like nothing better than to dine with Mrs Eliot and yourself . . .'

ᴔ

Early in the spring, the Lewises thought they would have to forego their summer vacation in Ireland. For once, health was not the consideration; it was money. In March they had been 'financially knocked flat by a huge surtax on royalties earned two years ago, which was a bumper year'; this was money long since spent and forgotten; careful budgeting for the next eighteen months would prevent bankruptcy. By April, however, they had got 'a fair amount of refund for erroneously paid tax,' and Barfield had discovered a way to retain more of the royalties.

In the last week of June, then, the Lewises voyaged to Ireland. They spent time in County Down at The Old Inn, Crawfordsburn, and in County Donegal at the Port Royal Hotel, Rathmullan. Greeves was both chauffeur and companion on much of the trip. 'We had a heavenly time; beautiful sunny weather, miraculous golden light over everything, clean air in which the mountains glowed like jewels — there isn't a speck of dust in the whole country,' wrote Joy to her former husband. 'The country is all rocks — granite hillsides like the roughest in New England, and dry stone walls everywhere — and completely lacks the lush garden quality of England; there's a good deal of austerity in its beauty, but it is the most beautiful place I've ever seen.'

ᴔ

'If we get out of here — I say "if" because it's beginning to seem rather doubtful,' said Lewis to Charles Wrong, whom he had met on the Broad before entering the stationer's, 'I should think we might go and have a pint.' Wrong had read history at Magdalen in the middle thirties; Lewis had been his tutor. He had served in the RAF during the late war and, contemplating a career in journalism, had even interviewed Lewis with a view to publication. Even now over a pint, far from the August Saturday crowd, he asked the questions.

'A complete flop, the worst flop I've ever had,' Lewis answered when *Till We Have Faces* came up. 'I must admit it's my favourite of all my books, but I suppose that's because it's the last.'

'When they asked me to do that, I was tremendously flattered,' he answered when *English Literature in the Sixteenth Century* came up. 'It's like a girl committing herself to marrying an elderly millionaire who's also a duke. In the end she finally has to settle down and live with the chap, and it's a hellish long time before he dies,'

'*Fantasy and Science Fiction* is the best of those magazines; there s sometimes some astonishingly good stuff in it,' he answered when the name Anthony Boucher came up. 'It's getting to be too difficult a field for me. There's less and less fiction and more science.'

Pints drained, they stood up to go. He was about to leave for America, said Wrong, where he planned to settle and to teach history at the University of South Florida.

'You, sir,' said Lewis in appreciation, 'are an adventurer!'

❧

What are you going to call it? asked Lewis.

'*Dear Wormwood*,' said James Forsyth. He and his wife had arrived at tea-time, apologized for being late, having miscalculated the time it would take them to drive from Sussex to Oxford. Joy poured tea and passed the cakes. Forsyth hastened to explain that his play *Heloise* had just closed in New York; the reason he was imposing on Lewis at this time was that the Dramatic Publishing Company in Chicago had asked him to dramatize *The Screwtape Letters*. He had already approached Bles and Curtis Brown, both of whom said that Lewis was less than keen on dramatization.

That was correct, said Lewis, remembering how he had to reject Douglas' radio dramatization of *Lion* last year; but he would try to listen with an open mind to what the playwright had to say.

Picking up her target rifle, Joy invited Mrs Forsyth to follow her out into the garden while the men talked. Mrs Forsyth followed somewhat reluctantly, Mrs Lewis having severely admonished her on the telephone not to be late for tea.

Picking up the cups and saucers, and urging Forsyth to collect the plates and the silver, Lewis led the way to the kitchen.

'All right, treat the story in your own way,' said Lewis, mopping the dishes with steaming water. 'But why not use another name, another title?'

Forsyth wouldn't agree to that, nor could he; there was copyright to respect and royalty to be paid.

'But you will have trouble,' said Lewis as they left the kitchen. 'Doing anything with the Devil, you are sure to have trouble.'

The wives returned from the garden, Joy leaning the rifle, unfired, against a bookcase.

'One thing the Devil can't stand,' said Lewis, ushering the Forsyths to the door, 'is humour.'

❧

'Mr Principal, your Imminence, your Disgrace, my Thorns, Shadies, and Gentledevils . . .'

After twenty years, Lewis was reviving Screwtape in order that he might speak to the world on the eve of the 1960s. The *diabolus emeritus* couldn't really write another letter, but he could address the annual Tempters' Training College for young devils. Dr Slubgob, principal, would propose a toast to the guests; Screwtape, guest of honour, would rise to reply.

The banquet was a gastronomic disaster, said Screwtape, feasting as they were on the anguish of poor souls. *Municipal authority with graft sauce* was flavourless. *Casserole of adulterers* was lukewarm. *Trade unionist stuffed with sedition* was palatable, but barely so. There were no great dishes such as the ones served at the banquets when he was a pupil; there was no Henry VIII, no Adolf Hitler. But, he was very quick to point out, 'Is the dullness of your present fare not a very small price to pay for the delicious knowledge that His whole great experiment is petering out?'

As Lewis was writing, Coghill dropped by for a visit and asked what he was doing.

Writing an article for the *Saturday Evening Post*.

How did he know what to write about or what to say?

'Oh, they have somehow got the idea that I am an unaccountably paradoxical dog, and they name the subject on which they want me to write; and they pay generously.'

'And so you set to work and invent a few paradoxes?'

'Not a bit of it. What I do is to recall, as well as I can, what my mother used to say on the subject, eke it out with a few similar thoughts of my own, and so produce what would have been strict orthodoxy in about 1900. And this seems to them outrageously paradoxical, avant-garde stuff.'

When they stopped laughing and Coghill had left, Lewis returned to the toast. He had Screwtape rehearse human history from the second half of the nineteenth century down to 1960, first distinguishing and then attacking varieties of liberty and democracy and such manifestations of social and educational theory as togetherness, being-like-folks, and I'm-as-good-as-you.

'Your Imminence, your Disgrace, my Thorns, Shadies, and Gentledevils: I give you the toast of — Principal Slubgob and the College!'

∝

'I stay miraculously well and active,' wrote Joy on 26 September to her former husband. 'My last X-rays showed a few holes here and there in my bones that won't vanish, but at least they don't grow.'

'Will you redouble your prayers for us?' asked a worried Lewis on 18 October of Shelburne. 'Apparently the wonderful recovery Joy made in 1957 was only a reprieve, not a pardon.'

'Joy's last X-ray check,' he wrote on 21 October to Walsh, 'revealed that cancer has returned on several parts of the skeleton.'

'It is like being recaptured by the giant,' he wrote in November to Green, 'when you have passed every gate and are almost out of sight of his castle.'

&

'The main objection to classical nomenclature in English poetics is already out of date,' he wrote in an essay on metre which he was preparing for *A Review of English Literature* and in which he was trying to distinguish the English iambus from the Latin iambus. 'We need not be afraid of encouraging our pupils to read Latin wrongly because we know they are not going to read Latin at all. We need no precaution against corns in a man who has already had both his legs amputated at the hip.'

&

'Haven't you discovered yet that I'm not a scholar but only a learned man?' he wrote on 16 November to Brewer. 'A Cambridge don asked me the other day whether the last syllable of *polymath* and *aftermath* were derived from the same word!'

&

' "Great Works" (of art) and "good works" (of charity) had better also be good work.' That was the conclusion he wanted to reach, the principle he wanted to enunciate in the article he was writing for the *Catholic Art Quarterly*, but the road to it was twisting and torturous, and he was having a hard time not going right off the cliff.

There were good works like almsgiving and helping in the parish. There was also good work, objects of utility and not a little beauty that were produced by cabinet makers, cobblers, and sailors. There were never enough of the former; the number of the latter was decreasing at an alarming rate. The villain of the piece was industrialized society with its diabolical stepchild, built-in obsolescence. In the nineteenth century a horse-drawn carriage was made to last a lifetime; but in the twentieth century the horse-powered car was made to last two years. The centuries-old button, because it always worked, had to be superior to the twentieth-century zipper that was always getting snarled and snaggled.

Another serpentine stepchild of industrialization was advertising, the sort that was plastered on a wooden fence to broadcast for sale what people didn't need but were made to feel they wanted. Some of that stuff he felt had invaded the Kilns when Joy went on an orgy of spending. Repair and refurbishing were the motives, but he could not help but feel that she had bought more than the household needed. The fact that she had approached the job with foreknowledge, that she had bought much of the stuff at bargain prices learned from one medium of advertising or another was no consolation to him. It had to have been more noble, less gross in the past.

'The only hopeful sign at the moment is the "space race" between America and Russia. Since we have got ourselves into a state where the main problem is not to provide people with what they need or like, but to keep people making things (it hardly matters what), great powers could not easily be better employed than in fabricating costly objects which they then fling overboard. It keeps money circulating and factories working, and it won't do space much harm — or not for a long time. But the relief is partial and temporary. The main practical task for most of us is not to give the big men advice about how to end our fatal economy — we have none to give, and they wouldn't listen — but to consider how we can live within it as little hurt and degraded as possible.'

∽

'You know what cogent reason I have to feel *with* you; but I can feel *for* you too,' he wrote on 3 December to Henry Willink, master of Magdalene, whose wife had just died. 'I know that what you are facing must be worse than what I must shortly face myself because your happiness has lasted so much longer and is, therefore, so much more intertwined with your whole life.'

∽

'I'm not as well as I was, a few new spots in my bones and lumps here and there,' wrote Joy on 15 December to her former husband, 'but so far they melt away beautifully before X-rays.'

'Despite the terrible news of which I told you, we hobble along wonderfully well,' he wrote on 22 December to Shelburne. 'I am ashamed (yet in a way pleased) to tell you that it is Joy who supports me rather than I her.'

'Can one without presumption even ask for a *second* miracle?' he wrote on 15 December to Milward.

∽ 1960 ∽

'The ghastly, daily grind of unavoidable letters leaves me a brain and hand very ill disposed to pleasanter and friendlier correspondence,' wrote Lewis from Magdalene on 17 January to Gebbert. 'For example, it is now 9.50 a.m., and I've already been writing letters as hard as I can drive the pen across the page for an hour and a half; and when on earth I shall get a chance to begin my own day's work, I don't know.'

&

'I need not say that your article on the Narnian books gave me much pleasure,' he wrote on 21 January to John Warwick Montgomery who had sent him a copy of his article on the *Chronicles* as they pertained to the adolescent reader. 'I had thought of children rather than adolescents as my readers, but have found (which confirms your view) that they are read also by schoolboys.'

&

'You could not have chosen a better present,' Lewis wrote on 31 January to Schofield. 'My wife (who is an American) loves maple syrup and, as it is a pretty rare commodity, her heart leapt up as yours and mine would at the sight of white man's food in the depths of China.'

&

'It looks as if we shall after all be able to manage a lightning air trip to Greece, which was arranged in happier times,' he wrote on 13 February to Shelburne. The Greens had made just such a trip in April last year; when June and Roger described to the Lewises their peregrinations in the land of Apollo and Aphrodite, Joy said she wanted to go. Jack agreed; the Greens made reservations for a Wings tour that would depart in April. 'It would mean a great deal to both of us to have stood even once on the Acropolis.'

&

'If you want people to weep by the end, make them laugh in the beginning,' he wrote on 7 March to Milward, congratulating the young Jesuit on his ordination in Tokyo, and offering him some advice on preaching. 'I hope your priesthood will be blessed.'

&

'I sometimes feel I am mad to be taking Joy to Greece in her present condition, but her heart is set upon it,' wrote Lewis on 26 March to Shelburne. Latest X-rays showed cancer advancing on his wife's skeleton. As soon as radiation eradicated one lump, another lump appeared. But she was in pain only occasionally; almost always she was cheerful. 'They give the condemned man what he likes for his last breakfast, I am told.'

&

The Lewises were the first to arrive at London airport on Sunday 3 April. Morris had been hired to drive them; Douglas went along for the ride and to wave them goodbye. Soon the Greens and a couple of dozen others on the Wings tour appeared. They all climbed into the Viking Hunter Clan, which laboured on take-off and staggered through heavy weather. With intermediate stops at Lyons, Naples, and Brindisi, the aircraft finally settled down in Athens after midnight. First venture into the vernacular secured for them the Greek word for 'wheelchair.' With the Hotel Cosmopolis as their base for the next few days, they explored ancient Athens, climbing to the Acropolis and Parthenon where, standing between fluted pillars that were old when Britain was young, they looked down on modern Athens.

On Wednesday 6 April the Lewises and the Greens absented themselves from the tour and took a limousine, which drove them past classical ruins and Byzantine churches, through groves and vineyards, to the Gulf of Corinth, where they repaired to a taverna by the shore. Ouzo was poured; pickled octopus was served. There followed, in no particular hurry, red mullets just snatched from the blue waters of the gulf, fried in olive oil, and fillets of squid. For hours they sat conversing and contemplating, cicadas susurring in the sunlight. 'A supreme day,' said Lewis to Green.

On Thursday 7 April they flew to the island of Rhodes, where the Greens climbed aggressively to the Citadel and the Lewises sauntered slowly about the villages. It was 'an earthly paradise — all orange and lemon orchards and wildflowers and vines and olives, and the mountains of Asia on the horizon.' Joy knew she was dying; Jack knew she was dying; but when they heard the shepherds' flutes filtering down from the hills, 'it seemed to make no difference.' On Sunday, which was Easter, they visited the Orthodox cathedral. After lunch, they caught a plane for Crete. Dinner was not available at their hotel, so they set out for the harbourside. There at the Glass House they waited to be seated; once seated, they waited to order; once they had ordered, they waited to be served. The musicians were loud and smiling and seemingly unstoppable. Joy broke some bread, pinched the pieces into pellets, and flicked them with ferocity if not accuracy at the nearest musician.

To immortalize the moment, Jack suggested they compose a poem. He would start with the first line, and each in turn would have to add a line. Iambic pentameter with rhyme; couplets, if you please.

A pub crawl through the glittering isles of Greece,
I wish it left my ears a moment's peace!
If once the crashing Cretans ceased to bore,
The drums of England would resist no more.
No more they *can* resist. For mine are broken!
To this Curetes' shields were but a token,
Our cries in silence still above the noise —

> He has been hit by a good shot of Joy's!
> What aim! What strength! What purpose and what poise!

On Wednesday 13 April the party flew from Crete to Pisa, and the following day they flew to London. Morris was awaiting them with his car; he drove them north to the Kilns as fast as the law allowed. Both Lewises were exhausted; Joy was in pain. She had brought little medication with her on the trip, but she managed to keep the pain at a tolerable level by frequent and generous drafts of ouzo and Chianti, of the wine of Nemea called Lion's blood and Minos wine just off the wood.

〰

'It is indeed an occasion for disgust, but nothing to worry about,' wrote Lewis on 3 May to Jane Douglass. She had heard George MacDonald, his disciple C. S. Lewis, and Christianity attacked in a lecture at Yale University by Robert Lee Wolff. 'The "smuthounds" have done this to author after author, but the libels are soon fogotten, and the authors remain where they were.'

〰

Joy hadn't died with a bang on the steps of the Parthenon as she half-suspected she might, but new X-rays revealed that the cancer had spread while she was away. 'Joy's cancer has returned,' wrote Lewis on 16 April to Vanauken, 'and the doctors hold out no hope.' 'Pray for us,' he wrote on 19 April to Shelburne; 'the sky grows very dark.'

She was well enough on the morning of 25 April for him to make an appointment at the Bird and Baby where he was greeted warmly and ushered towards the glowing grate.

'There was a new waiter being instructed in a hotel by an old waiter as to his duties,' he said, launching into a story before they could ask about his wife's health. 'And the most important thing, my boy, is tact.'

'How do you mean, tact?' asked the new waiter.

'Well, I'll give you an example,' said the old waiter. 'A few days ago I went up to the bathroom to leave a fresh cake of soap — and there was a lady in the bath, who had forgotten to lock the door. So I said, "A fresh cake of soap, sir," and went straight out as if nothing were wrong.'

'How are you getting on,' asked the old waiter a week or two later, 'particularly in the matter of tact?'

'Oh, splendidly,' answered the young waiter. 'I'll give you an example. A few mornings ago I took a tray of tea into the bridal suite, and there were the bride and bridegroom in bed together — in the very act. So I put down the tray by the bed and said, as I turned to go, "Your early morning tea, gentlemen." '

On Saturday 14 May the Lewises entertained the Nickolas Zernovs at the Kilns; Joy dressed for tea and was crocheting a quilt when the guests arrived. But on 19 May she was returned to the hospital, where on the following morning her right breast was removed. The surgeon seemed pleased with the result, the cancer having been stemmed at least in that one area.

∽

'Don't bother about thinking *quickly*,' wrote Lewis on 5 June to the Rev. Brian D. Doud of Fort Matilde, Pennsylvania. 'People who think *clearly* will come in the end to think quickly, but people who think quickly do not necessarily come to think clearly.'

∽

'No, I'm afraid I'm not even an Anglo-Catholic,' he wrote on 17 June to a correspondent; 'I'm a Protestant.'

∽

When the day nurse at the Kilns had completed Joy's toilette on the morning of Tuesday 14 June, she greeted Warren warmly. He rolled her wheelchair first to the library and then outside and up the slope to the pond. On the way down she looked at a flower bed and paused in the greenhouse. No, she didn't want anything to eat; she seemed to have indigestion. On Thursday she surprised Warren with a dozen handkerchiefs for his sixty-fifth birthday. The indigestion worsened, causing her to want to retch; gastric infection, diagnosed the doctor; there was a lot of that going around. On Friday she cancelled the end-of-term trip to Cambridge, which she had planned to make on Saturday. On Saturday she cancelled the taxi that would take her and Jack to Studley Priory for dinner on Sunday. She couldn't sleep on Sunday night, again trying to throw off what was disturbing her intestinally. Jack stayed up with her, doing what he could to help, holding the tray for her; nothing but saliva was coming up.

'This is the end, I know I'm dying,' she said to the day nurse. 'Telegraph Doug.'

'I've got enough cancers now to form a trades union of the damned things,' said Joy to the doctor who had come to give her an injection. 'Finish me off quick; I won't have another operation.'

The ambulance arrived at 4.00 p.m., and Jack rode with her to the hospital. David arrived from Dane Court; Warren met him at the foot of the drive and posted him on his mother's condition. Douglas arrived later, having been driven from Montgomeryshire, Wales, by the headmaster of Ludley Grange; he broke into tears at the news.

On watch in her room at the Radcliffe Infirmary, Jack began a sonnet: 'All this is flashy rhetoric about loving you . . .'

∽

'A spiteful or merely jocular journalist would certainly make us for a week or two malodorous in the public nostril,' he wrote on 17 June to Willink, master of Magdalene, who was trying to decide whether the diary of Samuel Pepys, which was about to be published, should be expurgated or unexpurgated. 'But a few weeks, or years, are nothing in the life of the college. I think it would be pusillanimous and unscholarly to delete a syllable on that score.'

∽

On Monday 27 June Joy returned to the Kilns, looking rested and refreshed. On Sunday 3 July she and Jack were driven to Studley Priory for dinner, which she seemed to enjoy. On Monday 4 July she was taken by Hibbie the nurse for a drive through the nearby Cotswolds. But by Tuesday her energy ebbed, her shoulders ached. For the next week she couldn't get out of bed.

∽

They had done the crossword during the day; in the evening they were about to embark on Scrabble when Warren appeared, bearing the last cups of tea of the day. Late into the tranquil night husband and wife talked, nourishing each other's loves and fears. She was dying, and he was dying with her.

'If you can, if it is allowed, come to me when I too am on my deathbed.'

'Allowed! Heaven would have a job to hold me,' she said; 'and as for Hell, I'd break it into bits!'

Early the next morning, Warren awoke with a start. In the room below him Joy was screaming. But she never screamed, he thought as he careered down the stairs. The pain was in her stomach, she said. Warren ran upstairs and woke his brother, who telephoned the doctor. Before seven the doctor had arrived and given her a heavy shot. The pain was probably coming from the spine, the doctor said, not the stomach. Jack pleaded with the doctor to admit her to the Radcliffe Infirmary. The doctor agreed; the ambulance arrived before Joy was ready for the trip.

It was only a matter of hours, perhaps even of minutes before the end would come. Did Lewis want to tell his wife, asked the doctor, or should they keep the information to themselves?

No, said Jack, he'd tell her.

It was good news, not bad, she said.

The doctor's instructions were to keep the woman as comfortable as possible until the end came.

'Don't get me a posh coffin,' she murmured as the afternoon wore on; 'posh coffins are all rot.'

'We humbly commend the soul of this thy servant, our dear sister, into thy hands,' read Austin Farrer over Joy; he had come when Jack called.

Yes, he would officiate at the crematorium, he said when she asked.

'You have made me happy,' she said to Jack as the afternoon became evening.

He thought she was gone, but she said, to no one in the room, 'I am at peace with God.'

At ten o'clock or thereabouts she heaved a great sigh; another; a third, and she was gone.

How was he getting home? asked the infirmary. Morris; Lewis told them to call Clifford Morris. It was a short drive to the Kilns; Morris drove slowly; Lewis stayed for a while and talked with his gentleman driver.

'What news?' asked Warren, emerging from his bath; it was 11.40 p.m.

'She died about twenty minutes ago,' said Lewis, having lost all track of time.

'God rest her soul.'

❧

That night Lewis dreamed so vividly that he felt he was still awake; on Thursday morning he walked around the Kilns as though he were still asleep. He didn't want to read or write or even talk.

'What do we do now?' asked Douglas.

'I suppose we carry on somehow,' he said, hugging his stepson.

He did force himself to write to the vicar at Holy Trinity, asking for his prayers and the prayers of his congregation for the repose of the soul of Helen Joy Lewis.

On Friday morning he felt somewhat better. He was able, if not eager, to sit down at his writing table. 'Alas, you will never send anything along "for the three of us" again,' he wrote to Gebbert, "for my dear Joy is dead.' 'I can't describe the apparent unreality of my life since [Wednesday],' he wrote to Shelburne. 'Joy died on the 13th July,' he wrote to Gresham; 'this need make no change in your plans, but I thought you should arrive knowing it.'

❧

On Monday 18 July the Lewises and the two boys emerged from the Kilns at 11.15 and climbed into a taxi. Mollie Miller and her husband Len, Hibbie the nurse, and Wilk the housekeeper boarded a second taxi. It was a sunny day, wind strong, clouds racing. The cars rolled down Kiln Lane; at the roundabout they fell in behind the hearse. At the Headington Crematorium the Farrers greeted them when they arrived. The chapel was non-sectarian, austere if not sterile. There was no music, but there was sunlight. 'I am the resurrection and the life, saith the Lord,' read Farrer from the Book of Common Prayer as soon as he saw that no one else was coming. He prayed with emotion and several times was nearly overcome. When he finished, the coffin rolled from sight. Joy was still there — Jack felt her presence vividly even as her cold remains were being reduced to warm ash, and so did Warren. Their father had lingered after death, they remembered, and so had Williams.

❧

'No one ever told me that grief felt so like fear,' he scribbled into an empty notebook. 'I am not afraid, but the sensation is like being afraid. The same fluttering in the stomach, the same restlessness, the yawning. I keep on yawning . . .'

'Her mind was lithe and quick and muscular as a leopard,' he sat down to write again. 'Passion, tenderness, and pain were all equally unable to disarm it. It scented the first whiff of cant or slush; then sprang, and knocked you over before you knew what was happening . . .'

'I have no photograph of her that's any good,' he wrote again. 'I cannot even see her face distinctly in my imagination . . . But her voice is still vivid. The remembered voice — that can turn me at any moment to a whimpering child.'

❧

It was a week since Joy died; he hadn't heard from Coghill or Dyson or the Tolkiens, friends of his he might have expected to call; when the telephone revealed an American who wanted to visit, he accepted. The Eastgate it was, on the morrow. He hadn't seen Starr for ten years or so; he had never met his wife. Introductions in the dark parlour were warm enough; beer was ordered; the Starrs said they were on their way to Bayreuth where they would see *Parsifal*. Lewis told them what they already knew, his fondness of Wagner, romance, nothernness. As Nathan chattered about the forthcoming meeting of the International Arthurian Society in Brittany, Nina snapped away with her camera. Then Lewis told them of his wife, her death, her two sons, now his stepsons, and what a new and sad life it was going to be.

❧

'Today I had to meet a man I haven't seen for ten years,' he wrote in a second notebook, the first one having been filled. 'And all the time I had thought I was remembering him well — how he looked and spoke and the sort of things he did. The first five minutes of the real man shattered the image completely. Not that he had changed. On the contrary. I kept on thinking, "yes, of course, of course. I'd forgotten that he thought that, or disliked this, or knew so-and-so, or jerked his head back that way.' I had known all these things once, and I recognized them the moment I saw them again. But they had faded out of my mental picture of him, and when they were all replaced by his actual presence, the total effect was quite astonishingly different from the image I had carried about with me for those ten years. How can I hope that this will not happen to my memory of Joy?'

※

'She loved you both very much,' wrote Lewis on 22 July to the Farrers, telling them also that Joy had left her fur coat to Kay, 'and getting to know you both better is one of the many permanent gains I have got for my short married life.'

※

'I wonder do we blame TV and the comics too much?' he wrote on 18 August to the Rev. B. Ginder of Old St. Mary's, a Catholic seminary in Baltimore, Maryland. 'Was not a certain sort of boy in a certain sort of home wasting his time just as badly in other ways before they were invented? It annoys me when parents who read nothing but the newspapers themselves — i.e. nothing but lies, libels, poppycock, propaganda, and pornography — complain of their children reading the comics! Upon my soul, I think the children's diet is healthier than their parents'!'

※

'I cannot talk to the children about her,' he wrote again in the quiet of the Kilns. 'The moment I try, there appears on their faces neither grief, nor love, nor fear, nor pity, but the most fatal of all non-conductors, embarrassment. They look as if I were committing an indecency. They are longing for me to stop. I felt just the same after my own mother's death when my father mentioned her. I can't blame them. It's the way boys are.'

※

He began to read again. *Rider Haggard: His Life and Works* by Morten Cohen he found excellent. It even moved him to write a short piece for *Time and Tide*. Even though Haggard's writing style was nil and his philosophy a hotchpotch, his openings were full of alluring promise, promise that was kept by triumphant catastrophe. What kept winning new readers to his works was 'the story itself, the myth. Haggard [was] the textbook case of the mythopoeic gift pure and simple.'

'For the first time I have looked back and read these notes,' he began in a third notebook. 'They appal me. From the way I've been talking, anyone would think that Joy's death mattered chiefly for its effect on myself. Her point of view seems to have dropped out of sight. Have I forgotten the moment of bitterness when she cried out, "And there was so much to live for"? . . .

'Is it rational to believe in a bad God? Anyway, in a God so bad as all that? The cosmic sadist, the spiteful imbecile? . . .'

∽

The next book he picked up was *The Phenomenon of Man* by Pierre Teilhard de Chardin, a French Jesuit priest and anthropologist, which had been published in England the year before with an introduction by Julian Huxley and which spoke of such things as Christogenesis and cosmogenesis. 'How right your society was to shut up de Chardin!' he wrote on 21 September to Frederick J. Adlemann, an American Jesuit priest who had invited him to give a lecture series at Boston College. 'The enormous boosts he is getting from scientists who are very hostile to you,' he wrote on 26 September to Milward, the Jesuit in Tokyo, 'seem to me very like the immense popularity of Pasternak among anti-Communists. I can't for the life of me see his merit.'

∽

'The agonies, the mad midnight moments, must in the course of nature, die away,' he wrote in the third notebook. 'But what will follow? Just this apathy, this dead flatness? Will there come a time when I no longer ask why the world is like a mean street because I shall take the squalor as normal? Does grief finally subside into boredom and fatigue? . . .

'She was my daughter and my mother, my pupil and my teacher, my subject and my sovereign; and always, holding all these in solution, my trusty comrade, friend, shipmate, fellow-soldier. My mistress; but at the same time all that any man friend (and I have good ones) has ever been to me. Perhaps more. If we had never fallen in love, we should have nonetheless been always together, and created a scandal . . .'

'Tonight all the hells of young grief have opened again; the mad words, the bitter resentment, the fluttering in the stomach, the nightmare unreality, the wallowed-in tears . . .'

∽

At the beginning of September he invited Green to spend a few days at the Kilns. He showed his young friend and future biographer the notebooks he had filled with random thoughts. Green immediately thought of publication. Lewis didn't want that; his only purpose was to exorcise the grief that was bedevilling him. What about publication under an assumed name? asked Green. After all, Lewis already had one, N. W., Nat Whilk, Anglo-Saxon for 'I know not whom,' which he had been using in *Punch* and elsewhere. The only thing Lewis would have to do with the manuscript, besides having it typed, would be to change the names. Lewis said he would think about it.

❦

'This is the fourth — and last — empty manuscript book I can find in the house,' he wrote after Green had gone. 'I resolve to let this limit my jottings. I *will not* start buying books for the purpose. Insofar as this record was a defence against total collapse, a safety valve, it has done some good . . .

'Today I have been revisiting my old haunts, taking one of the long rambles that made me so happy in my bachelor days. And this time the face of nature was not emptied of its beauty and the world didn't look (as I complained some days ago) like a mean street . . .

'It doesn't matter that all the photographs of Joy are bad. It doesn't matter — not much — if my memory of her is imperfect. Images, whether on paper or in the mind, are not important for themselves. Merely links . . .'

❦

'Thank you very much for the photos,' he wrote on 1 November to Nina Starr. 'I can't judge the likeness of myself, of course, but if I've come out as well as Nathan, it must be very good. Your own absence from the group is much to be regretted. *Whose was the third glass?* might well be engineered into a research question!'

❦

At 4.00 p.m. on Thursday 24 November he left Magdalene and walked towards Milton Street. He had been invited to tea by H. C. Chang, who had translated a chinese allegory into English in 1952 and who had published a fairly sensible book entitled *Allegory and Courtesy in Spenser* in 1955. The roundabout at Mitcham's corner was murderous; Lewis had to dance through the traffic to avoid being hit. They had corresponded when Chang was lecturer in English at the University of Malaya in Singapore; when not many months before he was appointed lecturer in Chinese at Cambridge, he renewed the acquaintance in person.

At Chang's, Lewis bowed to the family and was introduced to several guests, Miss Hiro Ishibaski among them. Ever since he heard Lewis describe himself in his inaugural lecture as Old Western man, said Chang, he had considered himself as the example of old Eastern or old Chinese man. Mrs Chang asked that she be excused if she burst into tears; she was just recovering from a long bout of postnatal depression. He too had been subject to fits of tears, said Lewis to comfort her. Once, when he had completed a particularly difficult examination, seemingly for no reason, he began to blubber in a most embarrassing way. Even now, he said, reaching for his handkerchief, tears seemed to come without warning . . .

❧ 1961 ❧

'We do now have a decent spare room with a double bed nearly as broad as it's long,' wrote Lewis on 25 January to Greeves, who was planning a vacation in England. 'Or, if it is term time, this college has a good guest suite, sitting-room as well as bedroom (with TV), and you can have breakfast in it by yourself unshaved at any hour you like.'

'I have done, and am doing, what I can for her with advice and a little money,' he wrote on 17 February to Hugh Kilmer about Aunt Mary Willis Shelburne. 'But a little help and friendship from co-religionists on the spot is badly needed. Could you or anyone in your circle — perhaps a really nice nun — get in touch with her and lend a hand?'

Ten or twenty years' abstinence both from the reading and the writing of literary criticism, wrote Lewis in *An Experiment in Criticism*, a book that Cambridge University Press planned to publish in the autumn, would do a great deal of good. He had managed to finish the manuscript the year before; now he was perusing the proofs for errors. 'Thanks for noting misprint,' he wrote to Greeves to whom he had sent a set of the proofs; 'I'm very bad at spotting them.'

'For meditative and devotional reading (a little bit at a time, more like sucking a lozenge than eating a slice of bread), I suggest *The Imitation of Christ* (astringent) and Traherne's *Centuries of Meditation* (joyous),' he wrote on 9 May to Margaret Gray. 'For Christian morals I suggest my wife's (Joy Davidman) *Smoke on the Mountain*; Gore's

The Sermon on the Mount and (perhaps) his *Philosophy of the Good Life*. And possibly (but with a grain of salt, for he is too puritanical), William Law's *Serious Call to a Devout and Holy Life*. I know the title makes one shudder, but we have both got a lot of shuddering to get through before we're done!'

∽

'*Lady Chatterly* has made short work of a prosecution by the Crown,' he wrote. 'It still has to face more formidable judges. Nine of them, and all goddesses.' Lawrence's novel had been published in a limited edition in Florence in 1929 and in Paris in 1932. It was published in London in 1932 with the tabooed sex words deleted. In unexpurgated form the novel was published in New York in 1959; in 1960, after *Regina versus Penguin Books Limited*, it was published in London with all the tabooed sex words intact. That Lawrence's vocabulary constituted a grave moral danger, was not upheld in the court. But Lewis couldn't agree with certain literary critics that the vocabulary constituted a reverential and enthusiastic treatment of sex. To confirm this view, he decided to check the history of the four-letter, or obscene, word. Perusing the glossary of Skeat's edition of Chaucer, he found eight words, which were used in a variety of contexts. Thumbing through Lewis and Short's *Latin Dictionary*, he found five words used in the poetry of Horace, Martial, Catullus, and Apuleius. Fingering Liddell and Scott's *Greek-English Lexicon*, he found seven words, almost all of which were used in the plays of Aristophanes, where one could find 'a four-letter word about once in every twenty lines.' Not once did he find a four-letter word used seriously in erotic or lyric poetry; each usage was intended to provoke belly laughter or snarls of hatred. 'Lawrence's usage is not reckoned a return to nature from some local or recent inhibition,' he wrote for publication in *The Critical Quarterly*. 'It is, for good or ill, as artificial, as remote from the linguistic soil, as Euphuism or, a closer comparison, the most desperate parts of *Lyrical Ballads*. Here, as in them, the words may be earthy, but the use of them is not. It is a rebellion against language.'

∽

On the morning of Thursday 22 June Lewis hurried outside the Kilns to climb into the taxi he had hired. He wished Morris had been able to make the round trip to and from London; he was almost a member of the family. Instead, his Jehu of the day was a talkative person who, if he hadn't been such a bore, Lewis would gladly take with him into a hotel dining-room for lunch. Instead, he made sandwiches and brought them along. If all were known, his indigestion recently had been so severe that he wanted to make sure he had something bland for lunch.

In London he directed the driver to Ealing Broadway under-ground station. There, at noon, near the refreshment room he found Greeves. As they settled into the back of the car for the drive to Oxford, Lewis unwrapped the sandwiches and uncapped the bottles of beer. What kind of disease was 'hunt poggines', he asked, and how long had Arthur been suffering from it? 'Heart grogginess,' said Greeves; his handwriting couldn't have been that bad. Palpitations, breathlessness, that sort of thing.

At the Kilns they had the house to themselves; Warren was in Ireland on vacation. Mrs Miller did the honours at dinner on Thursday and Friday evenings. On Saturday, Greeves returned to London, noting, however, that his friend did not look at all well; in fact, he looked very ill.

◎

'The trouble turns out to be (what's very common to our age and sex) a distended prostate gland,' he wrote on Friday 30 June to Greeves. 'I go into the Acland Nursing Home on Sunday for the operation.' On Monday morning, however, the doctors didn't oper-ate. Samples of fluids taken from his body the night before indicated that his kidneys and heart may have been damaged, and his blood count was not normal. Until his biochemistry was stabilized, it would not be safe to operate. No, he couldn't go home; he should stay in the hospital for observation and continued testing. Suddenly he was without energy. Warren brought his mail each day, but he was capable of giving no more than a comment on each piece. 'I saw him yesterday and mentioned that a letter had arrived from you,' wrote Warren on 12 July to Shelburne, 'and he asked me to explain why there will be no answer to it for quite a time.' Shelburne demanded to know more. 'He is, so far as a sick man can be, in the best of spirits, eating well, hungry,' wrote Warren on 20 August, 'and what we all take to be a splendid sign, is beginning to complain of being *bored*.'

◎

Was the Devil 'personal' or 'corporeal'? a working man wanted to know. Did magistrates administer justice 'indifferently' as the old Prayer Book said, or 'impartially' as the revisers of the Psalter wanted to say? a sexton in a country church wanted to know. Before trying to communicate with either party, and indeed before a person tried to communicate with Christianity or the world at large, he or she had better find out the specific meanings of all key words. In other words, he wrote for publication in the October issue of *Breakthrough*, the communicator had to 'listen and note and memorize.'

'I am awaiting an operation on my prostate,' he wrote in September to Green; 'but as this trouble upsets my kidneys and my heart, these have to be set right before the surgeon can get to work.' His movements were restricted to the ground floor of the Kilns. Protein was eliminated from his diet. He slept in a chair, the better for the urine to flow through the catheter. 'Jack has had a series of blood transfusions in hospital,' wrote Warren on 7 October to Shelburne, who was impatient for news, 'and the result was that he came home a week ago most definitely improved.' He could eat a hearty breakfast now; he went out each day for half an hour's walk. But return to Cambridge for the Michaelmas term was out of the question. 'I grow quite homesick for college,' he wrote on 9 October to Ladborough, 'and very much hope that, though not good for much, I'll be allowed back in January.' But his kidneys were not functioning well; they continued to contaminate his blood supply. 'I'll write more, but I've just had a blood transfusion and am feeling drowsy,' he wrote on 21 October to Raine; 'Dracula must have led a horrid life!'

⁓

'The most important thing is to *keep on*, not to be dismayed however often one yields to the temptation, but always to pick yourself up again and ask forgiveness,' he wrote on 13 October to Harvey Karlsen, a senior at Fort Hamilton High School, Brooklyn, New York, who had read *The Screwtape Letters* and accepted Jesus Christ as his personal saviour. 'In reviewing your sins don't either exaggerate them or minimize them. Call them by their ordinary names and try to see them as you would see the same faults in somebody else — no special blackening or whitewashing.'

⁓

'I always thought Herbert Read an ass,' he wrote on 24 November to Greeves after reading Read's review of *An Experiment in Criticism* in the 16 November issue of *The Listener*, 'so I don't know whether to conclude that my book is bilge or to revise my opinion of H.R.'

⁓

'By all means let us have an end to acrimony,' wrote the anonymous reviewer in the 3 November issue of *The Times Literary Supplement*, assessing Lewis' *An Experiment in Criticism*. Lewis had opposed his own view — that literary criticism did not much help the appreciation of a literary work — to the view often expressed by F. R. Leavis of Cambridge University — that 'all the great names in English literature — except for the half-dozen protected by the momentary critical 'establishment' — are as so many lamp posts for a dog.' Lewis' views were not so far from Leavis', noted the *TLS* reviewer; 'if the critical alliance is led by a compound figure, it does not matter whether we call him C. S. Leavis or F. R. Lewis.'

∽

'The real question is whether a murderer is more likely to repent and make a good end three weeks hence in the execution shed or, say, thirty years later in the prison infirmary,' he wrote in a letter to the *Church Times*, contributing to the debate on capital punishment. 'No mortal can know.'

∽

'I prayed when I buried my wife, my whole sexual nature should be buried with her, and it seems to have happened,' he wrote on 20 December to Griffiths. 'Thus one recurrent trial has vanished from my life — an enormous liberty. Of course, this may only be old age . . .'

∽

'Thank you very much for your kind and most cheering letter. I cannot tell you how much I appreciate your kind interest in the whole matter.' Lewis had written to Cecil Roth, reader in post-biblical Jewish studies at Oxford, about his stepson. David, it seemed, was becoming interested in his Jewish heritage, associated with Jewish undergraduates although he was still in Magdalen Day School, and was visiting the Roths' house on Sabbath afternoons; he found Orthodox belief attractive, was teaching himself Yiddish, and was even experimenting with Hasidic garb; but he had not yet confided in his stepfather. 'If David opens out and gives me the least encouragement, I'll try to say something much as you suggested. Otherwise it would be like trying to open an oyster with a paper knife.'

∽ **1962** ∽

'I seemed to have turned a bio-chemical corner,' he wrote in January to Green, 'and shall soon be ready for the surgical one.'

'No later than a week ago we were going to ask you down,' he dictated to Warren on 29 January, and Warren typed to Vera Gebbert, who was visiting London with her son, 'when, alas, I got the bad news that my blood count had fallen back; which means another course of blood transfusions.'

'Locomotion, as well as protein, is one of the things I must cut down to a minimum,' he wrote in March to Green.

During the waking moments of his convalescence, he was able to read *War and Peace*, the *Odyssey*, *Modern Painters*, *The Prelude*, and *Orlando Furioso*. The best new spiritual reading he came across, he told Sister Penelope, was *No Man Is an Island* by an American Trappist named Thomas Merton. *World's Apart*, which Barfield sent him, he found so exciting that he read it 'far too quickly.'

༄

At the end of March he was still not healthy enough to undergo the prostate operation. If he took the medication as prescribed, continued the low-protein diet, and avoided stair-climbing as much as possible, he could go to Cambridge for the beginning of Easter term. Collecting his papers and books before going from one level to another was like 'planning an expedition to the North Pole or central Africa,' but he managed the experiment with increasing aplomb.

'You need not sympathize too much,' he wrote on 25 May to Eliot; 'if my condition keeps me from doing some things I like, it also excuses me from doing a good many things I don't.' The commission on revising the Prayer Book Psalter continued during Easter term with Eliot and the others; it was 'delightful work with delightful colleagues,' he wrote on 23 June to Sister Penelope, and he was learning a lot.

Vacation in Ireland, however, was out of the question because of the tubes and pouches, which needed continued and professional maintenance. 'I need to be near a lifeline,' he wrote on 18 June to Greeves; 'the plumbing often goes wrong.' 'I am now as convalescent as (apparently) I am ever likely to be,' he wrote on 30 June to Vanauken; 'loneliness increases as health returns.'

༄

'In my opinion [*The Pilgrim's Progress*] would be immeasurably weakened as a work of art if the flames of Hell were not always flickering on the horizon,' he read into the BBC microphone; he was recording for broadcast in October a programme entitled 'The Vision of John Bunyan.' 'I do not mean merely that if they were not, it would cease to be true to Bunyan's own vision and would therefore suffer all the effects which a voluntary distortion or expurgation of experience might be expected to produce. I mean also that the image of this is necessary to us while we read. The urgency, the harsh woodcut energy, the continual sense of momentousness, depend on it.'

༄

In July Masefield wrote to ask if he would serve on a committee that would survey the work of modern poets and eventually award a prize. The most modern poets he read for pleasure, he replied, were Masefield himself and Walter de la Mare. How ironic it was that Lewis should know less about the moderns than Masefield, who was twenty years his senior; perhaps they were like apples in a barrel, decaying at different rates.

In July also he was putting the finishing touches on the manuscript of *The Discarded Image* and wrote the preface. For some years now, he had been asked to put into book form the lectures prolegomena to the study of medieval and Renaissance literature, which he had given at Oxford. A nice touch, he thought, was dedicating the work to Roger Lancelyn Green, who in 1938 sat in the front row of the hall and whose pocket-watch Lewis plucked off the pupil's desk and plunked down on the lectern, to be returned only as he walked from the hall at the end of the lecture.

∽

Supine in bed, he was prone to dream. Medication served only to make the nocturnal productions more elaborate. One of these had to do with Purgatory, which in the light of day he considered, if not a doctrinal necessity, then at least an aesthetic need. In the dark of night he envisioned 'a great big kitchen in which things are always going wrong — milk boiling over, crockery getting smashed, toast burning, animals stealing.' That was Purgatory, he knew, because 'the women had to learn to sit still and mind their own business'; because 'the men have to learn to jump up and do something about it.' He put this down in a letter of 31 July to Shelburne; he explained it to Pitter when she came to call at the Kilns on 15 August. The drug visions left nothing behind, he surmised, but the real ones, though equally transitory, seemed to contain glints of the future. Indeed the purgatorial dream was an everpresent reality. Making breakfast for himself, something he had done with pleasure for decades, was now a nightmare. Not being able to put the lid properly on the kettles was enough to send him into a rage.

∽

'Certainly I shall be happy to see you when you visit England,' he wrote in July to Walter Hooper of the University of Kentucky. 'But I feel very strongly that a man is ill advised to write a book on any living author.'

∽

'I am in favour of your idea that we should go back to our old plan of having a more or less set subject — an *agendum* — for our letters,' wrote Lewis to one of his friends. 'Prayer, which you suggest, is a subject that is a good deal in my mind. I mean, private prayer. If you were thinking of corporate prayer, I won't play. There is no subject in the world (always excepting sport) on which I have less to say than liturgiology . . .'

Lewis had read Loyola and De Sales and indeed drew some fruit from *Spiritual Exercises* and *Introduction to the Devout Life*, but no one in the history of ascetic literature had written a book for middle-aged, middle-class academics. He had attempted such a project several times before. This time, with *Screwtape* as a model, he thought he could succeed.

First he invented an *alter ego*, Malcolm, a person with whom he would have corresponded since undergraduate days on such topics as Plato's *Republic*, classical metres, and the new psychology. By 1962 Malcolm has been married for twenty-five years; what Betty lacked in intellectuality, she more than made up for with practicality; their son George, Lewis would reveal in the course of the correspondence, had been cured from a severe gastric ailment — was it miraculously? — after a siege of petitionary prayer.

Like De Sales and Loyola before him, Lewis had to discuss the mechanics of prayer. When? Any time; at the end of the afternoon; just before dinner; never before bedtime. Where? Never in a church; churches are too cold nine months of the year; in the other three, there was either a woman in rubber boots swabbing the sanctuary floor or a mad organist practising in the loft. In what position? It mattered not a whit whether the orant knelt, sat, or stood, for it mattered not to the Person prayed to.

At the beginning of each meditation De Sales suggested that the meditand should put himself into the presence of God; an easy task for a peasant, wrote Lewis, but for intellectuals like himself and Malcolm, this was an intricate, if not an impossible task. Loyola recommended that the meditand should transport himself to the geographical and historical locale where the mystery took place; this piece of advice Lewis thought helpful only to the archaeologically inspired or the imaginatively impaired, neither of which he or Malcolm was.

There was something theatrical about prayer. A person appeared on the stage of life as an actor, strutting back and forth, mouthing words of a character created by another. Underneath the costume and the grease paint was a person who lived a real life in a real world. It was not necessary to leave the stage to pray, wrote Lewis to his imaginary friend, but it was necessary from time to time to remember that one was indeed acting. 'This situation is, at every moment, a possible theophany. Here is holy ground; the Bush is burning now.'

In the course of the letters Lewis elucidated two kinds of prayer, the prayer of adoration and the prayer of petition. There would be consolation and desolation, the one following the other as surely as waves hitting a shore. He would even reveal his practice of festooning, garlanding some formula like the Lord's Prayer with all sorts of personalized reflections and particularized petitions.

'Thank Betty for her note,' he wrote in the last paragraph of the twenty-second letter. 'I'll come by the later train, the 3.40. And tell her not to bother about a bed on the ground floor. I can manage stairs again now, provided I take them "in bottom." Till Saturday.'

∽

Reading *Margin Released*, which had been sent to him by Heinemann's, provoked a flood of memories about boarding schools, broadcasting at the BBC during the war, and acquaintances like George Gordon; on 12 September he wrote a letter of appreciation to J. B. Priestley, whose reminiscences and reflections they were. Priestley replied on the 17th, apologizing for the publisher's having imposed on him for a prepublication quote, and inviting him for a visit. It was not an imposition in this case, replied Lewis on the 18th; he went on to deplore the direction that the study of literature had taken at Oxford and Cambridge; F. R. Leavis was the villain; he seemed to control the intellectual press. A visit would indeed be nice if only his health did not prohibit it.

∽

When asked to contribute an article on 'Medieval Romance' to *The Catholic Encyclopedia*, he refused. When the editors of *Christianity Today* asked him, one among a number of scholars, to write a paragraph about the chief obstacle to the advance of Christianity, which they would print in their 12 October issue, he accepted. 'Next to the prevalent materialism, for which we are not to blame, I think the great obstacle lies in the dissentiences not only between Christians but between splinter groups within denominations. While the name 'Christianity' covers a hundred mutually contradictory beliefs, who can be converted to it?'

∽

'I shan't be at the festschrift dinner,' he wrote on 20 November. He had just received a very nice letter from Tolkien inviting him to celebrate the publication by Allen & Unwin of *English and Medieval Studies Presented to J. R. R. Tolkien on the Occasion of his Seventieth Birthday*, to which Lewis had contributed the chapter entitled 'The Anthropological Approach.' 'I wear a catheter, live on a low-protein diet, and go early to bed. I am, if not a lean, at least a slippered, pantaloon.'

~~~

'Would you describe Abbott's *Flatland* as science fiction?' asked Lewis. It was 4 December; Kingsley Amis and Brian Aldiss were in his rooms at Magdalene to record a conversation on science fiction, its past and its future. 'There's so little effort to bring it into any sensuous — well, you couldn't do it, and it remains an intellectual theorem.' Amis rose and moved towards the sideboard. 'Are you looking for an ashtray? Use the carpet.'

'I was looking for the Scotch, actually.'

'Oh, yes, do, I beg your pardon,' said Lewis, who tried to pick up the strand of argument. 'But probably the great work of science fiction is still to come. Futile books about the next world came before Dante, Fanny Burney came before Jane Austen, Marlowe came before Shakespeare.'

'We're getting the prolegomena,' said Amis.

'If only the modern highbrow critics could be induced to take it seriously,' said Lewis.

'Do you think they ever can?'

'No,' said Lewis, 'the whole present dynasty has got to die and rot before anything can be done at all.'

'Splendid!' said Aldiss.

'What's holding them up, do you think?'

'Matthew Arnold made the horrible prophecy that literature would increasingly replace religion,' said Lewis. 'It has, and it's taken on all the features of bitter persecution, great intolerance, and traffic in relics. All literature becomes a sacred text. A sacred text is always exposed to the most monstrous exegesis; hence we have the spectacle of some wretched scholar taking a pure *divertissement* written in the seventeenth century and getting the most profound ambiguities and social criticisms out of it, which, of course, aren't there at all . . . It's the discovery of the mare's nest by the pursuit of the red herring,' he said, to the laughter of Amis and Aldiss. 'This is going to go on long after my lifetime; you may be able to see the end of it; I shan't.'

~~~

The editor of *Show* magazine in New York had asked Lewis, as a writer who had sucessfully combined science fiction with religion, to comment on the Russian claim that, as sputniks circled the earth, the cosmonauts did not find God. 'Space travel has nothing to do with the matter. To some, God is discoverable everywhere; to others, nowhere. Those who do not find him on earth are unlikely to find him in space. (Hang it all, we're in space already; every year we go a huge circular tour in space.) But send a saint up in a spaceship, and he'll find God in space as he found God on earth. Much depends on the seeing eye . . .'

∽

'I discovered only the other day that Christmas presents had begun in the time of St Augustine, and he called them "diabolical" because they originated not in Christmas but in the pagan saturnalia,' he wrote on 10 December to Allen. ' "Diabolical" is a bit strong; perhaps "a damn nuisance" would be more accurate.'

Cards if not presents emanated from the Kilns during the Christmas season, wishing 'a happy Christmas and a very prosperous New Year.' A sleigh, two horses, and a man and woman right out of Dickens raising Pilsener glasses in toast to the season, was on the front of the card, a rendering by a member of the Mouth and Foot Painting Artists Publishing Company.

∽ 1963 ∽

Lewis woke with a start about midnight on Saturday 19 January. In some discomfort he reached for the medication at his bedside. Biscuits had a soothing effect; it was a shame that pharmacology had not discovered this. But this night the biscuits didn't help. The pain was a flaming sensation; he couldn't wait until morning for help. He telephoned his surgeon, who said the hospital could repair the damage; all he had to do was telephone for the ambulance. When he called, they said they could come, but because of deep snow on the path up to the Kilns, he would have to meet them at Kiln Lane. Swathing himself in flapping woollen things, he left the house; the snow was drifting, but the moon was full as he walked the two hundred yards to the lane. His extremities grew numb in the whistling cold; his ears had frozen into china by the time the ambulance appeared and took him to the hospital. The damage was redressed easily enough, but it was 6.00 on Sunday morning before he was back at the Kilns, defrosting under the covers.

∽

At 2.30 in the afternoon of 7 February, he had a visitor, Juliet Pannett. She had been commissioned by *The Illustrated London News* to do a likeness of Lewis. Yes, she had just come up to Cambridge on the train and no, she had no trouble finding Magdalene. To catch the fading light, she sat him down by a window and got him talking; in the next half hour she was able to pencil a number of sketches. He admired her work and offered to make tea. When he served it himself, he explained that the reason he didn't make an appointment to see her in London was that he had a heart condition and had to limit his travel. The crooked stairs to his room, she said, were enough to make even a young person's heart flutter.

⌒⌒

In the 17 March issue of *The Observer*, Lewis read an article that inflamed him. The author was John A. T. Robinson, former dean of Clare College, Cambridge, now bishop of Woolwich; his article was entitled 'Our Image of God Must Go'; it was a summary of his book *Honest to God*, which had just been published. What had to be dismissed, said Robinson, was the image of a God out there, if not up there, who came to earth like a visitor from outer space; this sort of image was just as erroneous as the bearded old God who sat on the jewelled throne in a localized heaven; perpetrators of the image, and most successfully so, were D. L. Sayers, J. B. Phillips, and C. S. Lewis. Better to err on the side of Sayers and Phillips, Lewis thought to himself, than on the side of the bishop of Woolwich. 'Must Our Image of God Go?' he wrote at the top of a piece of paper, hoping that *The Observer* would print his reply in the 24 March issue. 'We do not understand why the bishop is so anxious to canonize one image and forbid the other. We admit his freedom to use which he prefers. We claim our freedom to use both.'

The Episcopalian, the official laymen's publication of American Anglicans, wrote to Lewis to ask him for a 1,500 to 2,000-word introduction to and critique of the bishop's book. 'I should find it hard to write of such a mess with charity,' he replied on 22 April to the Rev. Edward T. Dell, Jr., associate editor of the magazine, 'nor do I want to increase his publicity.'

⌒⌒

'Professor Lewis, if you had a young friend with some interest in writing on Christian subjects, how would you advise him to prepare himself?'

'I would say if a man is going to write on chemistry, he learns chemistry. The same is true of Christianity . . .'

He was being interviewed by Sherwood E. Wirt of the Billy Graham Evangelistic Association on 7 May. Lewis remembered having a pleasant dinner with Graham during the evangelist's Cambridge crusade in November 1955.

'Can you suggest an approach that would spark the creation of a body of Christian literature strong enough to influence our generation?'

'There is no formula in these matters. I have no recipe, no tablets. Writers are trained in so many individual ways that it is not for us to prescribe. Scripture itself is not systematic; the New Testament shows the greatest variety. God has shown us that he can use any instrument. Balaam's ass, you remember, preached a very effective sermon in the midst of his "hee-haws." '

'What is your opinion of the kind of writing being done within the Christian church today?'

'A great deal of what is being published by writers in the religious tradition is a scandal and is actually turning people away from the church. The liberal writers who are continually accommodating and whittling down the truth of the gospels are responsible. I cannot understand how a man can appear in print claiming to disbelieve everything that he presupposes when he puts on the surplice. I feel it is a form of prostitution.'

'What do you think of the controversial new book *Honest to God* by John Robinson, the bishop of Woolwich?'

'I prefer being honest to being "honest to God." '

On Thursday morning, 16 May, Lewis greeted Chang, who had come to call at Magdalene. He wanted to dispose of two books in Chinese, said Lewis; copies of *The Magician's Nephew* in translation. Chang accepted courteously, even though he saw that they were in Japanese. He'd been ill, said Lewis; had to miss last term and the term before that. He had to watch his diet now, but he could drink all he liked. When was the old Western man going to grow a beard? asked Chang. Facial hair was coming into fashion again, Lewis had to admit; perhaps not shaving had something to do with existentialism.

On Friday 7 June he admitted to the Kilns the American who had so seriously and so insistently sought an interview. He wanted to write a book about Lewis, said Walter Hooper, which would be one of an American series on English authors. How dangerous it was to write about an author who was still alive! said Lewis as he poured the tea. One cup became two; two cups became four; Hooper asked to be shown to the bathroom. Lewis rose and led him to the bathroom, threw towels on the floor, and politely closed the door. A bath there was in the room, but nowhere was there a toilet. 'Well, sir, *that* will break you of those silly euphemisms,' roared Lewis with laughter as Hooper, unrelieved, returned to the sitting-room. 'And now, where was it you wanted to go?'

One hour became two before Lewis rose and said he would walk Hooper to the bus. They stopped for further chat and a drink at the Ampleforth Arms. As the bus finally approached, Hooper thanked Lewis for the interview, which was so much longer than he had hoped for.

'But won't I see you again? You're not getting away. Meet me at the Lamb and Flag on Monday as I want to talk with you some more.'

∽

'My brother is away in Ireland,' he wrote on 10 June to Shelburne. 'This throws a lot of extra work on me, besides condemning me to — what I hate — solitude. God help us all.' At least it was Monday morning; he headed towards Oxford where he hoped to find Hooper and an Inkling or two, hoisting a pint at the Lamb and Flag.

∽

'Of course this may not be the end,' wrote Lewis on 17 June to Shelburne, who seemed to die a thousand deaths in her letters. 'Then make it a good rehearsal.'

'Yours (and like you a tired traveller, near the journey's end),' he signed it, 'Jack.'

∽

On Tuesday 9 July he noticed that his ankles were swollen; that was a sign of kidney failure. On Wednesday he went to see the doctor, who heard irregularities in his heart and suggested that, for his health's sake, he cancel his trip to Ireland. On Thursday he complained to a correspondent of 'a splitting headache.' On Saturday, he scrawled to Green, 'I am now suffering a relapse and at present waiting to be admitted to hospital as soon as there is a vacancy. I am but a *fossil* dinosaur now.'

On Sunday Hooper arrived at the Kilns about 7.30 in the morning. He expected to find Lewis up and dressed and ready for the stroll down the hill to Holy Trinity for the eight o'clock communion service. But Lewis wasn't dressed. He was still in his dressing gown. He asked for tea, but when it came, he couldn't hold the cup. The cigarette, once lighted, trembled from his fingers. He had seen the doctor, he told Hooper; he was going into the Acland for a blood transfusion. Hooper helped as much as he could, but then he didn't know whether he should leave or stay. Stay, pleaded Lewis, and be my secretary; Warren is drunk in Ireland and may never return. I've got no one to help me; I'll pay whatever the University of Kentucky pays you. Yes, said Hooper, he would stay.

'I'm going into the hospital this afternoon,' he wrote to Shelburne on Monday 15 July, the day he and Doug had planned to depart for their Irish vacation. 'I fell asleep three times during your letter and found it very hard to understand!' At 5.00 p.m., shortly after being admitted to the Acland, he had a heart attack and lapsed into unconsciousness. Still in a coma at 2.00 the following afternoon, the curate of St Mary Magdalene's, Michael Watts, gave Lewis extreme unction. To the hospital's surprise, the patient awoke at 3.00, took off the oxygen mask, and asked for tea. A nurse ran to the telephone; Hooper and the Farrers rushed to the hospital.

'Is there anything wrong?'

'You have been asleep for quite a while,' said Farrer, not telling him how frazzled he looked; 'we were concerned about you.'

'I do not think,' replied the patient, 'that it could be urged,' summoning up all the baritone he could, 'that I am a very *well* man!'

Lewis asked Farrer to hear his confession and to bring him the sacrament. The following day he asked if Hooper could receive too. No, said Farrer; he wasn't the one sick. Then he'll have to do the kneeling for me, said Lewis. The sacrament consumed and prayers said, he dispatched the Farrers, who had postponed the start of their holiday in Wales by a day, and he sent Hooper out to buy stationery; he felt like tackling his correspondence.

∽

Dressed in pyjama bottoms and sports jacket and looking about for his hat, Lewis demanded to be taken to the Bodleian. Hooper arrived at the hospital just in time to escort him back to his room without embarrassment. Poisons from the kidneys, explained the doctor, were getting into the bloodstream and affecting the brain.

∽

'Don't you think you should be getting along to the station?'

'What for?' asked Douglas who had come to visit.

'To meet the *au pair* girl,' said Lewis. 'Didn't Mrs Miller tell you?'

Delighted at the prospect of a French maid at the Kilns, Douglas went to call a cab.

'What cab?' asked Lewis when Douglas returned for money to pay the cabby. Lewis had forgotten, and when Douglas explained, he looked up at the ceiling. 'You know, my mind's all I have left, and now that's going.' He could have cried, but he laughed.

∽

'Jack, it's Maureen.' She had tiptoed into the room and taken his hand. Hooper warned her that he hadn't recognized Tolkien earlier in the day.

'No,' he said smiling, his eyes still closed; 'it is Lady Dunbar of Hempriggs.'

'Oh, Jack, how could you remember that?' Only recently and quite unexpectedly, she had succeeded to a baronetcy in Scotland, with a castle and a vast estate.

'On the contrary, how could *I* forget a fairy tale.'

∞

A week went by; Lewis was improving. One thing Hooper had to tell him was that he had had a heart attack, gone into a coma, and was expected to die.

'Dear Walter, I am glad that you have not left me a stranger to that which concerns me most deeply.'

When Hooper looked as though he were about to grieve for what might have happened, Lewis consoled him for what would surely happen to all men. He even credited the anointing for turning the tide.

'You really do *believe* all the things you've written.'

'Of course!' said Lewis, closing his eyes. 'That's why I wrote them.'

∞

Cigarettes, said the matron, but no matches. Lewis could smoke in bed, but only when there was someone else in the room. Otherwise he would fall asleep, and the glowing fag would set the hospital ablaze.

'Give me a box of matches I can hide under my bedclothes!' He badgered Hooper until the guileless young American finally gave him a box.

When Hooper left the room in search of the facilities, the nurse appeared and casually tidied up until she discovered the box and with a yell of triumph confiscated it.

'How do they know?' asked Lewis when Hooper returned.

He was not only the supplier, Hooper confessed; he was also the informer.

'I have what no friend ever had before!' roared Lewis. 'I have a private traitor, my very own personal Benedict Arnold. Repent before it is too late!' He appreciated the practical joke, but he also demanded another box of matches.

∞

'Remember Helen Joy Davidman, died July 1960, loved wife of C. S. Lewis.' Before he died Lewis wanted to have a stone plaque installed at the Headington Crematorium to commemorate his wife; he was dictating to Hooper what should be inscribed on it:

> Here the whole world (stars, water, air
> And field, and forest, as they were
> Reflected in a single mind)
> Like cast off clothes was left behind
> In ashes, yet with hope that she,
> Reborn from holy poverty,
> In lenten lands, hereafter may
> Resume them on her Easter Day.

～

As his health improved, he asked for books, which Hooper brought. The incoming correspondence he also brought into the room, and he laboured, insofar as Lewis' mind could concentrate, to answer the more pressing letters first. Soon there were four tables in the room, each loaded with books and papers. They were not to be moved or dusted or even touched, proclaimed Lewis to the hospital staff who paraded in and out of the room, on pain of death!

～

'Thanks for the photo,' he wrote on 11 July with the help of Hooper. He commented favourably on Joan Lancaster's progress as a poet. 'I hoped you were the centre one; it would have been horrid if you were Morna Glaney. I'd write a better letter if I had not got a splitting headache.'

～

He would need a nurse when he returned to the Kilns. Hooper could cover the days, but who would cover the nights? There were few male nurses in England, Lewis learned; they seemed to gravitate towards celebrities. Alec Ross was highly recommended, but he wanted to know more.

'Was the great mon in that big boke?' asked Ross of Hooper.

'Ay, ay, Alec,' said Lewis who had overheard. "I am in what you in Scotland call *Wha's Wha*.'

All laughed, and a deal was struck. On the morning of 6 August Morris picked up the party and drove them to the Kilns. There, Ross was shocked by what he saw. The kitchen was a pigsty according to his standards and had to be scoured and disinfected before he'd put a foot in the place. Mrs Miller and the housekeeper hopped to; soon Ross was ensconced in the music room on the first floor. Hooper had already moved into the Kilns.

The following morning, and many mornings after that, Hooper brought a cup of tea to the sitting-room at seven. Lewis sipped it and dozed for perhaps another hour. Then he rose and went to the kitchen where he attempted breakfast. After that, he and Hooper worked at the correspondence.

Almost the first letter had to be to Cambridge University. Regretfully, but with a sense of urgency, he had to resign the chair and fellowship, retaining at the same time all of his affection for Magdalene College.

∽

What did VPR mean? Hooper was looking at the initials written at the top of a letter Lewis had received.

'Very polite refusal,' said Lewis. An American university had offered him £100 if he would speak, via a transatlantic telephone hookup to a classroom, on any subject of his choosing for half an hour.

Why did he want to refuse? asked Hooper.

'Because I can write much better than I can speak.'

The next letter Lewis asked Hooper to handle himself. 'Professor Lewis regrets,' he wrote to Shelburne, 'that he is unable at this time (and probably for a long time) to answer your letters.'

'I can't blame you for not knowing I had been so ill,' Lewis wrote himself on 11 August to Green, 'seeing how I didn't know myself until it was all over. I am now unofficially an extinct volcano.'

At the end of August, he sent Hooper and Douglas to Cambridge. There, in his rooms at Magdalene, they packed his books, perhaps two thousand of them, and belongings into boxes and loaded them onto a lorry they had hired. 'Where'll we store the books?' asked Hooper when they arrived back at the Kilns. Bookcases already lined most of the walls that had no windows. Lewis picked up a handful of books and motioned to them to follow him to the music room. In a bed, which was in the far corner, lay Ross; he was asleep and snoring. For the next hour or so, walking softly, the three of them carried books from the truck into the room, building higher and higher walls, reaching almost to the ceiling. Awaking finally, Ross panicked. He screamed and tried to flail his way out. Books fell, concussing him and causing him to curse. Lewis and Hooper were sick with laughter by the time the nurse had finally extricated himself. 'Best damned joke' he had ever seen played on anyone, Ross had to admit, but not before several whiskys were coursing through his veins.

∽

The Farrers were coming to tea; Hooper was worried about the sugar. Paxford, who did the shopping for the Kilns, bought only half a pound at a time and could not be coaxed into buying more.

'Well, you never know when the end of the world will come,' said Paxford, 'and we don't want to be left with sugar on our hands.'

Would it make any difference what was in the larder when the end came? asked Hooper. All that mattered was that Mr Jack's guests enjoy their tea *with* sugar.

They might not take sugar.

But they might.

They might not, replied Paxford, the inspiration for Lewis' Puddleglum the marshwiggle in *The Silver Chair*, and then where would they be?

When the Farrers arrived, Kay assumed the role of hostess. She sliced and served the cake, and poured the tea. The conversation was nimble and witty. She wrote novels; he wrote sermons and had appeared as speaker at the Socratic. Lewis had asked her to evaluate *Till We Have Faces* when it was in manuscript; he had written an introduction to one of Austin's books.

'Jack, Austin and I always thought you guarded very jealously your private life,' said Kay when Hooper left the room. 'Is it uncomfortable having Walter . . . living in your house?'

'But Walter is *part* of my private life.'

Watching the Farrers a short time later insert themselves into their battered Mini — she was small, but he was tall and slim — Lewis said to Hooper, 'It was like entertaining elves.'

⁓

Ross had left the Kilns, his services as night nurse no longer needed; Hooper was about to leave for the United States. He had to explain his new job to his family in North Carolina and to conclude his relationship with the University of Kentucky, but he would return. He would handle all but Lewis' most personal correspondence. Lewis would be freed to write books. Together they would explore the French sources of Malory's *Morte d'Arthur* . . .

'Warren . . . has completely deserted me. He has been in Ireland since June and doesn't even write, and is, I suppose, drinking himself to death,' he wrote on 11 September to Greeves. 'But Paxford and Mrs Miller look after me very well, and if it weren't for that horrid amount of letter writing I now have to do, we could really get on very well without him.'

'When you die, and if "prison visiting" is allowed,' he wrote on 17 September to Sister Penelope, 'come down and look me up in Purgatory. It *is* all rather fun, solemn fun, isn't it?'

'Death would have been so easy,' he told Green when he stayed the night of 26 September at the Kilns; 'I was nearly there — and almost regret having been brought back!'

'Yes, autumn is really the best of the seasons,' he wrote on 3 September to Jane Douglass; 'and I'm not sure that old age isn't the best part of life. But, of course, like autumn, it doesn't last.'

Sober now and remorseful, Warren came back, grateful that he himself was alive, more grateful still that his brother was alive. They embraced; Lewis called out to Mrs Miller to make an early tea. 'The wheel had come full circle,' Warren would write. 'Once again we were together in the little end room at home, shutting out from our talk the ever-present knowledge that the holidays were ending, and that a new term fraught with unknown possibilities awaited us both.'

∽

'Perhaps I might be able to make up what is lacking of your hospital coverage,' wrote Lewis in great haste on 17 October to Shelburne. 'How much would it be?'

∽

'I'd like to have a try at that article but must warn you that I may fail,' wrote Lewis on 7 October to the editor of the *Saturday Evening Post* in New York. He had just finished proof-reading *The Discarded Image*, and Bles was preparing *Letters to Malcolm: Chiefly on Prayer*; he needed something to do. 'It would be impossible to discuss "the right to happiness" without discussing a formula that is rather sacred to Americans about "life, liberty, and the pursuit of happiness." I'd do so with respect. But I'd have to point out that it can only mean "a right to pursue happiness by legitimate means," i.e. "people have a right to do whatever they have a right to do." Would your public like this?'

A parable came to mind when he sat down to write. Mr A divorced his missus of many years because she had lost her looks and her liveliness; Mrs B divorced her mister because he had lost his virility and his job; to live happily ever after Mr A and Mrs B married each other. 'A man has a right to happiness,' said Mr A when asked to comment on his first wife's suicide. He had to take his one chance when it came.

'At first this sounds to me as odd as a right to good luck,' he wrote in comment. 'For I believe — whatever one school of moralists may say — that we depend for a very great deal of our happiness or misery on circumstances outside all human control. A right to happiness doesn't, for me, make much more sense than a right to be six feet tall, or to have a millionaire for your father, or to get good weather whenever you want to have a picnic.'

∽

'Send them a very polite refusal,' he said, his academic career slowly slipping from his grasp. In looking through the morning's post Warren had opened an invitation to his brother to deliver the next Romanes lecture at Oxford.

'Yes, I would like to have seen much more of you than I did,' he wrote on 22 October to Willey at Cambridge. 'But at our age terms flash past like telephone posts seen from an express.'

'It was lovely to feel that I need not read Rouse on the sonnets!' he wrote on 7 November to Bonamy Dobrée. 'Instead I reread the *Iliad, The Daisy Chain, Bleak House,* and *In Memoriam*: a good balanced diet.'

'I am constantly with you in imagination,' he wrote on 25 October to the master and colleagues of Magdalene on learning that he had been made an honorary fellow of the college. 'If in some twilit hour anyone sees a bald and bulky spectre in the combination room or the garden, don't get Simon to exorcize it, for it is a harmless wraith and means nothing but good.'

∽

The Starrs had visited him in October, and so had Griffiths, renewing a friendship that had begun thirty-five years before. His illness had been announced in the newspaper, which only increased the number of items in the morning mail.

'I am, as you say, house-bound, even floor-bound,' he wrote on 7 November to Kathleen Raine; 'but no reason why *you* shouldn't come and see *me* whenever you are in these parts.'

On Friday 8 November Ladborough travelled from Cambridge to Headington, having accepted an invitation to lunch at the Kilns. Fish was served; it was a devotional practice with not much devotion in it, said Lewis; he loved fish, and Paxford cooked fish particularly well. 'What a very *rum* book!' Somebody had lent him a copy of *Les Liaisons Dangereuses*. It was 'like reading a Mozart libretto seriously: a blood-curdling experience.'

∽

The next Friday, 15 November, Green arrived in time for dinner. Lewis' day had been stressful. He was correcting proofs of 'We Have No "Right to Happiness" ' when he found that the last paragraph had been tampered with. In a fury he telephoned New York to tell the *Saturday Evening Post* to publish the article as it was written or not to publish it at all.

'Though the "right to happiness" is chiefly claimed for the sexual impulse, it seems to me impossible that the matter should stay there,' read Green aloud from the last paragraph as Lewis had written it. 'The fatal principle, once allowed in that department, must sooner or later seep through our whole lives. We thus advance towards a state of society in which not only each man but every impulse in each man claims *carte blanche . . .*'

'I rarely venture further afield than a stroll in the garden,' he wrote on 16 November to a correspondent; 'once a week I attend a reunion of old friends at one of the Oxford taverns.'

On Monday 18 November, he was driven down to the Lamb and Flag in St Giles'; beer was not one of the things denied him on his diet; he had a pint; the conversation with Hardie, the only one who showed up, flowed with animation.

On Wednesday 20 November he greeted Kaye Webb of Puffin Books at the Kilns. They talked about Green, who had arranged the meeting, and about his trip to Greece, which Green had also arranged. There were many loose ends and ambiguities in *The Chronicles of Narnia,* she said; he agreed to make some corrections and emendations. But when she left, he thought again and said to Warren, 'I have done all that I was sent into the world to do, and I am ready to go.'

On Friday 22 November, he answered four letters in his own hand. Warren answered others, the last one being the four-hundred-and-seventy-sixth he had typed since the beginning of the year. Lewis fell asleep in his chair after lunch. Warren suggested he might be more comfortable in his own bed. There, at 4.00 p.m., Warren brought him tea. Jack roused himself to say thank you, but drowsed off again. At 5.30 Warren heard a crash. Jack had fallen to the floor. Warren shouted for help, but before it could come, his brother had stopped breathing. Warren telephoned the doctor and the vicar; Havard was on his way, but Head wasn't home. The telephone rang; it wasn't Head; it was Jill Freud asking which night next week would be the most convenient for her and her children to come to dinner at the Kilns. Warren told her the terrible news.

The wording of the death notice for the newspapers — 'On Friday, 22 November 1963. Professor C. S. Lewis. No flowers, please.' — Warren had decided on by the time the vicar arrived at the Kilns on Saturday morning. The reason Head hadn't come sooner was that he was saying evensong when Warren called the night before; from the church he had proceeded to the village hall for a supper commemorating the one-hundred-and-fourteenth anniversary of the dedication of Holy Trinity Church. Warren wanted the funeral to be as private as possible, with no notice of day or time published. Would Tuesday morning at ten o'clock be acceptable? asked Head; the professor could be received into the church the night before. Warren agreed; but no flowers, he warned, and no music.

On Saturday in Cambridge, Chang felt unaccountably depressed, but the burden was lifted on Sunday, he noted in his diary, when he heard on the 1.00 p.m. BBC news that Lewis had died. In Swanage, Dorset, Phillips was watching television when he saw Lewis sitting in a chair a few feet away, ruddy and grinning and glowing with health. He had seen Lewis only once before; he knew what he was seeing now. He didn't look up to the ceiling, as the bishop of Woolwich thought people did, to see if Lewis had come down through a hole. 'It's not as hard as you think, you know,' said Lewis; Phillips knew what he meant.

Obituaries and evaluations began to appear, crowded in by stories of John F. Kennedy's assassination in Dallas and Aldous Huxley's death in Los Angeles, all on 22 November. 'Christian apologist, literary historian, scholar, critic, writer of science fiction children's books, he was one of the more prolific authors of his time,' read the fifth paragraph of *The Times* obituary, which had been patched together by Mathew, Bayley, and Green and published on Monday 25 November. 'As a Christian writer his influence was marked: he caught and held the attention of those usually apathetic to religion, of lapsed churchgoers, and of people who liked to think themselves agnostics; with J. B. Phillips he made religious books bestsellers and, in a nice sense, fashionable.'

Early on Tuesday morning at Holy Trinity, Lewis' coffin in the centre aisle, Head said a Requiem Mass. Soon thereafter Tolkien, Havard, and Dundas-Grant walked into the churchyard; they had just come from St Aloysius' Catholic Church where Tolkien had had a mass offered for the repose of the soul of their friend. Arriving intermittently were Lewis' peers Barfield and Harwood, former pupils Sayer and Bayley; Tolkien's son Christopher; Anglican priest Bide and Dominican priest Mathew; the president and vice-president of Magdalen; and Zernov, with a great sheaf of flowers. Lastly, from the Kilns, came Douglas, who was accompanied by his mother's friend Jean Wakeman; Maureen and her husband Leonard; and Paxford the marshwiggle.

When Head learned that the major would not be in attendance, he had Zernov's flowers placed at the foot of the coffin. 'I am the resurrection and the life, saith the Lord,' he began; he was assisted by the Rev. E. J. Payne. The Rev. Dr. A. M. Farrer read the lesson. After the service, they moved out to the graveyard, their feet crunching the hard frost on the ground. It was a cold, sunny, brilliant day. Cloud puffballs were everywhere. A single candle burned on top of the coffin as it was carried from the catafalque and put over the open grave, which lay, Tolkien noticed, under a larch. After the final prayers, as earth was being returned into the hole, people talked. Some paid their respects to Douglas; he would be off now with Jean

Wakeman; Bide said there would always be a place for him at his home.

'We've certainly lost a friend,' said Dundas-Grant to Havard as they passed out through the churchyard gate.

'Only for a time, D. G.'

Only for a time.

ACKNOWLEDGMENTS

May I express my profoundest gratitude. . . .

First, to Walter Hooper.

Second, to the Wade Collection at Wheaton College for naming me recipient of the 1983 Clyde S. Kilby Research Grant in recognition of my work on *A Dramatic Life*; to Marjorie Mead, Evelyn Brace, Brenda Phillips, Pat Hargis, and Lyle Dorsett.

Third, to the Bodleian Library, Department of Western Manuscripts, and Dennis Porter.

Fourth, to Norman Bradshaw.

Fifth, to Owen Barfield, Peter Bide, Harry Blamires, David Cecil, Dan Davin, Christopher Derrick, E. L. Edmonds, B. J. Findlay, W. R. Fryer, June and Roger Lancelyn Green, Douglas H. Gresham, Bede Griffiths, Ronald E. Head, R. T. Hewitt, Clyde S. Kilby, Peter Milward, Martin Moynihan, Bob O'Donnell, W. Norman Pittenger, Caroline Rakestraw, Stephen Schofield, Arthur P. Strong, Priscilla Tolkien, Eva and Chad Walsh, Charles Wrong.

Sixth, to John Breslin, Roy M. Carlisle, Jesse Core, Alexia Dorszynski, Paul Ford, Robert J. Muldoon, Jr., John O'Dell, Wallis Windsor, Ken Stuart.

May I hereby express my gratitude to the following: Owen Barfield for permission to quote from 'Abecedarium Philosophicum,' from *Mark vs Tristram: Correspondence between C. S. Lewis and Owen Barfield,* and from *A Cretaceous Perambulator (The Re-examination of).* Harry Blamires for permission to quote from his unpublished essay 'C. S. Lewis.' Bodleian Library for permission to quote from the unpublished writings of C. S. Lewis deposited therein. BBC Data, Written Archives Centre for permission to quote from the correspondence between the BBC and C. S. Lewis. The Bodley Head for permission to quote from *Out of the Silent Planet* by C. S. Lewis. Bridge Publishing, Inc., for permission to quote from *In Search of C. S. Lewis* compiled and edited by Stephen Schofield (copyright © 1983 by Bridge Publishing, Inc.). Cambridge University Press for permission to quote from *Studies in Medieval and Renaissance Literature* (© Cambridge University Press 1966) and *Selected Literary Essays* (©Cambridge University Press 1969). *Canadian C. S. Lewis Journal* for permission to quote from several numbers. Chappell/Intersong Music Group for permission to quote 'Twentieth

CLIVE STAPLES LEWIS

Century Blues' by Noel Coward (Copyright © 1931 by Chappell &
Co., Ltd; copyright renewed, published in the USA by Chappell &
Co., Inc.; international copyright secured; all rights reserved).
Collins Publishers for permission to quote from *The Screwtape
Letters*; *The Problem of Pain*; *The Abolition of Man*; *The Lion, The Witch
and The Wardrobe*; *George MacDonald — An Anthology*; *The Great
Divorce*; *Mere Christianity*; *The Pilgrim's Regress*; *Fernseed &
Elephants, Screwtape Proposes a Toast*. Curtis Brown Group Limited,
on behalf of C. S. Lewis Pte Ltd, for permission to quote from 'Our
English Syllabus' as it appears in *Rehabilitations*; 'Awake, My Lute!';
C. S. Lewis' contributions to *A Cretaceous Perambulator* and
Abecedarium Philosophicum; *God in the Dock*; *Essays Presented to
Charles Williams* and *The Personal Heresy*; *The Lewis Papers*; material
held in the Wade Collection and the Bodleian Library. Wm. B.
Eerdmans Publishing Co. for permission to quote from *Letters to an
American Lady* (© 1967 Wm. B. Eerdmans Publishing Co.) and
Christian Reflections (© The Executors of the Estate of C. S. Lewis,
1967). The Episcopal Radio–TV Foundation, Inc., for permission to
quote from the 'Four Talks on Love,' recordings made from radio
talks by C. S. Lewis. Harcourt Brace Jovanovich, Inc., for permission
to quote from *The World's Last Night*; *Surprised by Joy*; *The Dark Tower
and Other Stories*; *Letters to Malcolm*; *On Stories*; *Spirits in Bondage*;
Poems; *Narrative Poems*; from *Letters of C. S. Lewis* edited by
W. H. Lewis; from *Light on C. S. Lewis* edited by Jocelyn Gibb; from
C. S. Lewis: A Biography by Roger Lancelyn Green and Walter
Hooper; from *Murder in the Cathedral* by T. S. Eliot. Harper & Row,
Publishers, Inc., for permission to quote from *Brothers and Friends:
The Diaries of Major Warren Hamilton Lewis* edited by Clyde S. Kilby
and Marjorie Lamp Mead, and *A Severe Mercy* by Sheldon Vanauken.
Houghton Mifflin Company for permission to quote from *The Letters
of J. R. R. Tolkien* edited by Humphrey Carpenter (copyright © 1981
by George Allen & Unwin [Publishers] Ltd); from *The Hobbit* by
J. R. R. Tolkien (copyright © 1966 by J. R. R. Tolkien); from *The
Inklings* by Humphrey Carpenter (copyright © 1978 by George
Allen & Unwin [Publishers] Ltd); from *W. H. Auden: A Biography* by
Humphrey Carpenter (copyright © 1981 by the Estate of W. H.
Auden, copyright © 1981, by George Allen & Unwin [Publishers]
Ltd). Hutchinson Publishing Group Limited for permission to quote
from *The Collected Poems of Ruth Pitter*. Macmillan Publishing
Company for permission to quote from *Out of the Silent Planet* by
C. S. Lewis; *They Stand Together: The Letters of C. S. Lewis to Arthur
Greeves* edited by Walter Hooper (copyright © 1979 by The Estate of
C. S. Lewis; introduction and notes copyright © 1979 by Walter

416

Hooper); from *Letters to Children* by C. S. Lewis, edited by Walter Hooper (copyright © 1985 by C. S. Lewis Pte Ltd); from 'On Forgiveness,' 'A Slip of the Tongue,' and the 'Introduction' by Walter Hooper as they appear in *The Weight of Glory, and Other Addresses*, revised and expanded edition (copyright © The Trustees of the Estate of C. S. Lewis 1975, 1980). The New York Public Library for permission to quote from correspondence relating to the Macmillan Company and C. S. Lewis (Macmillan Company Records, Rare Books and Manuscripts Division, The New York Public Library, Astor, Lenox and Tilden Foundations). Oxford University Press for permission to quote from *English Literature in the Sixteenth Century; the Allegory of Love*; and *A Preface to 'Paradise Lost'*. Random House, Inc., for permission to quote from *Selected Poetry of W. H. Auden*, Second Edition. Templegate Publishers for permission to quote from *The Golden String* by Bede Griffiths. Viking Penguin, Inc., for permission to quote from *The Auden Generation: Literature and Politics in England in the 1930's* by Samuel Hynes (copyright © 1972 by Samuel Hynes). The Marion E. Wade Collection, Wheaton College, Wheaton, Illinois, for permission to quote from the unpublished writings of C. S. Lewis and Warren Hamilton Lewis deposited therein. Chad Walsh for permission to quote from *Apostle to the Skeptics* by Chad Walsh. Winston Press for permission to quote from *A Grief Observed* by C. S. Lewis (copyright © 1961 by N. W. Clerk). A. P. Watts, Ltd, Literary Agents for permission to quote from 'Unreal Estates,' an interview of C. S. Lewis by Brian Aldiss. Sherwood Eliot Wirt for permission to quote from his interview of C. S. Lewis as it appeared in the September and October issues of *Decision* magazine (© 1963 Billy Graham Evangelistic Association). The Zondervan Corporation for permission to quote from *C. S. Lewis: Speaker and Teacher* compiled by Carolyn Keefe (copyright © 1971 by Zondervan Publishing House).

Additionally for the British edition:

The Bodley Head for permission to quote from *The Auden Generation: Literature and Politics in England in the 1930s* by Samuel Hynes (copyright © 1972 by Samuel Hynes). Collins Fount for permission to quote from 'On Forgiveness', in *The Weight of Glory, and Other Addresses*, revised and expanded edition (copyright © The Trustees of the Estate of C. S. Lewis, 1975, 1980). The C. S. Lewis Company Ltd for permission to quote from *Letters* by C. S. Lewis copyright © C. S. Lewis Pte. Ltd; *Of This and Other Worlds* by C. S. Lewis copyright © C. S. Lewis Pte. Ltd 1982; *Letters to Malcolm* by C. S. Lewis copyright © C. S. Lewis Pte. Ltd

1963, 1964; *The Dark Tower* by C. S. Lewis copyright © C. S. Lewis Pte. Ltd 1977; *The Four Loves* by C. S. Lewis copyright © C. S. Lewis Pte. Ltd 1960; *Surprised by Joy* by C. S. Lewis copyright © C. S. Lewis Pte. Ltd 1955; *Fernseed and Elephants* by C. S. Lewis copyright © C. S. Lewis Pte. Ltd 1975; *Letters to Children* by C. S. Lewis copyright © C. S. Lewis Pte. Ltd 1985; *Screwtape Proposes a Toast* by C. S. Lewis copyright © C. S. Lewis Pte. Ltd 1959; *Christian Reflections* by C. S. Lewis copyright © C. S. Lewis Pte. Ltd 1967, 1980; *Poems*; *Narrative Poems*. Curtis Brown Limited, on behalf of C. S. Lewis Pte. Ltd, for permission to quote from *Letters to an American Lady* (© 1967 Wm B. Eerdmans Publishing Co.). Faber and Faber Ltd for permission to quote from *A Grief Observed* by C. S. Lewis (copyright © 1961 by N. W. Clerk). George Allen & Unwin [Publishers] Ltd for permission to quote from *The Letters of J. R. R. Tolkien* (copyright © 1966 by J. R. R. Tolkien); from *The Inklings* by Humphrey Carpenter (copyright © 1978 by George Allen & Unwin [Publishers] Ltd); from *W. H. Auden: A Biography* by Humphrey Carpenter (copyright © 1981 by the Estate of W. H. Auden, copyright © 1981 by George Allen & Unwin [Publishers] Ltd). HarperCollins Publishers Ltd for permission to quote from *A Biography* by Roger Lancelyn Green and Walter Hooper; *On Stories*; from *Light on C. S. Lewis* edited by Jocelyn Gibb; *The World's Last Night*; *Spirits in Bondage*; from *The Golden String* by Bede Griffiths. Hodder & Stoughton Ltd, for permission to quote from *A Severe Mercy* by Sheldon Vanauken.

Every effort has been made to trace and contact copyright owners. If there are any inadvertent omissions in the acknowledgments we apologize to those concerned, and ask them to contact us in order to make appropriate amendments for any future editions.

BIBLIOGRAPHY

For a comprehensive bibliography of Lewis' writings, which includes not only books but seven other categories of publication, the reader is referred to Walter Hooper's masterful compilation in *C. S. Lewis at the Breakfast Table, and Other Reminiscences* edited by James T. Como (New York: Macmillan, 1979), pages 245–88.

What follows is a chronicle only of Lewis' books, their publications in both England and the United States.

1919
Spirits in Bondage: A Cycle of Lyrics
London: William Heinemann. Published under the pseudonym Clive Hamilton.

1926
Dymer
London: J. M. Dent. New York: E. P. Dutton. Published under the pseudonym Clive Hamilton.

1933
The Pilgrim's Regress: An Allegorical Apology for Christianity, Reason and Romanticism
London: J. M. Dent

1935
The Pilgrim's Regress
London and New York: Sheed and Ward

1936
The Allegory of Love: A Study in Medieval Tradition
Oxford: Clarendon Press

1938
The Allegory of Love
London: Oxford University Press. Reprinted with corrections.
Out of the Silent Planet
London: John Lane, The Bodley Head

1939
Rehabilitations, and Other Essays
London: Oxford University Press, 1939
The Personal Heresy: A Controversy
London: Oxford University Press. Coauthored with E. M. W. Tillyard.

1940
The Problem of Pain
London: The Centenary Press

1942
The Screwtape Letters
London: Geoffrey Bles

A Preface to 'Paradise Lost'

London: Oxford University Press. 'Being the Ballard Matthews Lectures, delivered at University College, North Wales, 1941.' Revised and enlarged.

Broadcast Talks

London: Geoffrey Bles and The Centenary Press. 'Reprinted with some alterations from two series of Broadcast Talks ('Right and Wrong: A Clue to the Meaning of the Universe' and 'What Christians Believe') given in 1941 and 1942.'

1943

The Pilgrim's Regress

Third edition. London: Geoffrey Bles. 'With the author's important new Preface on Romanticism, footnotes, and running headlines.'

Out of the Silent Planet

New York: Macmillan

The Problem of Pain

New York: Macmillan

The Screwtape Letters

New York: Macmillan

The Case for Christianity

New York: Macmillan. American edition of *Broadcast Talks*.

Christian Behaviour

London: Geoffrey Bles and The Century Press. New York: Macmillan. 'A further series of Broadcast Talks.'

Perelandra

London: John Lane, The Bodley Head

The Abolition of Man, or Reflections on Education with Special Reference to the Teaching of English in the Upper Forms of Schools

London: Oxford University Press. 'Riddell Memorial Lectures, Fifteenth Series.'

1944

The Pilgrim's Regress

Third edition. New York: Sheed and Ward.

Perelandra

New York: Macmillan

Beyond Personality: The Christian Idea of God

London: Geoffrey Bles and The Centenary Press

1945

Beyond Personality

New York: Macmillan

That Hideous Strength: A Modern Fairy-tale for Grownups

London: John Lane, The Bodley Head

The Great Divorce: A Dream

London: Geoffrey Bles and the Centenary Press

1946

The Abolition of Man

London: Geoffrey Bles and The Centenary Press

The Tortured Planet (That Hideous Strength)

New York: Avon Books. 'A paperback specially abridged by the author with a different Preface.,'

The Great Divorce: A Dream

New York: Macmillan

That Hideous Strength
   New York: Macmillan
George MacDonald: An Anthology
   Edited by C. S. Lewis. London: Geoffrey Bles.

1947

Miracles: A Preliminary Study
   London: Geoffrey Bles and The Centenary Press
The Abolition of Man
   New York: Macmillan
George MacDonald: An Anthology
   New York: Macmillan
Essays Presented to Charles Williams
   Edited and with a preface and chapter by C. S. Lewis. London: Oxford University
   Press.

1948

Arthurian Torso
   London: Oxford University Press. 'Containing the posthumous fragment of 'The
   Figure of Arthur' by Charles Williams and 'A Commentary on the Arthurian Poems
   of Charles Williams' by C. S. Lewis.'

1949

Transposition, and Other Addresses
   London: Geoffrey Bles. New York: Macmillan; published as *The Weight of Glory, and
   Other Addresses.*

1950

Dymer
   New York: Macmillan
The Lion, the Witch, and the Wardrobe: A Story for Children
   Illustrations by Pauline Baynes. London: Geoffrey Bles. New York: Macmillan.

1951

Prince Caspian: The Return to Narnia
   Illustrations by Pauline Baynes. London: Geoffrey Bles. New York: Macmillan.

1952

Mere Christianity
   London: Geoffrey Bles. 'A revised and amplified edition, with a new introduction,
   of the three books 'Broadcast Talks,' 'Christian Behaviour,' and 'Beyond
   Personality'.
Mere Christianity
   New York: Macmillan. 'A revised and enlarged edition, with a new introduction, of
   the three books, 'The Case for Christianity', 'Christian Behaviour', and 'Beyond
   Personality'.
The Voyage of the 'Dawn Treader'
   Illustrations by Pauline Baynes. London: Geoffrey Bles. New York: Macmillan.

1953

Voyage to Venus (Perelandra)
   London: Pan Books
The Silver Chair
   Illustrations by Pauline Baynes. London: Geoffrey Bles. New York: Macmillan.

1954

The Horse and His Boy
Illustrations by Pauline Baynes. London: Geoffrey Bles. New York: Macmillan.
English Literature in the Sixteenth Century, Excluding Drama
Volume III of *The Oxford History of English Literature.* Oxford: Clarendon Press. 'The Completion of "The Clark Lectures," Trinity College, Cambridge, 1944.'

1955

That Hideous Strength
London: Pan Books
The Magician's Nephew
Illustrations by Pauline Baynes. London: Geoffrey Bles. New York: Macmillan.
Surprised by Joy: The Shape of My Early Life
London: Geoffrey Bles.

1956

The Last Battle: A Story for Children
Illustrations by Pauline Baynes. London: The Bodley Head, 1956. New York: Macmillan; published as *The Last Battle*
Till We Have Faces: A Myth Retold
London: Geoffrey Bles
Surprised by Joy
New York: Harcourt, Brace & World

1957

Till We Have Faces
New York: Harcourt, Brace & World

1958

The Allegory of Love
New York: Oxford University Press
Miracles
The Association Press. 'An abridgment with a specially written preface by the author.'
Reflections on the Psalms
London: Geoffrey Bles. New York: Harcourt, Brace & World.

1960

Miracles
With revision of Chapter III. London: Collins-Fontana Books.
The Four Loves
London: Geoffrey Bles. New York: Harcourt, Brace & World.
Studies in Words
Cambridge: Cambridge University Press
The World's Last Night, and Other Essays
New York: Harcourt, Brace & World

1961

The Screwtape Letters, and Screwtape Proposes a Toast
London: Geoffrey Bles. 'With a new and additional Preface.'
A Grief Observed
London: Faber and Faber. Published under the pseudonym N. W. Clerk. Reprinted in 1964 under C. S. Lewis.

An Experiment in Criticism
Cambridge: Cambridge University Press

1962

They Asked for a Paper: Papers and Addresses
London: Geoffrey Bles
The Screwtape Letters, and Screwtape Proposes a Toast
New York: Macmillan

1963

A Grief Observed
Greenwich, Connecticut: Seabury Press. Published under the pseudonym N. W. Clerk.

Beyond the Bright Blur
New York: Harcourt, Brace & World. '*Beyond the Bright Blur* is taken from *Letters to Malcolm: Chiefly on Prayer* (Chapters 15, 16, 17) by C. S. Lewis, which will be published in the year 1964. This limited edition is published as a New Year's greeting to friends of the author and his publisher.'

1964

Letters to Malcolm: Chiefly on Prayer
London: Geoffrey Bles. New York: Harcourt, Brace & World.
Poems
Edited by Walter Hooper. London: Geoffrey Bles.

1965

Screwtape Proposes a Toast, and Other Pieces
With a Preface by J. E. Gibb. London: Collins-Fontana Books.
Poems
New York: Harcourt, Brace & World

1966

Studies in Medieval and Renaissance Literature
Collected by Walter Hooper. Cambridge: Cambridge University Press.
Letters of C. S. Lewis
Edited, with a Memoir, by W. H. Lewis. London: Geoffrey Bles. New York: Harcourt, Brace & World.
Of Other Worlds: Essays and Stories
Edited by Walter Hooper. London: Geoffrey Bles.

1967

Studies in Words
Second edition. Cambridge: Cambridge University Press. Three additional chapters.
Of Other Worlds
New York: Harcourt, Brace & World
Christian Reflections
Edited by Walter Hooper. London: Geoffrey Bles. Grand Rapids, Michigan: Eerdmans.
Spenser's Images of Life
Edited by Alistair Fowler. Cambridge: Cambridge University Press.
Letters to an American Lady
Edited by Clyde S. Kilby. Grand Rapids, Michigan: Eerdmans.

1968

A Mind Awake: An Anthology of C. S. Lewis
  Edited by Clyde S. Kilby. London: Geoffrey Bles.

1969

Letters to an American Lady
  London: Hodder and Stoughton.
Narrative Poems
  Edited by Walter Hooper. London: Geoffrey Bles.
Selected Literary Essays
  Edited by Walter Hooper. Cambridge: Cambridge University Press.

1970

God in the Dock: Essays on Theology and Ethics
  Edited by Walter Hooper. Grand Rapids, Michigan: Eerdmans.

1971

Undeceptions: Essays on Theology and Ethics
  London: Geoffrey Bles. British edition of *God in the Dock*.
Arthurian Torso as it appears in *Taliessin Through Logres* [and] *The Region of the Summer Stars* by Charles Williams and *Arthurian Torso* by Charles Williams and C. S. Lewis
  Introduction by Mary McDermott Shideler. Grand Rapids, Michigan: Eerdmans.

1972

Narrative Poems
  New York: Harcourt, Brace & World

1975

Fern-seed and Elephants, and Other Essays on Christianity
  Edited by Walter Hooper. London: Collins-Fontana Books.

1977

The Dark Tower, and Other Stories
  Edited by Walter Hooper. London: Collins. New York: Harcourt, Brace, Jovanovich.
The Joyful Christian: 127 Readings from C. S. Lewis
  With a Foreword by William Griffin. New York: Macmillan.

1978

Miracles
  With revision of Chapter III. New York: Macmillan.

1979

God in the Dock: Essays on Theology
  Edited by Walter Hooper. London: Collins-Fontana Paperbacks. Abridgement of *Undeceptions*.
They Stand Together: The Letters of C. S. Lewis to Arthur Greeves (1914–1963)
  Edited by Walter Hooper. New York: Macmillan. London: Collins.

1980

The Weight of Glory
  Revised and expanded edition, with a new Introduction by Walter Hooper. New York: Macmillan.

1981

Mere Christianity
  Anniversary edition edited and with an introduction by Walter Hooper. New York: Macmillan.

The Lion, the Witch, and the Wardrobe
  Illustrations by Michael Hague. New York: Macmillan.
The Visionary Christian: 131 Readings from C. S. Lewis
  Selected and edited by Chad Walsh. New York: Macmillan.

1982

On Stories, and Other Essays in Literature
  Edited by Walter Hooper. New York: Harcourt Brace Jovanovich.
The Grand Miracle, and Other Selected Essays on Theology and Ethics from God in the Dock
  Edited by Walter Hooper. New York: Ballantine Books.

1984

The Business of Heaven: Daily Readings from C. S. Lewis
  Edited by Walter Hooper. London: Collins. San Diego: Harcourt Brace Jovanovich.
Spirits in Bondage: A Cycle of Lyrics
  Edited by Walter Hooper. San Diego: Harcourt Brace Jovanovich.

1985

Boxen: The Imaginary World of the Young C. S. Lewis
  Edited by Walter Hooper. London: Collins. San Diego: Harcourt Brace Jovanovich, 1985
Letters to Children
  Edited by Lyle W. Dorsett and Marjorie Lamp Mead. New York: Macmillan. London: Collins.

1986

Mere Christianity
  New York: Collier Books
The Seeing Eye, and Other Essays from 'Christian Reflections'
  New York: Ballatine Books

INDEX

Also available from Lion:

FAITH IN THE AGE OF REASON

Jonathan Hill

'It was the best of times, it was the worst of times, it was the age of wisdom, it was the age of foolishness . . .' So starts Charles Dickens' *A Tale of Two Cities*. And without doubt The Age of Reason — or the Enlightenment — was a period unlike any other. In many ways it was during this time that the modern world was forged.

It was an age when world views clashed and new ways of seeing and understanding emerged. It was in religion, above all, that this clash took place. Our modern views of religion, like our modern understanding of science and the interaction between the two, were developed as the Enlightenment gathered pace and hit opposition.

This book examines what these powerful new ideas were, and how they impacted on Christianity. It offers a wonderfully rich and enjoyable portrait of one of the great periods of human history.

'This book is part of the excellent Lion Histories series . . . Jonathan Hill offers a clearly-written introduction to the Enlightenment period. The content is accessible, the style is readable and the research that has been undertaken is thorough. As always with Lion books, the illustrations are an outstanding feature . . . For those who want a concise introduction to a key era in the development of Western thought, this book is ideal.'
The Baptist Times

'Hill's deceptively slim volume in the attractively produced Lion Histories series makes for an engaging introduction to that sea of change in European thought . . . an excellent and attractive production.'
Anvil

ISBN 0 7459 5130 9

AUGUSTINE AND HIS WORLD

Andrew Knowles and Pachomios Penkett

Augustine is one of the giants of the Christian Church. From his birth in North Africa and his days as a relatively permissive young man, through his midlife conversion to Christianity and career as bishop of Hippo, his story has intrigued and inspired every generation for over 1,600 years.

It is as a thinker, teacher, writer and debater that Augustine has exerted the most influence. His greatness lay in his ability to relate the philosophies of Ancient Greece and Rome to the precepts of the Christian faith. Augustine also saved the church itself from disintegrating into rival factions by forging sound doctrine in the fires of controversy.

Augustine and His World tells the story of Augustine's life. It helps readers to understand the world he came from and the enormous contribution he made to the church both of his day and of the future.

'A superb introduction with lots of quality archive illustrations, maps and an easy-to-read prose style.'
Christian Marketplace

'It is a great companion for a beginner in Augustine studies . . . every library that serves undergraduate students, including local town libraries, would benefit from this rich resource.'
Catholic Library World

ISBN 0 7459 5104 X

THE INTIMATE MERTON

Thomas Merton

Thomas Merton (1915–68) is undoubtedly one of the greatest spiritual masters of the twentieth century, whose influence and appeal has reached far beyond the confines of his monastic world. The publication in 1948 of his classic memoir *The Seven Storey Mountain* established him as a highly successful and prolific writer, whose searingly honest and visionary writing has the power to inspire believers and non-believers alike.

From within one of the strictest of monastic orders, he campaigned for social justice and peace, wrote poetry, a play and popular books on the spiritual life, as well as essays engaging his passionate interests in contemplative traditions of the East and the West, world literature, politics and culture. His writing continues to have enormous influence on readers of all ages, who respond to it as both a window and a mirror.

This selection from his journals (which were originally published in seven volumes) is a powerful and chronological presentation of his life and its major themes as he expressed them in this most intimate of forms. Writing was the way in which he came to understand life and his vocation, and it is in his journals that readers find him at his most self-exploratory. By turns inspiringly profound, breathtakingly beautiful and hauntingly moving, Merton here describes the daily sadnesses and joys of his relentless search to know God. It is certain to become a classic, the first and best book for all seeking to understand the life and writing of this extraordinary personality.

'Patrick Hart and Jonathan Montaldo are to be congratulated on the marvellous work they have achieved together in what could have been a fictional task. With great skill and discernment they have put together those elements from each of the seven journals which, in their view, best reflect the core of Merton's writing at that time.'
The Door

'Searingly honest and visionary, this selection from his journals is certain to be a classic, the first and best book for an understanding of the life and writing of this extraordinary man.'
The Watkins Review

ISBN 0 7459 5017 5

JOHN WESLEY

Stephen Tomkins

On 24 May 1738, John Wesley's heart was 'strangely warmed' as he listened to a reading from Luther's *Preface to Romans* at a meeting in Aldersgate Street, London. 'Then it pleased God,' he declared, 'to kindle a fire which I trust shall never be extinguished.'

From this time on, Wesley's life was devoted to one goal: 'to promote as far as I am able vital, practical religion; and by the grace of God to beget, preserve and increase the life of God in the souls of men.' He became an evangelist, travelling the length and breadth of Britain to spread the good news of salvation. He and his brother, Charles, preached wherever they could — in pulpits, in the marketplace and on the common. Extraordinary phenomena, such as convulsions, laughter and healings, accompanied their missions. They drew crowds of thousands and suffered savage persecution. To conserve the gains of evangelism, Wesley formed societies in the wake of his missions. These societies were organized to become Methodism, the great nonconformist movement that spread across the British Isles and made a significant impact in America.

John Wesley: A Biography tells the dramatic story of Wesley's life, covering all the key aspects, including his relationships with his powerful mother, Susanna, and his hymn-writing brother, Charles; his university Holy Club; his early mission to Georgia, as well as his Methodist missions to Britain; and his disastrous relationships with women. Written in a colourful and accessible style, this is a book for all those wanting to know more about one of the greatest Englishmen of the 18th century.

'Tomkins colourfully retells the story of his dramatic life, bringing this great man of faith alive for a new generation.'
Publishing News

'A rounded and well-documented account of a complex personality.'
Methodist Recorder

ISBN 0 7459 5078 7

PAUL AND HIS WORLD

Stephen Tomkins

We know little about Paul, yet he has had a greater impact on the development of Christianity than any other person except Christ. For some, his influence has been largely negative. For others, he is simply the greatest mind in Christian history.

Stephen Tomkins argues that Paul would have been quite at home with such a mixed reception. He had his share of hero worship in his lifetime, but was also more reviled than any other Christian. What no one ever accused Paul of, however, was being half-hearted. His Christian life was a constant arduous missionary journey, enduring shipwrecks, prison, mob violence and the depressing politics of church life.

Paul and His World is a lively and lucid attempt to portray the man behind the controversy and the drama. As the author says: 'Two billion people today are followers of Jesus, and every one of them sees him through a lens crafted by Paul. A person of that influence is worth getting to know.'

'[Stephen Tomkins] has produced a penetrating, readable and exciting guide to Paul. He makes him human — an ordinary person, child of his age and place, called by God to an extraordinary role. [He] probes Paul's ideas with sympathy and critical acumen.'
Steve Motyer, Lecturer in New Testament, London Bible College

'A simple introduction to the figure of Paul: short, written in an easy style, well-illustrated and based largely on the story Luke tells in Acts.'
Methodist Recorder

ISBN 0 7459 5129 5

All Lion Books are available from your local bookshop,
or can be ordered via our website or from Marston Book
Services. For a free catalogue, showing the complete list
of titles available, please contact:

Customer Services
Marston Book Services
PO Box 269
Abingdon
Oxon
OX14 4YN

Tel: 01235 465500
Fax: 01235 465555

Our website can be found at:
www.lionhudson.com